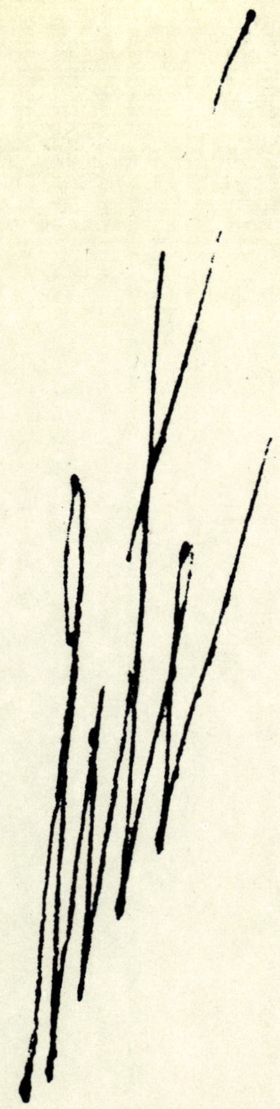

The Last Works

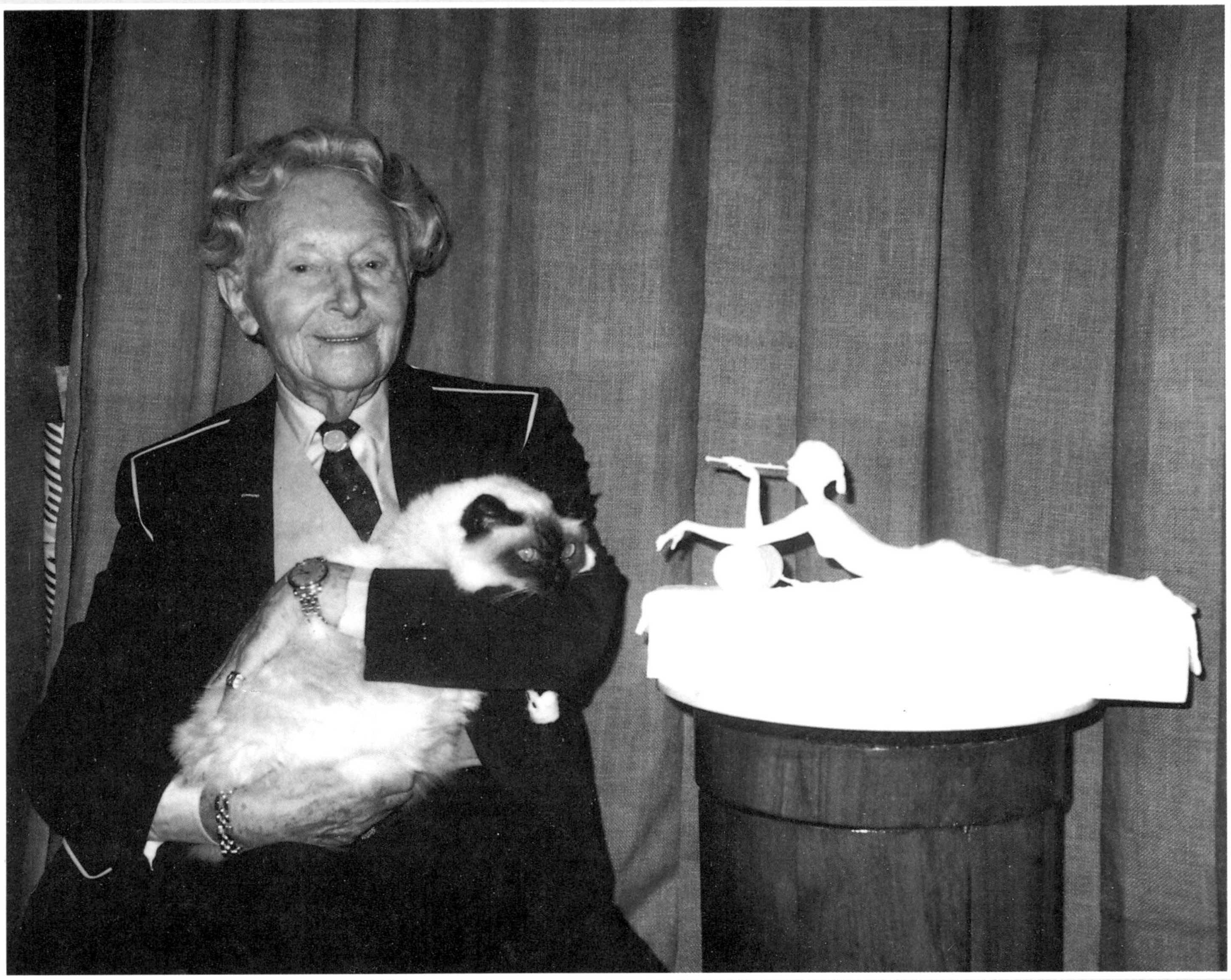

Erté with Caramelle and a plaster cast of Daydreams.

ERTÉ

THE LAST WORKS

GRAPHICS
SCULPTURE

BY

Eric Estorick

CONTRIBUTIONS BY

RAY PERMAN AND DAVID ROGATH

Photographed by
DANIEL KRAMER

Additional photography by Ron Krisel

DUTTON STUDIO BOOKS

New York

DUTTON STUDIO BOOKS

First published by Dutton Studio Books, an imprint of
Penguin Books USA Inc.

The Penguin Group

Penguin Books USA Inc., 375 Hudson Street.
New York, New York, 10014, U.S.A.
Penguin Books Ltd, 27 Wrights Lane,
London W8 5TZ, England
Penguin Books Australia Ltd, Ringwood,
Victoria, Australia
Penguin Books Canada Ltd, 2801 John Street,
Markham, Ontario, Canada L3R 1B4
Penguin Books (N. Z.) Ltd, 182-190 Wairau Road,
Auckland 10, New Zealand
Penguin Books Ltd, Registered Offices:
Harmondsworth, Middlesex, England

First printing, October 1992
10 9 8 7 6 5 4 3 2 1
Library of Congress
Catalog Card Number: 91-76575
ISBN: 0-525-93439-1

Printed in Italy

All photographs of the sculpture and graphics are by Daniel Kramer except those on pages 110, 117, 135, 140, 152, 171, and 176, and the top photos on pages 129 and 162, which are by Ron Krisel; those on page 122, which are by Ciaran Tully; those on pages 147, 188, and 192, and the bottom photos on pages 129 and 162.

The photographs on pages 45 and 47 are by Robert Skinner

CONTENTS

Note

Erté's creation of graphics and bronze sculptures dates back to the publication of the lithograph series of the *Numerals* in 1968, but the publication of these works in book form has a much shorter history. A relatively small number of graphics appeared in Charles Spencer's book *Erté* in 1970, and some were reproduced in the artist's 1975 autobiography, *Things I Remember.* Both of these books were relatively modest productions in which the reproductions appeared largely as illustrative of the text. The first publication of the graphics in a large format was in two paperbacks published by Dover Publications, *Erté Graphics* (1978) and *New Erté Graphics* (1984). However, it was not until *Erté at Ninety* appeared in 1982, with 208 reproductions, that a major representation of the graphics was available.

Four years later, in 1986, the first book illustrating the sculptures, entitled *Erté Sculpture,* was published, with forty-one subjects, and a year after that appeared *Erté at Ninety-five,* containing 163 graphics. This was followed in 1988 by the *Extended Edition,* with another twenty-seven prints, for a total of 398 graphics published in book form. The present volume reproduces all seventy-one graphics that were executed since the publication of *Erté at Ninety-five: Extended Edition,* and all 105 sculptures made since the publication of *Erté Sculpture.*

PROLEGOMENA

Following the death of an artist, a controversy may arise regarding the authenticity of the attributed works that appear posthumously. This is particularly true in the case of an artist whose works have included such multiple images as graphics and sculptures published in editions of a few to a few hundred copies. Since these works may not be produced entirely by the artist's own hand, but rather can involve the participation of additional artisans who carry out the artist's expressed wishes, a question may emerge as to the degree of participation by the artist in executing the piece and, in turn, if that constitutes a sufficient basis for identifying it as a legitimate work by the artist.

The presence or absence of a signature on a multiple image should dismiss any doubt arising with respect to its validity, but the matter is more complicated than that. An artist who was active until death will probably leave works in various states of completion, ranging from those just initiated to those finished. Some of the latter may have been reviewed and approved by the artist in their final form but not yet signed. Others may have been executed to a penultimate state, completed according to the artist's revisions but, again, left unsigned. Still others may have been initiated by the artist and then completed by artisans.

In the graphics by Erté that are illustrated in this book there are examples from each of these categories: (1) works signed by him, (2) works approved but not signed by him (these bear a gold hot-stamped signature), and (3) works begun by the artist but not finally approved by him (they bear an "Erté Studio" imprimatur). Unsigned artworks in the following pages are identified by stars above their titles: two stars signify a gold hot-stamped facsimile signature print, and one star denotes an "Erté Studio" print.

The pattern of approval for sculptures differs from graphics because each piece is stamped with the artist's signature versus a direct signature placement. In the case of Erté's sculptures, the documentation form that accompanies each bronze indicates whether or not that particular edition number was cast posthumously.

The introductions to the Graphics and Sculptures sections, which were written respectively by Ray Perman and David Rogath, explain their working procedures with Erté in the creation and production of these works. Their remarks further elucidate the process of approval by the artist at various stages of execution. These introductions are accompanied by a number of letters and croquis containing comments and instructions for the production of his works in the artist's hand.

During the course of this past decade, my association with those who have contributed to the publishing of Erté's art has been rewarding. In their own time, a number became close friends of the artist, substantially advancing interest in his work due to their intellectual perception and faithful execution of his work. In particular, they are Ron Parker of RKP International, Co., Harris Shapiro of the Dyansen Corporation, David and Leslee Rogath of Chalk & Vermilion, Inc., and Ray Perman, my colleague at Sevenarts, Ltd. Jack and Carolyn Solomon of Circle Fine Art Corporation made similar contributions with Erté's jewelry and other objets de vertu.

I am deeply grateful to my friend Jean F. Tibbetts for her continuous assistance with the total project, including research and manuscript preparation. I am further indebted to my very dear friend and colleague Norman J. Alexander, who shared the Erté experience with Sal and myself from its inception. His own recall produced the critical observations that have so enhanced the vitality of *Erté: The Last Works.*

E.E.

PLATES

TEXT

GRAPHICS

PLATES

SCULPTURE

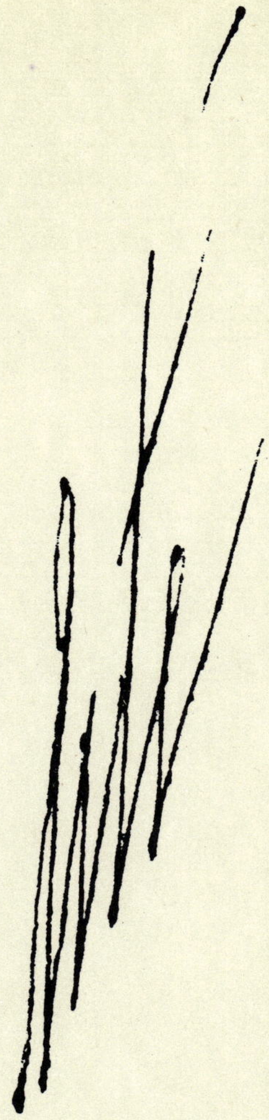

The Last Works

The original spelling of *Harper's Bazaar* was "*Bazar*". It was not until November 1929 that the third "*a*" was added. The present spelling is used throughout this book, regardless of the date of reference.

REFLECTIONS

on the occasion of an Erté centenary

Few people are fortunate enough to be able to reflect at length on their relationship with a creative artist in his own time. Such was the good fortune for me at the Grosvenor Gallery/Sevenarts with the artist Erté, because of our exceptionally close association with him, covering the past quarter century and until his demise. Since 1992 marks the centennial of his birth, I feel that this is the ideal time to celebrate Erté's creative works for fashions, magazine covers, musical revues, theater, opera, ballet, film, textiles, furniture, graphics, jewlery, sculpture, and objets de vertu. Remarkably, this extraordinary artist was productive for nearly the entire ninety-seven years of his life, which ended in the early hours of April 21, 1990.

Fortunately, Erté's visions, always contemporary, will continue to grace the world. Their timelessness assures pleasure to generation after generation, not only because of their uncanny sense of the moment, but for their incredibly varied modes of expression. In his life, Erté was equally at ease designing a luxurious, figure-flattering gown during his association with the Parisian haute couture house of Paul Poiret, a cover featuring a wind-swept ingenue for *Harper's Bazaar,* a bejeweled bird of paradise Bal Tabarin cabaret costume, or a sculpture of a sultry bronze mistress walking her panther.

An evocative, ethereal style characterizes Erté's work, especially in the way he clothed the female form. Historically speaking, his vision started as smart and savvy and progressed to exotic and extravagant. Closer observation of detail shows his keen intelligence about art, costume history, and humor when adapting and exaggerating period styles. In his *Numerals* series, the 6, for instance, is a classical Greek archer who carries the typical double-curved cupid's bow and wears a flexible corselet. Added flourish appeared with an elaborately emblazoned protective shield, high-crested Corinthian helmet variant, and wrist cuffs. In the Hollywood film *Restless Sex,* he dressed his Indo-Scythian dancer with an authentic belled girdle, armlets, and anklets. Frills and furbelows in this costume included an unusually long and fringed dipatta—the scarf worn across the chest and over the left shoulder—as well as an impressively tall tiered and jeweled turban. For the 1926 production of George White's *Scandals*, Erté's Nile princess was true New Kingdom in costume with her broad beaded collar and cuffs and Nefertiti's unique red crown permutation with its two-headed talismanic band. Likewise, the use of carnelian, turquoise, and gold, together with papyrus ornament, was historically accurate. Added embellishments included overall body beading in lieu of the more popular sheer, pleated sheath of the time, as well as an outrageously long, flowing cape, which was in the then-popular stylized feather pattern.

Of course, these were depictions of a unique, personal world that was quite apart from the one in which Erté lived. For here was a true twentieth-century man, whose lifetime witnessed such remarkable events and outstanding achievements as the Boer War and World Wars I and II; Marie and Pierre Curie's discovery of radium; the development of penicillin; Einstein's explanation of relativity; the introduction of radios, telephones, televisions, and computers; Robert Peary's polar assault, Edmund Hillary's Everest conquest, Neil Armstrong's walk on the moon; published first works of James Joyce and Ernest Hemingway; and the unearthing of a Minoan culture, Tutankhamen's treasures, and the Dead Sea Scrolls.

Erté (né Romain de Tirtoff) belonged to the Russian elite and the haut monde of France; he saw czars and commissars in power in his native land; he rode in carriages and on Concordes, and he illustrated beneath gaslights and spotlights. He practiced his art during a period that encompassed Constructivism, Cubism, Futurism, and Surrealism; he saw Bloomsbury, Bauhaus, and Happenings; Op Art and Pop Art likewise briefly coexisted as he created. But one would never have known this from the continuity of his style, which was transitional Art Deco. Indeed, the only way in which Erté enthusiastically adapted his unique artistic style was to apply his designs to new mediums—graphics, sculpture, and jewelry among them. Once he became aware of these and their potential for expressing his creative ideas to their maximum, he eagerly grasped the challenge of mastering them. His energy seemed boundless, and his enthusiasm for new modes of expression remained strong in him until the end.

Many of these applications occurred during Erté's last twenty-five years, when my late wife, Salomé, and I came to know, appreciate, and love him. He was a one-of-a-kind, special person whose passing truly marks the end of an era. Erté's distinct mark on this century's fine and applied arts remains unmatched, as does his effect upon each generation through which he passed.

It is a point of pride to be able to say that this gentle visionary was prolific, respected, and enormously popular during the period when we represented him. He was tireless in his pursuit of new visions and new ways to express them. His imagination seemed limitless. Here was an artist who always delighted in life and who, during the time of our association, achieved new fame with an entirely new public—a fame that equaled or even excelled that which he had enjoyed in much earlier days at *Harper's Bazaar.*

It is particularly easy to reminisce about Erté and his impact on the visual aspects of the performing arts because this was the period in which I grew up and appreciated the ongoing changes in ballet, theater, and opera. At that time, many popular performances were less realistically portrayed, in favor of the fantasy world in which Erté's work reigned. Much later, during the time when we represented him, he continued to execute designs for Roland Petit's Casino de Paris ballets, the Glyndebourne Opera Company's production of Richard Strauss's *Der Rosenkavalier,* and the Easter show at Radio City Music Hall. Prior to each performance, excitement would crackle in the air; anticipation would prevail as the orchestra struck its key, and then continue to crest as plaques flanking the proscenium would announce the next act. The visual impact that then followed was dependably memorable, for the movement was quick and fast and the colors were vibrant and beautiful.

The flow, movement, and life that was so prominent in those productions' costume and set designs was equally evident in the illustrations I saw for a few of them during the 1940's in those private collections that I was then viewing as a fine art dealer. I felt that Erté's depicted image of his ideal woman resembled that of the sixteenth-century master Lucas Cranach, an artist whom Erté revered. Both created distinctive faces with high cheekbones and wide-set almond eyes—but all similarities ended there, as Erté's illustrations were far more stylized, flamboyant, and fantastic, with a variety of emphatic Asiatic and Near Eastern art influences.

Admittedly inspired by the Russian Orthodox icons of his youth, Erté adapted the quiet dignity and flat, linear language of these paintings to his own images. Books on Persian miniatures that he found in the family library impressed him with their extraordinary technical refinement, lively rhythmic movement, bold designs, and extensive use of subtle and brilliant colors such as lapis lazuli and vermilion. Frequent visits to the Hermitage Museum in St. Petersburg, particularly its collections of Turkish majolica and Attic vases, also made their mark on Erté's stylistic development. He was intrigued by the geometric, floral, and interlace pattern combinations and the use of silver, copper, and gold on Turkish majolica, and equally by the elegant and delicate line, balance, and symmetry of Attic vases.

It is one thing to appreciate an artist from a distance and quite another to deal with him on a personal basis, and, as it happened, my relationship with this artist began in a curious, colorful way. Prior to our London gallery's grand exhibition of works by the eminent Art Nouveau artist Alphonse Mucha, in 1967 we staged a gala opening-night period-dress party to capture the spirit of the turn of the century. During the course of that evening, a Frenchman named Jacques Damase came to the gallery, announced himself, and said that he had something important to tell us that would represent a continuity with what we were doing in the Mucha exhibition. He said that he wanted us to meet an artist, named Erté, who represented the Art Deco generation that succeeded Mucha and Art Nouveau.

Damase, who was an art dealer, writer, and superb art historian (as well as a character of the times), was so eloquent, sincere, and convincing in his logic that my wife and I left for Paris almost immediately to meet Damase and Erté at the Galerie Jacques Perrin, where some of this artist's works were then on view.

That afternoon Erté invited us back to his studio in Boulogne-sur-Seine on the outskirts of Paris, where he had over a thousand perfectly preserved drawings representing his life's work. One cabinet contained designs from the operatic productions that he had produced during the past forty-five years. Here were striking gouaches of a prancing harlequin from *Don Pasquale,* forbidding Gothic maquettes for *Faust,* a wittily ruffled Sun King dancer from *Castor et Pollux.* Other folios held the work that Erté had produced according to the year of its execution. A file marked "1927" produced numerous designs for the Folies-Bergère, including an exotic blackamoor from *Queen of Sheba,* a fanciful fountain from *Parfums,* a malachite, lapis lazuli, gold, and ebony stage set for "Les Princesses de légende". Here, too, were chic day and evening ensembles for George White's production of *Manhattan Mary.* Elsewhere were designs for those costumes that he created for Mata Hari, Anna Pavlova, and Lillian Gish. *Schéhérezade,* Erté's first *Harper's Bazaar* cover, could also be seen in glorious detail. Cases in his basement displayed suits and shoes from the twenties together with costumes that he had made and worn to fancy dress balls. One could say that Erté—who never seemed to throw anything away—was a great continuing collector of his life.

This was a very exciting moment, in the sense that one was inspired and delighted by the technical dexterity and image knowledge of a world that Erté was making his own. And after viewing the unique style, extent, and range from his vast amount of work, one could actually track the development of this vivacious genius—from the time spent at La Maison Poiret to that of an independent couturier for export to an illustrator for magazines to a costume and set designer for film and stage.

At this point, I was as enthusiastic and confident about a new public's acceptance of this once-renowned artist's works as I had been by those of Mario Sironi, Umberto Boccioni, and El Lissitzky—those members of the Italian Futurist and Russian avant-garde movements whose careers the Grosvenor Galleries had also revived. Erté's work, like the others', had to be properly reintroduced. When I told him of my idea to present a series of exhibitions of his work in our London and New York galleries, which I believed would restore him to the eminence that he enjoyed prior to World War I, he was delighted with the proposal and agreed with enthusiasm to our plans.

It was obvious that time had not been fiscally generous to Erté, but that lack was not visible in his work. In fact, Erté seemed to be the classic example of an unswervable artist whose art was at the very core of his existence. He may have reminisced about such personal incidents as his radiant appearance at the very fashionable dress rehearsal for the play *La Phalène* at the Théâtre de Vaudeville in Paris in 1913, dressed in an ermine and scarlet velvet cloak with gloves and turban to match; virtually all members of *le grand monde* admiringly turned their heads his way. Then there was his dazzling entrance at the Paris Opèra Ball in 1926, when he dressed as a toreador in gold lamé. His magnificent cape, replete with its lining of fresh red roses, was included as part of his ensemble so that he could dramatically cast each flower, one by one, to the audience as he glided down the staircase. But even then, for all the theatrics, Erté remained an extraordinarily hardworking artist, who for decades spent every night, all night, at his desk. Here he sketched and painted beneath a single light to illuminate his work as soft strains of recordings of operas by Ravel, Rossini, Strauss, or Verdi wafted in the background. He may have been to the manor born and long ago enjoyed a footloose life that was balanced by diligent effort, but now he led a modest lifestyle with limited trappings—the latter of which seemed secondary to his life mission in art.

Upon our return to London from that introductory meeting, Sal and I promptly began to lay the groundwork for our forthcoming exhibitions of Erté's work. With a colleague, five hundred works were selected to represent Erté's entire *oeuvre* in order to show his broad diversity, convey stylistic development, and create visual interest. This dated from the time when he left Russia, prior to World War I, to the work that he was then doing for an outdoor extravaganza at the Montreal "Expo 67". Sal, whose immediate rapport with Erté in Paris was partially due to their shared multilingual facility, solicited background information on the selected works from him, assembled a chronology of his career, and supervised the catalogue's production. I, meanwhile, told friends and collectors of our reintroducing Erté to the international art world and contacted museum directors to explain why this master artist's works should be as justly recognized and rewarded through representation in their public collections as those by many of his contemporaries—Leon Bakst, Natalia Goncharova, and his friend Jean Cocteau among them.

The first exhibition was scheduled to take place in New York in June 1967, and, as events turned out, it was a glittering triumph. The day preceding the exhibition, the directors of the Martin Foundation, a charitable trust, purchased all 170 displayed works, then donated them to the Metropolitan Museum of Art, where they remained in the permanent collection of the Prints Department. As it happened, Erté stopped by the gallery on this particular day to see how his works were arranged, was told of this remarkable purchase, then ecstatically helped to arrange for more works to be air-freighted from his studio in Paris, while others were sent from London.

The opening itself was jubilant, with many members of the lively arts in attendance. Stars of ballet, opera, and symphony were there. So, too, were theater *costumiers, parfumiers,* and members of the fashion and society worlds. George Balanchine, Regina Resnick, and Roberta Peters were among those who appeared to both praise and pay their respects to this artist, who for five decades had further glamorized their performing arts with his resplendent work. Many young international art aficionados of the time were also there to welcome and acquire works by their effervescent genius. These included Andy Warhol and John McKendry, the superb curatorial director of the Metropolitan's Prints Department, who was responsible the following year for staging that museum's exhibition entitled "Fashions and Follies: Erté and Some of His Contemporaries", which included Georges Barbier, Georges Lepape, Étienne Drian, Sonia Delaunay, and Umberto Brunelleschi.

With the overwhelming success of the show in New York, a larger exhibition was arranged for London. There was a selection of eight hundred of Erté's works—of which six hundred were sold, including a pre-show sale to Lord Beaumont of Whitely of the entire Alphabet, the spirited twenty-six piece series based upon the moving figure.

Erté was so delighted with the success of these exhibitions and our reaction to it that he offered to give the Grosvenor Gallery an exclusive contract of the worldwide sale and exploitation of his work. At the age of seventy-five, when most people are well into their retirement, this man was actively looking forward to devoting many years to creating new projects.

Of course, we realized that by exhibiting Erté on the heels of our Mucha show in 1967 the Grosvenor Gallery would now be more identified with decorative as well as fine art. But in order to seriously promote Erté, we had to increase our work effort.

At this point, we were arranging one-man exhibitions of his works in scores of cities throughout Europe and the United States. We felt that Erté's designs—with their fine, hard lines that define and detail and clean, clear chroma and values in hues that are almost gradiently placed—would especially suit reproduction, and that, together with many requests for a particular design, led us to commence a graphics program. This began with the lithographic production of the ten *Numerals* in 1968, which was so successful that other series were developed, including *Six Precious Stones, Four Seasons,* and *Four Aces.* As with the *Alphabet,* which was conceived in 1924 and published as a graphics set in 1977, these serial designs were natural for Erté to develop because they were an embellishment of his all-encompassing opera, ballet, and theater productions. With these series, one might say that his entire *oeuvre* came into sharp focus: Erté's masterly style was already apparent, but now his design concepts for fashion, costume, and dance were fully integrated in their application to various single subjects.

Each of these initial editions was limited to a run of seventy-five plus a small number of artist's proofs, but they opened the door to acquisition by a vast audience of eager young collectors who could not afford to purchase original works. Editions of three hundred, plus proofs, followed in 1974, when we agreed to a proposal made by the Circle Fine Art Corporation of Chicago to reproduce expanded editions of Erté's work. This firm was known to offer moderately priced fine-quality graphic reproductions in their galleries throughout the United States. Eight years later this graphics program was further expanded when we granted a contract to the New York-based fine art publishing firm of Chalk & Vermillion, wherein an exceptionally enriching professional rapport developed between Erté and David Rogath, the owner of that company.

This was an exciting period for Erté. His art was being accepted by a new generation of admirers, he worked diligently to satisfy their growing demand, and he was becoming wealthy. To devote himself completely to creative development, Erté assigned ownership and title to his name and work to the Grosvenor Gallery. This included our undertaking all contract negotiations and ownership of Erté's copyrights.

It became obvious that because of the increasing time needed to devote to Erté's affairs, Sal and I restructured our business mode and relocated our firm to South Molton Street. It was here that numerous entrepreneurs contacted us who wanted to apply Erté's designs to their products. Some wanted to trim their belts, handbags, and costumes with his exuberant lines; others to embellish their towels, scarves, and hats. One producer created sweaters with Erté's high-keyed colors and lavish patterns, while another added them to their blouses. During this period Erté and Sal reviewed and revised prototypes for these projects and for those graphics that we had initiated.

Concurrently, I organized future publications about the artist's life and work. It was apparent that although Erté continually produced exquisite designs throughout the decades with all the skill and modesty of a confident, disciplined art worker, his efforts were accorded little acknowledgement in the historic press. He had been occasionally lauded for his spectacular costume and set designs upon those opening nights for George White's *Scandals* in New York, *Don Pasquale* and *La Traviata* in Paris, and *Castor et Pollux* in Lyons. Exhibitions of his India ink and gouache drawings likewise received written attention on both sides of the Atlantic during the twenties. Yet that was too little and too long ago, and with the now-burgeoning interest in Erté's work, his new public was eager to discover this artist's life story, admire more of his drawings, and study his period designs.

The first of these was an illustrative accompaniment to *Ermyntrude and Esmeralda,* a refreshingly naughty post-Edwardian novel that was written by Lytton Strachey and discovered posthumously among his papers. The London publisher Anthony Blond, who had been kindly granted the necessary permission to undertake this project by the author's estate and who was a friend of ours and a particularly good friend of Sal's, approached us in 1969 with respect to Erté's supplying the artwork for this story. We agreed, and Erté happily embarked upon the endeavor, the result of which was a handsome limited edition.

For broader consumption, the first book to encapsulate Erté's vast and varied creative output was written by our colleague Charles Spencer, under the title *Erté,* and published in 1970. Subsequent volumes published by Dover focused on the specific designs he created for fashion, theater costumes, and musical revues. Especially inspiring to fashion students, these books explained why the young Erté, who was both creator and artist, advanced further than his peers on the Poiret team who were either creators or depicters of costumes. Here, too, students could glean a sense of Erté's creative process—by his admission that he designed his provocative ensembles through one of two ways, i.e, to concentrate on an interesting or striking hairstyle, piece of jewelry, or other detail that might suggest the idea of a lavish costume or to build a costume by extending the lines of the naked body into decorative arabesques. Erté's autobiography, *Things I Remember,* published by Quadrangle/The New York Times Book Company, followed in 1975. This was succeeded by large-format books on Erté's *oeuvre,* produced by Marshall Lee and published by Dutton, under the titles *Erté at Ninety, Erté Sculpture, Erté at Ninety-five, My Life/My Art,* and *Erté: Art to Wear/The Complete Jewelry.*

At this point in time, one could no longer correctly call the amount of interest generated in Erté's career a revival or rebirth. It was, in fact, a sensation. Attendees at crowded exhibitions in art capitals of the world, including Tokyo, San Francisco, New York, Paris, London, Geneva, and Mexico City, stood alongside such luminaries as Claudette Colbert, Paloma Picasso, Gloria Vanderbilt, Bianca Jagger, Douglas Fairbanks, Jr., and the respected *New York Times* art critic John Russell.

In 1977 Erté was honored with the Ziegfeld Award for Excellence for his life's achievements, among them his dazzling "Gold" stage set, which was built for the *Ziegfeld Follies* of 1923 with six and a half miles of gold lamé. Diana Vreeland, who was then narrating a television film about Erté's life, said that no one in the twentieth century exerted more influence over fashion than Erté. During this period, whenever a new graphics edition of Erté's was released, it was oversubscribed within a matter of days. His major art books were repeatedly reprinted. Prices for Erté's works rose so steadily that some art dealers in New York used his gouaches as fiat for works by other artists.

The buildup to such phenomenal demand for Erté's linear art continued throughout 1979 as discussions were conducted with RKP International of New York to cast limited editions of sculptures by Erté. This was a natural avenue to pursue, as Erté's two-dimensional work on paper was always designated for three-dimensional application. His illustrations for a pearled and plumed confection, double-trained ermine ensemble, and turquoise-studded Byzantine tunic were assuredly decorative, but, first and foremost, they were patterns for those costumes worn by Mistinguette in *Marvels of the Orient*, Gaby Deslys in *La Marche à l'étoile*, and Lucrezia Bori in *Pelléas et Mélisande*. As the definitive draftsman, Erté understood clearly how the creations adapted from his designs would look long before their execution. He knew that they would be historically correct for a particular role, that their lines and colors would convey character and mood, and that invariably the recommended textile with specific texture, weight, and finish would drape as illustrated.

He also knew that his visual memory was extremely keen and that while he could easily recall and relish the momentary sweep of a diva's gown, the droll fling of a *danseur's* whip, or the breathtaking splendor of a long-gone Assyrian stage set, few others could. So the prospect of translating many of his now-coveted designs into permanent three-dimensional forms for others to enjoy fascinated the artist. He knew that the movements he so freely captured in his graphics—a coquette's flirtatious gait, the billow of a chanteuse's scarf, or the curves of his synchronic mermaids—could be realized in three dimensions.

The exciting challenge of applying his designs to sculpture is one that the experimentalist Erté tackled briefly two decades beforehand when he created his twenty-piece abstract series entitled *Formes Picturales*. Composed of aluminum, copper, iron, wood, and glass, with thickly applied oils and enamels to further effect bas-relief, these sculptures expressed thoughts and emotions rather than elucidate his more recognizable human forms.

For the proposed series of figurative bronzes that was to be produced in the United States beginning in 1980, the first problem to overcome was finding the time that Erté needed initially to create his clay models. According to his schedule, he would be in the country for only six weeks in order to sign graphics and attend gallery openings before his return trip to Paris, where more work awaited him. It was therefore suggested and Erté agreed to employ a modeler, who, under supervision, would produce clay prototypes for these sculptures from Erté's illustrations, much as Erté had hired artisans in the past to copy his original works for various productions.

Although pragmatic in theory, the initial clay models failed to convey the fresh definition and elegance of Erté's designs. Their scale and proportion were reproduced with precision, but their positioning and detailing required modification and articulation. It took Erté's own hand to correct this, with his modeler's wire loops and paddles as well as his personal comments and notations. For instance, he more deeply scored the helical headress of *La Plume;* more forwardly canted the arm of his

La Merveilleuse; more emphatically grooved the draped chiton in *An Evening in 1922.* The twenty-four-piece "Sculpture Collection" series that resulted from these and the other adjusted clay models was so popular that two subsequent editions were cast within the decade—an eighteen-piece "Images in Bronze" series and a three-piece "America" series, all of which were published by Fine Art Acquisitions, Ltd., of New York.

During this period Erté reveled in the exorbitant amount of international attention and affection that was bestowed upon him. He charmed Continental and American film crews that were producing documentaries on his life as he neared his ninetieth birthday. He was delighted with the major retrospectives of his work that were held in Paris, Copenhagen, London, and New York. And he was duly flattered when presented with the prestigious Order of Literature and Arts by the French Government at a Legion of Honor Awards ceremony.

Our friend Lisa Taylor, director of the Cooper-Hewitt Museum in New York, the national design affiliates of the Smithsonian Institution in Washington, D.C., has been actively aware since the early seventies of Erté's contribution to twentieth-century style and exhibited some of his works from time to time. Certainly, it was in part her influence that prompted the Smithsonian to organize a traveling exhibition of his gouaches and lithographs that toured the United States, Canada, and Mexico for three years. Indeed, this retrospective paid tribute to Erté's past contributions to all the visual arts; more specific recognition of his continued interest in the performing arts field came by way of a request made by Leonard Bernstein to Erté at a cocktail party. At that time, the master conductor was set to record a series of nine symphonies by Gustav Mahler for Deutsche Grammophon and asked if the same number of Erté's recently published works might be used as the individual dust jacket illustrations for those recordings. Deutsche Grammophon negotiated this with us, and we were delighted that Erté's works would be used. As a matter of course, it was Leonard Bernstein's recording of the Third Symphony with the New York Philharmonic from that series which won the coveted Grammy Award for classical music for 1989.

During the 1980s Erté again became an international celebrity and was fêted accordingly. Pierre Cardin organized a soigné party at Maxim's for him; Barbra Streisand entertained him at her home; Barbara Stanwyck, Elizabeth Taylor, and Cary Grant appeared at celebrations in his honor. He was recognized as a living legend wherever he went. With the arrival of 1985 a full seventy years had passed since Erté initially came onto the American scene with the first of some 250 covers that he had illustrated for *Harper's Bazaar.* A number of gallery attendees knew this and would often bring a past issue or two of this magazine for Erté to autograph. (He loved to do that, as the very sight of Harper's reminded him of the sweet and bittersweet memories of his association with that periodical: the mutual professional admiration he enjoyed with its publisher, William Randolph Hearst, and the unfortunate strong-arm editorial practices waged against him after his twenty-two-year tenure with that magazine by Carmel Snow, a fresh-from-*Vogue*, newly installed chief—the latter of which prompted Erté to sever his lucrative contract with the publication.) At gala openings, throngs of his devotees and enchanted collectors wanted to share such considerable time with him that Sal and my concern for his health and stamina prompted the use of guards in order to monitor the flow of well-wishers.

Understandably, the enormity of this workload exceeded our ability to deal with it. We therefore recognized an opportunity when Ray Perman agreed to join us in November 1985. He was the former chief operating officer at Christie's art auctioneers in New York and had recently returned to Christie's King Street headquarters in London. We had known Ray during the twenty-one years that he was at Christie's, were impressed by his professional mien, and, in fact, often relied on him to bid on paintings for us when we elected to keep our identity confidential.

Initially, we intended to have Ray manage the sale of our gallery's stock, which included a substantial collection of works by early-twentieth-century artists from Russia, Italy, Czechoslovakia, and England. However, it was not long before he, too, became involved in the growing Erté business matter. Posters were now being designed for the theater; ceramic dinnerware bore Erté's distinct illustrations; glass vases from Baccarat carried Erté etchings, as did French *lumières*. In the past, he had designed canes, umbrellas, fans, collars, flacon bracelets, scent bottles, screens, and cushions in addition to fashions and costumes, so this was much like a return to his vital postwar youth. As the range of products broadened, new designs needed to be created and approved, prototypes analyzed and adjusted, and trademarks safeguarded. With all this work, our concern for Erté's endurance continued. But, far from tiring, he accelerated his pace in applying his designs to these various mediums. Indeed, the prospect of a new project was like an elixir to him. He thrived on it because there was the added dimension in knowing that every project on which he now embarked could be completed and accepted.

As the amount of products increased, so did the number of unauthorized uses of Erté's name. A verbal understanding had existed from the onset of our relationship, but since this was not sufficient for us to legally protect the artist's interests, we acquired, with Erté's agreement, all his copyrights in 1974. He assigned all rights in his works to us in later agreements. Consequently, we were able to register his trademark in various countries and, through our diligent efforts, were able to protect the copyrights. He knew that if this were not done, the number of unauthorized works would have severely damaged the market and led to recriminations with our sanctioned licensees. With the help of various lawyers, we were therefore able to protect his designs and successfully bring suit against every offender. For my part, I increasingly enjoyed negotiating contractual terms as much as Sal and now Ray did helping Erté to analyze and adjust project prototypes. This entire working relationship was harmonious and rewarding, especially upon hearing that when secondary market sales were computed, total sales of Erté works probably exceeded $100 million a year at point of sale. The figure was astounding both in a monetary sense and as a gauge of the almost universal interest in Erté's work. Unfortunately, this felicitous collaboration had its frailty and would continue for only three years more.

During the early part of 1988 Sal was noticeably not well. Due to a protracted legal dispute concerning a number of Erté's works, she neglected her health, and sought medical attention only when those legal matters were finally resolved. At her consultation she was told that her diagnosis indicated that she had cancer, after which she underwent three major operations over the course of the next eighteen months. Needless to say, I was overwrought: first by the word of her illness and subsequently by the horror to which she would be subjected in attempting to cure her disease. This bore heavily on my mind during this entire period. Erté, who was as devoted to Sal as I, was similarly distraught by this sequence of events. He missed her companionship and thoughtful advice, particularly as he had just purchased a farm in Majorca and was looking forward to her help in renovating the farmhouse. Sal and Erté so complemented each other in their decorative tastes that he had hoped to recreate as welcome an environment for us at his new home as that

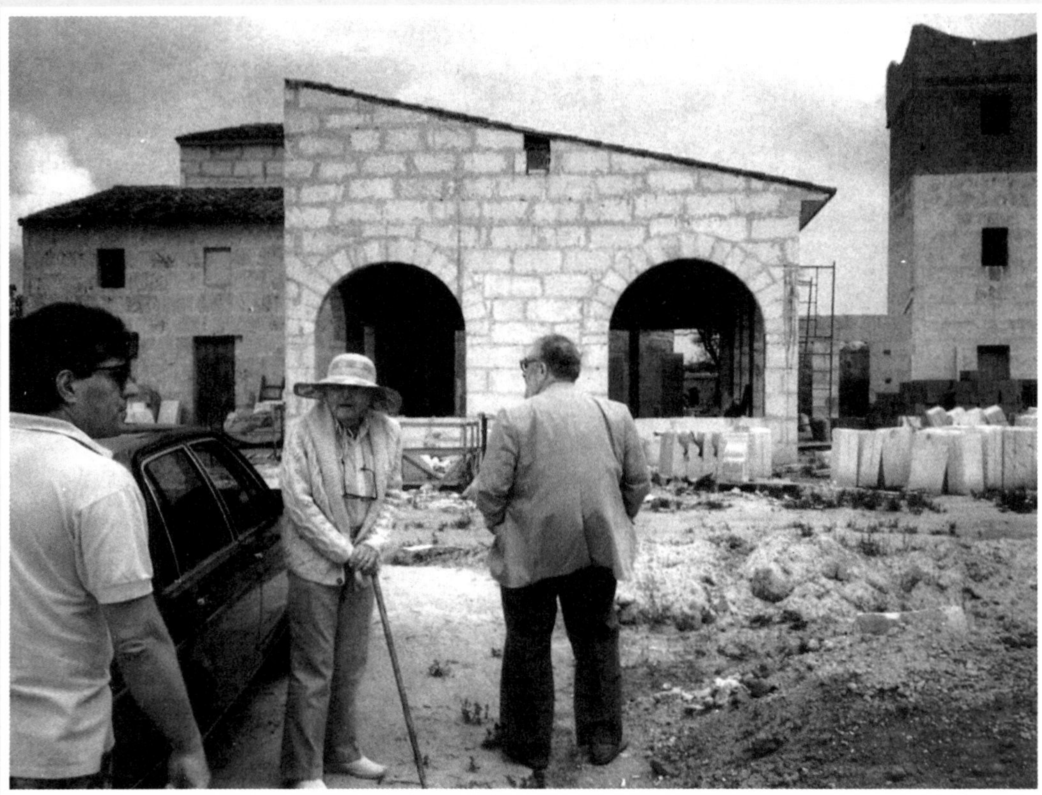

Erté and Eric Estorick watching the construction of Erté's finca *on Majorca*

which he enjoyed during his long visits with us at our winter home in Barbados. He even drafted plans for our personal guest quarters, which he hoped to furnish to Sal's taste. Fate, however, would see to it differently.

During Sal's illness, our associate Ray Perman proved to be invaluable because of his broad Christie's experience. He worked directly with Erté between London, Majorca, and New York to examine, amend, and approve product prototypes, while I continued to administer the business and work with him. Here again, Ray and the less ambulatory Sal functioned enormously well because of a very strong mutual bond emanating from genuine respect and devotion for each other and my becoming godfather to Ray's newborn son. In her lucid hours toward her end she maintained a continuing rapport with Ray and, in so doing, kept an affectionate watch over Erté while Ray produced splendidly. Sadly, Sal died in August 1989.

In the period of Sal's illness, Erté devoted a good deal of his time to the development of his newly acquired estate. He received substantial sums of money from us as and when he wanted it, and this enabled him to begin to renovate and furnish his new home without limitation. As Erté wanted me to see the work that was being undertaken on his farmhouse compound, I accompanied Ray on a brief trip to Palmas de Majorca. Erté had long dreamed of being landed, and now that he finally owned property on an island where he spent many a happy holiday, he let his creative sense of fancy run free in the plans he set forth for this house. As expected, his ideas were as spectacular as any stage set he had ever created for the Châtelet, Bal Tabarin, Ba-ta-Clan, or Opéra-Comique. His arched entrance was as sublime as his backdrop for *Au Soleil du Mexique*, his living room as lofty as his set for *Les Palais du bonheur*, his studio as sleek as his background for *Les Fleurs du mal*, and his interior as grand as his set for *Les Mamelles de Tirésias*, the opera written by his close friend Francis Poulenc. Outdoors, a number of his sculptures were to serve as fountains to grace his courtyard and to flank his uniquely formed swimming pool. The two tantalizing sirens that create his numeral *3* posed as the cynosure for the one, while a shell-toting mermaid and merman acted as the lodestar to the other. In passing, some of the dimensions I distinctly recall were that the living room was to rise to the impressive height of twenty-seven feet and extend thirty-six feet long and twenty feet wide.

Considering all the energy, experience, and foresight that Erté poured into his easy-to-execute plans, the renovations progressed at an alarmingly slow rate. Since Erté, characteristically, did not want to become involved in the noncreative aspects of his new venture, he asked us to assume that responsibility. Accordingly, we employed an English architect to oversee and hasten the work, and a local lawyer was hired to manage and disburse the appropriate funds.

Erté at ninety-six continued to be a whirlwind of productive imagination. As the construction of his house proceeded, he created two scenes for the Radio City Music Hall Easter show of 1990, a variety of objets de vertu and some jewelry for Circle Fine Art, and the costume and stage set designs for the musical Stardust, which was the brainchild of Louise Westergaard, the producer of *Sophisticated Ladies.* With Ray and David Rogath he reviewed, revised, and approved over sixty graphics and an even greater number of sculptures for Chalk & Vermilion, which now also published his sculptures, as well as another twenty-piece collection for Dyansen Corp., formerly Fine Art Acquisitions.

While most of these works were destined for Western collectors, a parallel demand in Japan had been developing during the eighties. This was not surprising, as Erté's illustrations had much in common with the linear fluency, color sense, and impeccable workmanship of Japan's *ukiyo-e.* The two eighteenth-century masters of that school of genre painting and printmaking to whom Erté is most often compared are Kitagawa Utamaro and Katsukawa Shunsho. Erté's statuesque, gracefully proportioned women suggest those of Utamaro, while his dramatic color schemes and sensuous lines are reminiscent of Shunsho.

To gauge the degree of the Japanese demand for Erté's work, Ray and I twice visited Tokyo. There we renewed our acquaintance with Masayuki Koreeda, who had been a collector of Erté's original work for some time, had recently purchased a number of Erté's graphics from our gallery, and whose company had been granted a license by us. We developed an association with Mr. Koreeda which led to two major exhibitions of Erté's gouaches and graphics in Tokyo and the opening of Sevenarts Tokyo, "The Erté Gallery". About the same time, our colleague David Rogath formed an association with Kiyotada Kadoya of Art Collection House that led to exhibitions in Osaka, Kyoto, Fukuoka, Sapporo, and numerous other cities in Japan.

The idea of having a gallery devoted entirely to his work in a country where he felt a kinship due to his Russian-Asiatic heritage so honored Erté that he promised to visit Tokyo in 1989 to open the new gallery's grand inaugural exhibition and to celebrate his ninety-seventh birthday.

Saluting Erté's birthday with feasts and fanfare in various cities across the globe had long been part of our overall practice to introduce this artist to his new audiences of international collectors. These celebrations were initially small and intimate, but they, too, blossomed over the years to a grand scale on par with Erté's acclaim. At the premier birthday dinner, which we hosted in Geneva, our entourage, including Erté, found itself dancing until dawn at a private club; a larger luncheon in Beverly Hills saw many of filmdom's smart set arrive in Erté-inspired dresses; a stately museum benefit ball in Miami was capped by a fireworks finale; and a sensational gala sponsored by Chalk & Vermilion in New York City was replete with acrobats and masquerading mannequins.

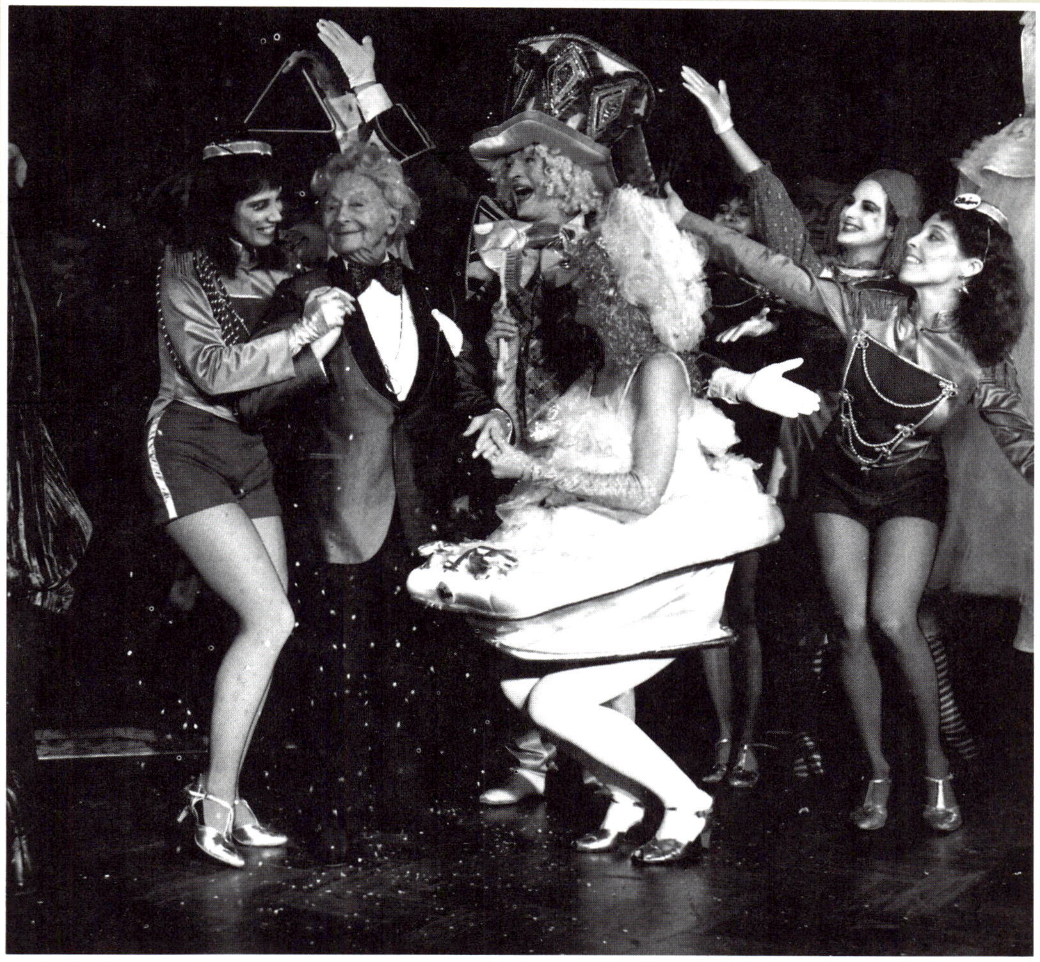

Erté at his 94th birthday celebration at the Plaza Hotel, New York, 1986

As we started to arrange plans for Erté's ninety-seventh birthday celebration in 1989, the artist proposed that the event be held in Paris at Régine's. Not only was she a fond acquaintance who had once hosted a birthday dinner for him in New York, her restaurant, Le Doyen, on the Champs-Élysées, held great sentiment for Erté. Built as a château a century before his birth, the palatial residence had become a fine restaurant and was often the place where Erté and his close friend Prince Nicholas Ouroussoff toasted special occasions together. For the birthday celebration, the room was flush with feathers and paste jewels, and the ever-gracious Erté was in his dependably high spirits. Those spirits rose even higher when I told him that I had concluded a deal the previous week to package an Erté perfume. He would use the fragrance of his choice in a variety of scent bottles that he had designed in the 1930s. Erté had long wanted to find his signature scent contained in his sleekly designed transparent white, black, and gilt glass flacons; the Surrealist Salvador Dalí and other artists saw their perfumes brought to market, and so this news was truly like icing on his soon-to-arrive birthday cake.

In his later years, Erté had been in the habit of spending his winters with us in Barbados, but shortly after that December party in Paris, he said

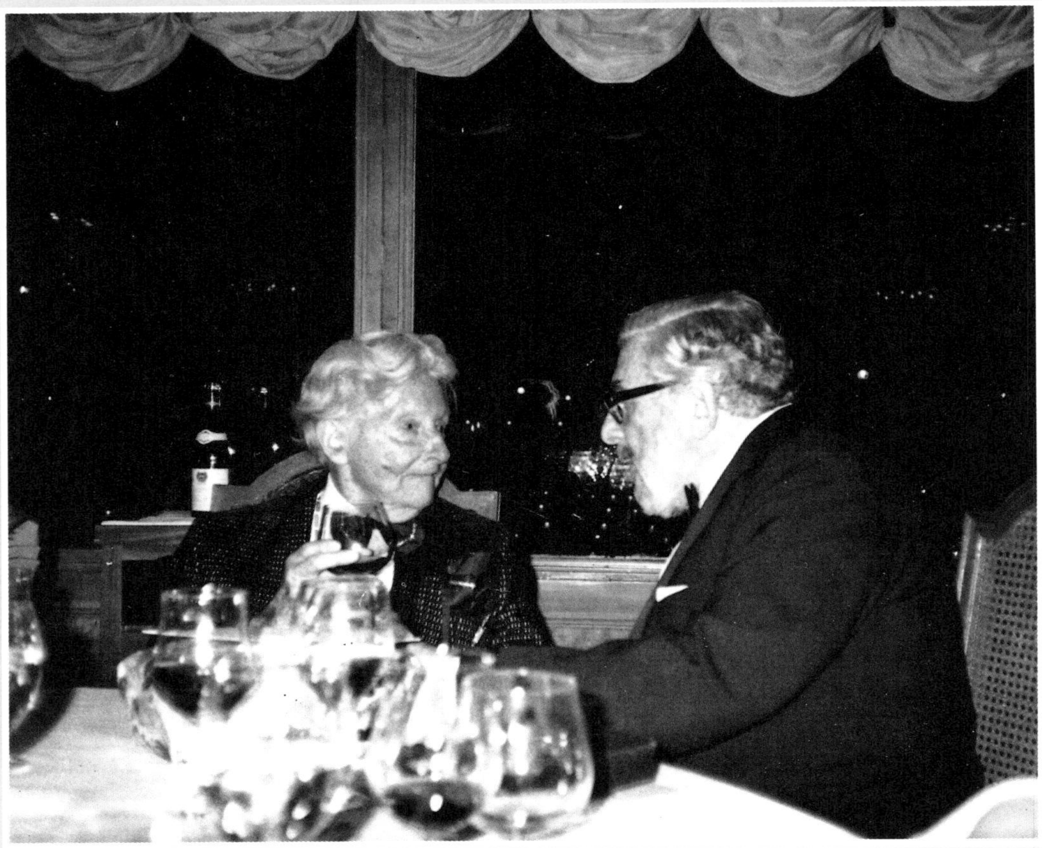

Erté with Eric Estorick at the 97th birthday celebration

that the memory of Sal would be too painful for him there. He would instead visit Majorca in January and Mauritius in March. This plan caused Ray and me much concern. Although Erté had always taken extremely good care of himself with his prudent diet and daily exercise regimen, he was careful to holiday at his customary resorts, where he was well known and could remain in close contact with us. We had no wavering doubts about his well-being in Majorca. He had vacationed there many times since 1948, and the island had a reliable communications network and dependable medical facilities should this near-centenarian require them. Mauritius, however, was unfamiliar territory. Other than its being a remote island east of Madagascar in the Indian Ocean, we were unaware of its telecommunications system and medical facilities. Obviously, this did not bode well, so I tried to dissuade him from embarking upon that trip. Erté, however, said that a friend suggested he must see "the most beautiful island on earth".

While in Mauritius with Serge Leeman, his chauffeur-companion, Erté became ill. A telephone conversation with Ray ensued during which Erté pleaded that he be brought back to Paris. Upon hearing of the condition and distress of my friend, I immediately asked Ray to organize a medical team, to schedule them to fly by air ambulance to the island, and for Ray to accompany them, which he did. Unfortunately, Erté had suffered from acute kidney failure, which had gone unattended for a number of days, and on Ray's arrival Erté had been taken to a local clinic, part of which time he lapsed into a coma. Fortunately, the plane and the medical team were able to transfer him without delay to the neighboring island of Réunion, where superior medical facilities were available for his treatment. Erté's doctors on Réunion released him from their care when his condition became stable, and at that time he returned with Ray to Paris, where he was admitted to the Hôpital Cochin. Here the doctors were astounded at Erté's rapid recovery and were on the verge of sending him home. However, his condition could not be sustained, and, despite medical efforts, Erté died suddenly on April 21, 1990. Certainly, the shock of his demise was enormous to me, for it was as if our long, devoted friendship and exciting business association had ended far too abruptly, prematurely, and tragically. We had shared so much together and looked forward to accomplishing so much more.

Like a family member whom one had always known to be reliably there, it remains difficult to accept the reality that Erté is no longer with us. When I consider the many years that we worked in collaboration, I distinctly recall his strength, energy, strong sense of responsibility, and personal heroism, which was evident at our first meeting. Erté then had very little and complained very little, but he continued to practice his skill and on occasion even exchanged his work for food and drink. I remain elated by the chance occasion that brought Erté and my family together, which caused me to expand my activity in the world of art dealing, for there was more vitality, excitement, and discovery in this one artist than there could have been through my association with a hundred others. His joie de vivre carried over and was shared individually by every member of my family. For example, he and my daughter, Isobel, enthusiastically occasioned to share a unisex-designed costume in which they were photographed for the press. Some years later, my son, Michael, who was similarly devoted, named his first-born after Erté. In retrospect, I am saddened, however, by the fact that his studio no longer exists. Not only was it pure period in style and exquisite to behold, its layout and library could have inspired young art students in their own flights of fancy, which is what Erté would have liked. As a matter of fact, part of the long plan that was so abruptly terminated was to develop a museum near his home that was to permanently display his personal collection of his own works. We had held previous discussions with the Louvre Museum in Paris with respect to acquiring the contents and collection of Erté's apartment, much to the artist's pleasure. During the course of our discussions, it was understood that a foundation would be formed with the artist as its permanent head and myself as chief officer. As Erté did not want to have his apartment disturbed or his possessions transferred during his lifetime, he tacitly agreed that upon his death this could be done. Unfortunately, this never came to pass. Nor did his pet projects that the artist expressed a desire to establish and support but for which provisions were never made. The last works that this artist reviewed and revised include the seventy-one graphics and 105 sculptures contained in this book. He also created jewelry, which has been previously published, as well as a variety of objets de vertu which will be illustrated in a future publication. The graphics that are reproduced in this book date from 1989 and the sculptures from 1986. None have been previously published in book form and all reflect a continuity of this master's creativity. Erté dared to explore the technical possibility of every medium in an effort to enhance his works-in-progress. For example, in graphics this meant the use of black paper instead of white; the addition of embossing for subtle relief and the use of foil-transfer for smart, sparkling effects. In sculpture, this included the use of gold-leaf and polished embellishments to add eye-catching splendor, and multi-patination to achieve a variety of textures, colors, and finishes per piece.

The period in which Erté applied these innovative procedures to his art was fascinating to observe. My fortunate colleagues, Ray Perman of Sevenarts and David Rogath of Chalk & Vermilion, were exhilarated as they worked in conjunction with Erté to produce his last designs. I have therefore imposed upon each to detail their own experiences with this artist. Their respective experiences in their own hand follow.

With respect to collectors, I am confident that they will derive as much pleasure from their ownership of these last works as Erté did in creating them. As for me, I join the collectors in their appreciation of the works, yet have in addition the deep and lasting pleasure of my quarter-century relationship with the extraordinary man and artist Romain de Tirtoff—known as Erté.

E.E.

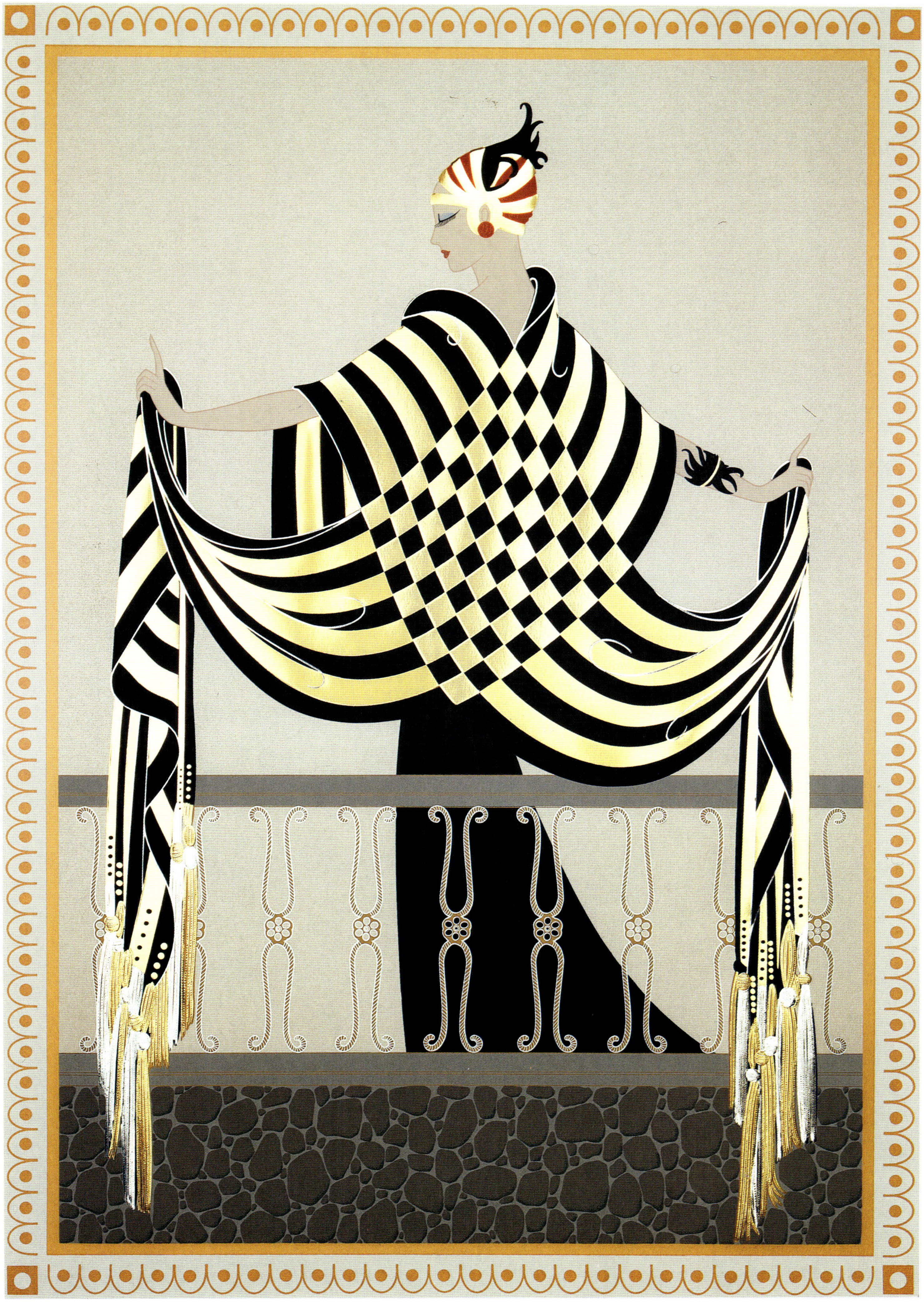

The Balcony
Le Balcon
Il balcone
Der Balkon

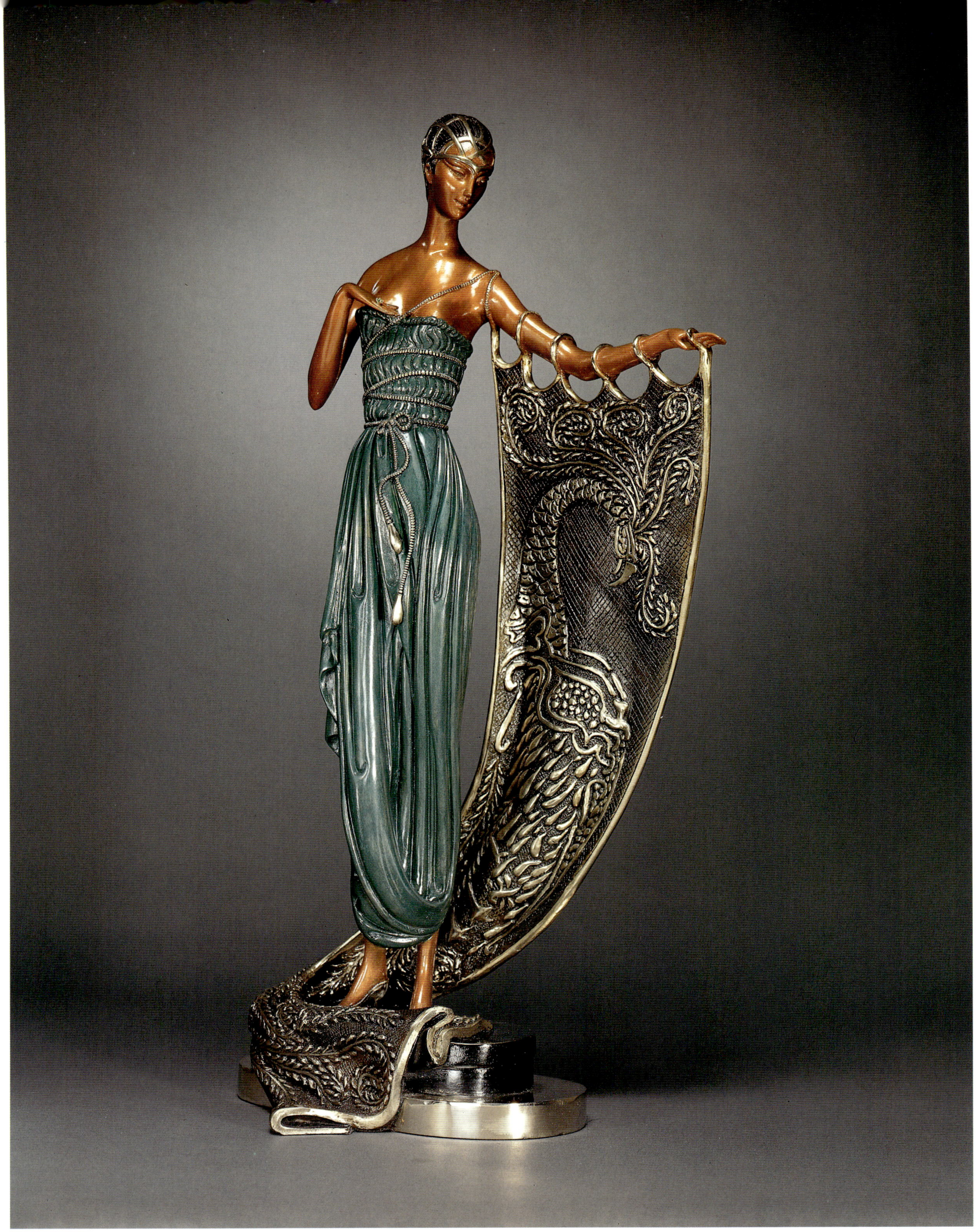

Emerald Night
Nuit d'emeraude
Notte di smeraldo
Smaragnacht

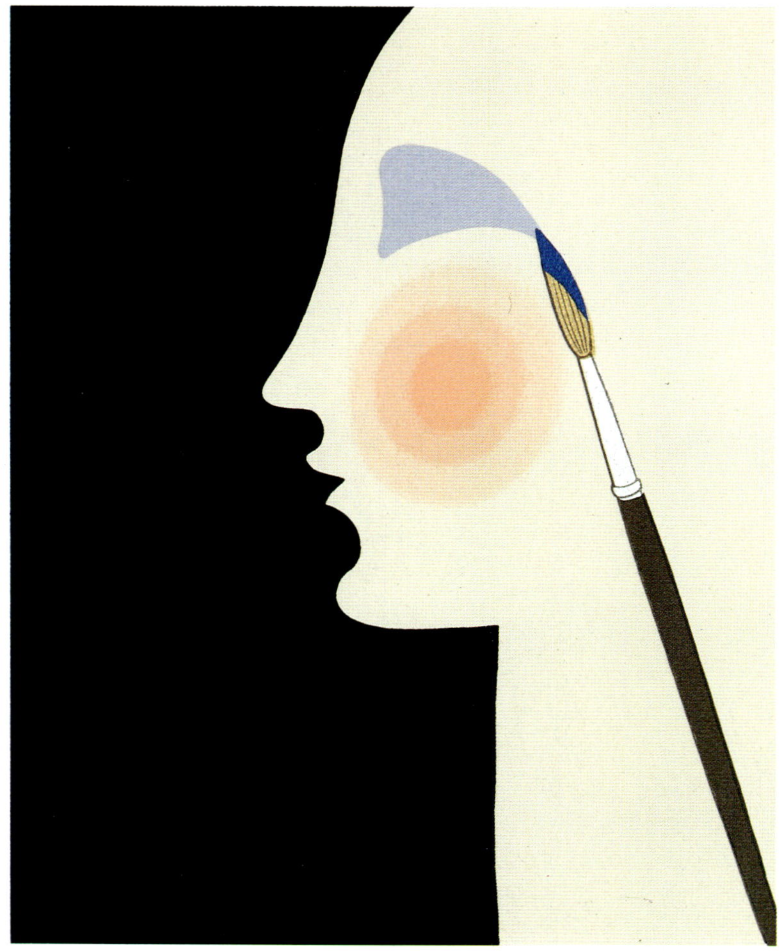

Cosmetic Brush
Pinceau à maquillage
Pennello da trucco
Schminkpinsel

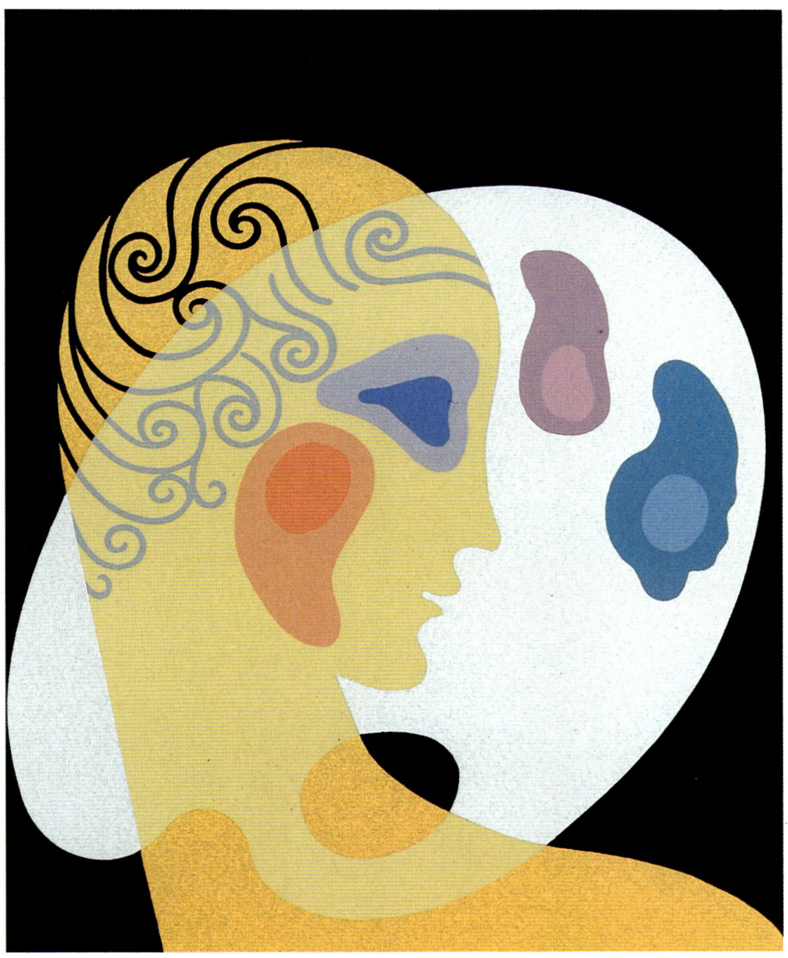

Cosmetic Palette
Palette à maquillage
Gamma di colori da trucco
Schminkpalette

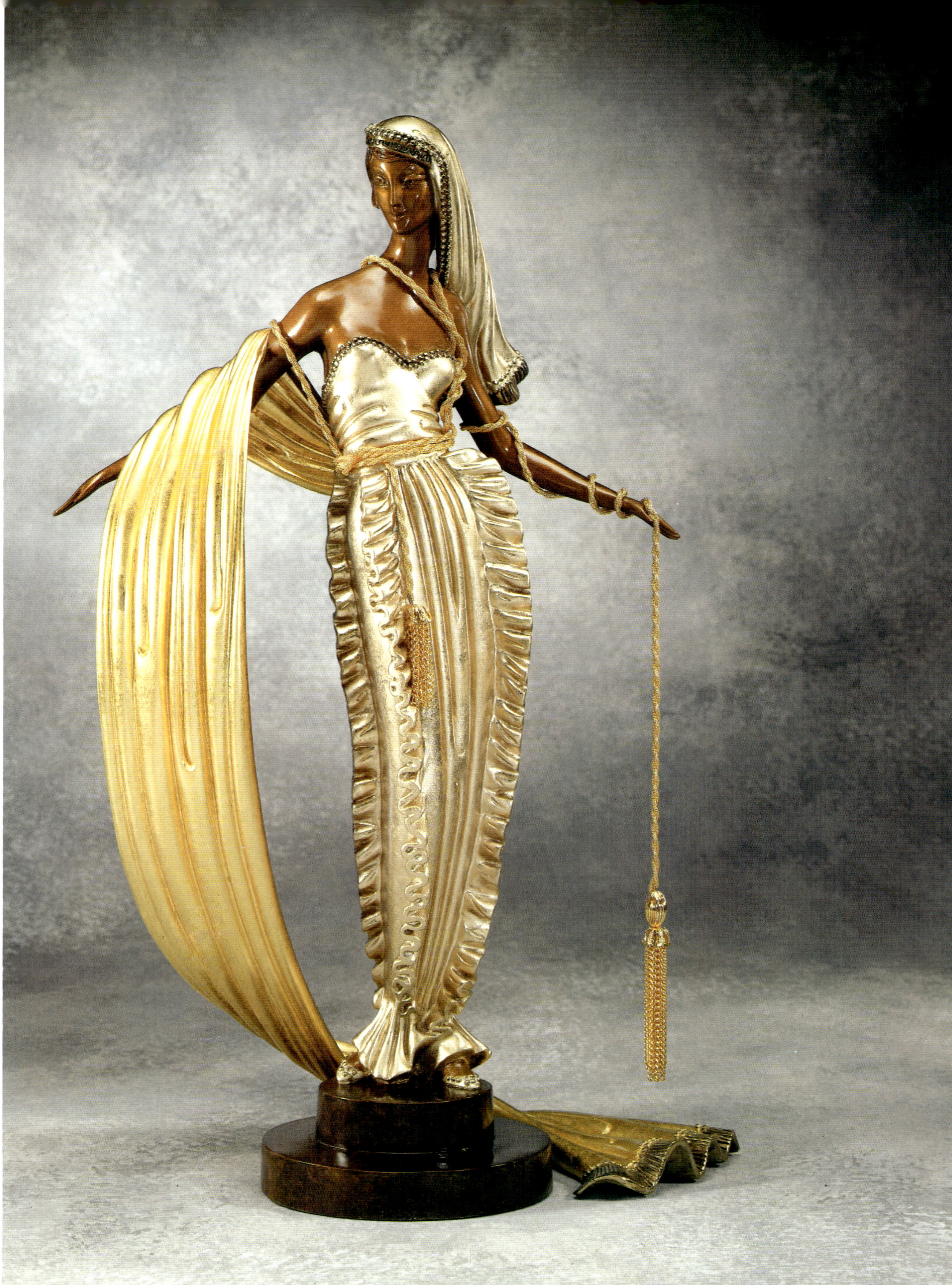

American Millionairess
Millionaire Américaine
Milionaria americana
Amerikanische Millionärin

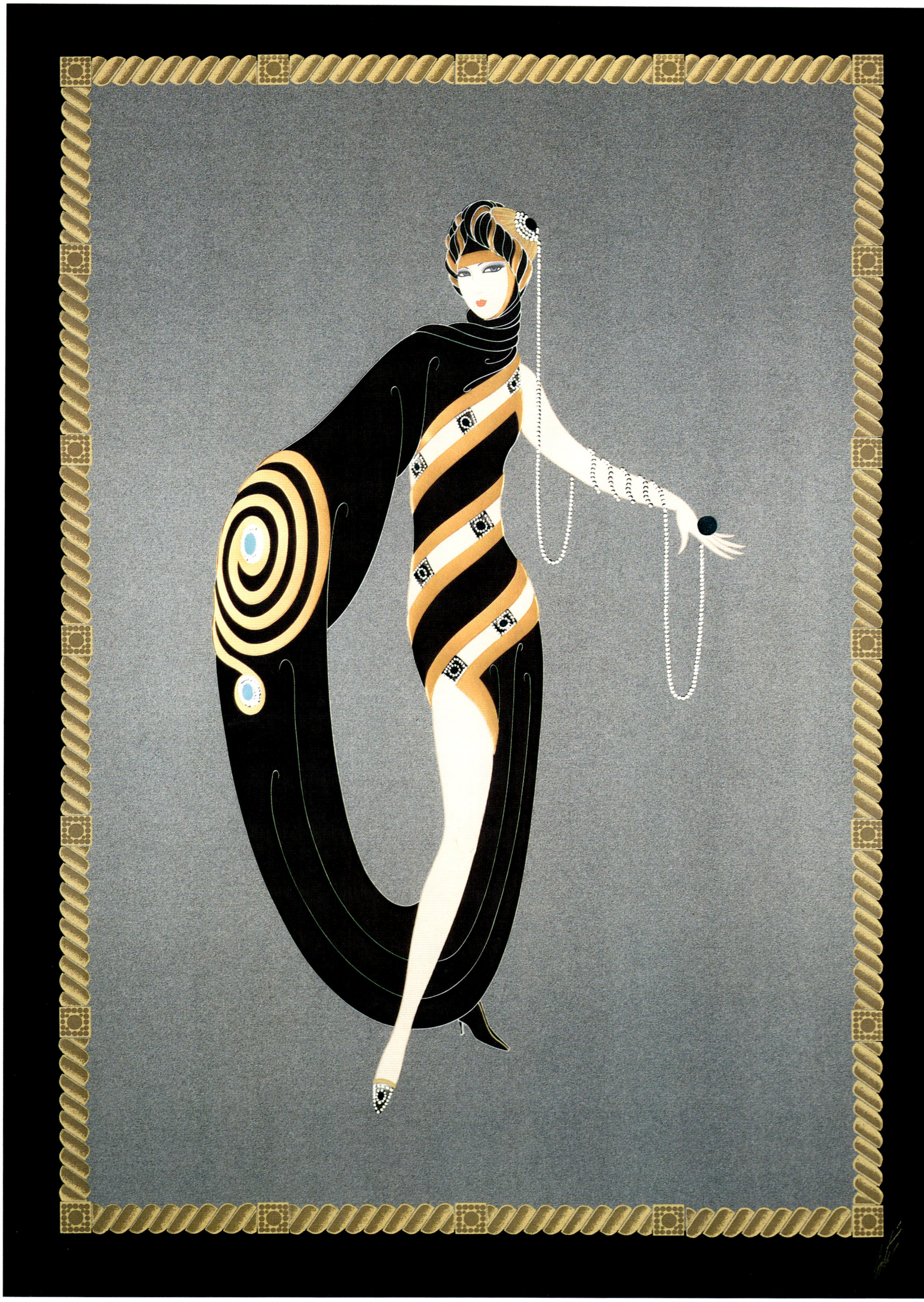

* *

Pearls and Emeralds
Perles et emeraudes
Perle e smeraldi
Perlen und Smaragde

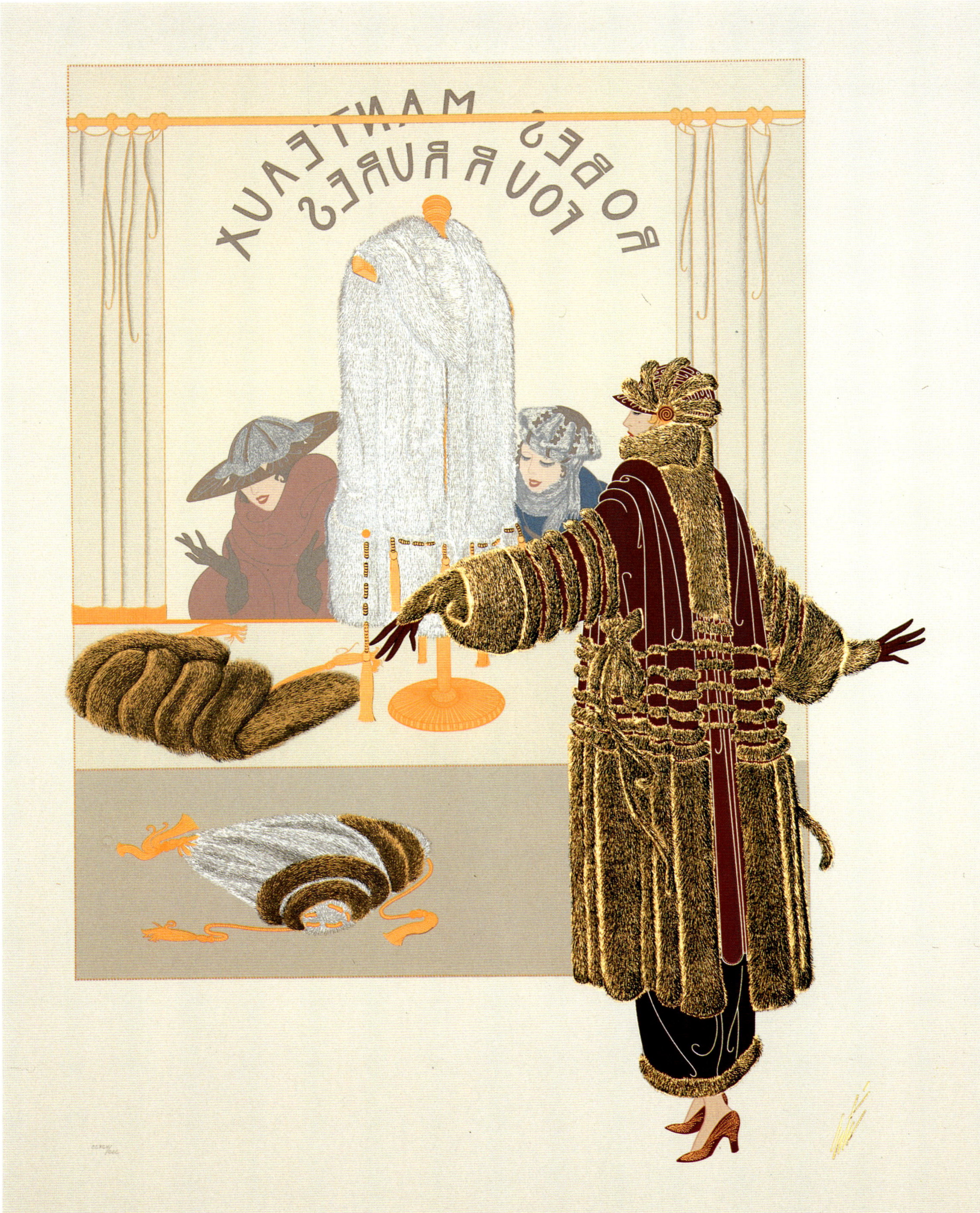

* *

Paris Boutique
Boutique de Paris
Boutique di Parigi
Pariser Modeladen

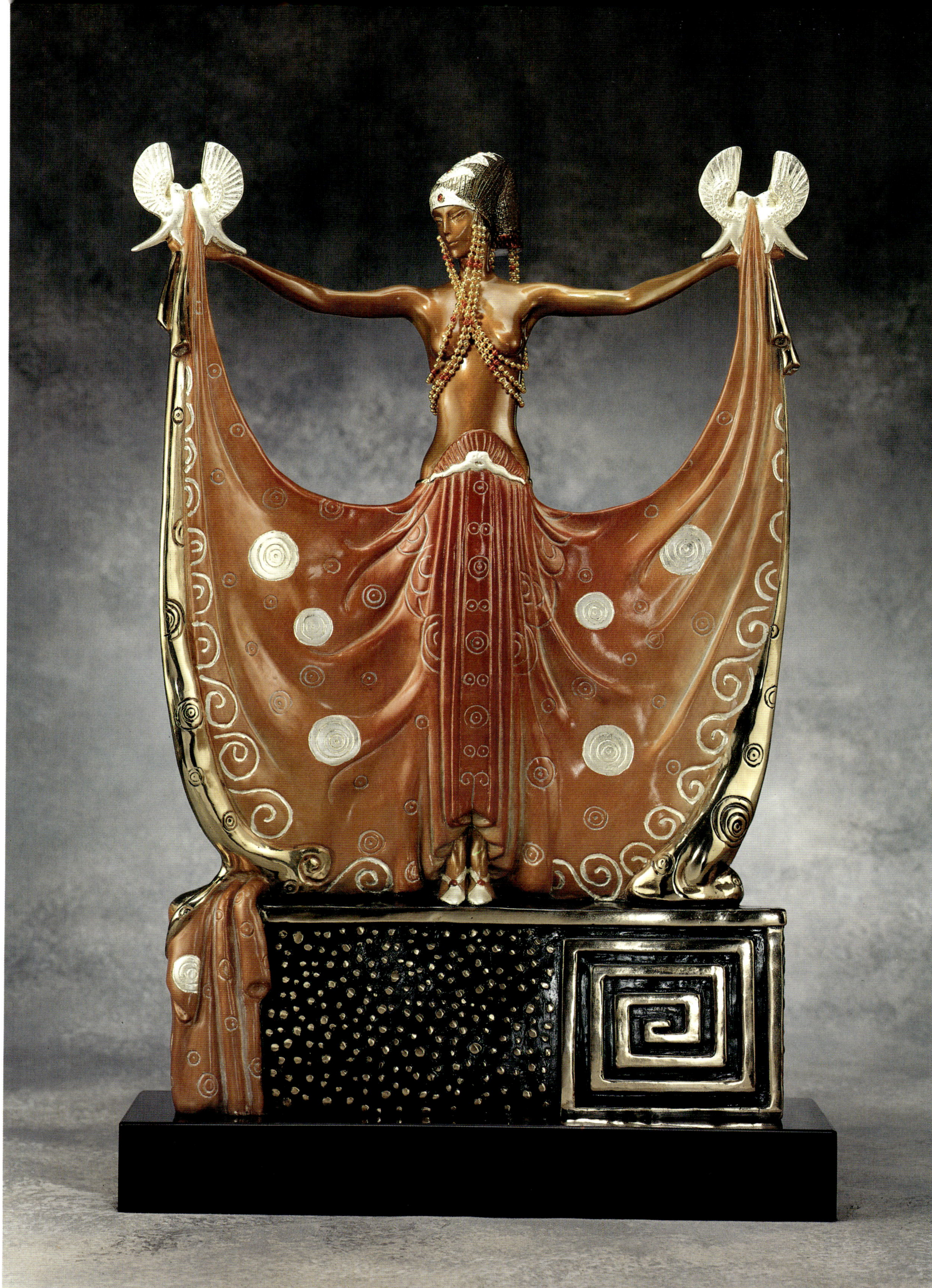

Venus
Vénus
Venere
Venus

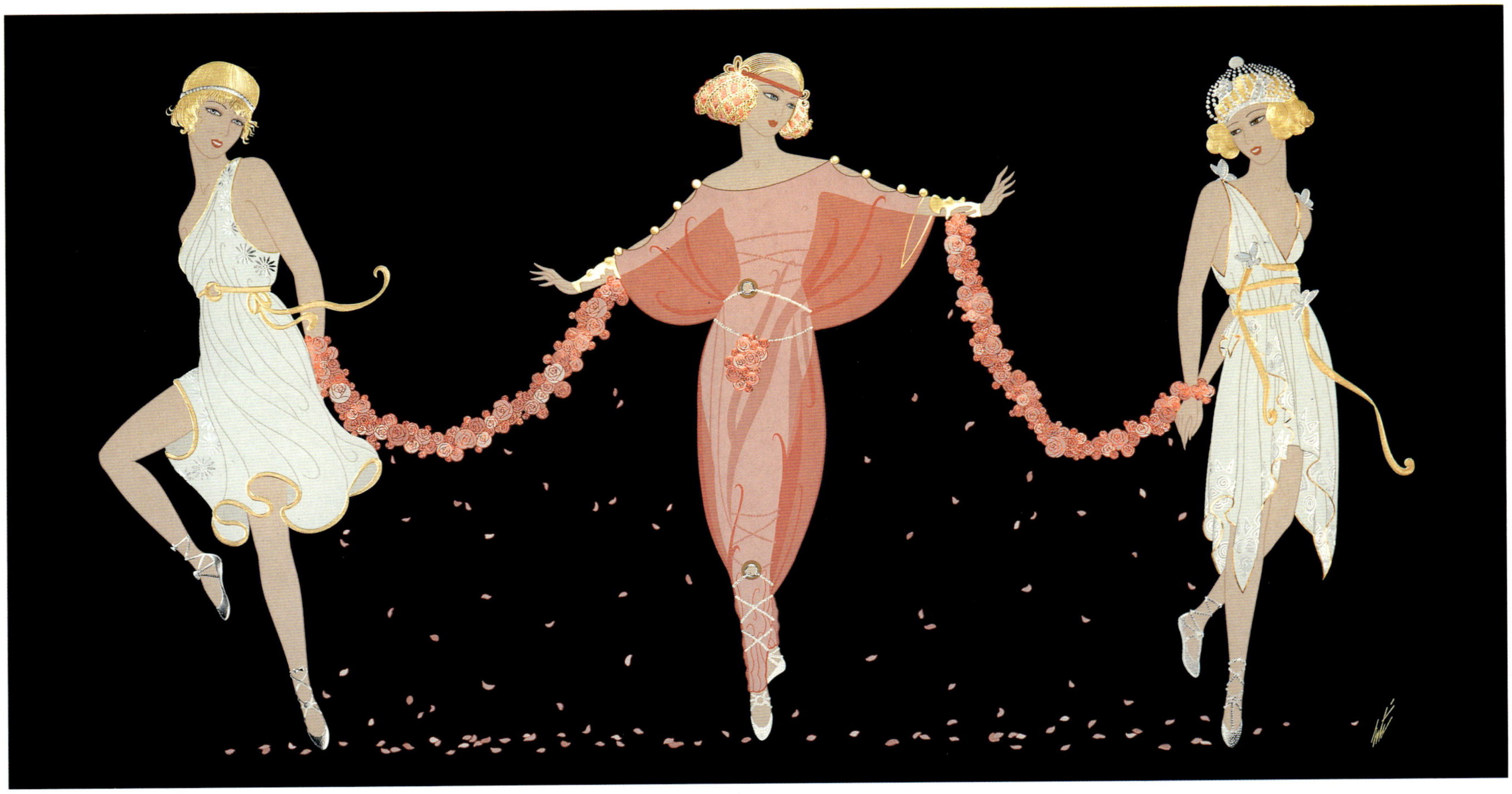

* *

Printemps
Printemps
Primavera
Frühling

GRAPHICS

INTRODUCTION

Erté at work on his last graphics

RAY PERMAN

Charles Sorlier, who collaborated with Marc Chagall to produce the artist's lithographs at the Parisian printing firm of Fernand Mourlot, once said, "I have had the rare privilege of seeing Chagall at work, and it cannot be denied that at times it seemed as if an angel had entered the workshop." Such was my opportunity and subsequent feelings as I acted on behalf of Sevenarts with the artist Erté and the publishers during the past four years to produce the serigraphs and sculptures that are illustrated in this book. It was impressive to watch this artist review a design conceived some time ago for a fashion magazine or a stage or film costume, then to see him carefully adapt that past-perfect rendering for its application to a different medium and, in the case of serigraphy, simultaneously assimilate its techniques and handle them with authority.

Prior to translating any artwork into the preliminary sketches needed to create the multiple images, I was quietly attentive as Erté selected those compositions whose lines were clean and precise, whose colors (or the promise thereof) were lush and beautiful, and whose overall designs lent themselves to accepting further color, embossing, and other printing techniques that were available. In short, the artist chose those works of which he was particularly proud and knew they would be enhanced in the transition. Once each selection was made, Erté then had his original design enlarged to the size that he had determined for the eventual print so that he could study it to make any necessary color adjustments or line refinements. In the graphics field, where I advanced his every decision to each work's appropriate printer or publisher, Erté relied on a set procedure to review and revise these croquis. He invariably took a long, hard look at the sheet that lay before him, we discussed his prospective modifications, and then he picked up his pen and began to work. Sometimes he simply noted the need for more vibrant hues and foil highlights, like the cobalt blue, jade green, and silver applied to his *Scandinavian Princess;* or recommended a color rendering of a formerly black-and-white drawing, as was done for his *Winter Promenade,* or perhaps a color substitution, like the blue-white palette that replaced the yellow-green one in *Angel Melody.* For the physical changes that Erté deemed necessary, he would place a near-transparent sheet atop the croquis, select his favorite pen, and use it to redraw the image. He might frame the alluring wide-brimmed hat in *Seduction* with a complementary background and border, or taper the fan-bearing arm of his *New Year's Eve* debutante.

As a master draftsman, Erté executed his alterations with extraordinary facility. He was delighted with their premier applications as designs for elegant ensembles, exotic raiments, or outrageous costumes for films or follies. In fact, he often recounted how these actually looked when produced, how they draped, and why certain accessories were critical elements in some of his compositions. He recalled how the form-fitting, slight red sheath of his Flapper with its sparkling web appliqué and pearl-stranded fan visually captured the giddy spirit of its Roaring Twenties musical *Manhattan Mary,* and why long draping sleeves or hand-held accessories were constants in those recherché costumes that he created for the aspiring opera singer Ganna Walska, known for her needling onstage habit of fidgeting with her hands. Erté tried to cover or curb that distraction with the additions that remain evident in the works entitled *Fedora Fur, Fedora Butterfly,* and *Fedora Fan.*

Much of the rationale behind Erté's current modifications to his work stemmed from the fact that he intended to incorporate various serigraphic procedures and their use dictated the need for further enhancement. We discussed the possibilities of adding relief to raise the surface of a billowing fold of fabric of plaited lock of hair, wherein Erté might suggest darker tones to emphasize the recessed areas of his pasha's throne in Casbah and ingenue's coif in *Flower Petal Gown.* Erté would avert the possibility of embossing's visually restricting an area by supplementing the illustration, such as his adding extra roses to the garland linking his three *Printemps* sylphs, then scattering petals below it. For those works in which he planned to add eye- catching gold or silver highlights, Erté checked the chance of excessive local accent by muting or removing any probable overbearing color, much as he eliminated the emphatic blue eye shadow on his *Balinese* dancer.

Once these preliminary adjustments to each work were completed, Erté would discuss the specific changes with me. I would make notes of any further alterations, then present these to the printer, where they were translated into the master screens needed to print each trial proof. These were then individually checked for image accuracy and transfer; the initial proof was made and, in turn, analyzed by the printer for its uniformly clear, crisp registry and color fidelity. Upon review of the proof, if Erté elected to make an adjustment such as to alter the background color, this was done. If he was pleased with that result, he might elect to print it or, occasionally, to print different editions of the same design, as was the case in *Tanagra,* with its individual red, blue, and turquoise fields. Black paper would alternately be used in instances like Le Harem moderne, where it provided a denser background than could be accomplished through inking. For many of these and the additional adjustments he suggested, a new proof would be pulled and reviewed by Erté until he was completely satisfied with the work. The artist would then sign this *bon à tirer* (literally, "good to pull"), which the printer would use as the definitive guide to each subsequent print in the edition. When the printing was completed, any plates required for embossing and foil stamping would be made, and the edition would then be embossed and stamped.

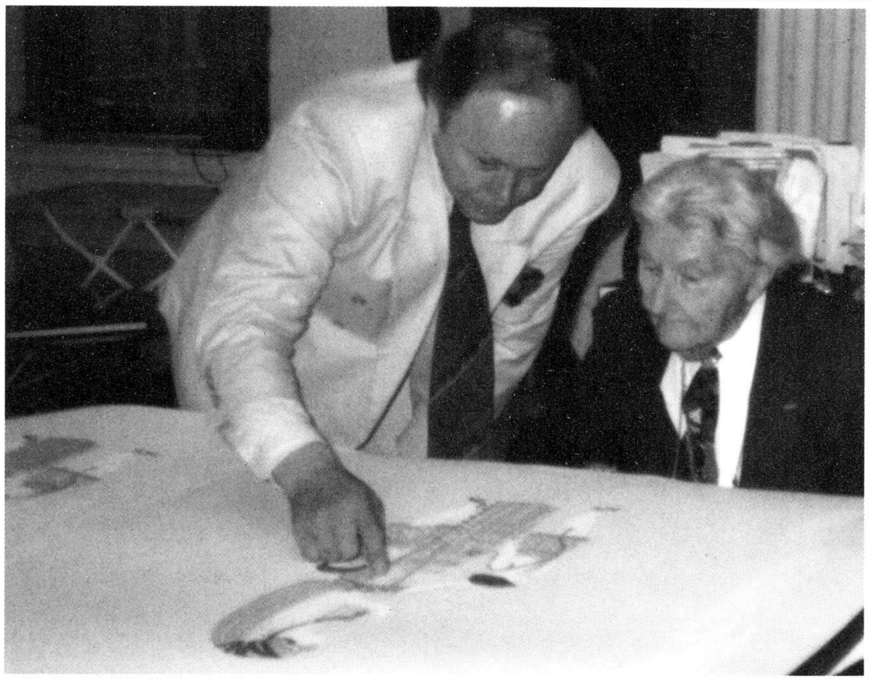

Ray Perman and Erté discussing corrections on Motherhood

Erté considered serigraphy a new avenue for creative expression rather than simply a means of transferring his designs to another medium. As he readily admitted, his spontaneous modifications and revisions imparted a true freshness to his original designs, while those accepted suggestions made by his publisher or printer regarding the application of such state-of-the-art techniques as multiple pigment layering and transparent ink use produced even greater results than what the artist working alone could achieve.

Erté worked diligently during the last three years of his life on the seventy-one graphics that are illustrated in this book and was able to complete and sign nineteen editions. There are forty-two works that bear Erté's gold hot-stamped signature stamp where the artist gave the instructions for its hot-stamping and foil transfer but had yet to place his own signature on the final result. With respect to the ten graphics that are designated "Erté Studio", the artist had selected the design of which he wished to create multiples and gave the initial color instructions. To all intents, the work that could have been completed by the artist had been done prior to his death. The production work sequence that followed thereafter was left to either me, the printers, or the publishers, and in each case the completion was faithfully executed.

The drawings and gouaches that serve as the basis for these works were produced over a fifty-six-year period dating from 1915, and they show Erté's extraordinary efforts as an independent couturier, fashion magazine and book illustrator, and costume and set designer for musical revues and opera. They also shed light on his broad intellectual scope and spirited personality. For example, his knowledge of classical art is clearly manifested in the *April, May,* and *June* images he created for the Folies-Bergère production of *Les Rois des légendes,* and his awareness of Eastern mythological specters remains apparent in *Masks and Mosques.* Closer inspection of his work likewise conveys Erté's wit, flair, and innovative mind. In *Cosmetic Brush,* which the artist executed for a 1932 *Harper's Bazaar* cover, he cleverly transformed his sleek brush head into his mannequin's arched eyebrow, while *Conte Hindou,* a stage set design for a sumptuous lotus land, illustrates Erté's unbridled imagination.

His constant state of creativity, resolve to produce his best, and, when accomplished, complete pride in effort are the virtues that I will always remember about Erté. He was so vital when considering a newly posed concept, eloquent and quick to develop it, and infectiously enthusiastic when seeing the final results.

In fact, his dedication to work never waned. He was the consummate artistic creator all of the time. Even after I accompanied him by air ambulance from a clinic on Mauritius to a hospital on Réunion, where his condition stabilized briefly. Erté asked for a progress report on a number of his graphics and complementary sculptures. Two weeks later, when his seemingly improved condition allowed me to move him to the Hôpital Cochin in Paris, we agreed to the artist's expressed wish to review the strike-offs for those graphics and photographs of the sculptures. One proof was for *Paris Boutique,* originally a pen-and-ink drawing of a scene at a fashionable furrier's; Erté's specified colors heightened its already luxurious nature. It was then that the artist gave instructions for its gold blocking and embossing.

It has been a genuine privilege for me to have been associated with a man distinguished by such grace in work and grace in character. Our mutual interest in the success and enjoyment of his work caused us to become inordinately good friends which was shared with his love for my family. I shall always miss him.

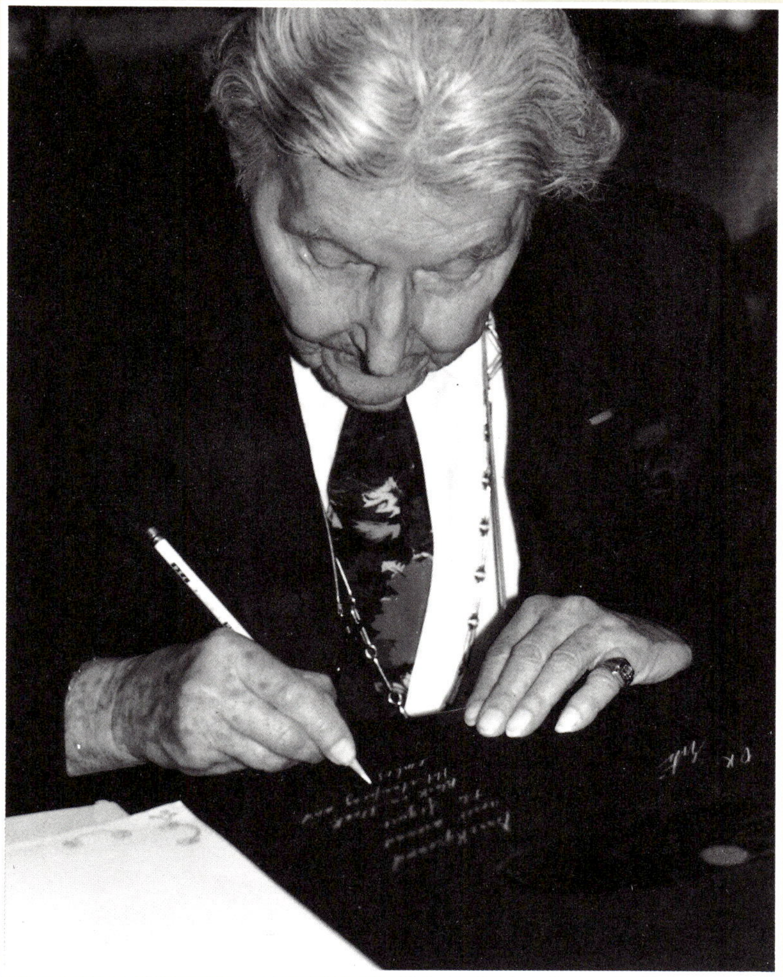

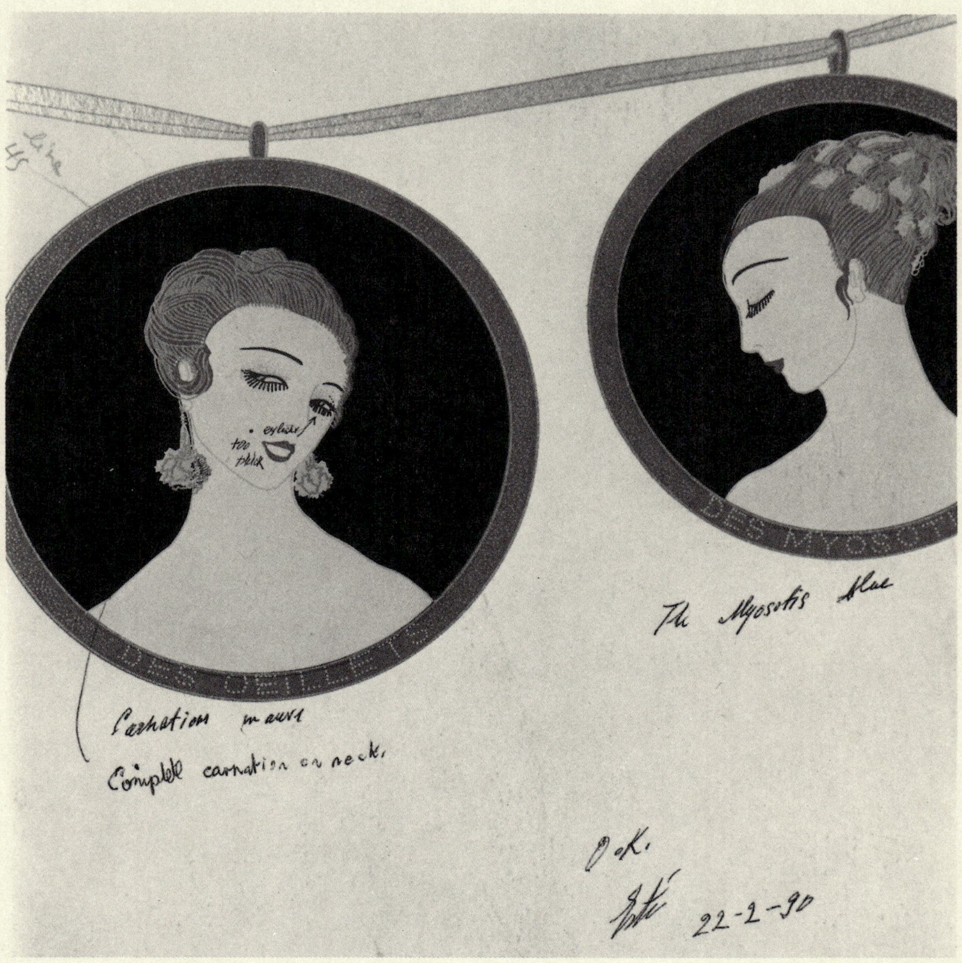
DES OEILLETS
The Myosotis blue
Carnation mauve
Complete carnation on neck.
O.K.
22-2-90

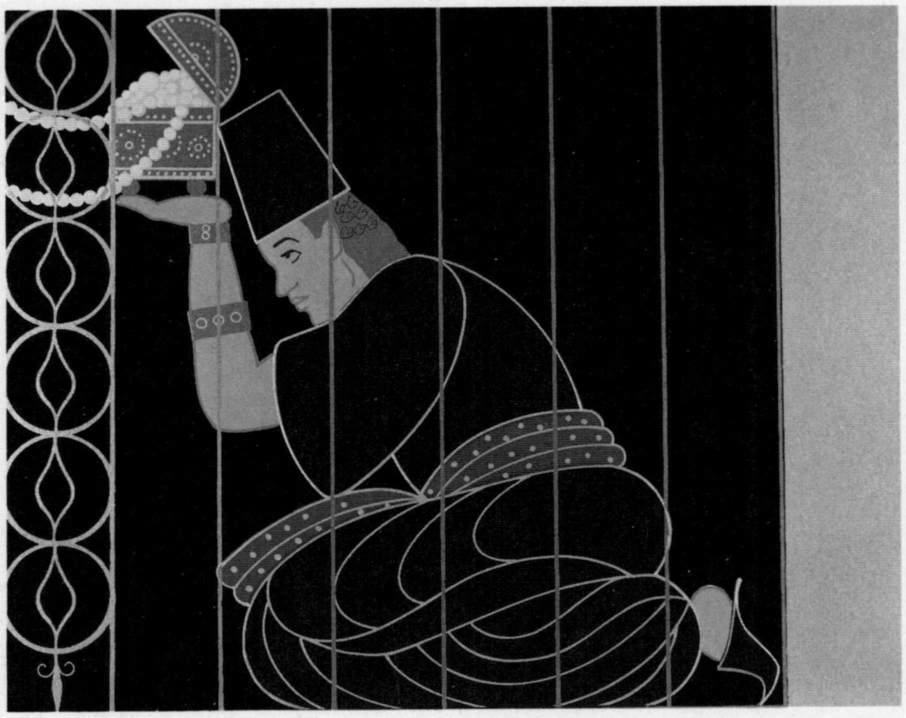

The skin of the eunuque should ~~should~~ be brown and the hair a little darker than the skin and with curly design. Otherwise O.K.

Erté

Dear David,

. . .

Graphics

Spider's Web

This is approved with the red version on the silvery background with black border. Erté requests that all the pearls and the fan and spider are embossed. The right-hand should be made a little smaller. He has also made an alteration to reduce the left forearm, which is also shown. This reduction will necessitate the completion of the pearl strings. Erté does not wish the hair to be made any longer and prefers that the right breast remains as shown with no indication, or at best a faint line.

Mirror Circle

Erté has approved the red version on black background. The ring on the hand in front of the mirror has to be obviously the same as the ring on the left-hand of the lady with her back shown in the mirror image. The neck of the lady outside of the frame needs to be amended as shown. Erté also suggests a complete colour to the edition and not the fading image as shown as present.

. . .

Yours ~~sincerely~~,

Best regards

Ray

Ray Perman

(The titles "Spider's Web" and "Mirror Circle" referred to in the letter were changed to "Flapper" and "The Looking Glass" respectively.)

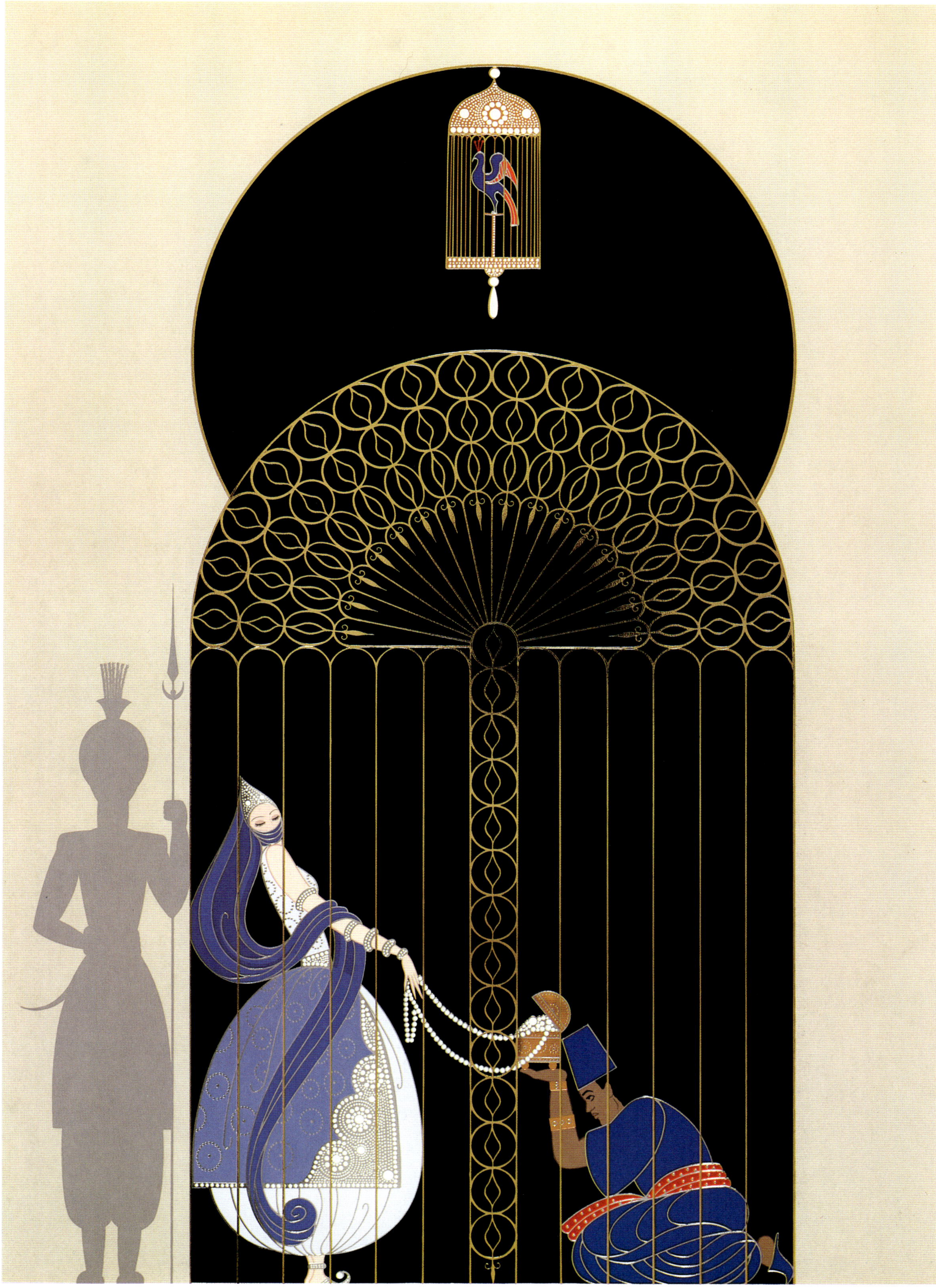

Bird in a Gilded Cage
L'Oiseau dans la cage dorée
Uccello in una gabbia dorata
Vogel im vergoldaten Käfig

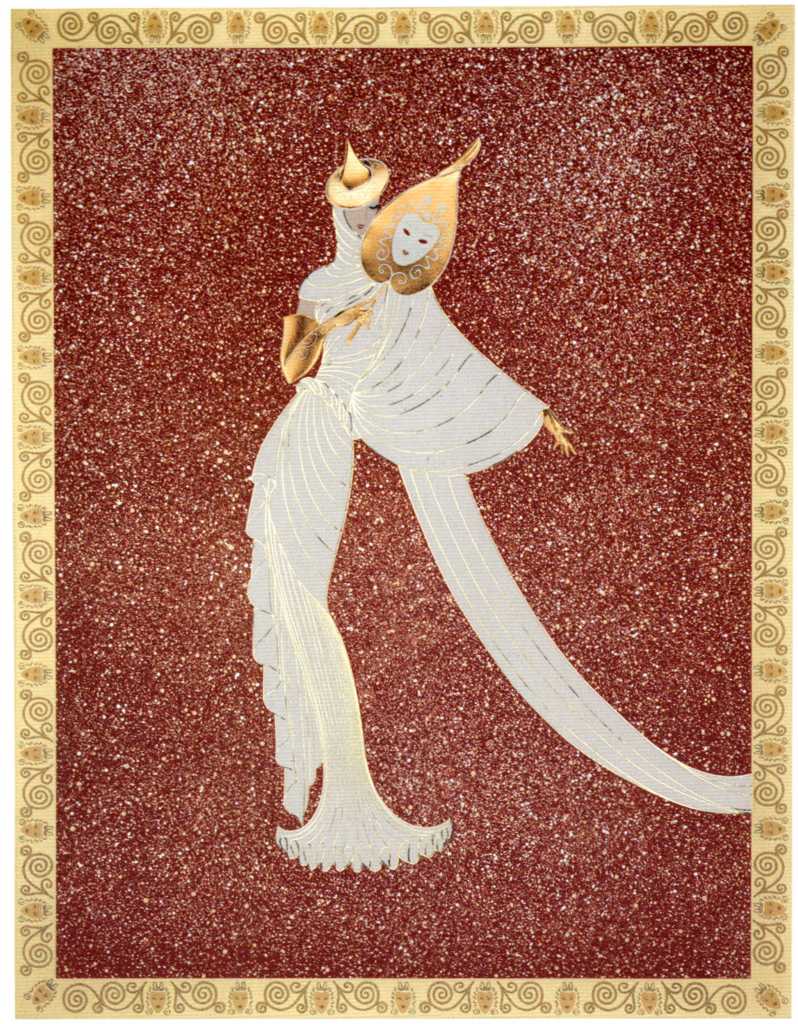

Tanagra (Red)
Tanagra (rouge)
Tanagra (rosso)
Tanagra (Rot)

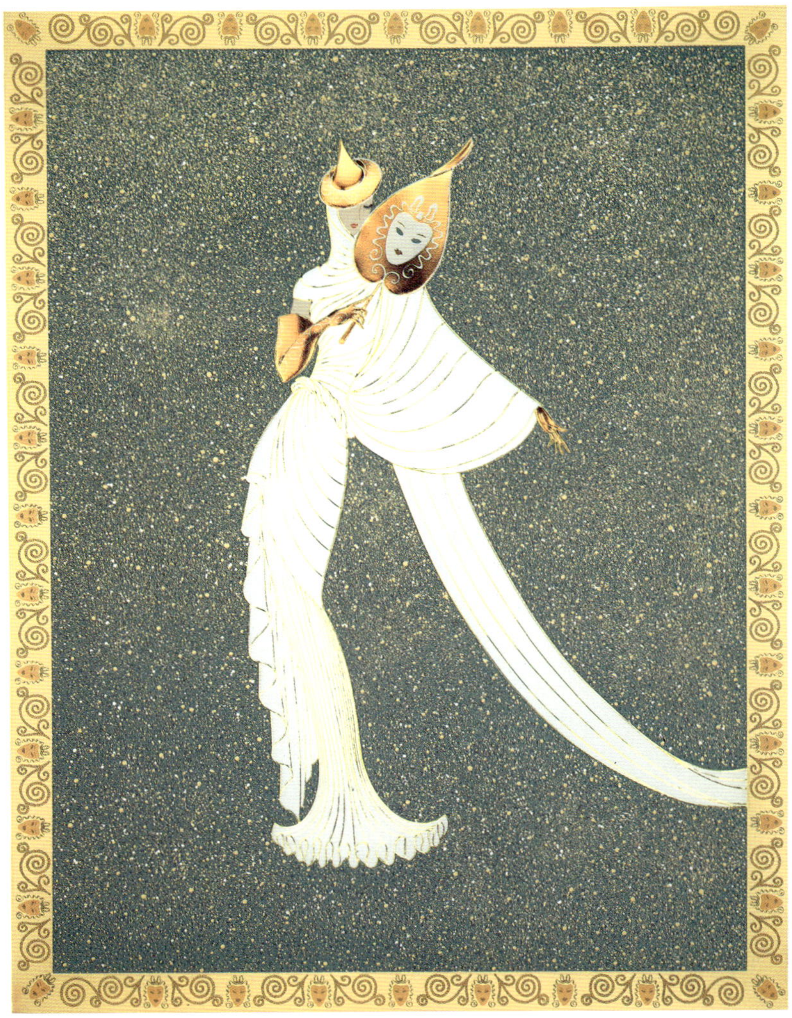

Tanagra (Turquoise)
Tanagra (turquoise)
Tanagra (turchese)
Tanagra (Türkis)

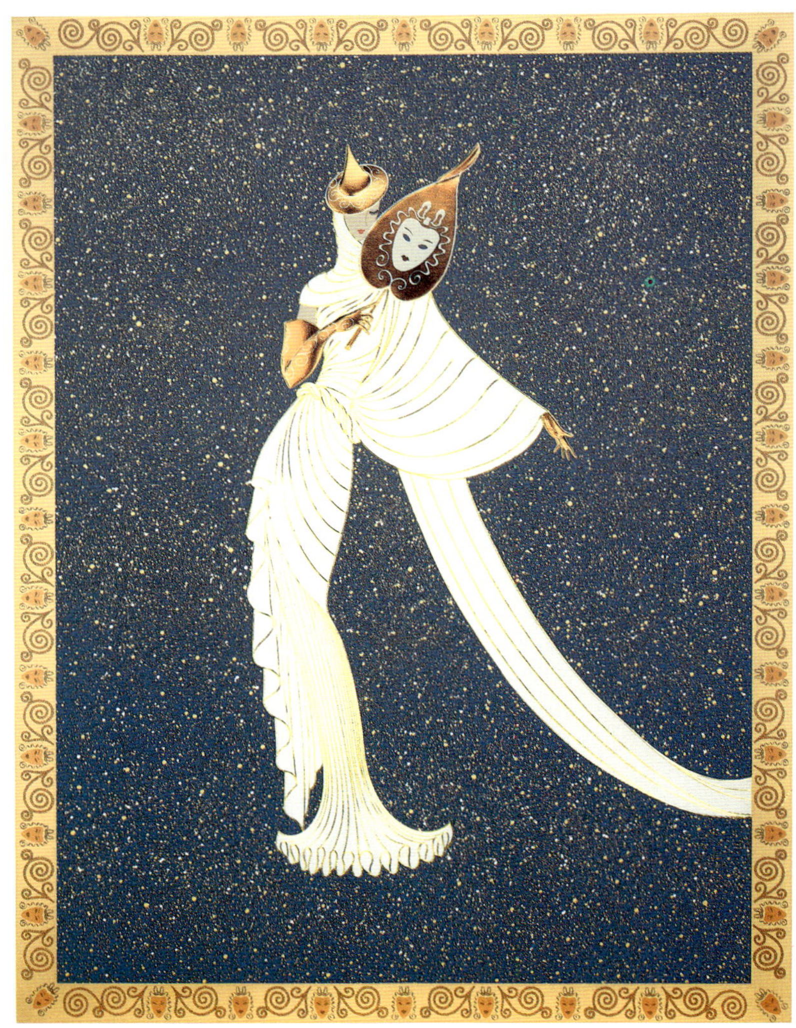

Tanagra (Blue)
Tanagra (bleu)
Tanagra (blu)
Tanagra (Blau)

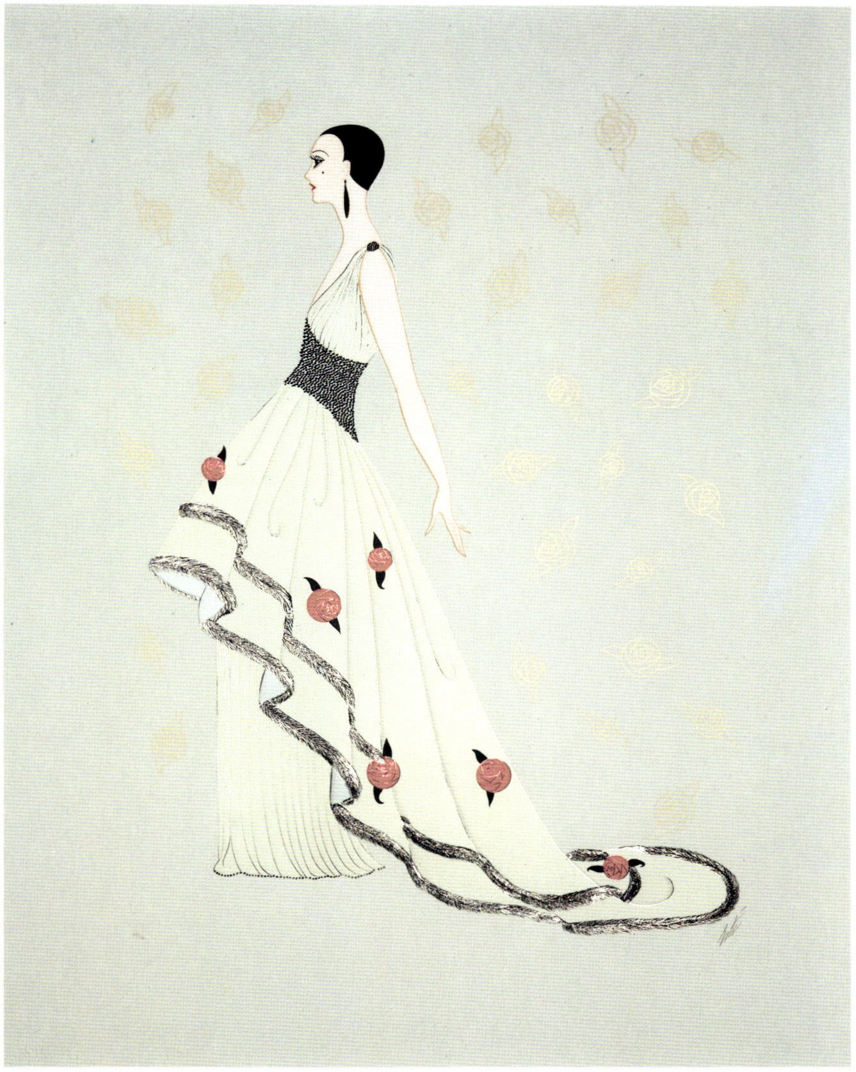

Rose Gown
Robe avec des roses
Abito con rose
Rosenkleid

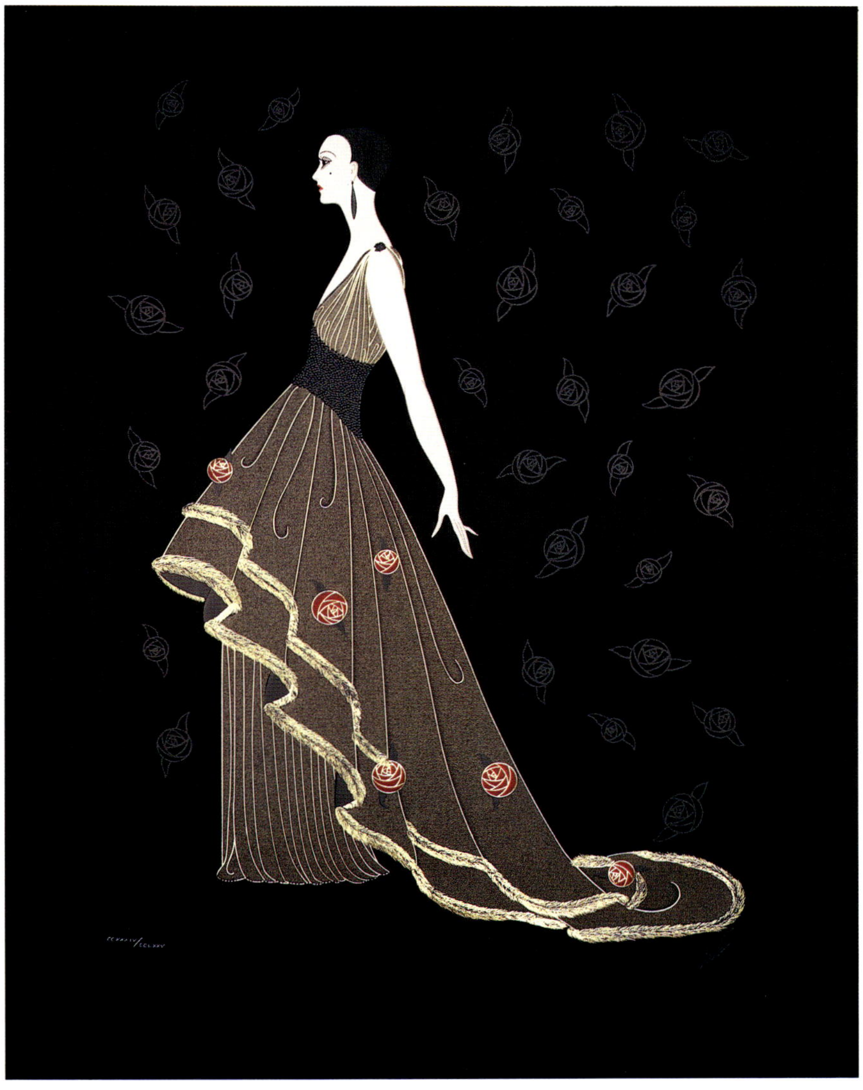

Roses de nuit
Roses de nuit
Rose di notte
Nachtrosen

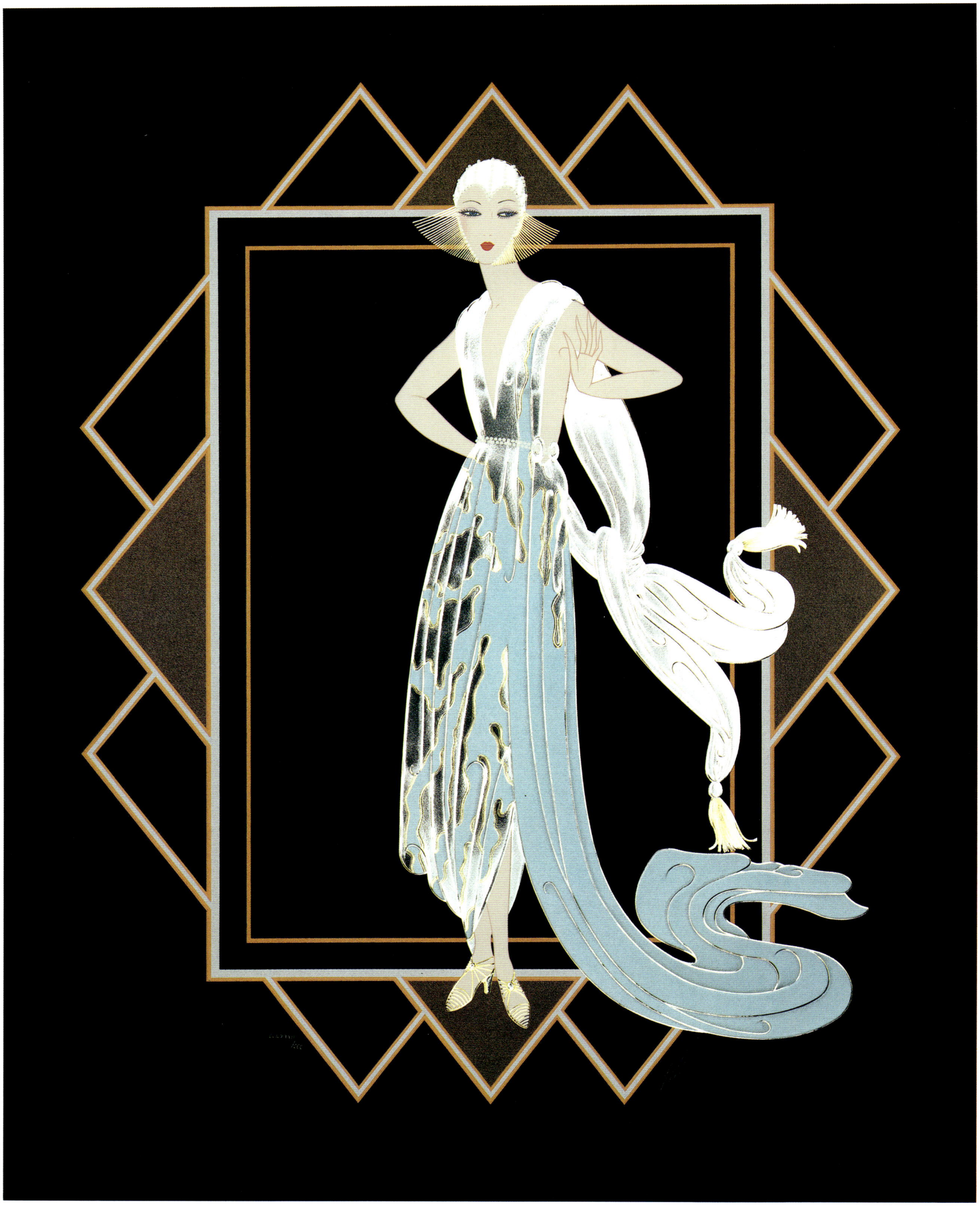

AMERICAN MILLIONAIRESSES

REVISITED SUITE

California (Turquoise dress)
Californie (Robe turquoise)
California (Abito turchese)
Kalifornien (Türkises Kleid)

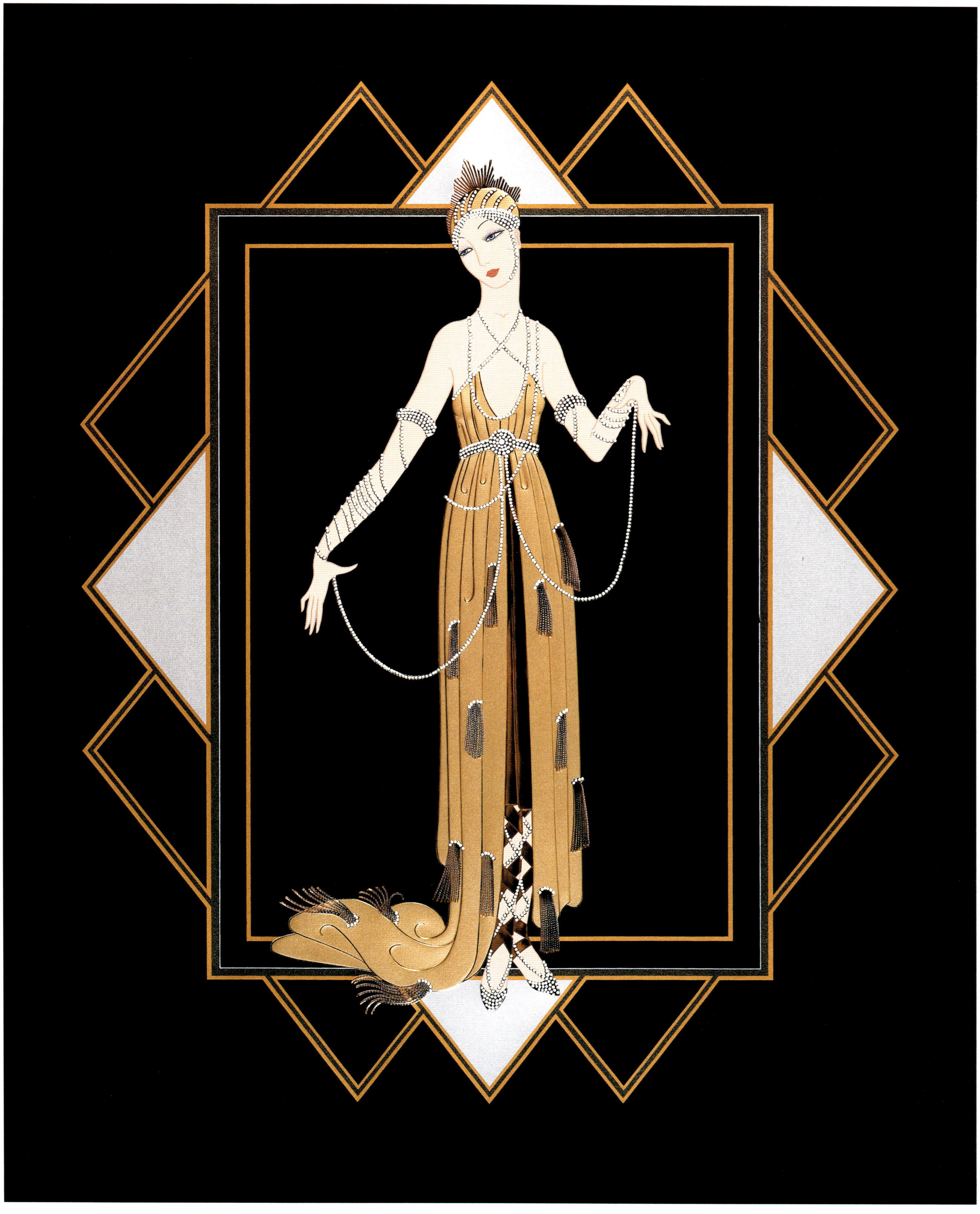

Florida (Pearl dress)
Floride (Robe de perle)
Florida (Abito di perle)
Florida (Perlen Kleid)

AMERICAN MILLIONAIRESSES
REVISITED SUITE

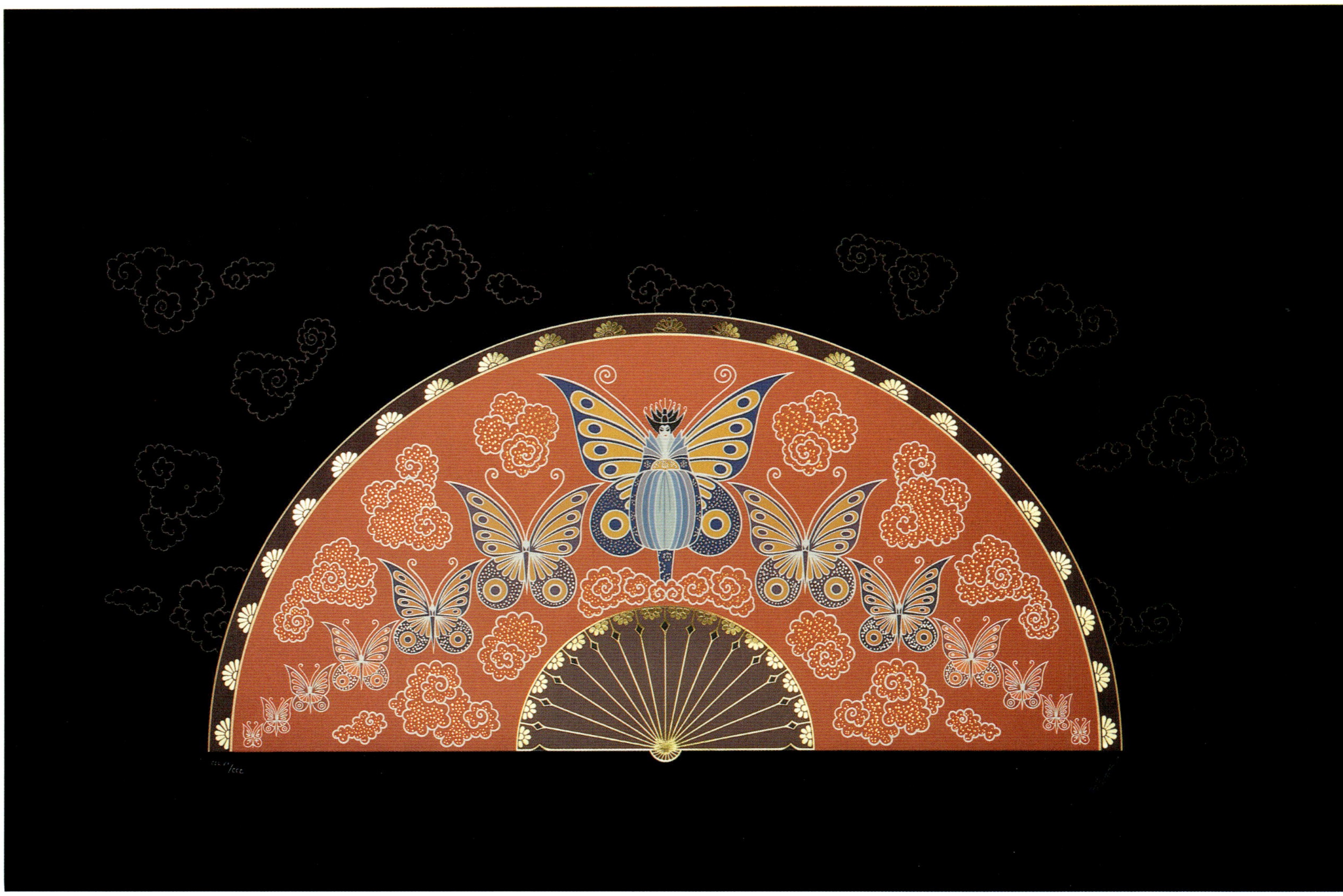

Madame Butterfly
Madame Butterfly
Madame Butterfly
Madame Butterfly

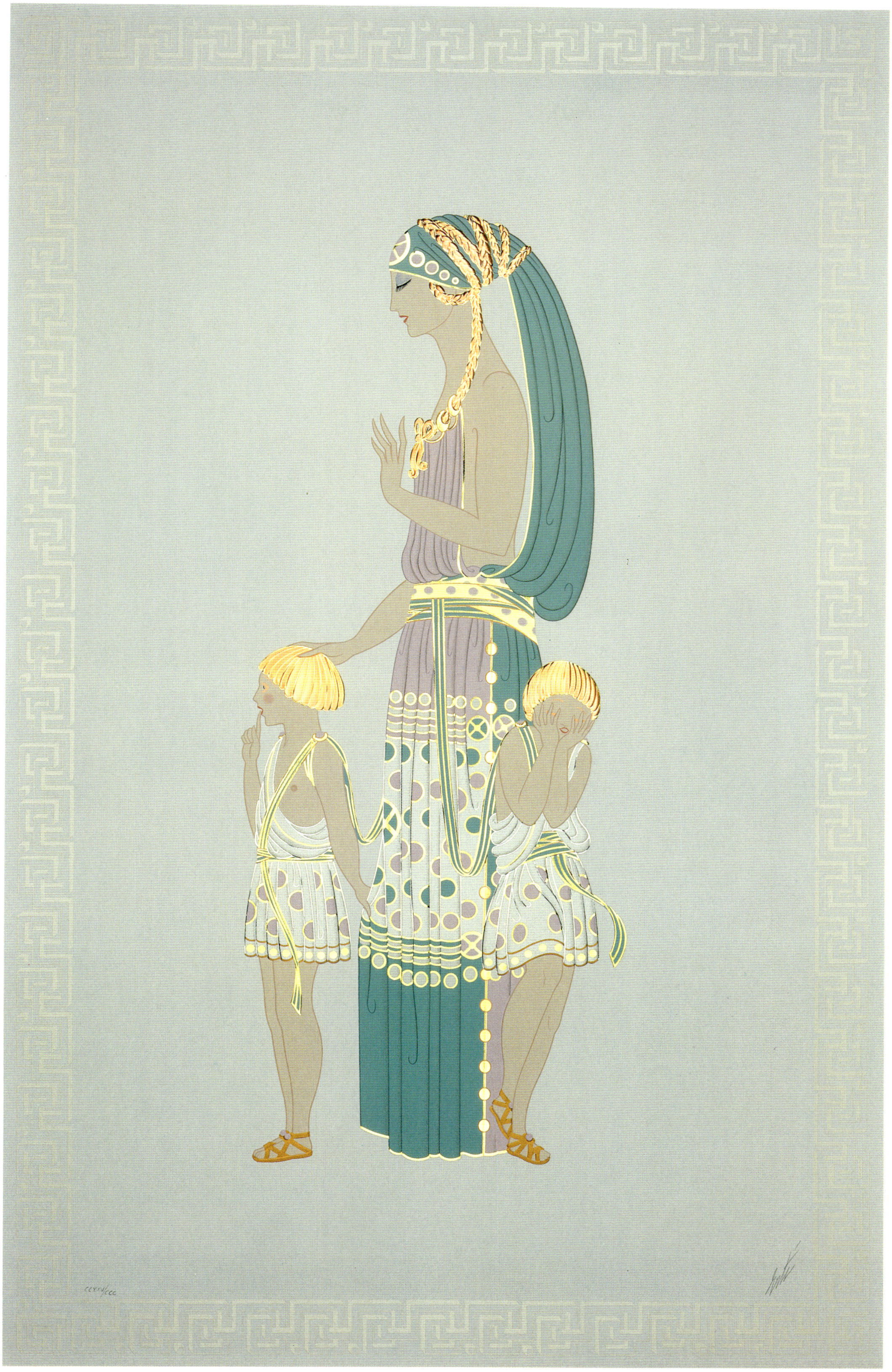

Motherhood
Maternité
Maternitá
Mutterschaft

Manhattan Mary IV
Manhattan Mary IV
Manhattan Mary IV
Manhattan Mary IV

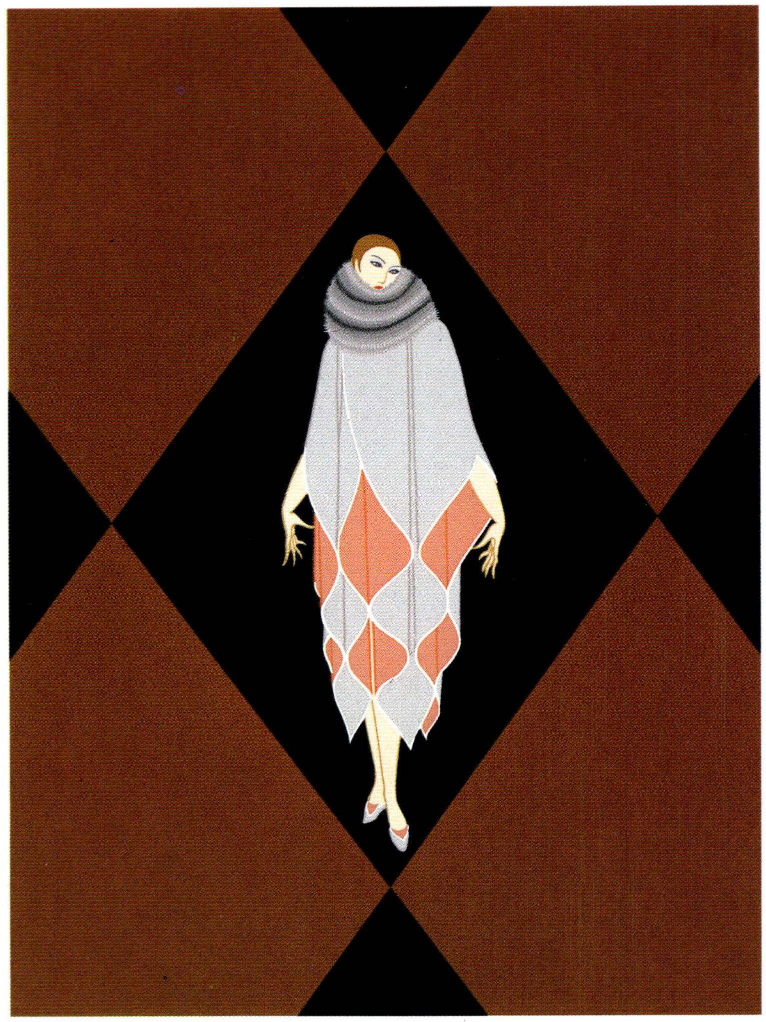

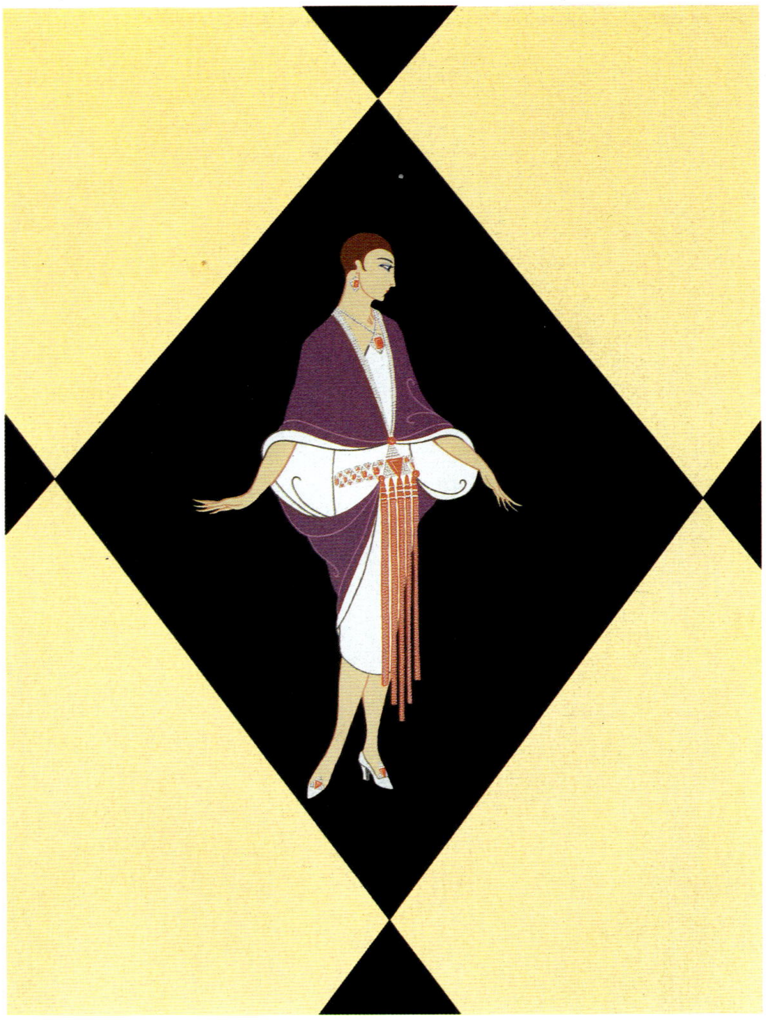

Manhattan Mary III
Manhattan Mary III
Manhattan Mary III
Manhattan Mary III

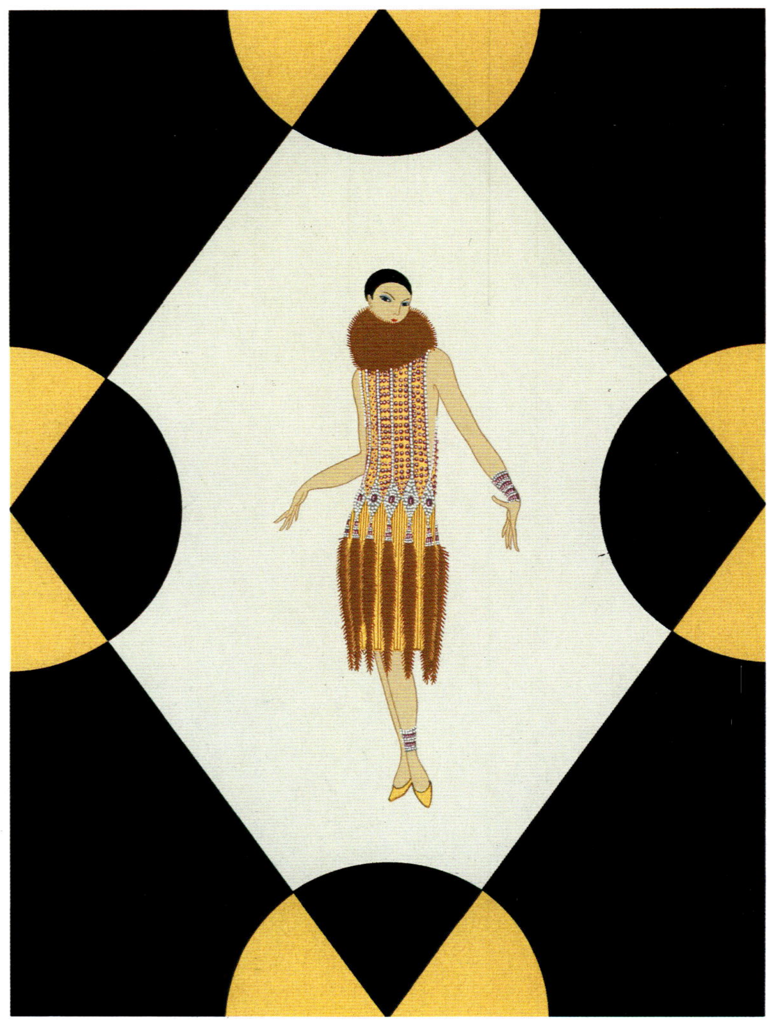

Manhattan Mary V
Manhattan Mary V
Manhattan Mary V
Manhattan Mary V

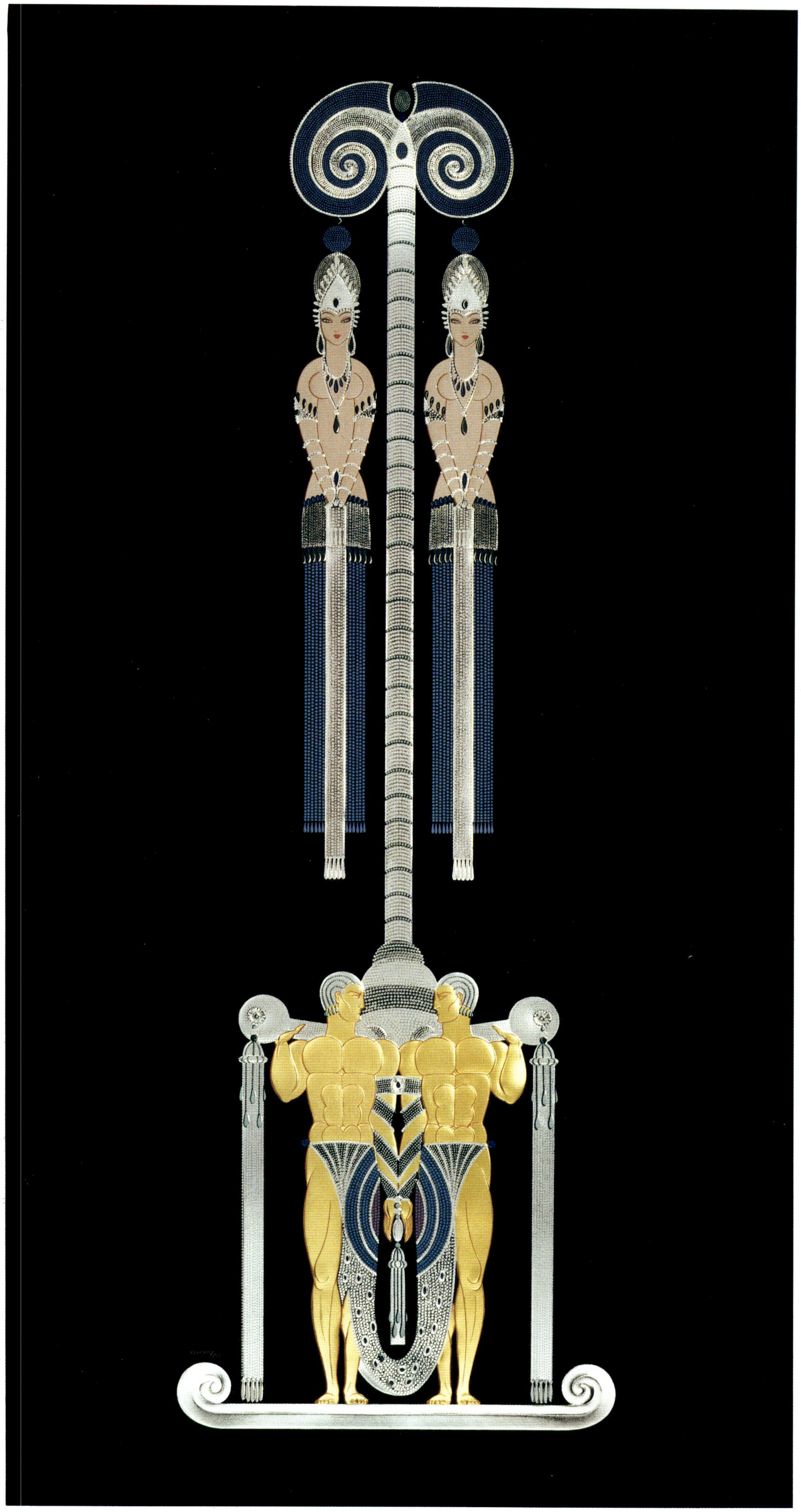

Les Prêtresses
Les Prêtresses
Le Sacerdotesse
Die Priesterinnen

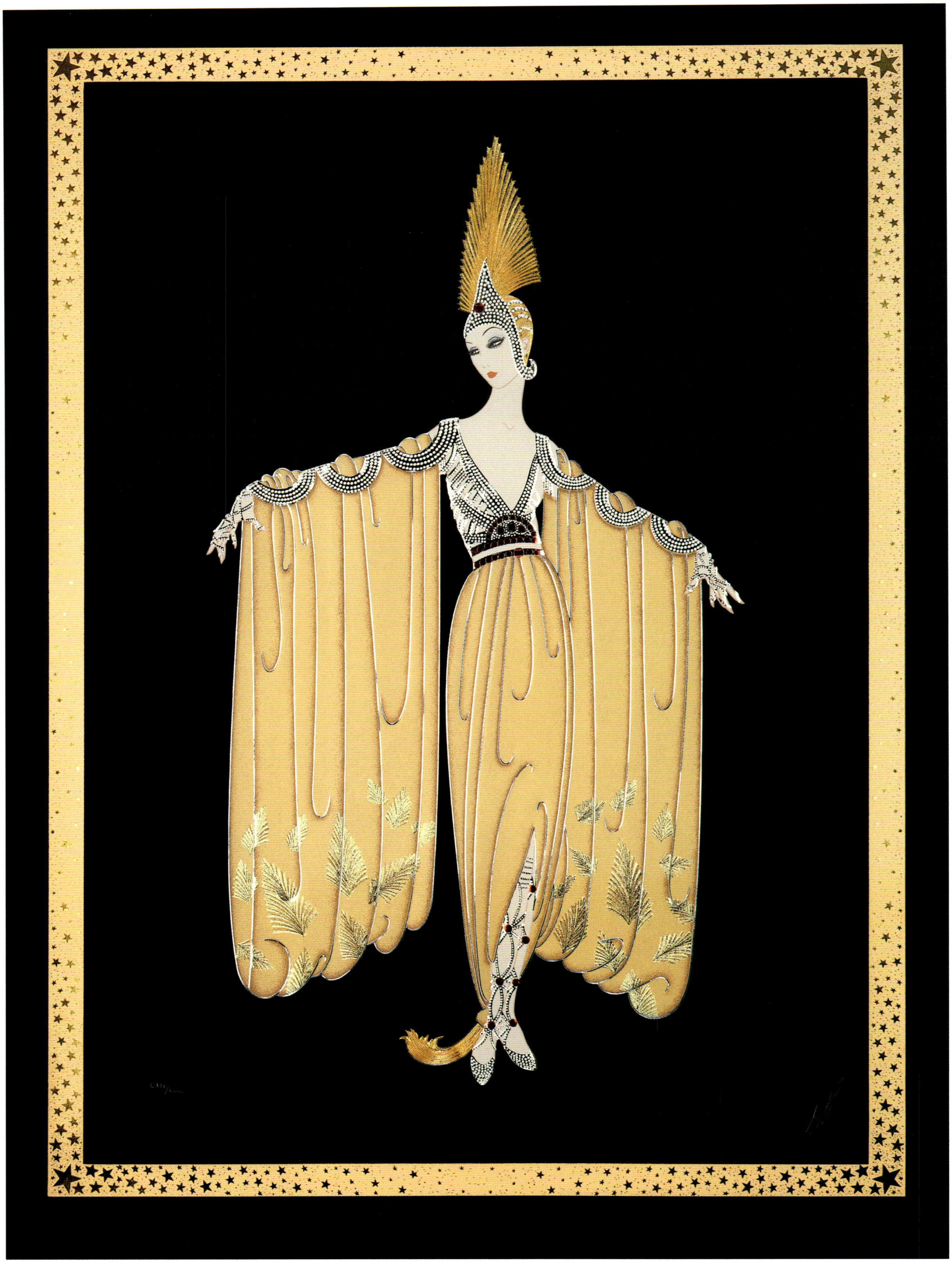

Gown Orientale
Robe Orientale
Abito orientale
Orientalisches Abendgewand

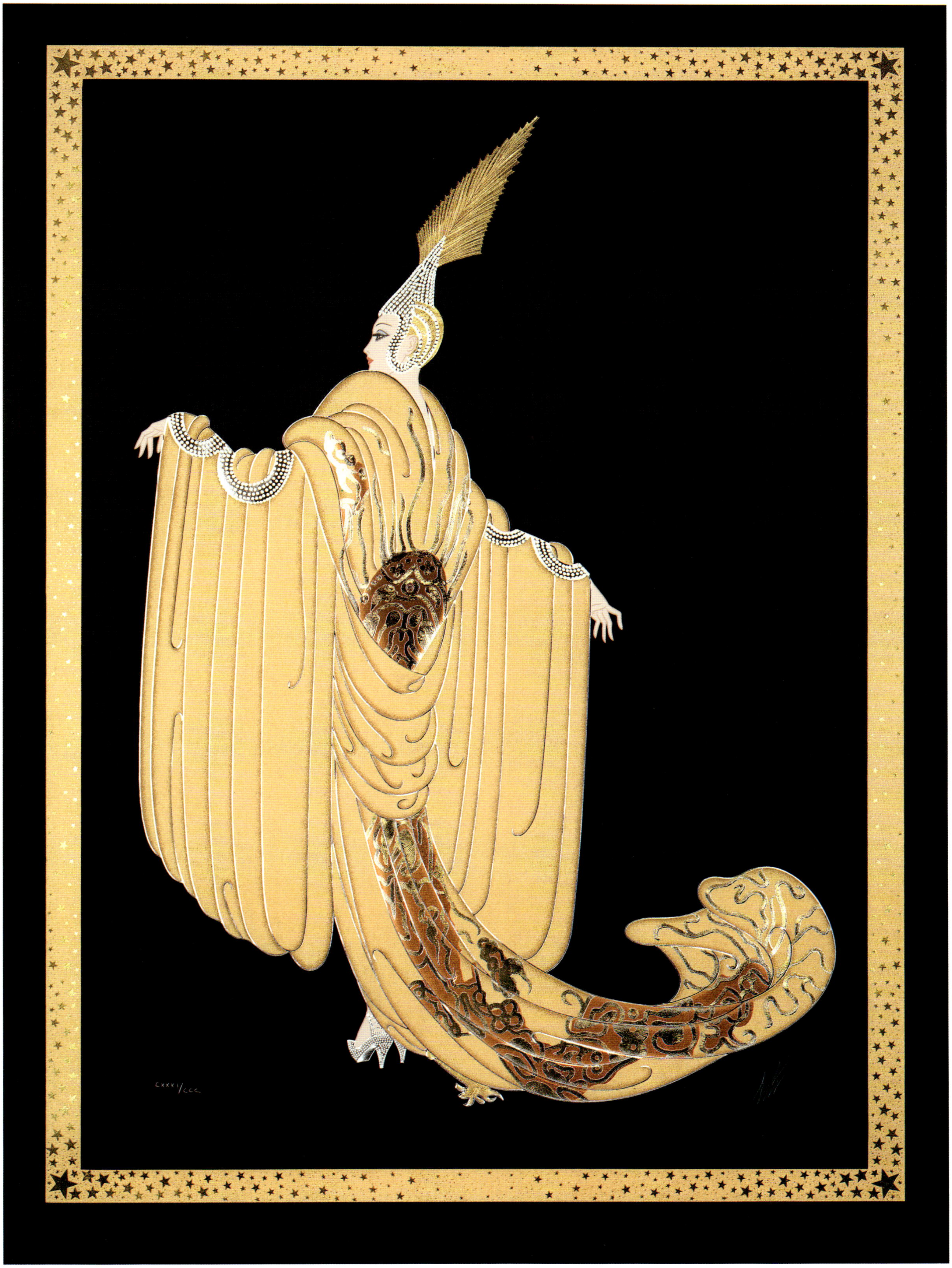

Cape a la Russe
Cape à la Russe
Cappa alla russa
Russisches Abend Cape

ENSEMBLE DU SOIR SUITE

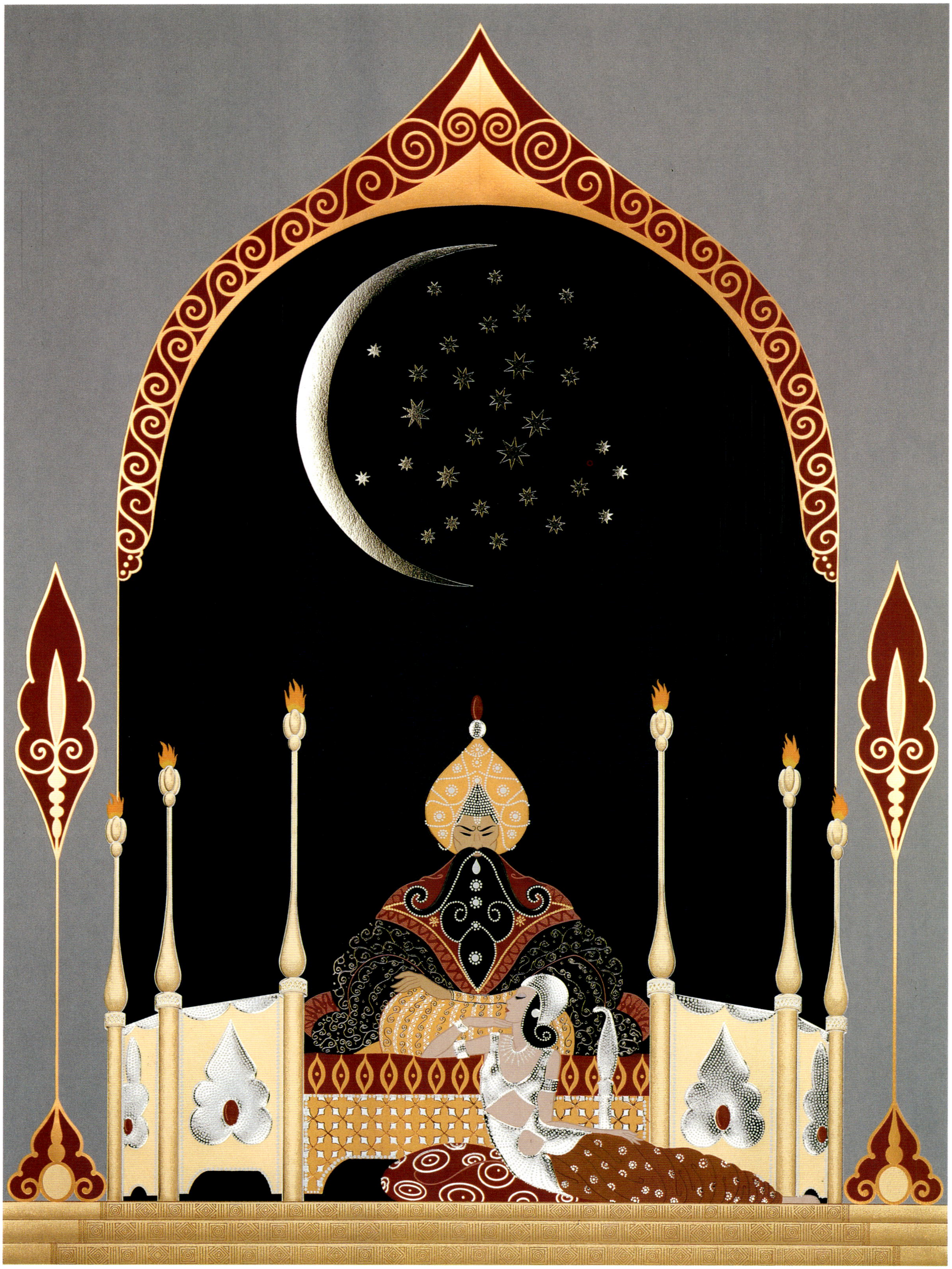

* *

Casbah
Casbah
Casba
Kasbah

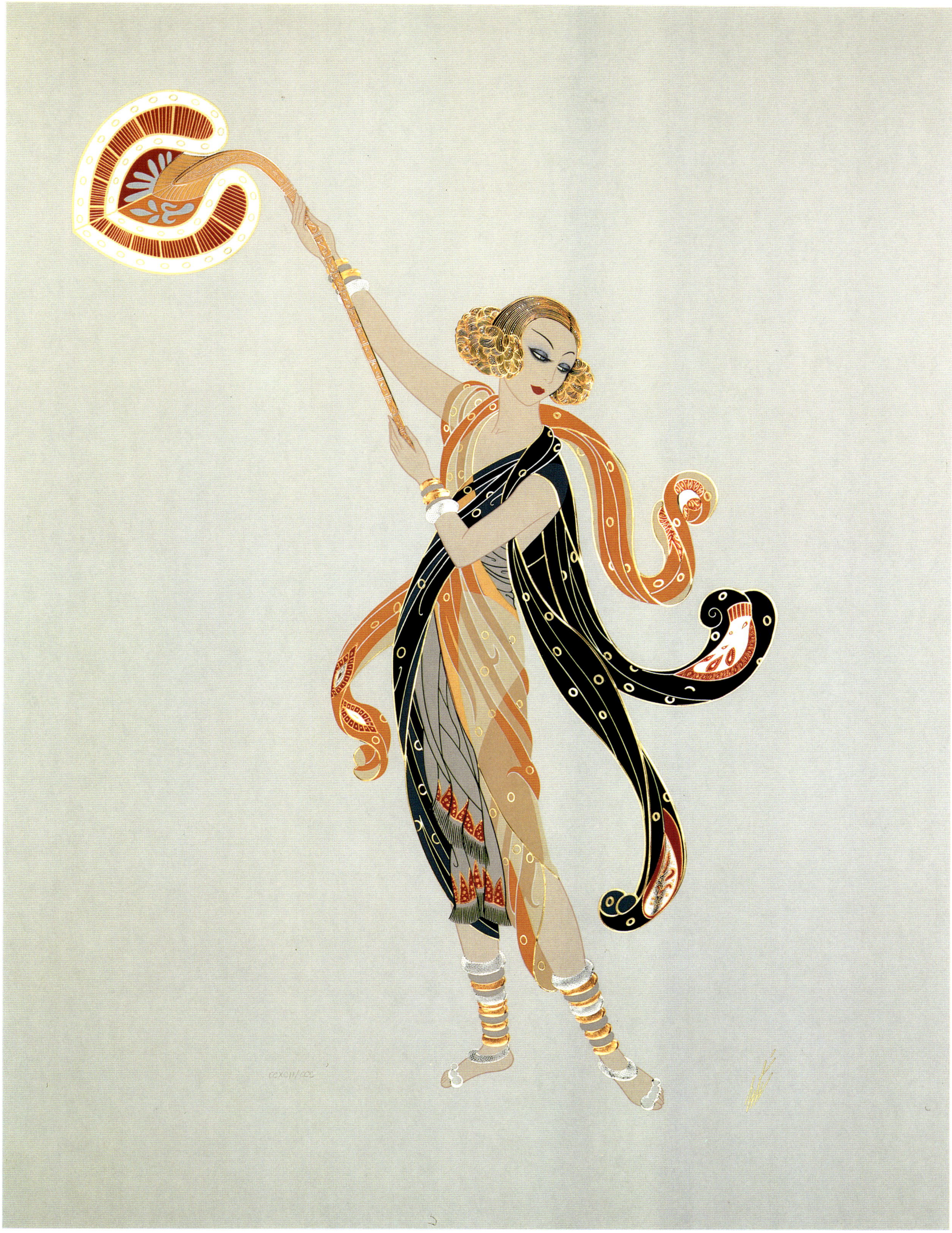

* *

Balinese
Balinaise
Balinese
Balinese

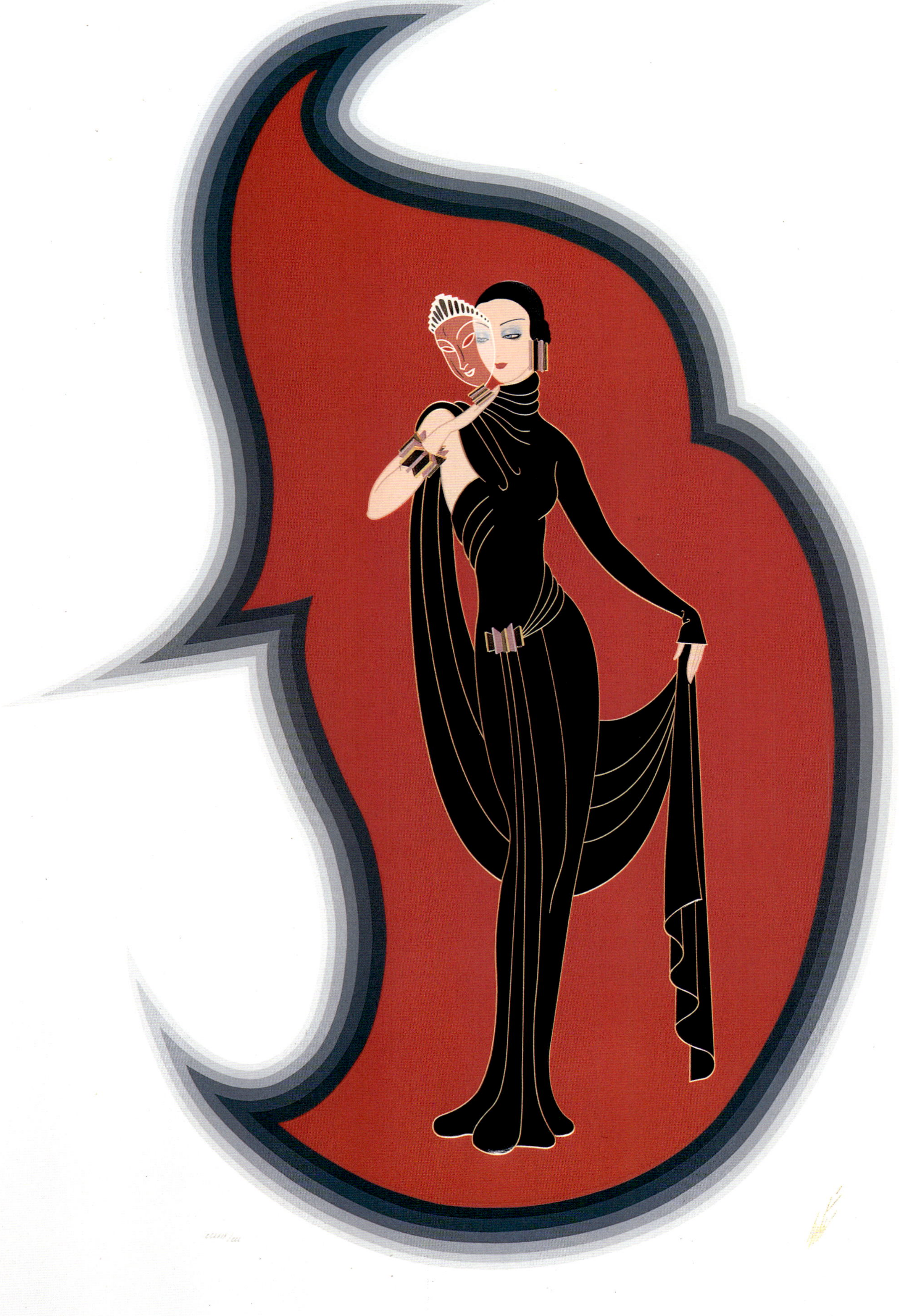

* *

Crystal Mask
Masque en cristal
Maschera di cristallo
Kristallmaske

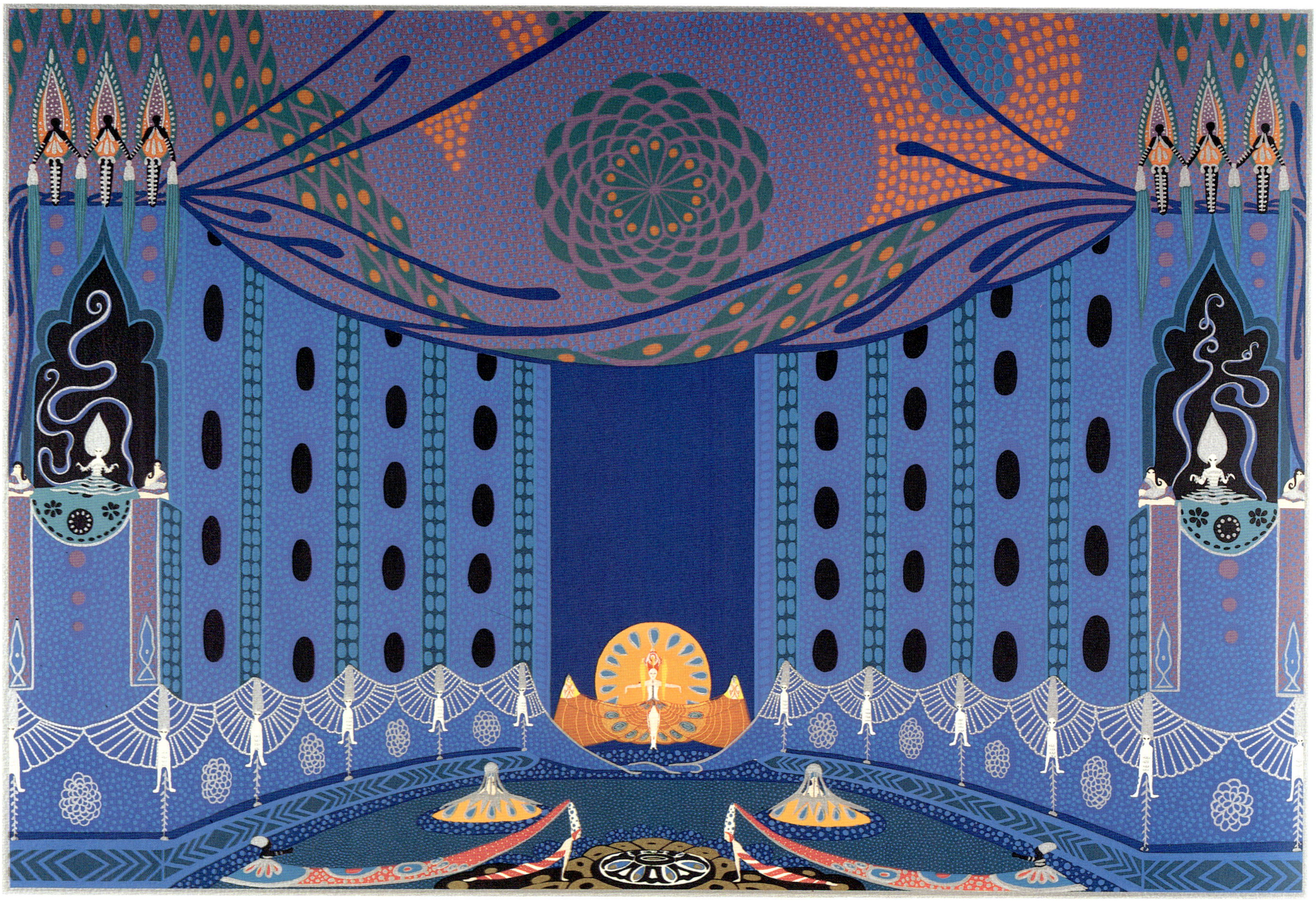

* *

Conte Hindou
Conte Hindou
Conte Hindou
Conte Hindou

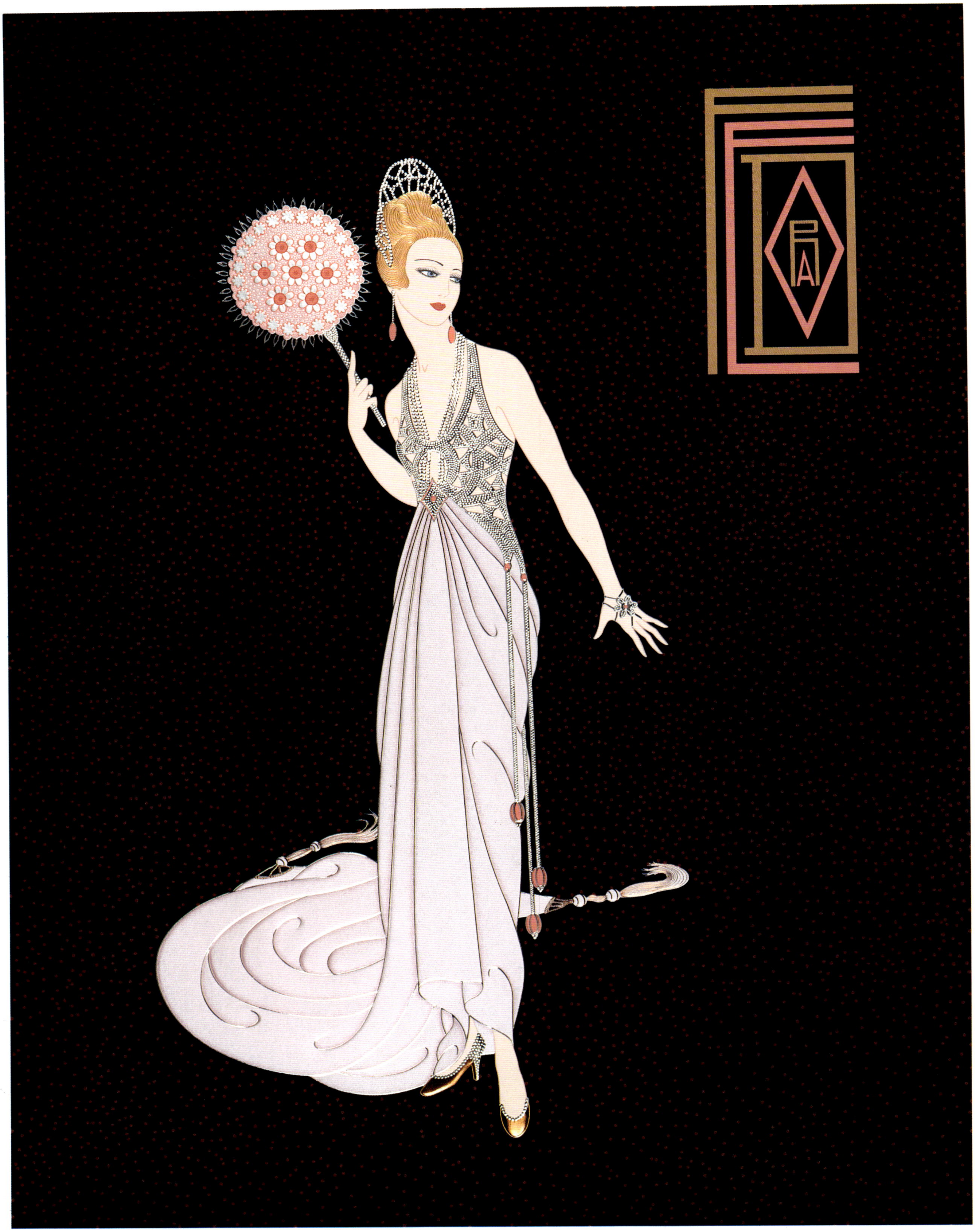

* *

Fedora Fan
L'Eventail pour Fedora
Il ventaglio per Fedora
Fedora Fächer

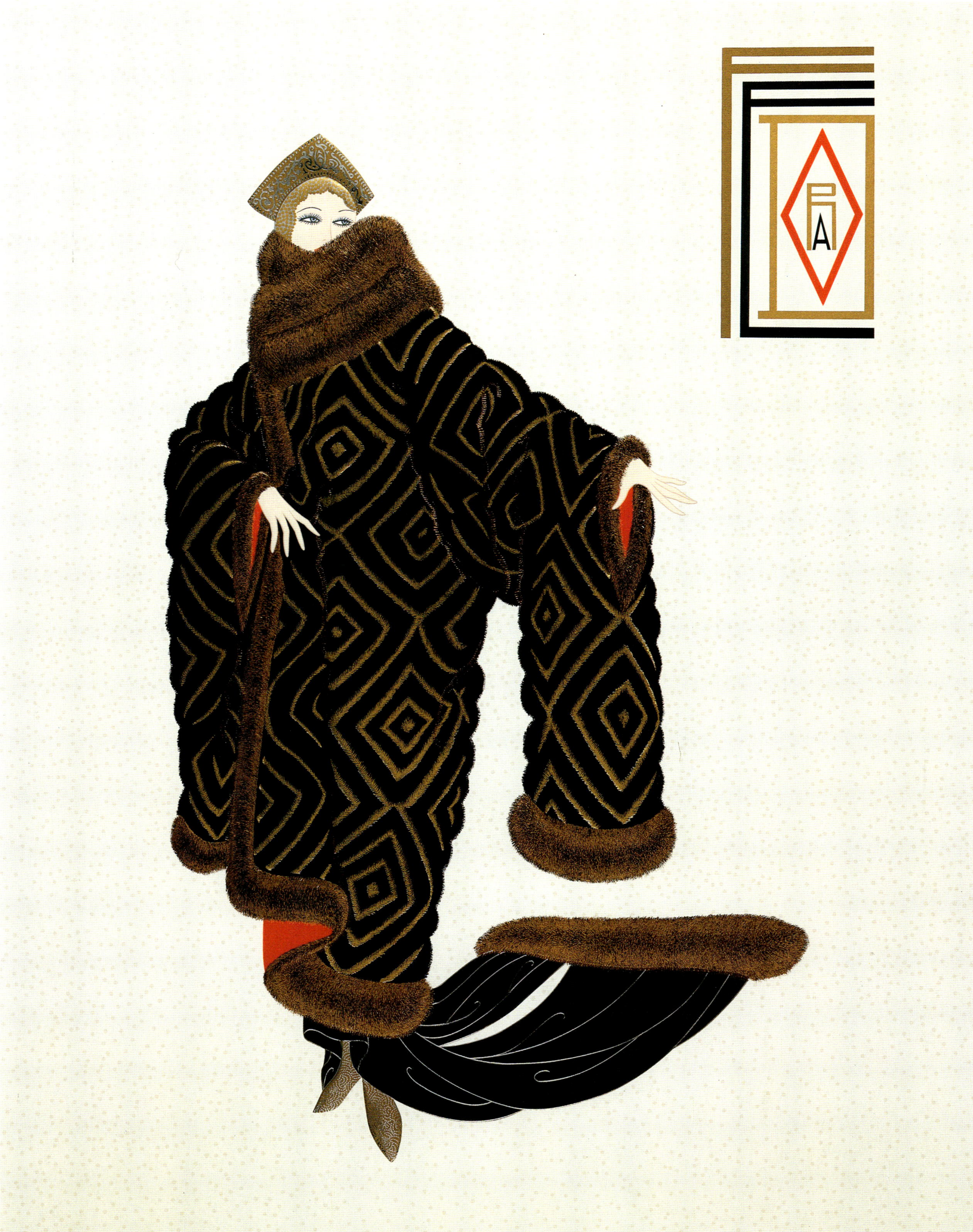

* *

Fedora Fur
La Fourrure pour Fedora
La pelliccia per Fedora
Fedora Pelz

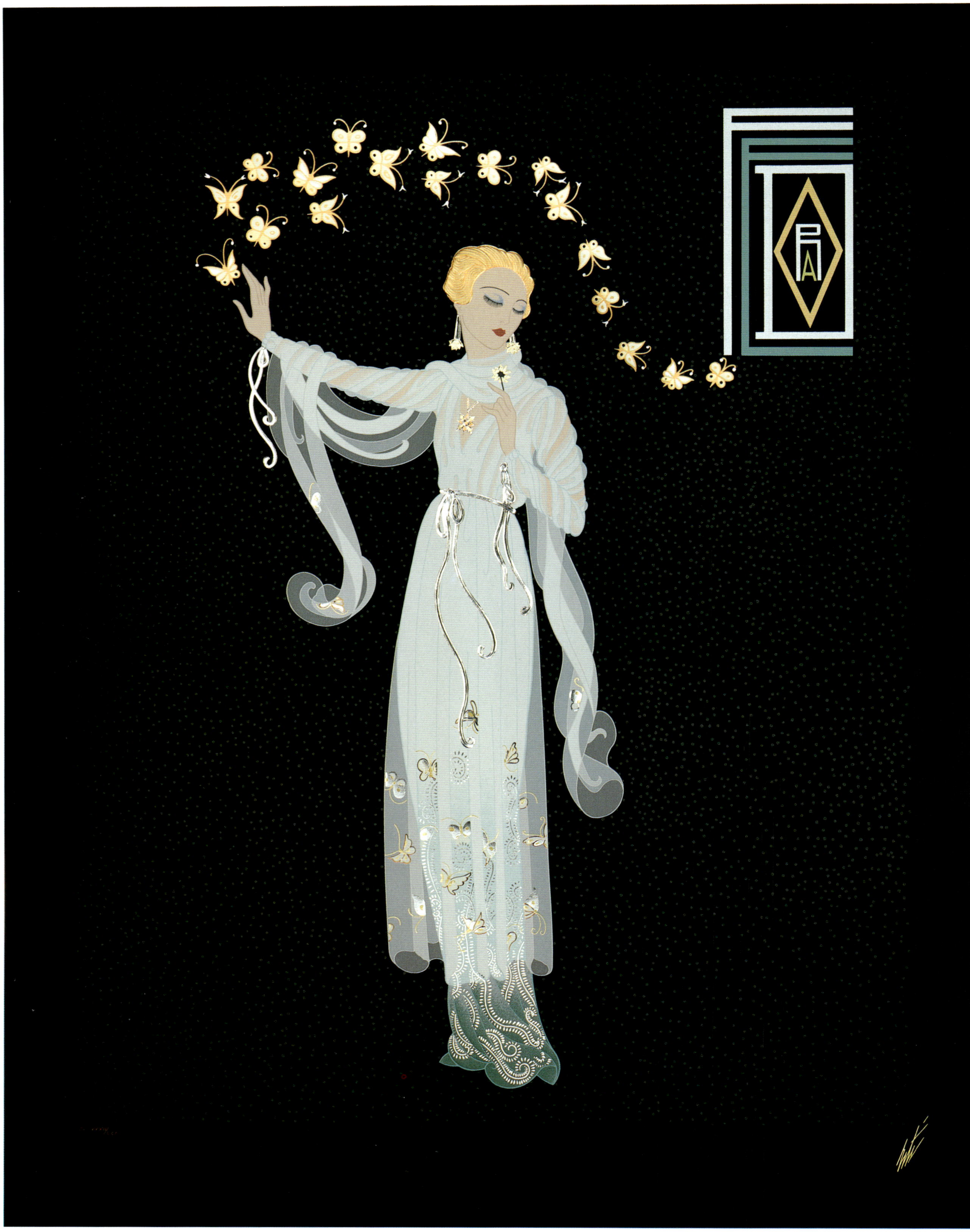

* *

Fedora Butterfly
Le Papillon pour Fedora
La farfalla per Fedora
Fedora Schmetterling

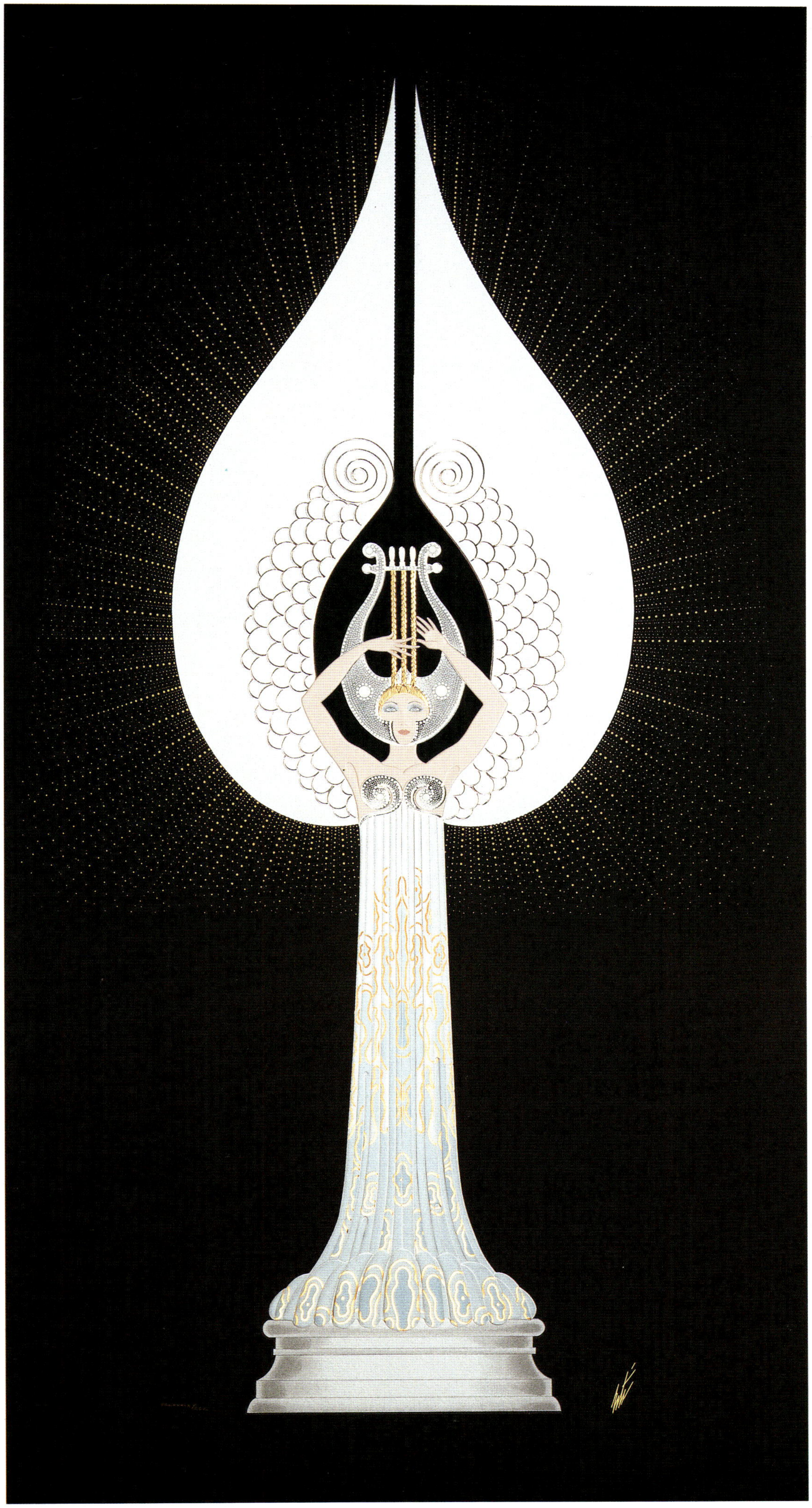

* *

Angel Melody
Melodie angélique
Melodia angelica
Engelsgesang

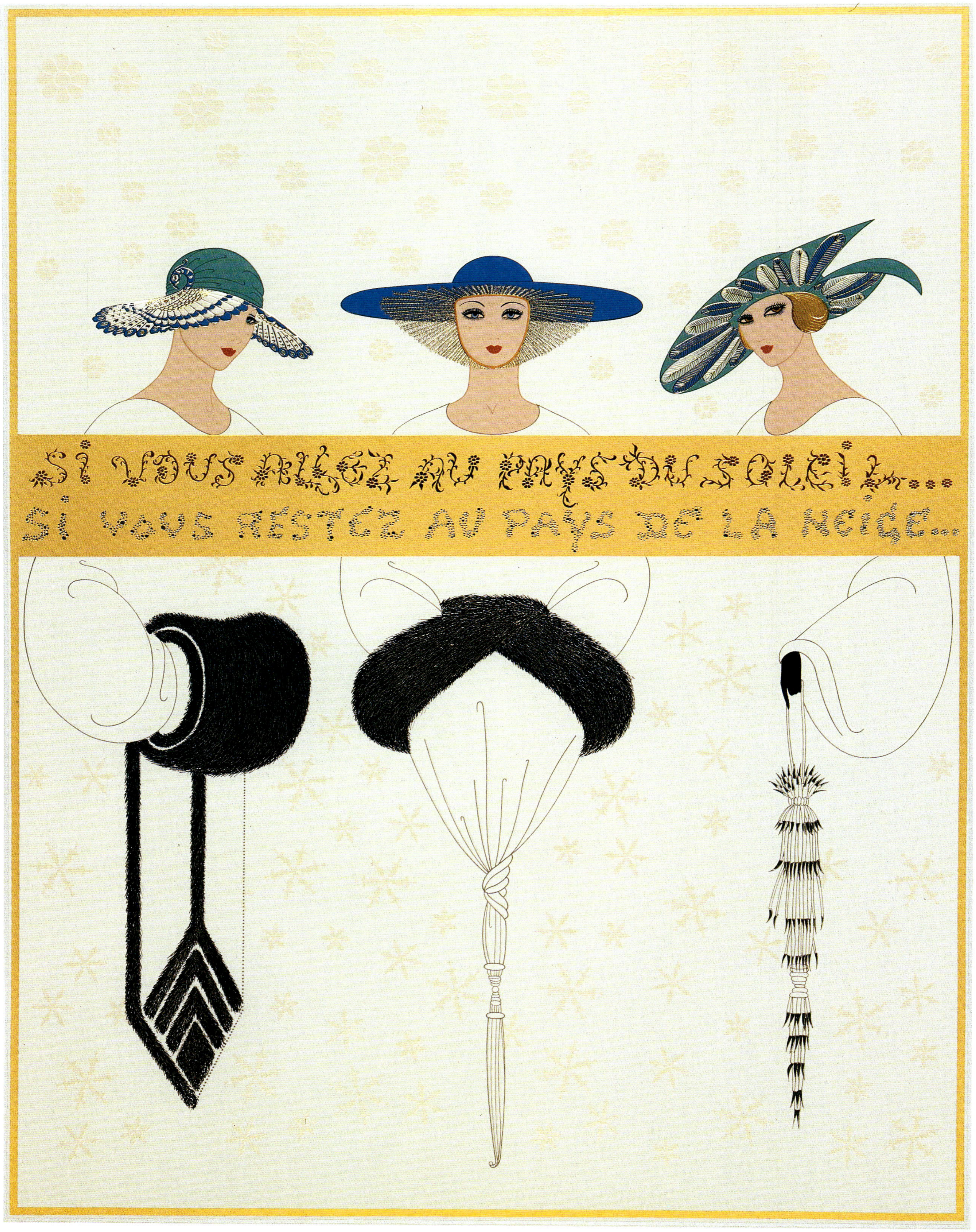

* *

Summer/Winter
Été/Hiver
Estate/Inverno
Sommer/Winter

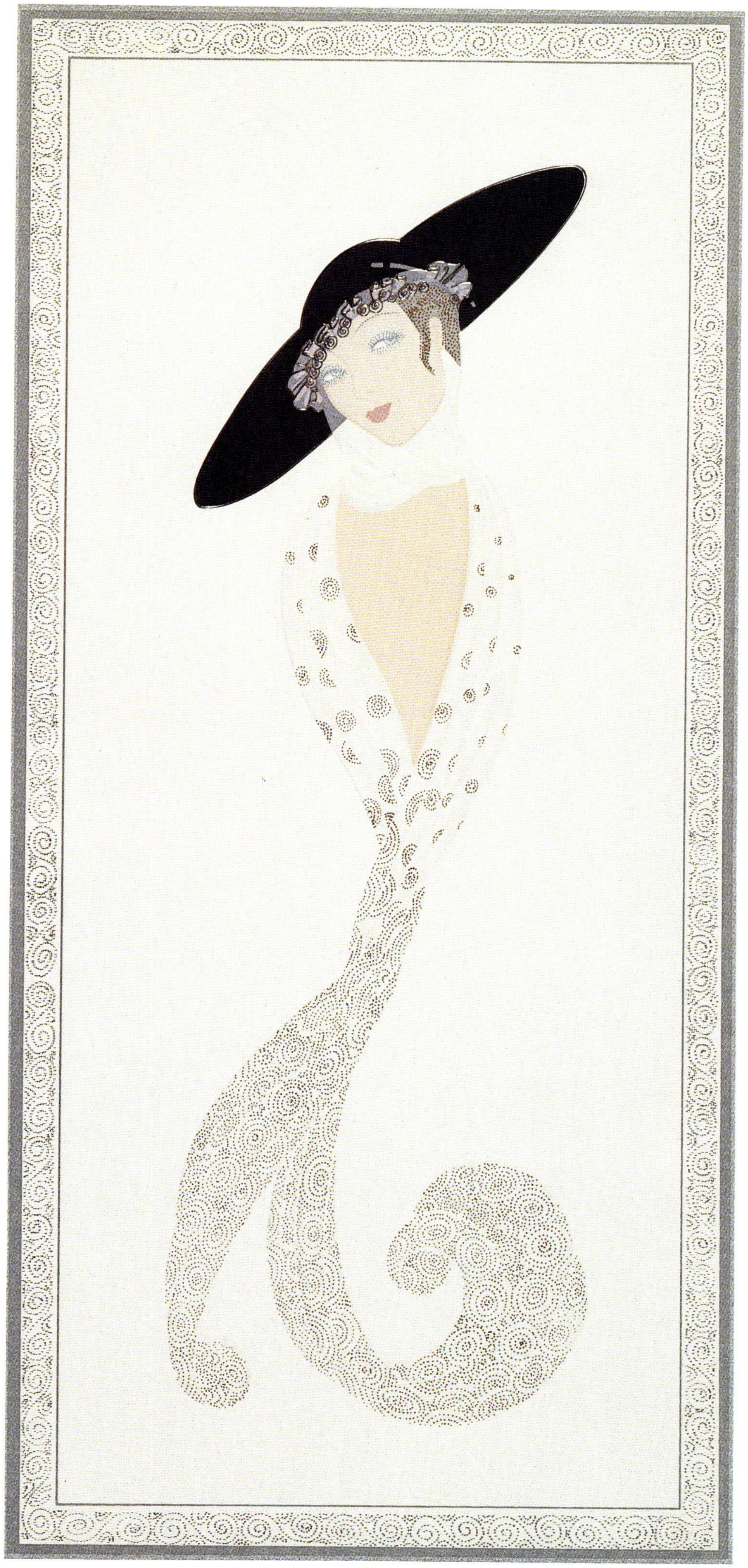

* *

A Glance
Un Coup d'oeil
Uno sguardo
Ein Blick

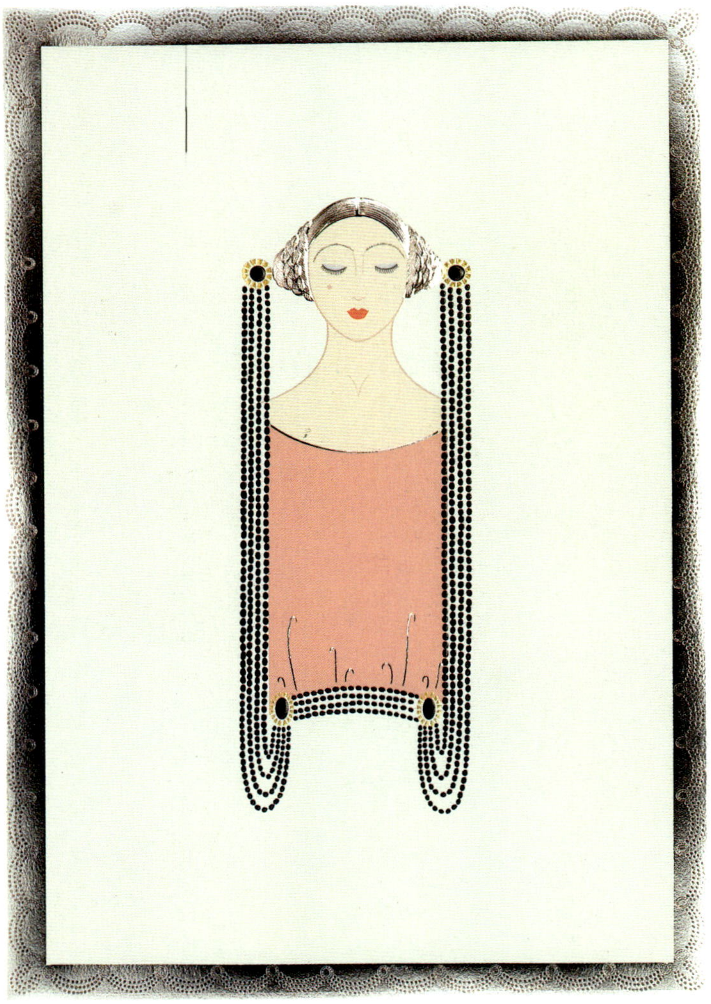

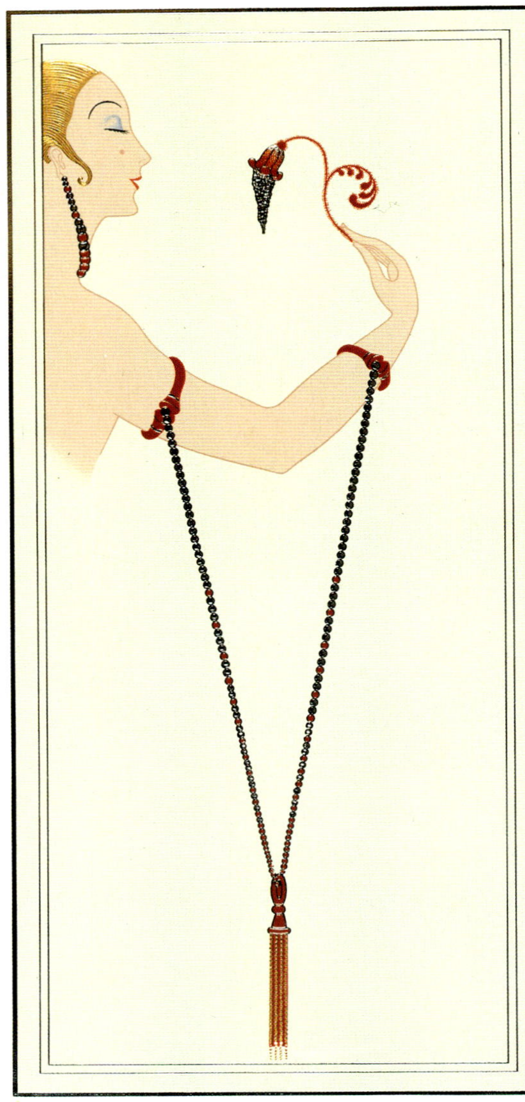

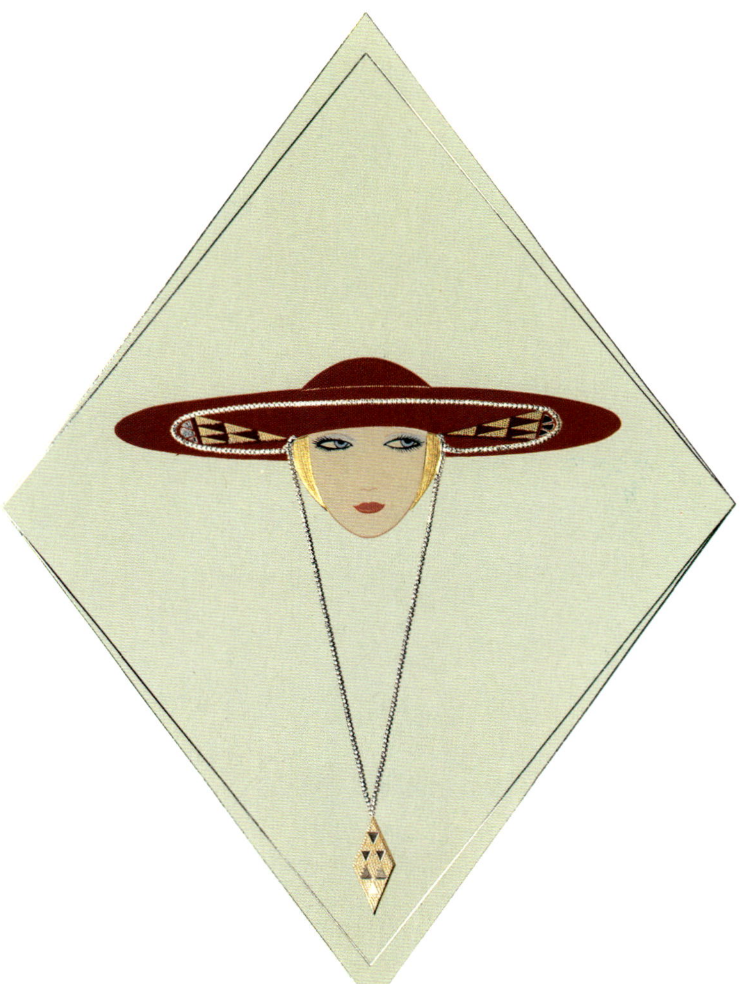

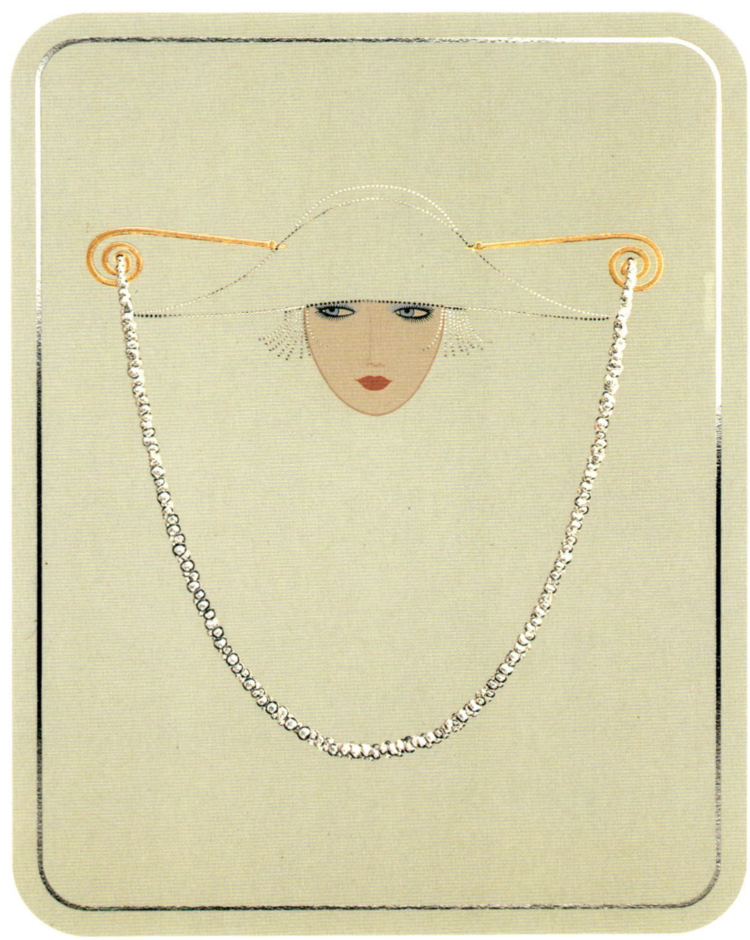

* *
Onyx Coiffure
Coiffure d'onyx
Acconciatura di onice
Onyx Haartracht

* *
Red Hat
Chapeau rouge
Cappello rosso
Der rote Hut

* *
Bracelets
Bracelets
Braccialetti
Armbänder

* *
Hat and Chain
Chapeau et chaine
Cappello e catena
Hut und Kette

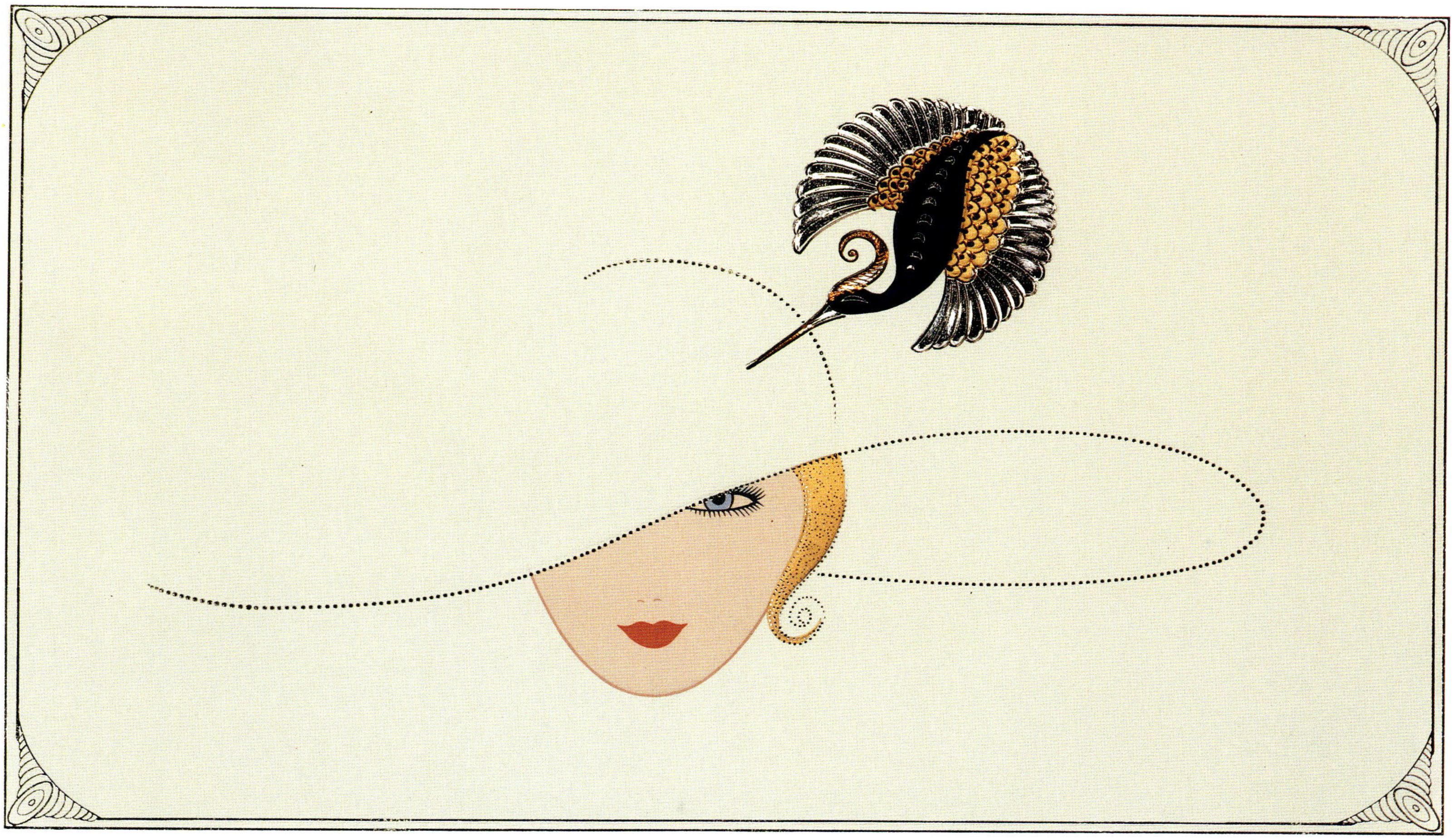

* *
Bird Pin
Broche en forme d'oiseau
Spilla a forma d'uccello
Vogelbrosche

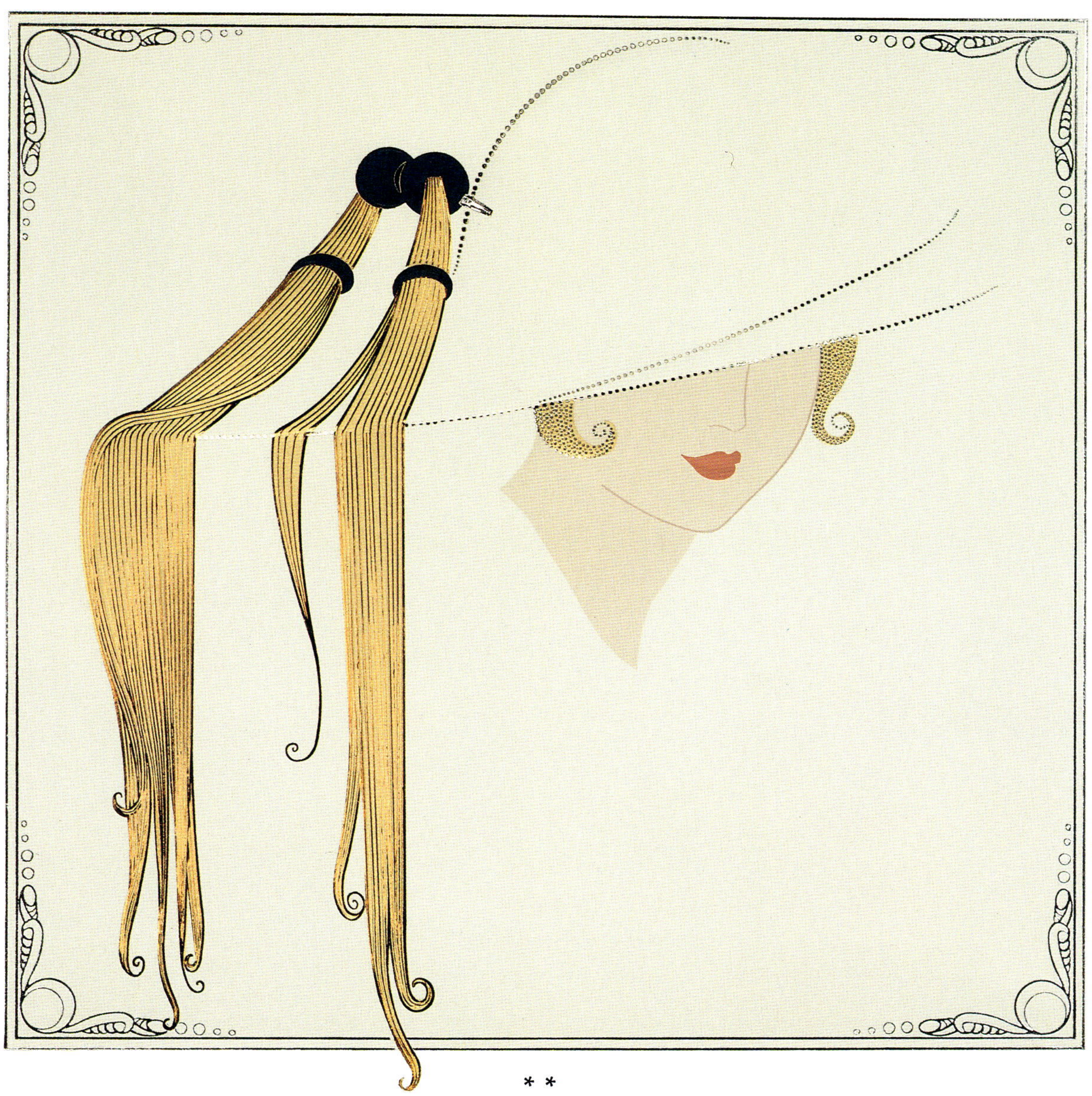

* *
Tassel Hat
Chapeau à pompon
Cappello con pompon
Trottelhut

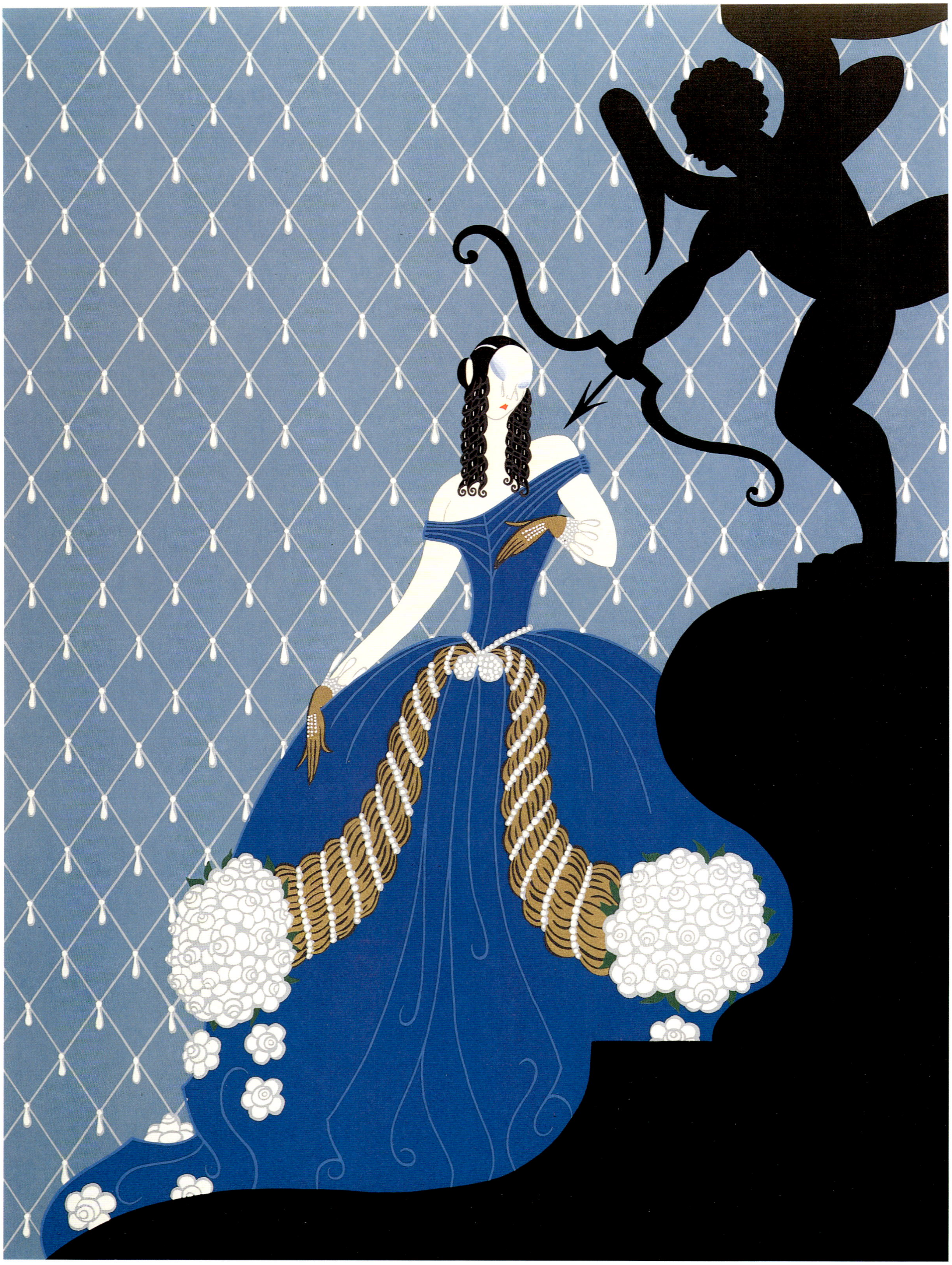

* *

Violetta
Violetta
Violetta
Violetta

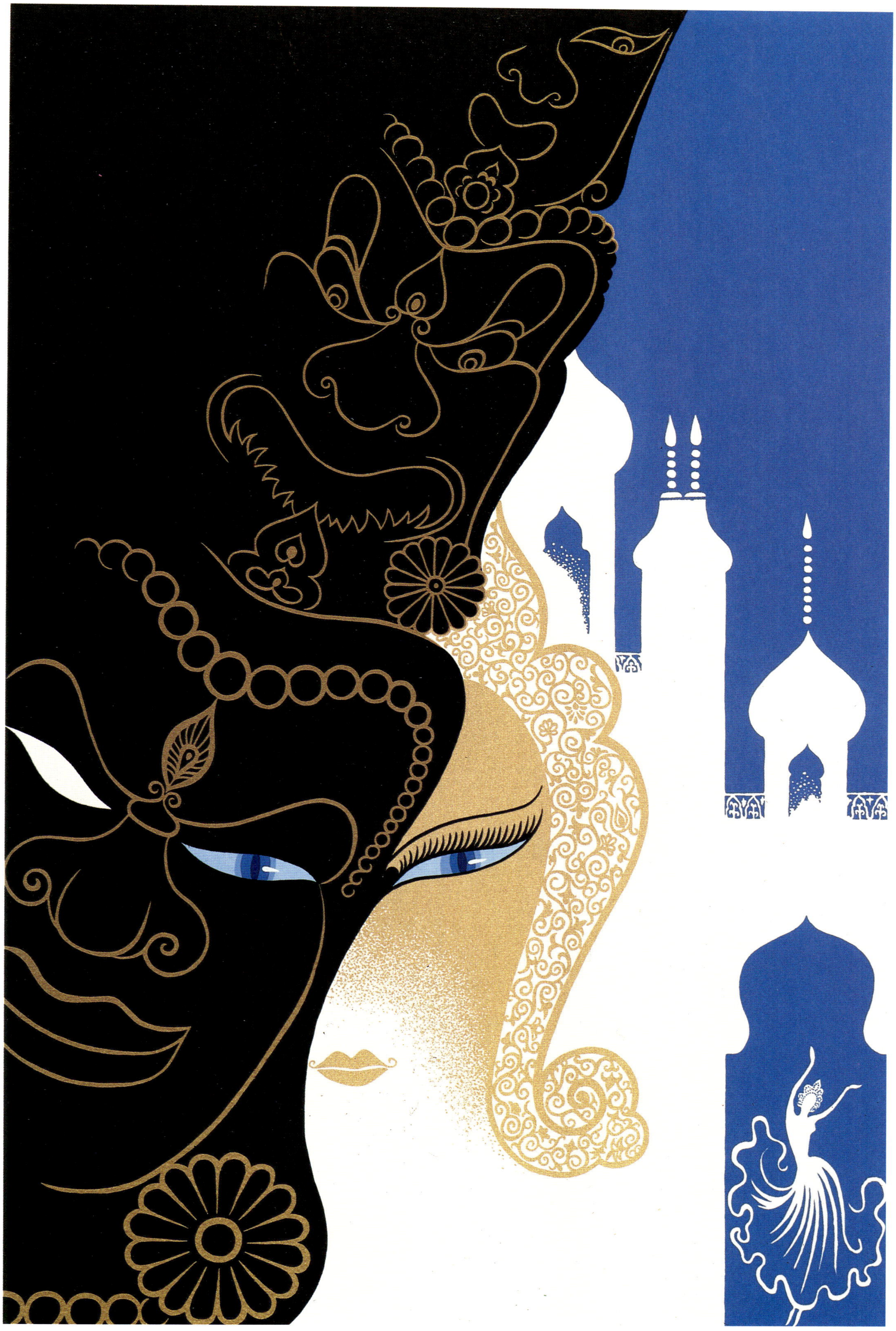

* *

Masks and Mosques
Masques et mosquées
Maschere e moschee
Masken und Moscheen

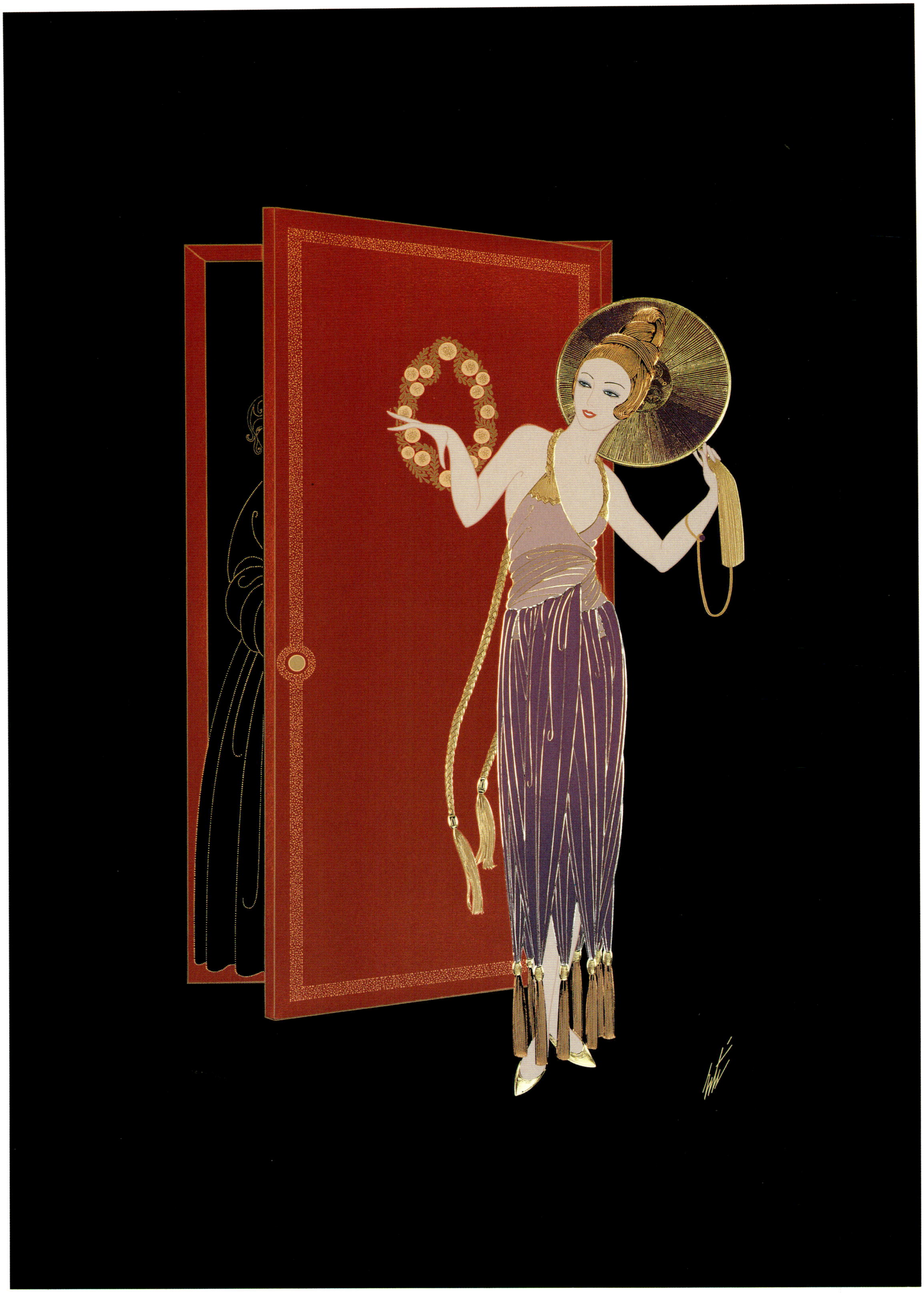

* *

New Year's Eve
Le Jour de l'an
Capodanno
Silvesterabend

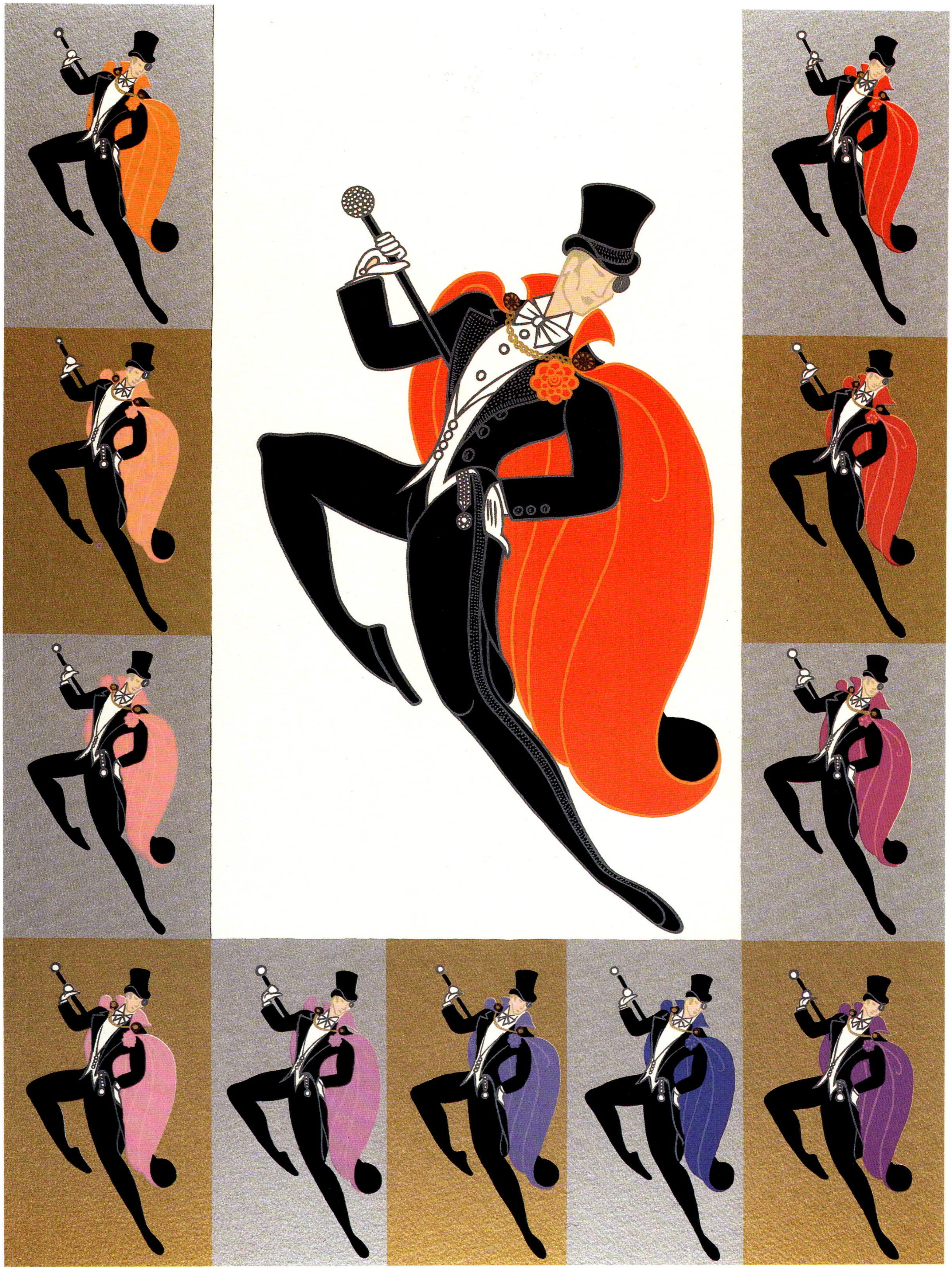

* *

White Tie
Cravate blanche
Cravatta bianca
Weisse Krawatte

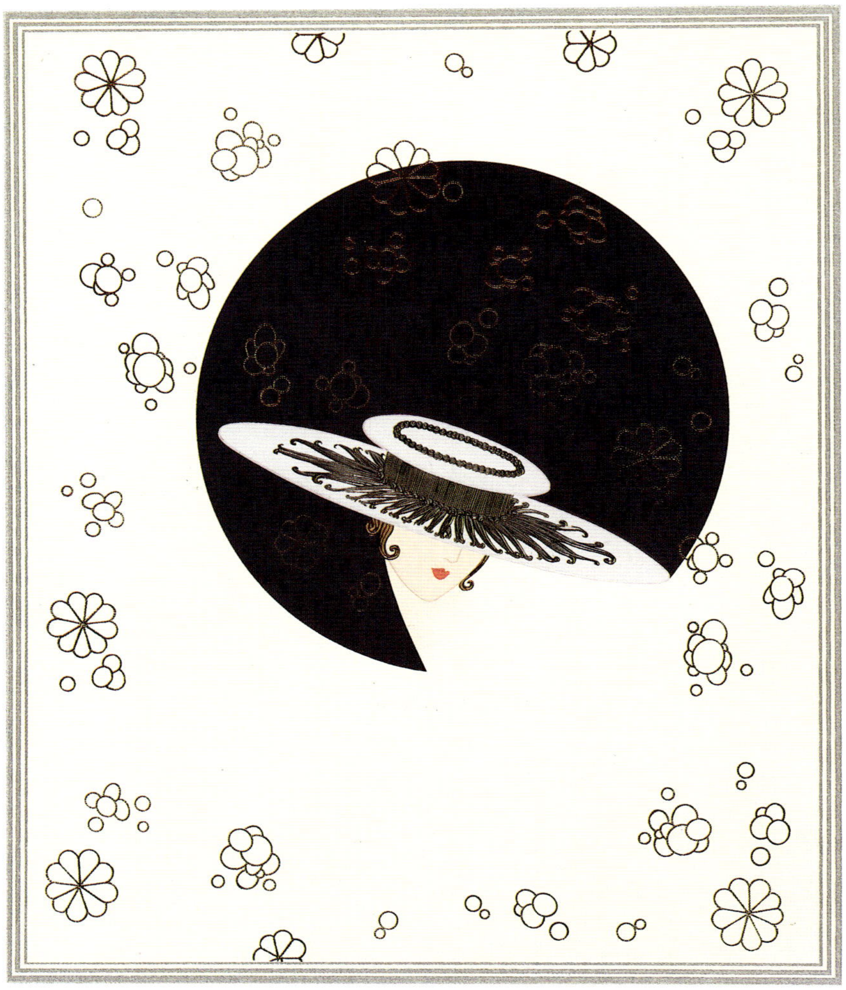

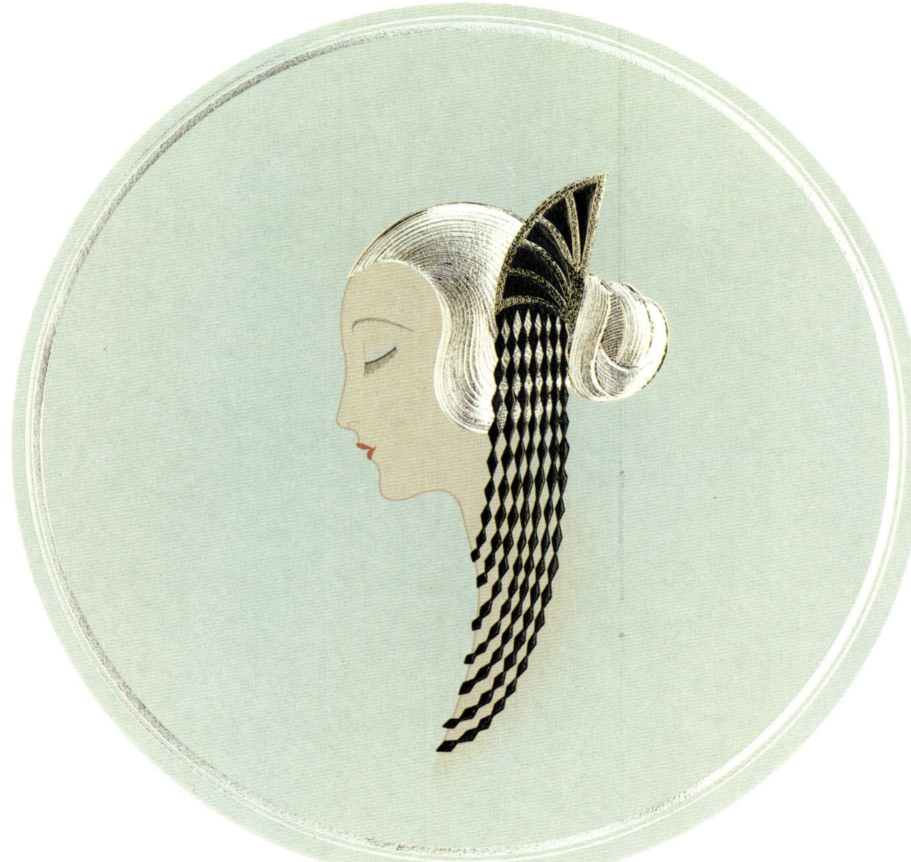

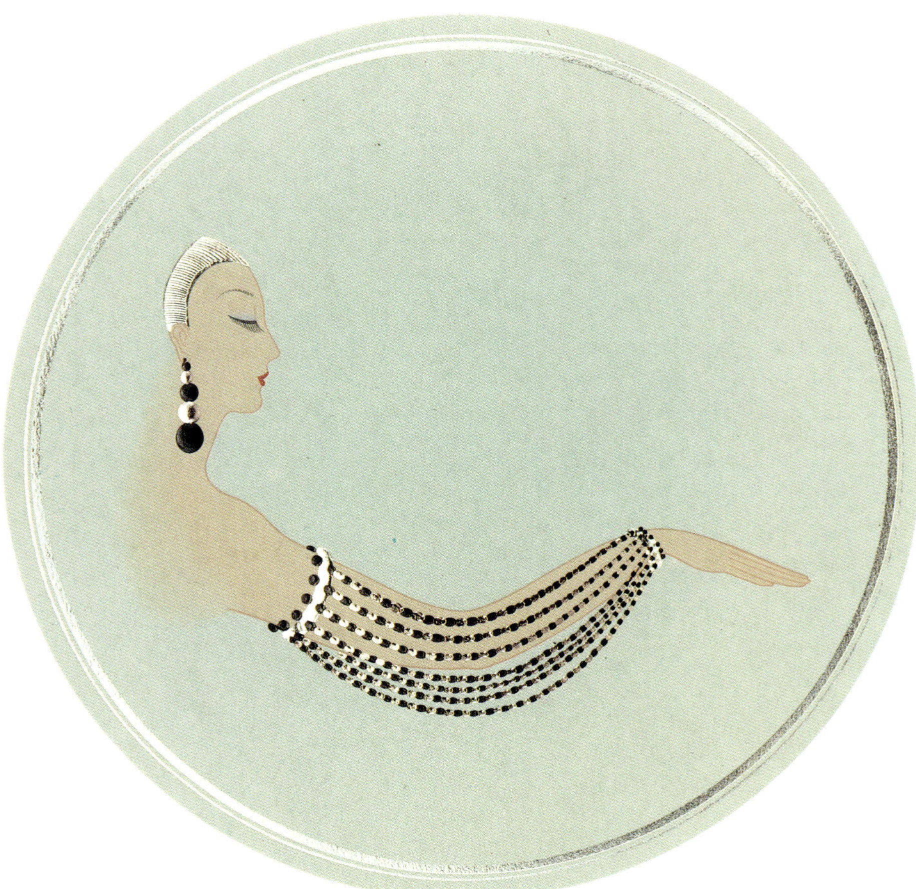

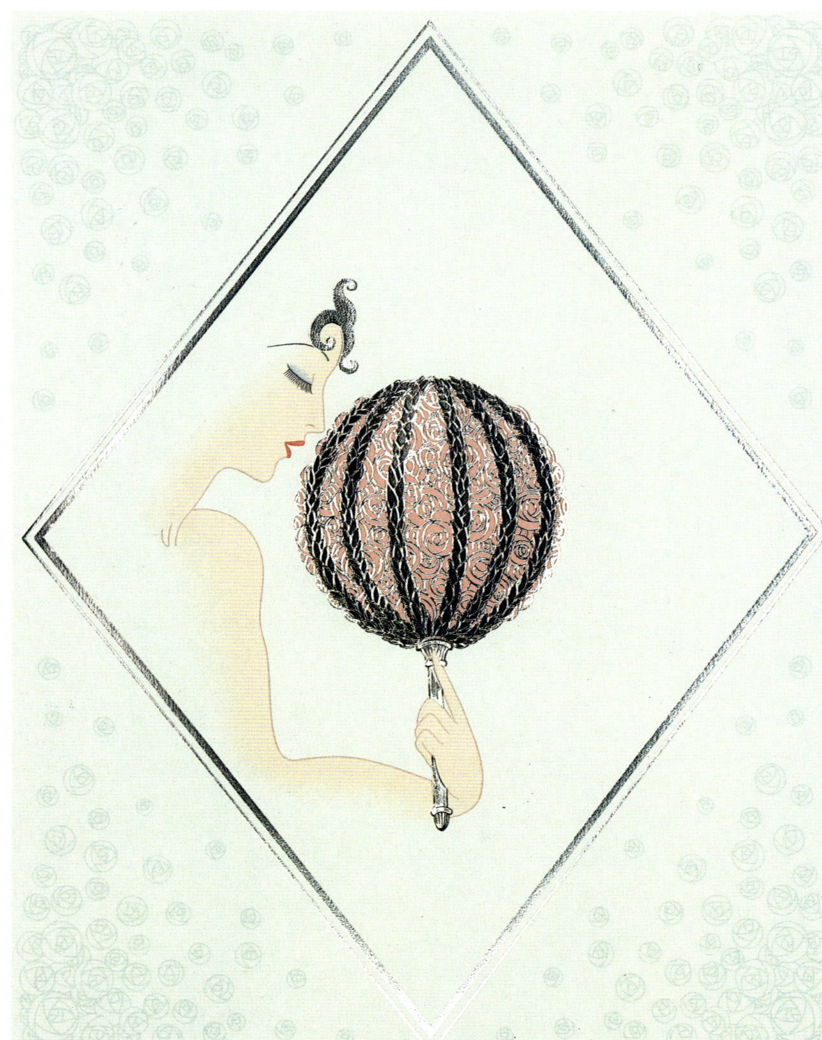

* *
Seduction
Séduction
Seduzione
Verführung

* *
Onyx Sleeve
Manche d'onyx
Manica di onice
Onyx-Ärmel

* *
Chignon
Chignon
Chignon
Chignon

* *
Rose Fan
Eventail rose
Ventaglio rosa
Rosenfächer

* *

Cameos
Camées
Cammei
Gemmen

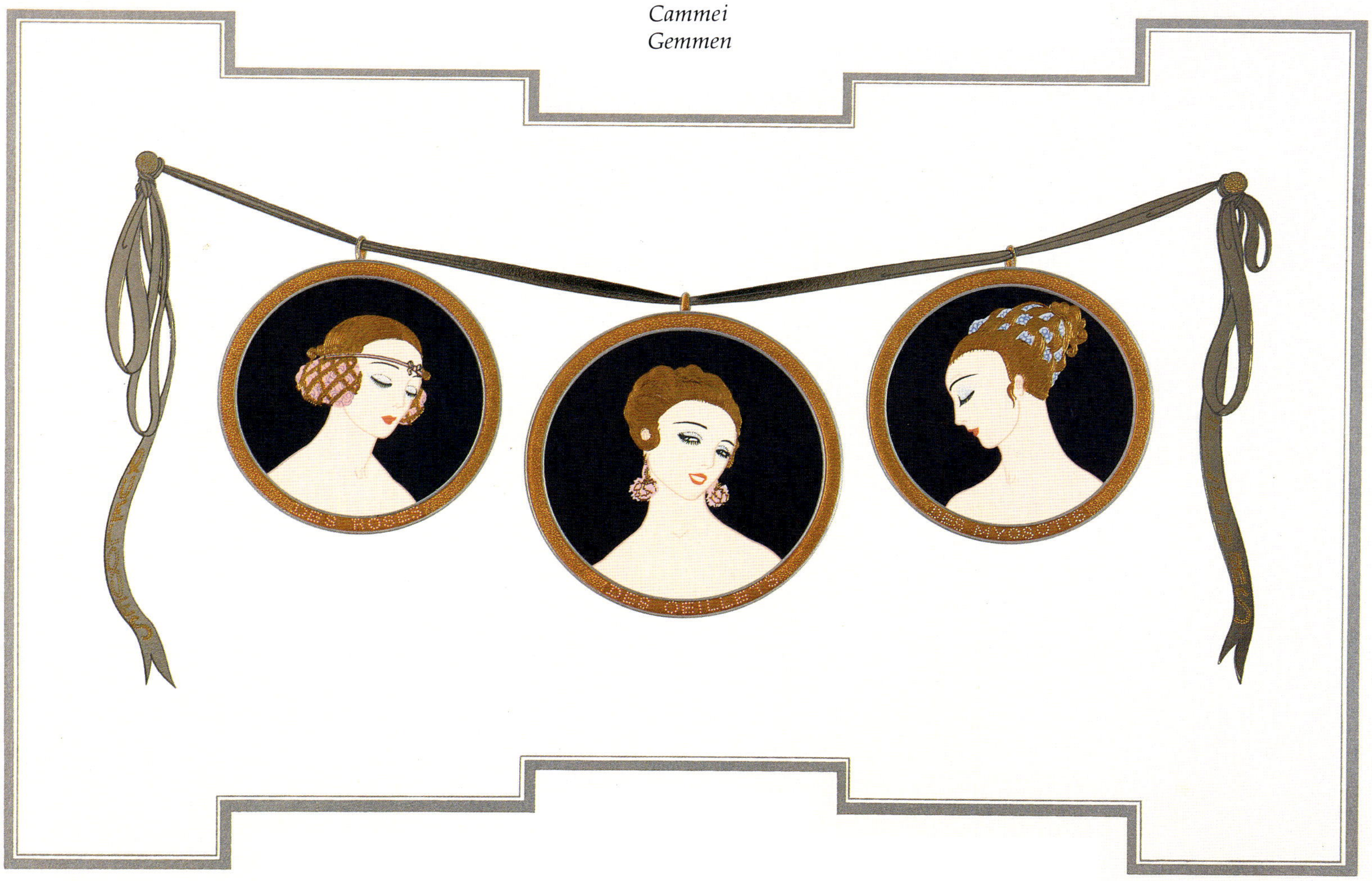

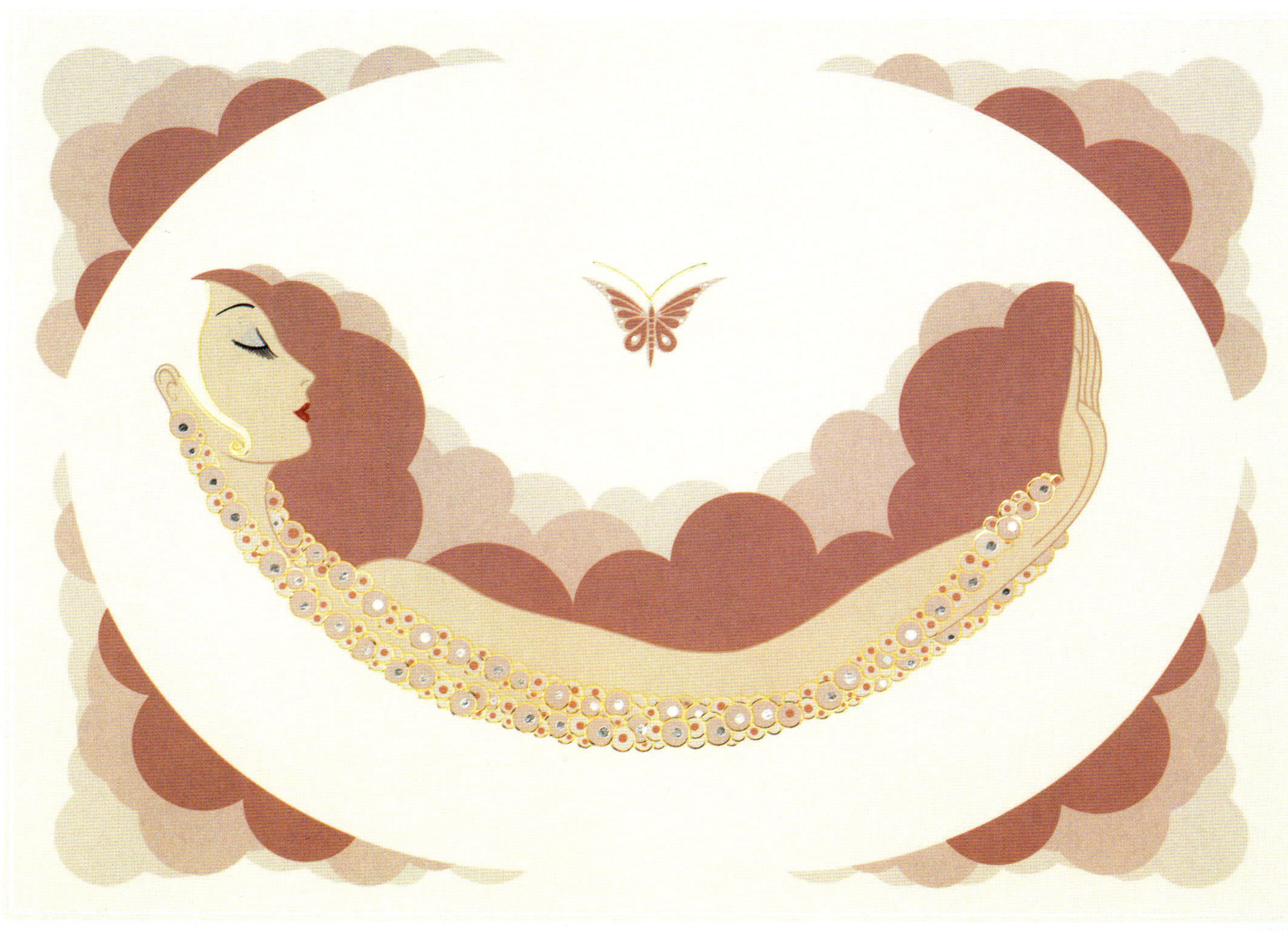

* *

Repose
Le Repos
Il riposo
Ruhepause

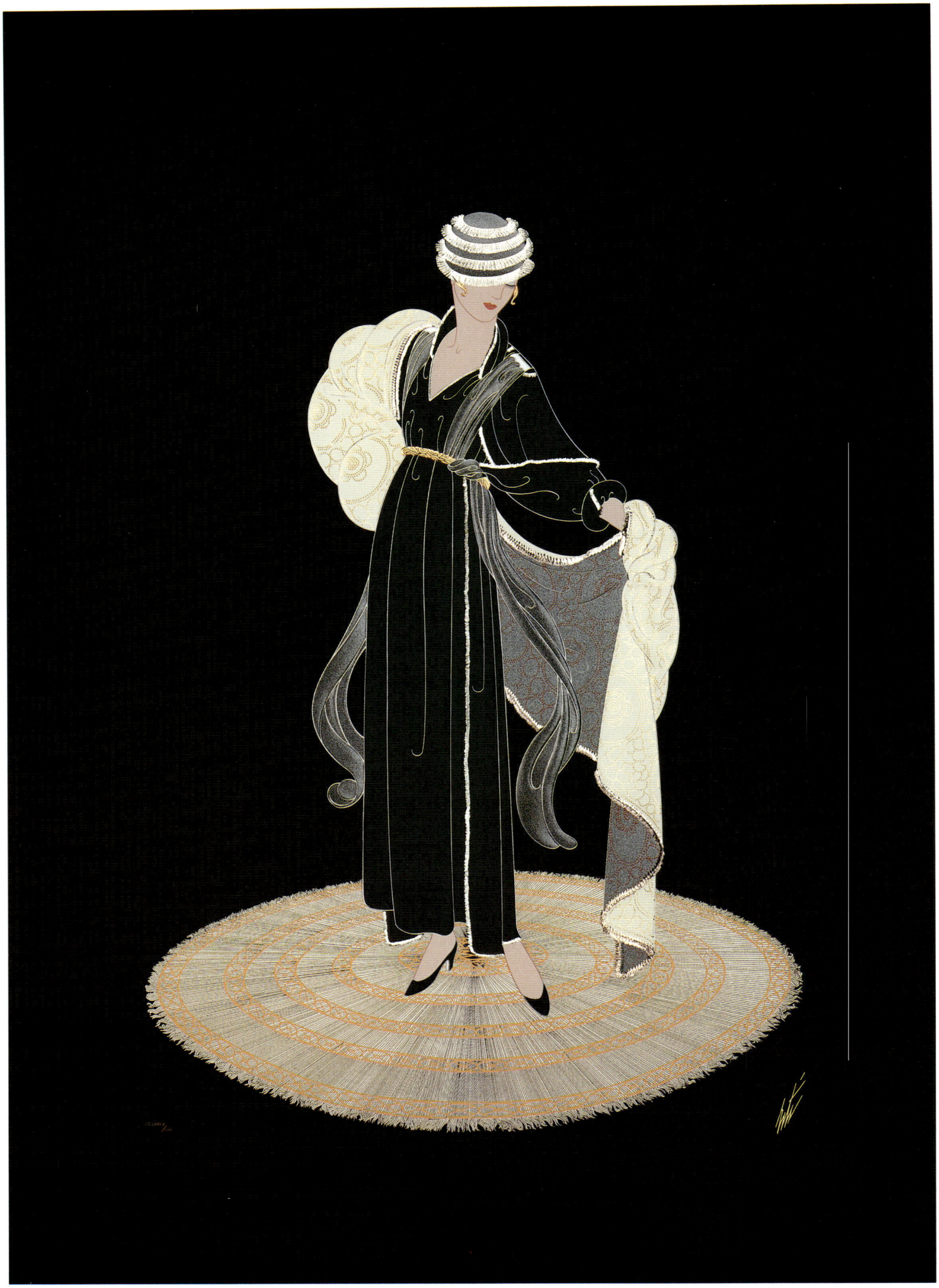

* *

Winter in Paris
L'Hiver à Paris
Inverno a Parigi
Winter in Paris

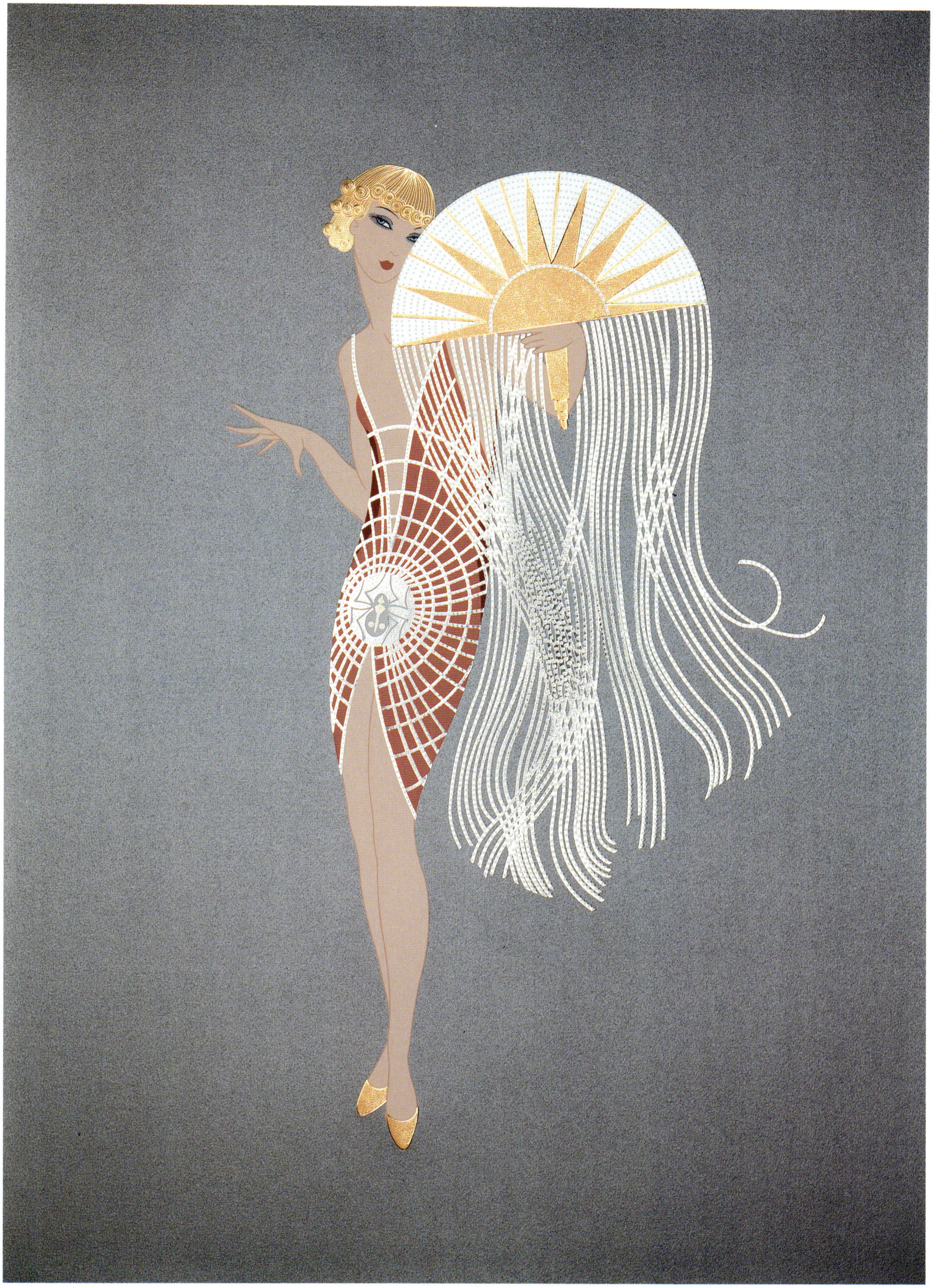

* *

Flapper
Flapper
Flapper
Flapper

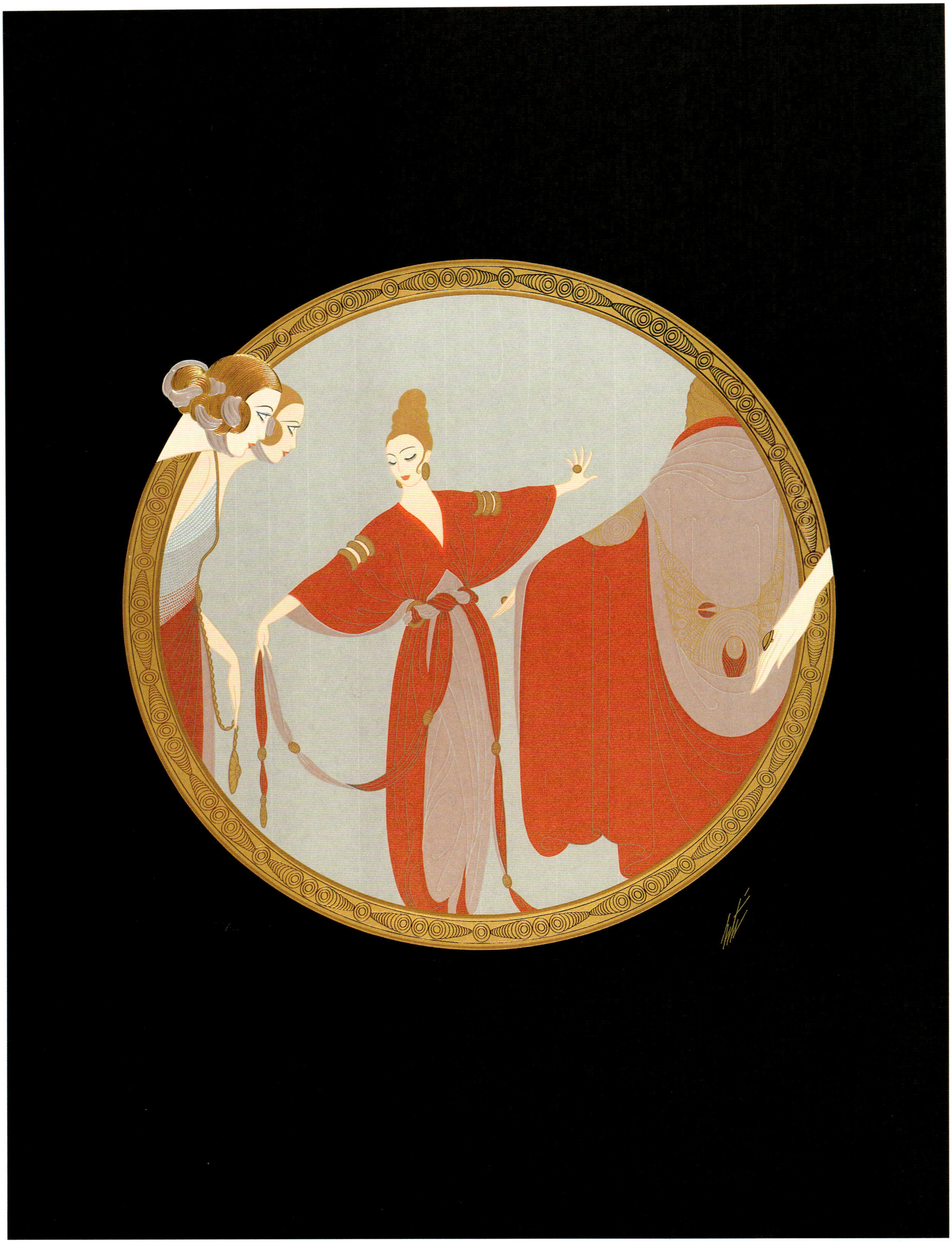

* *

The Looking Glass
Le Miroir
Lo specchio
Der Spiegel

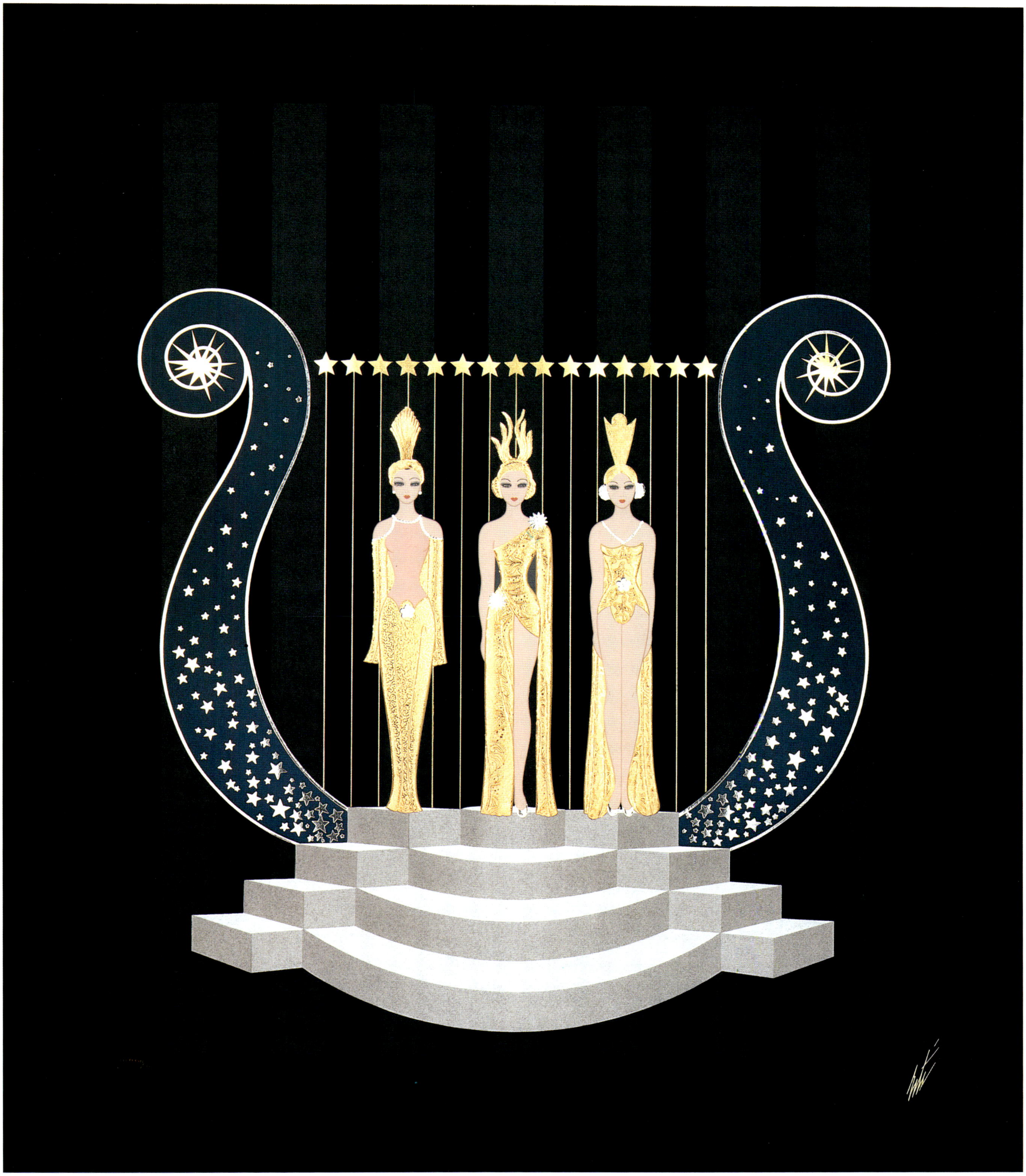

* *

Lyre

Lyre

Lira

Leier

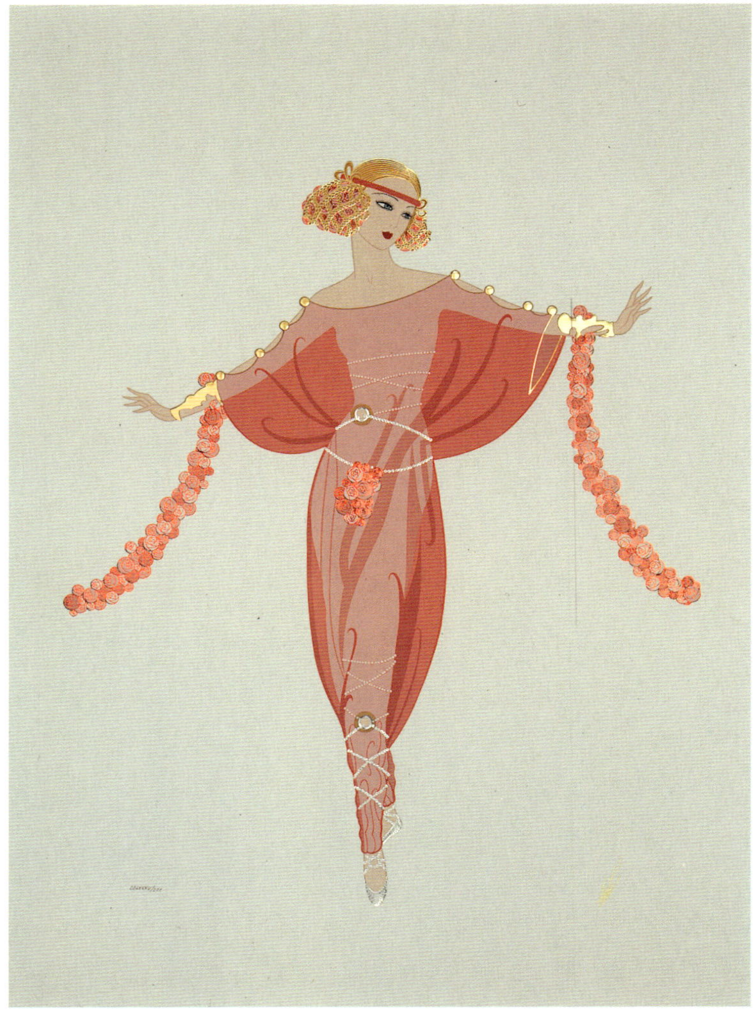

* *
May
Mai
Maggio
Mai

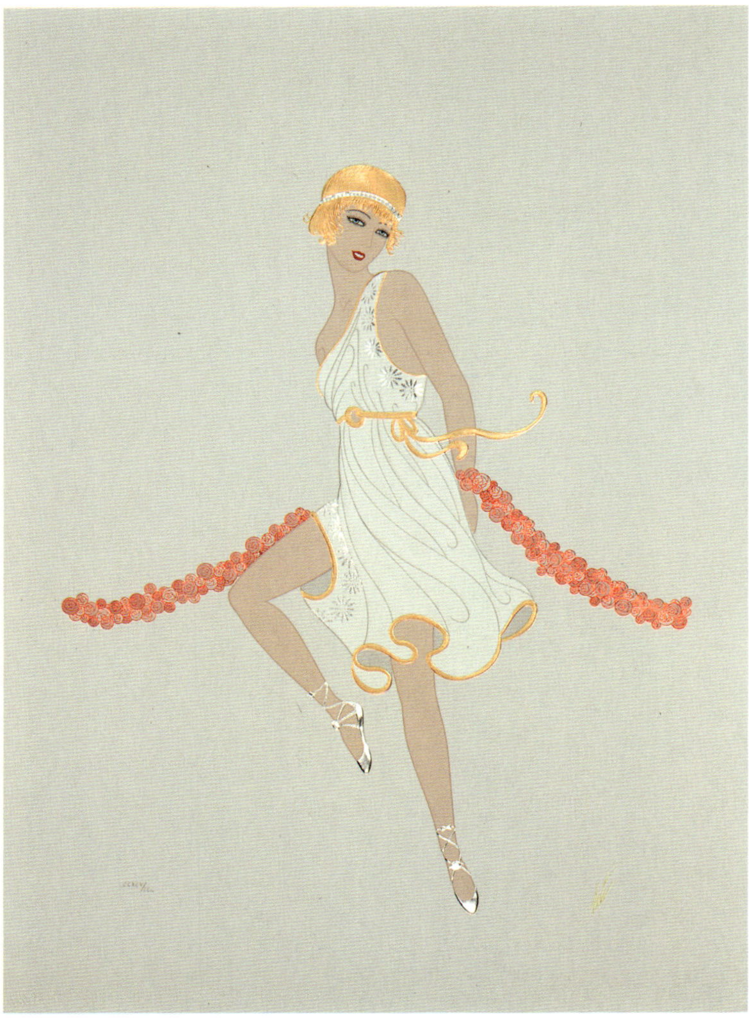

* *
April
Avril
Aprile
April

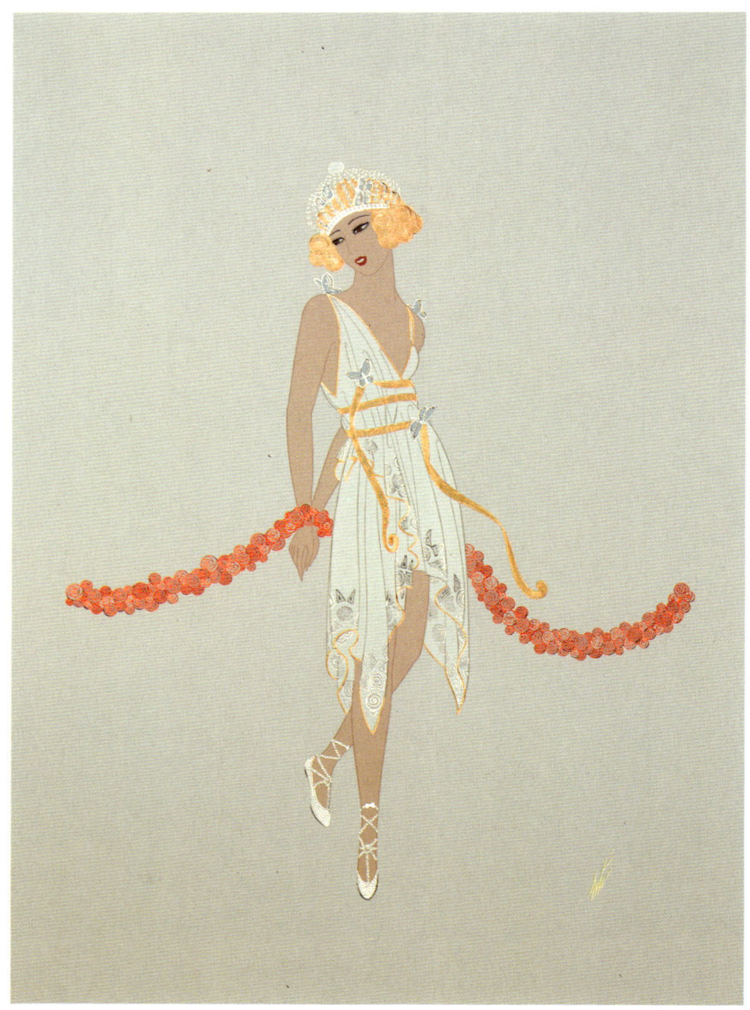

* *
June
Juin
Giugno
Juni

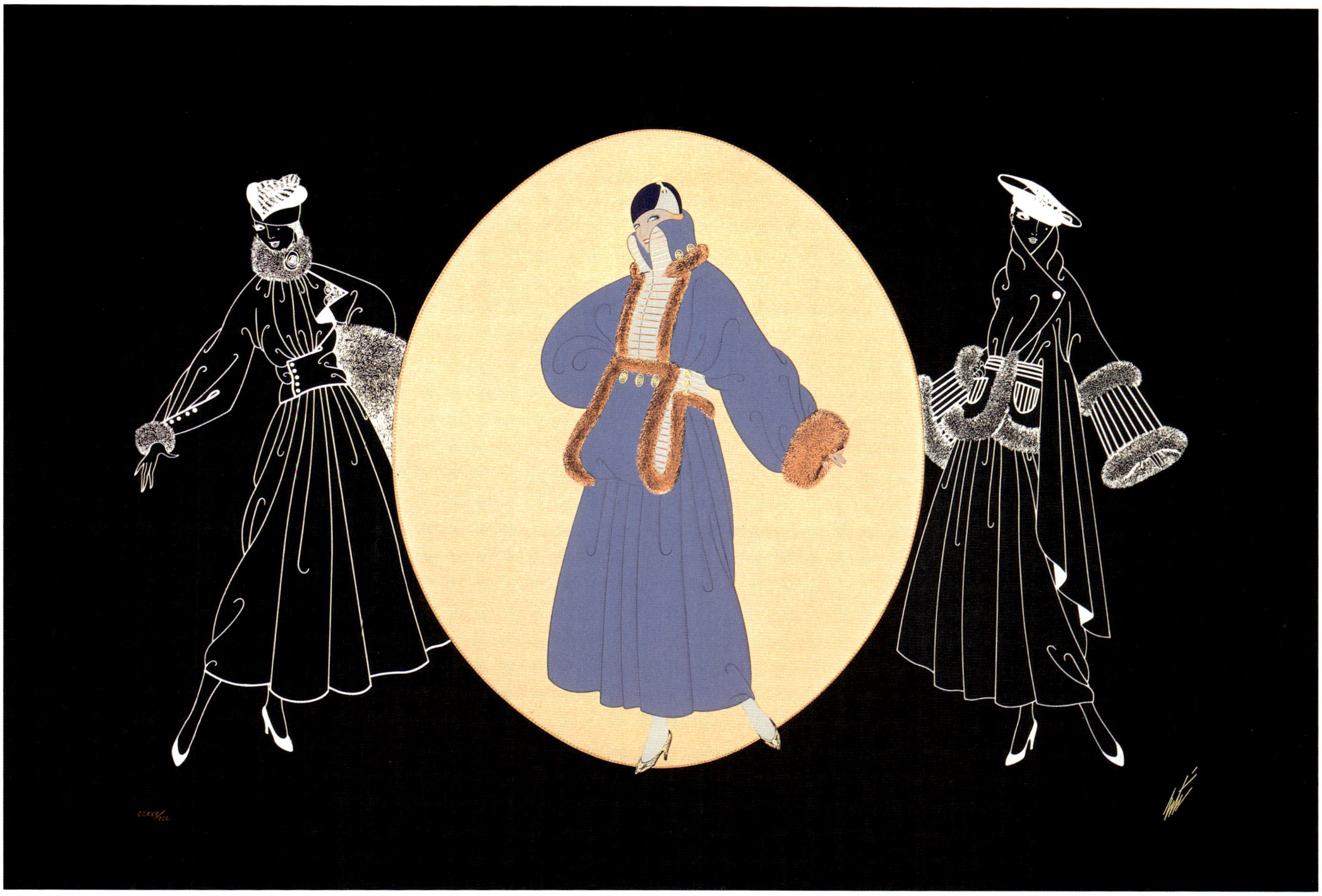

* *

Winter Promenade
Promenade en hiver
Passeggiata invernale
Winterpromenade

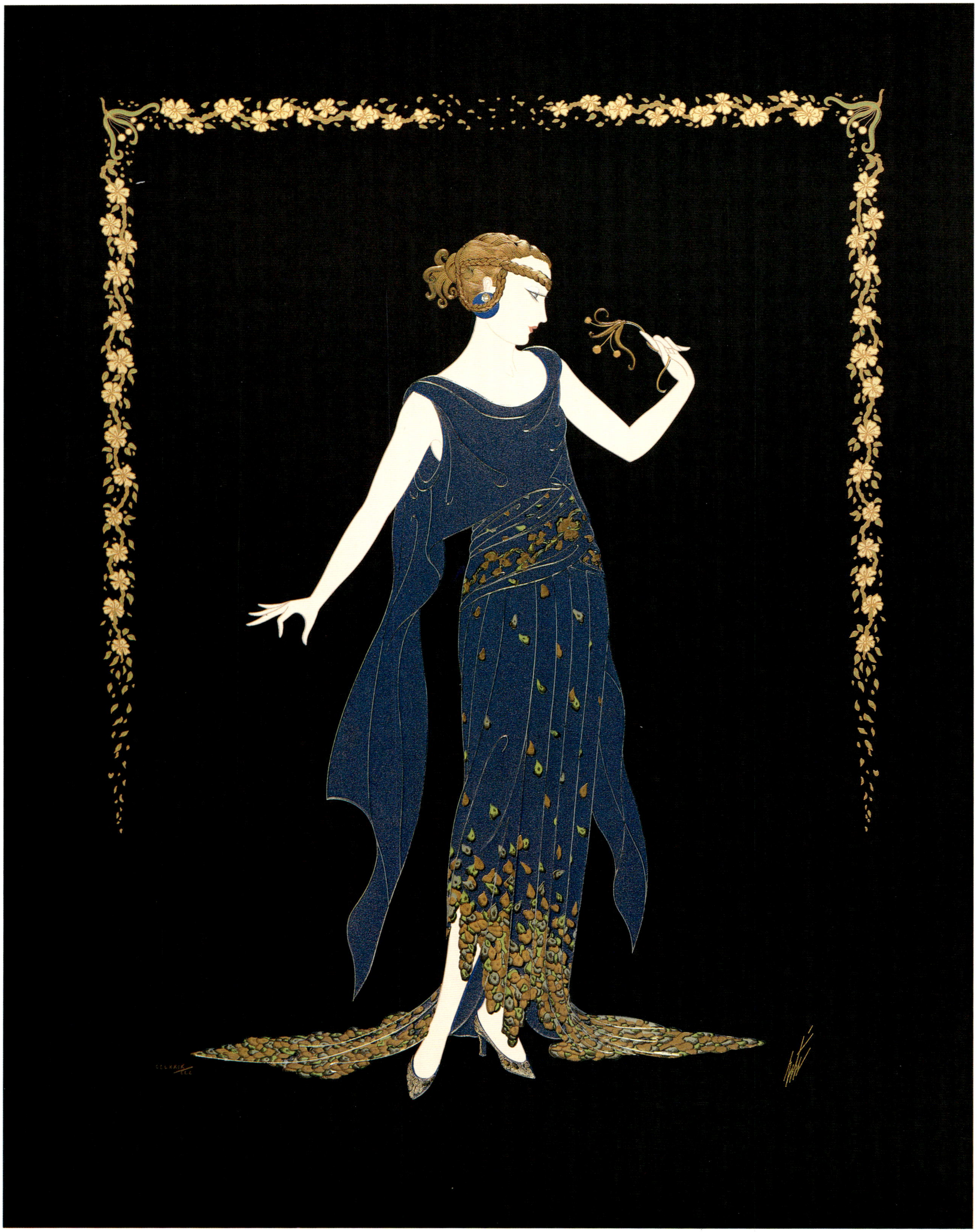

* *

Flower Petal Gown
Robe à pétale de fleurs
Abito con petali di fiore
Gewand aus Blütenblättern

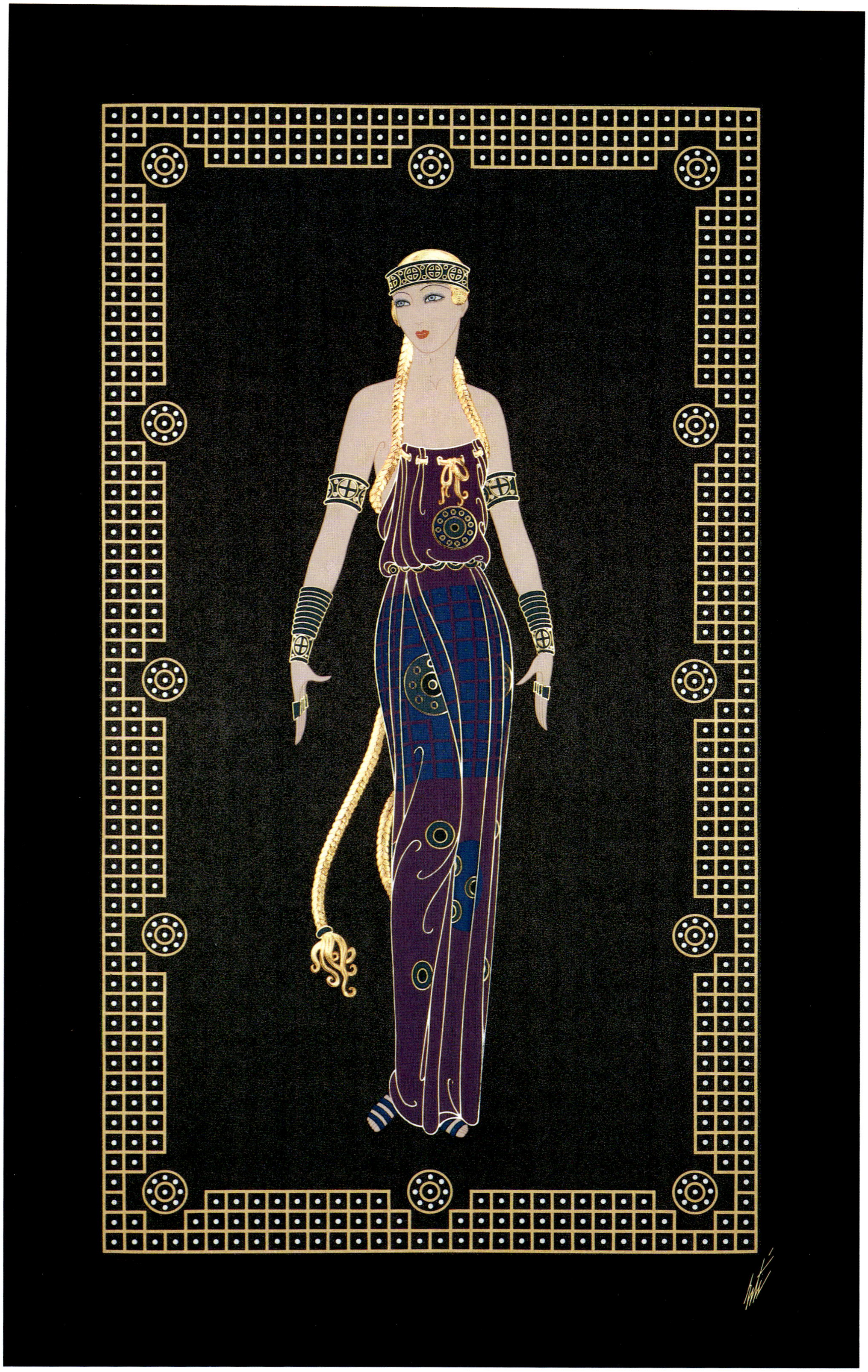

* *

Scandinavian Princess
Princesse Scandinave
Principessa scandinava
Skandinavische Prinzessin

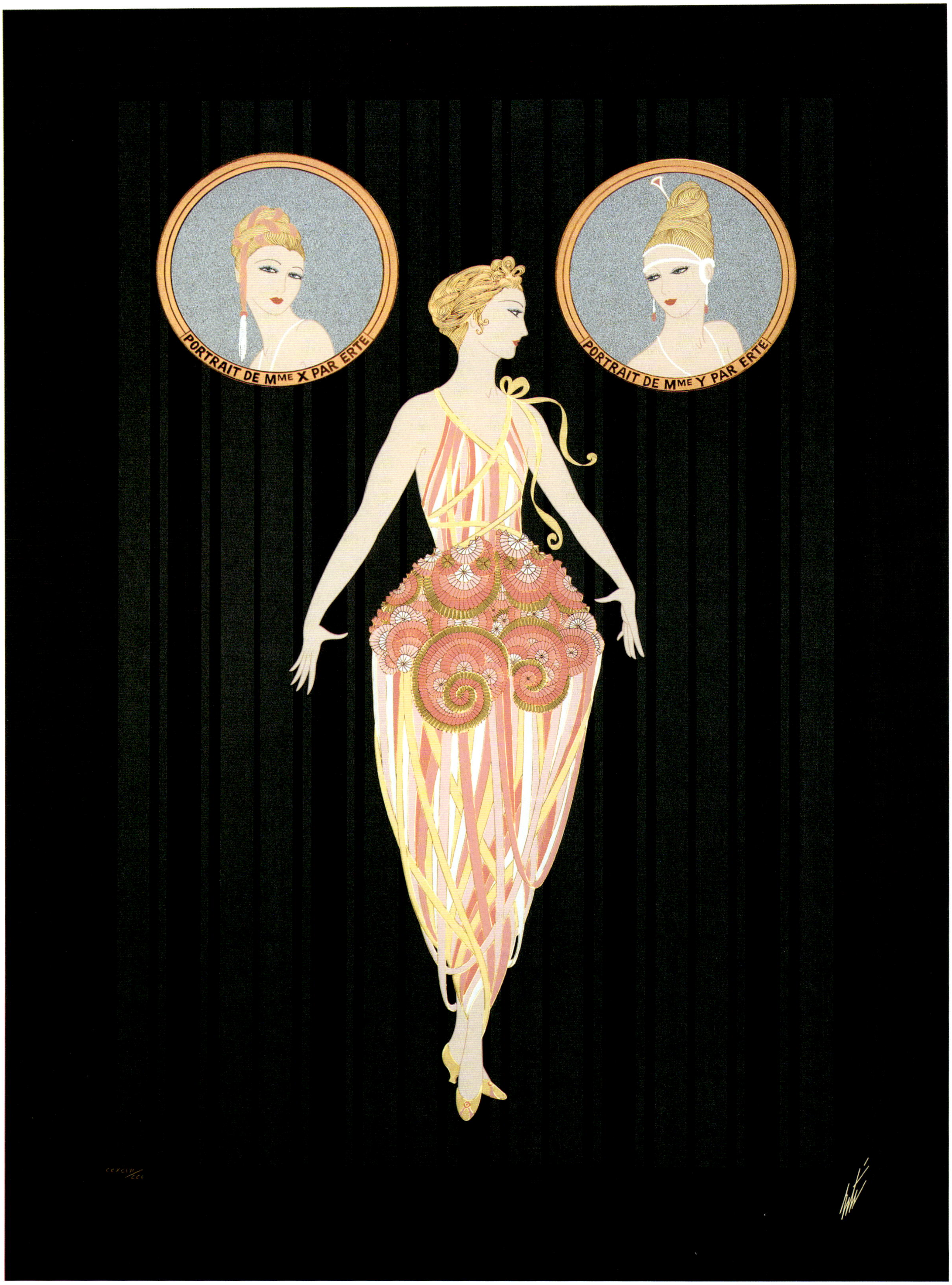

* *

Ribbon Dress
Robe en rubans
Abito con nastri
Bortenkleid

* *

Ingenue
Ingénue
Ingenuo
Unbefangen

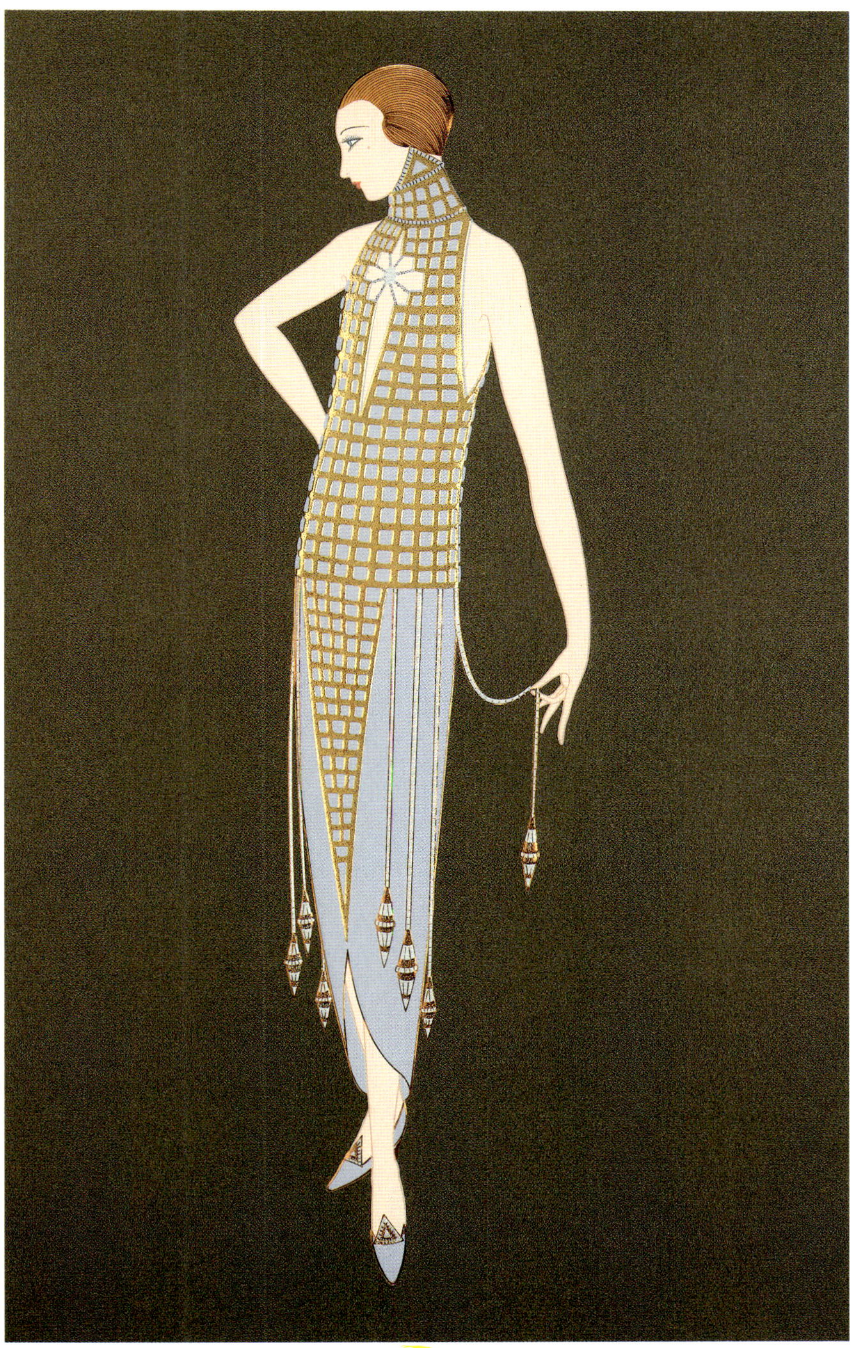

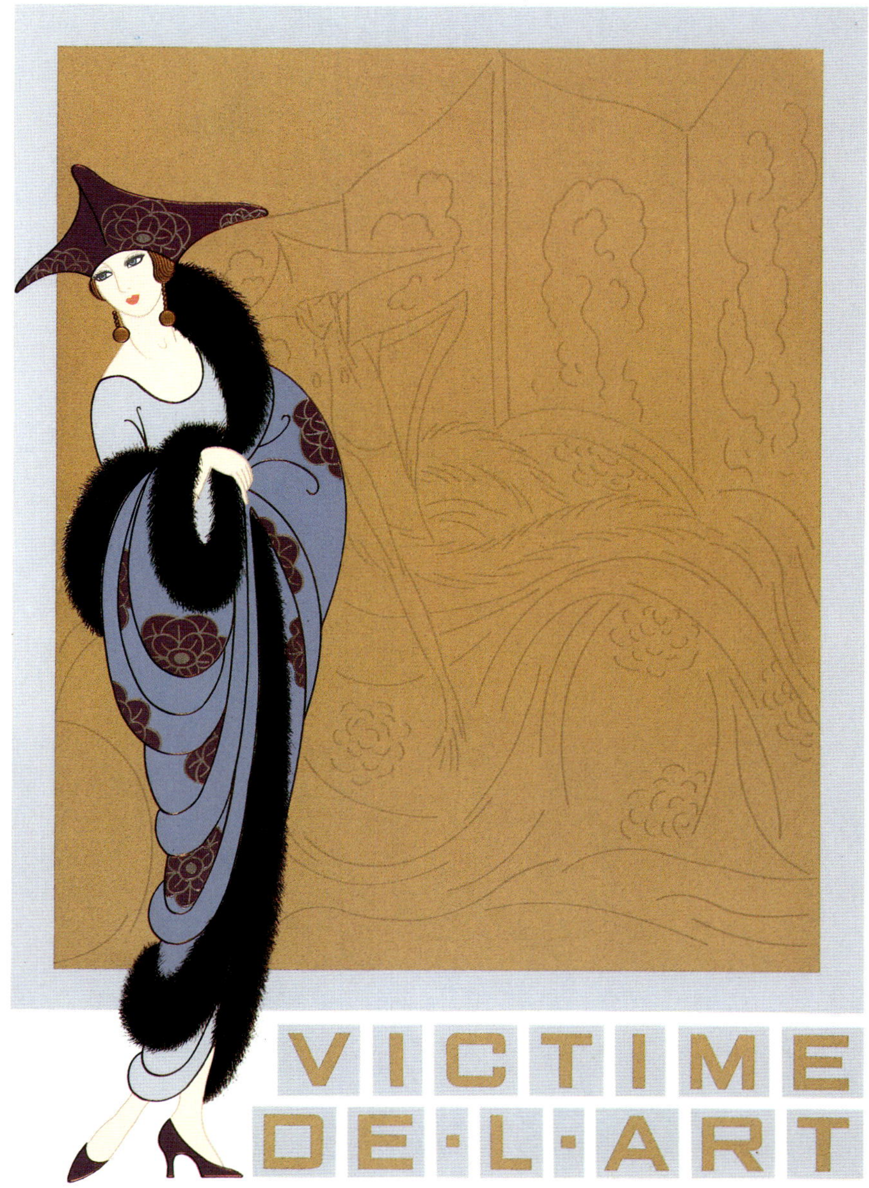

* *

Victime de l'art
Victime de l'art
Vittima dell'arte
Opfer der Kunst

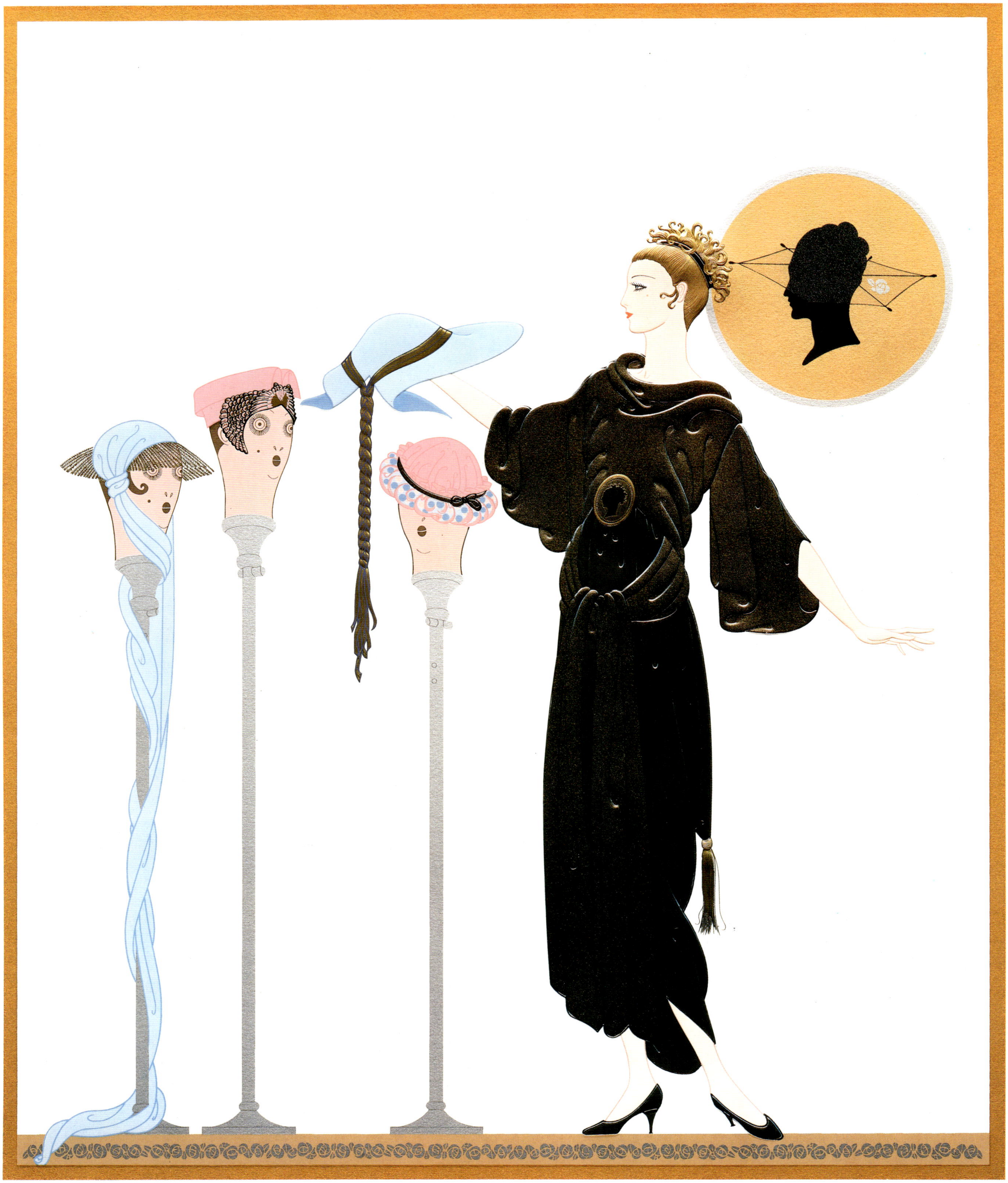

*

Millinery Shop
Boutique de mode
Modisteria
Hutladen

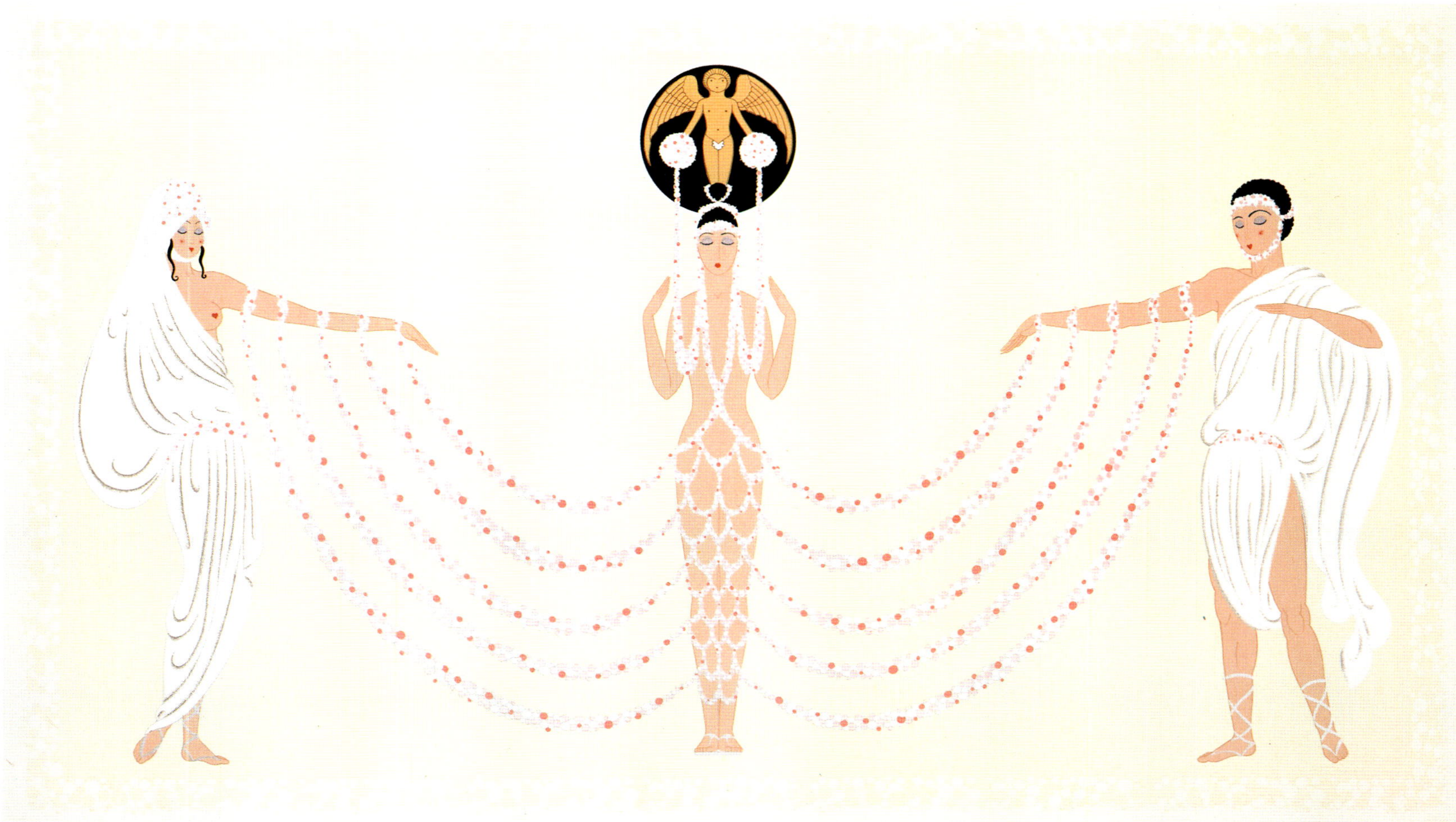

*

Arcadia
Arcadie
Arcadia
Arkadien

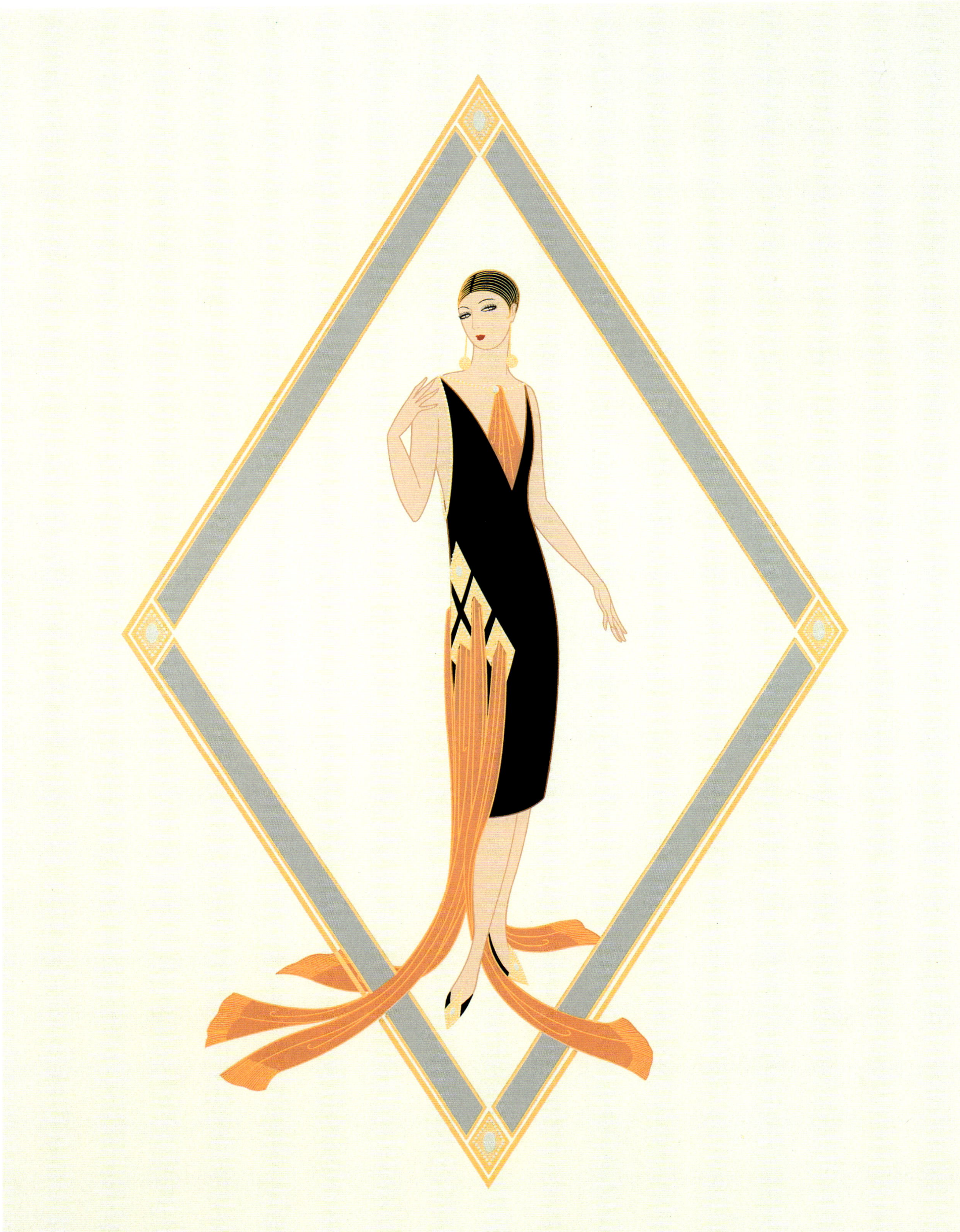

*

Maxim's
Maxim's
Maxim's
Maxim's

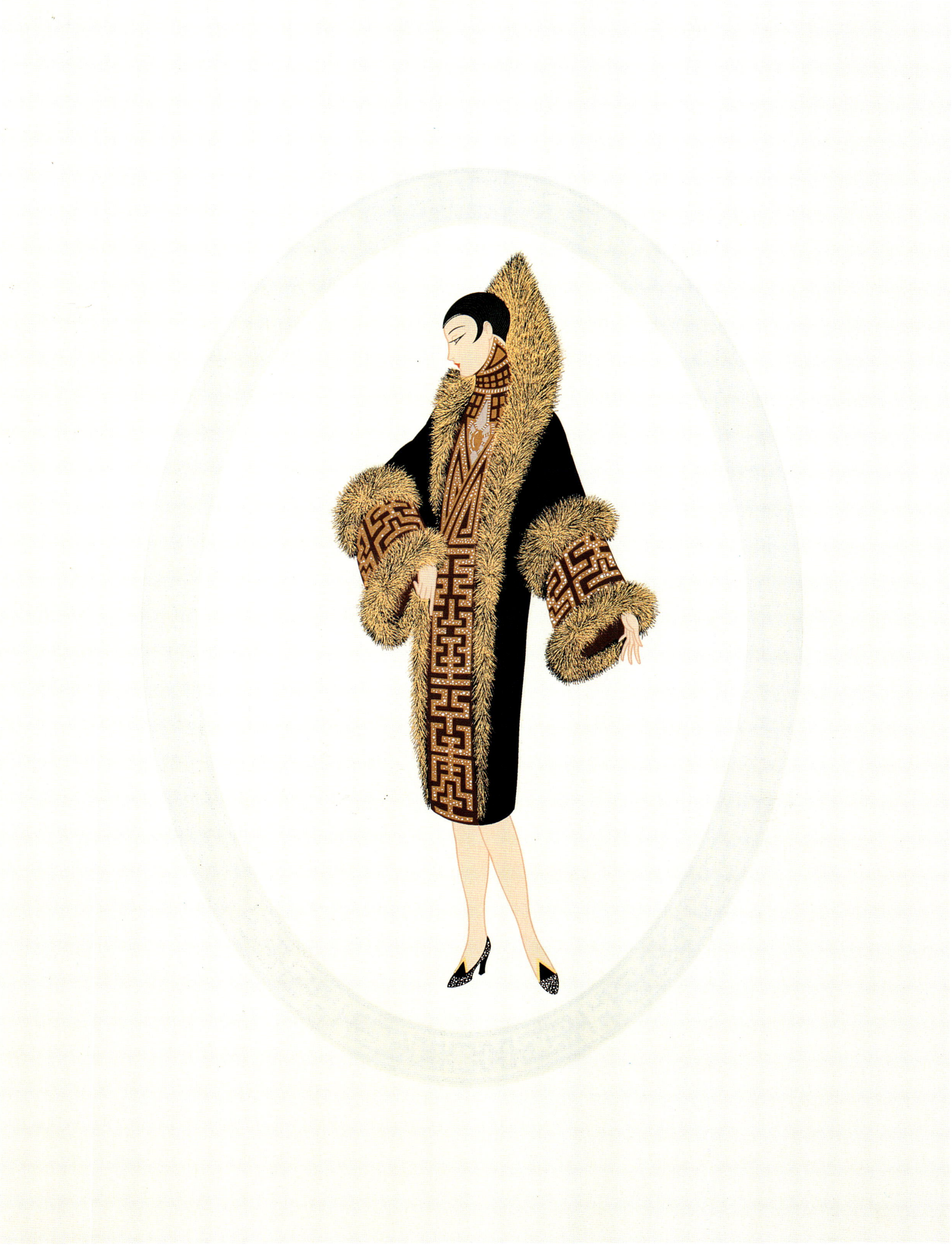

*

Le Cirque

Le Cirque

Le Cirque

Le Cirque

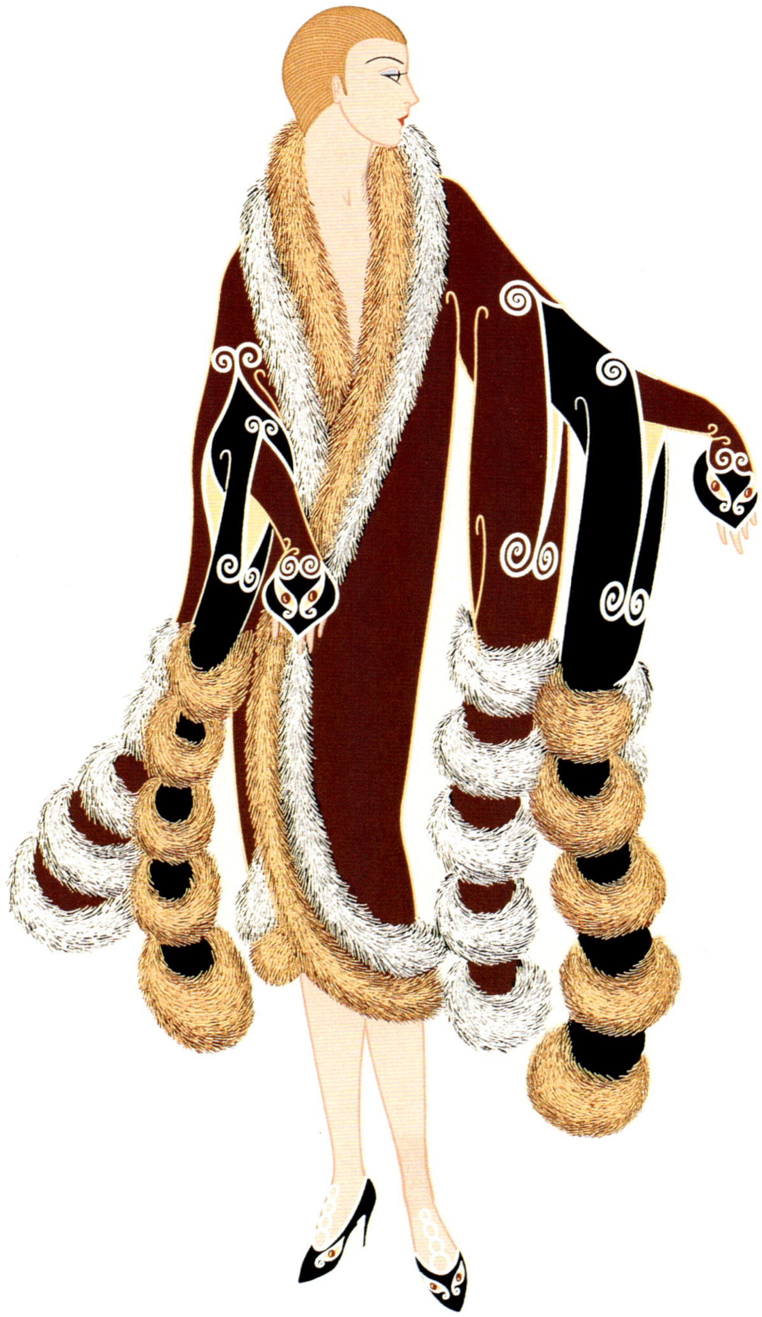

*

Laurent
Laurent
Laurent
Laurent

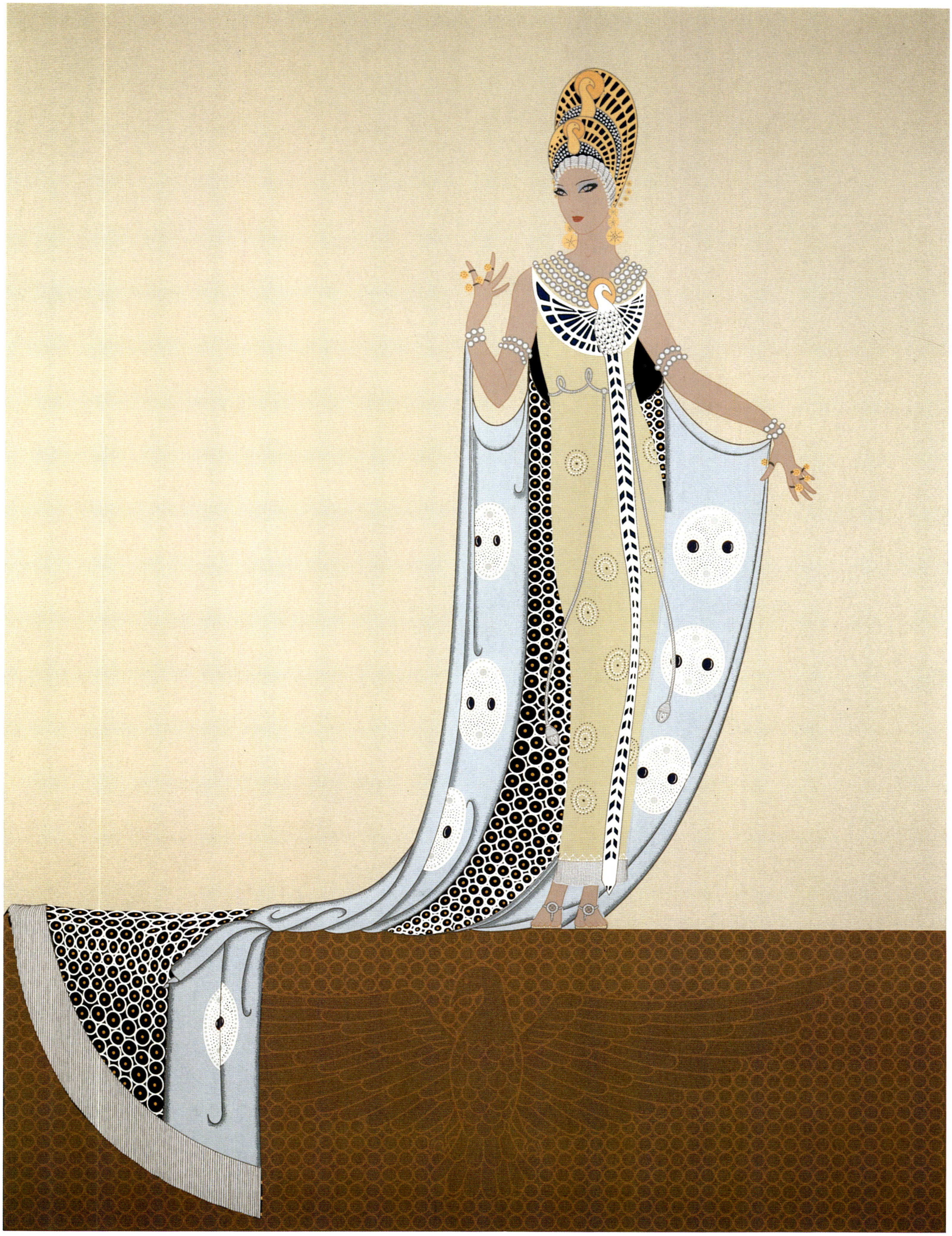

*

Isis
Isis
Iside
Isis

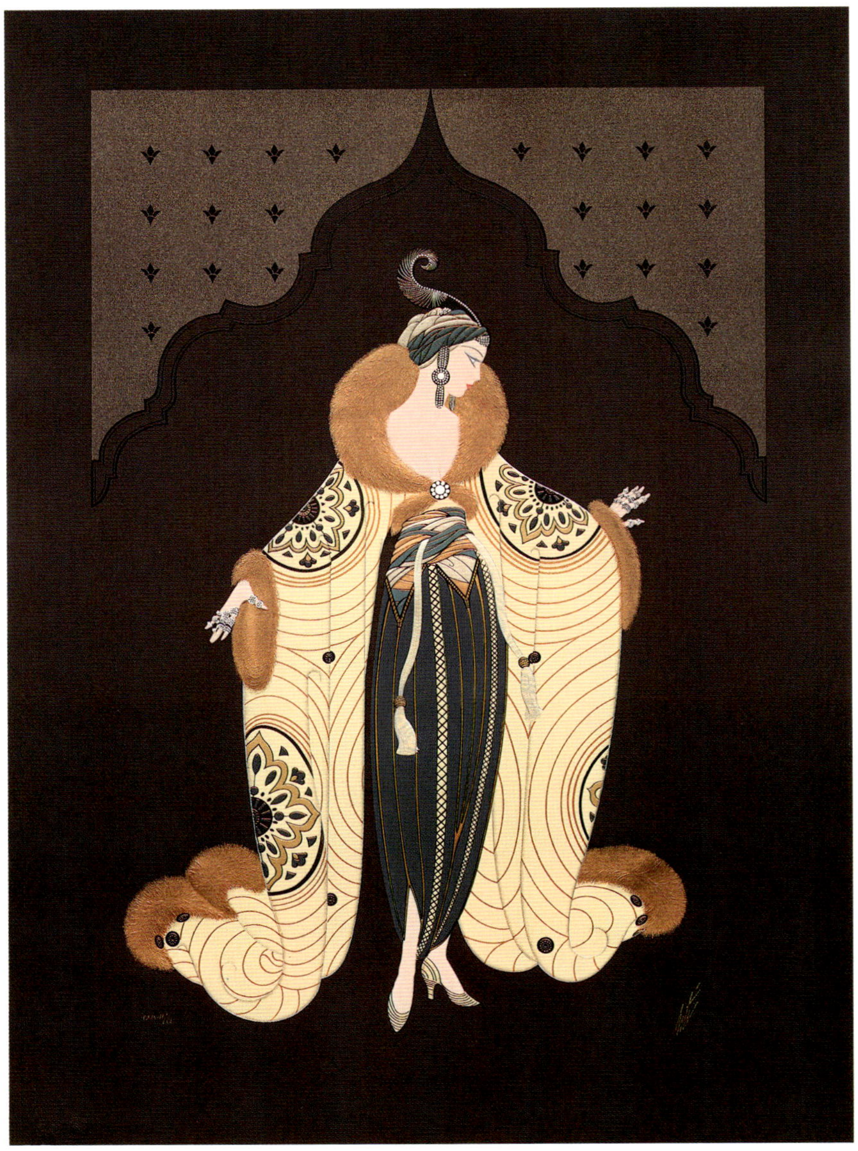

*

Le Harem moderne I
Le Harem moderne I
L'harem moderno I
Das moderne Harem I

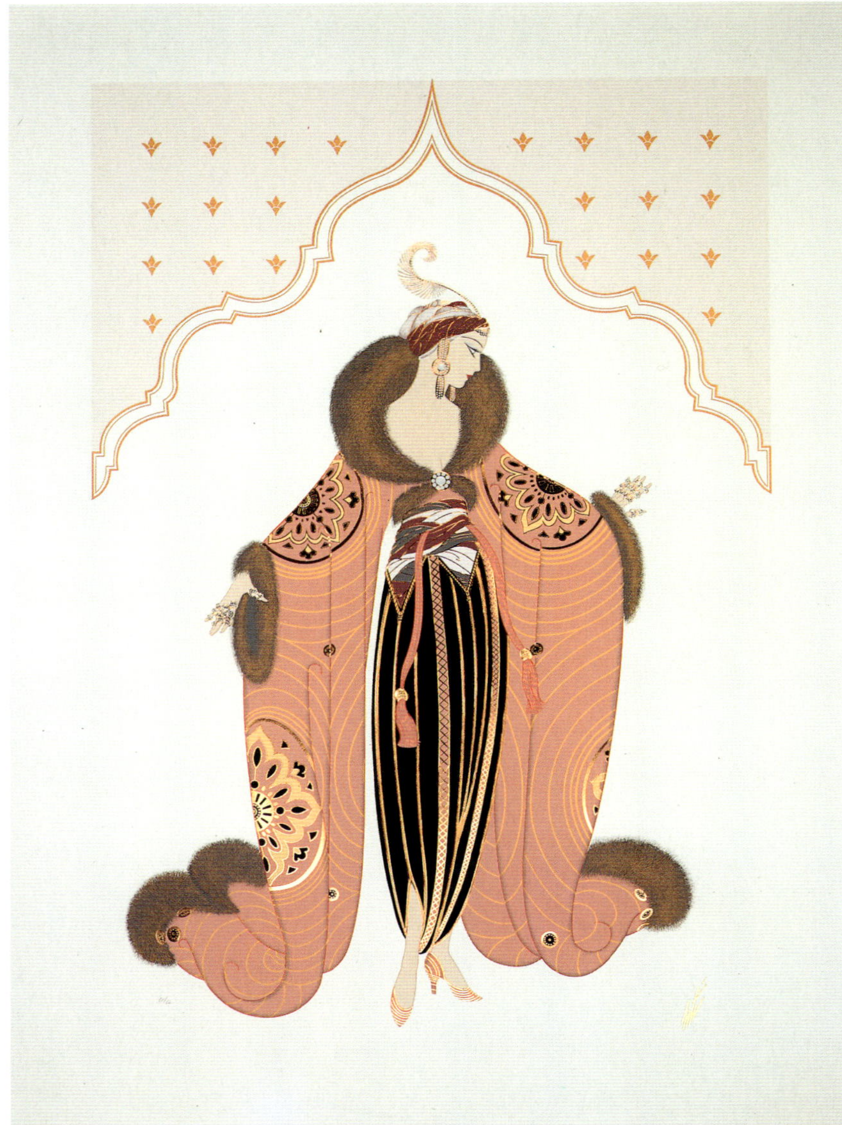

*

Le Harem moderne II
Le Harem moderne II
L'harem moderno II
Das moderne Harem II

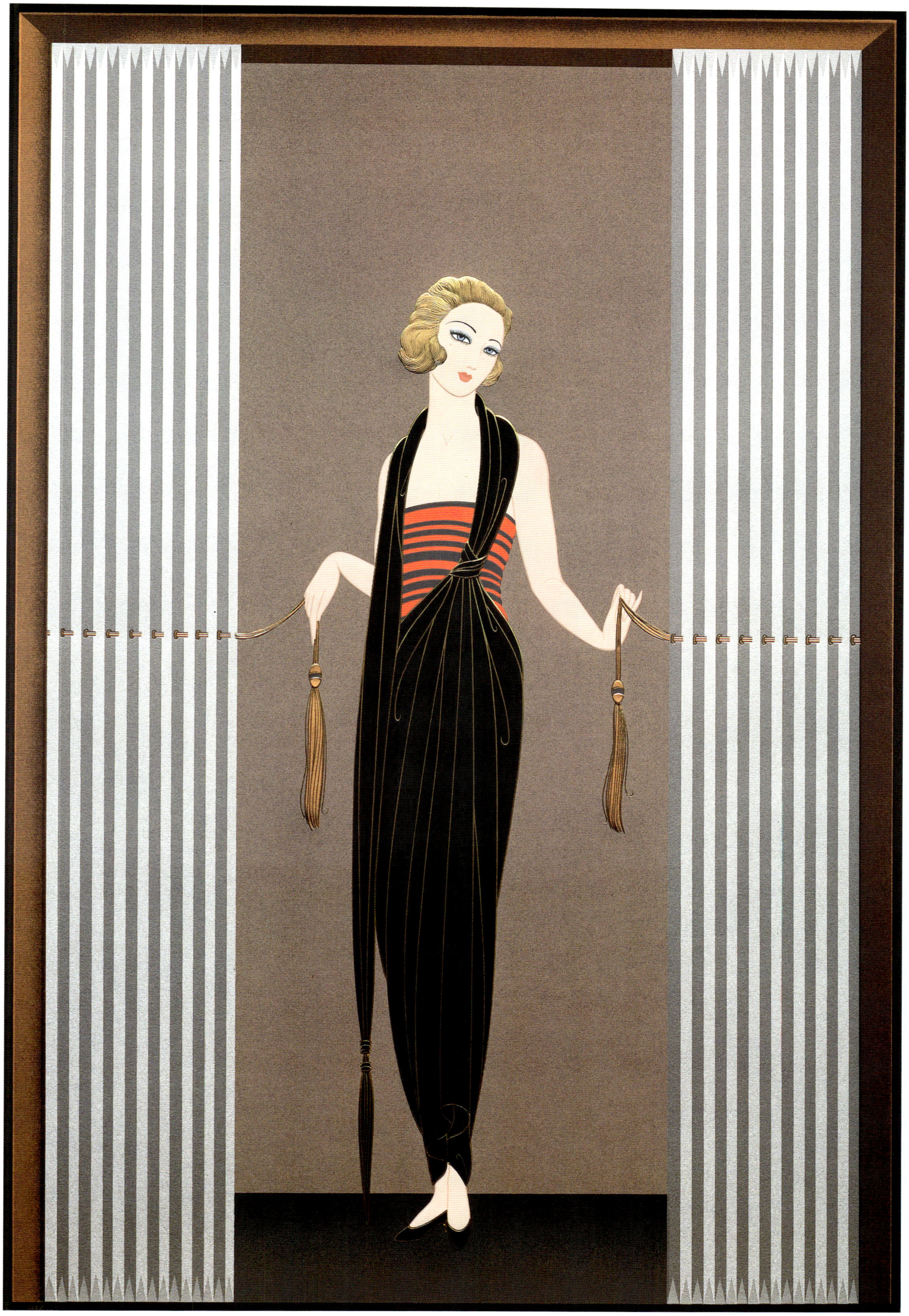

*

Boudoir
Boudoir
Boudoir
Boudoir

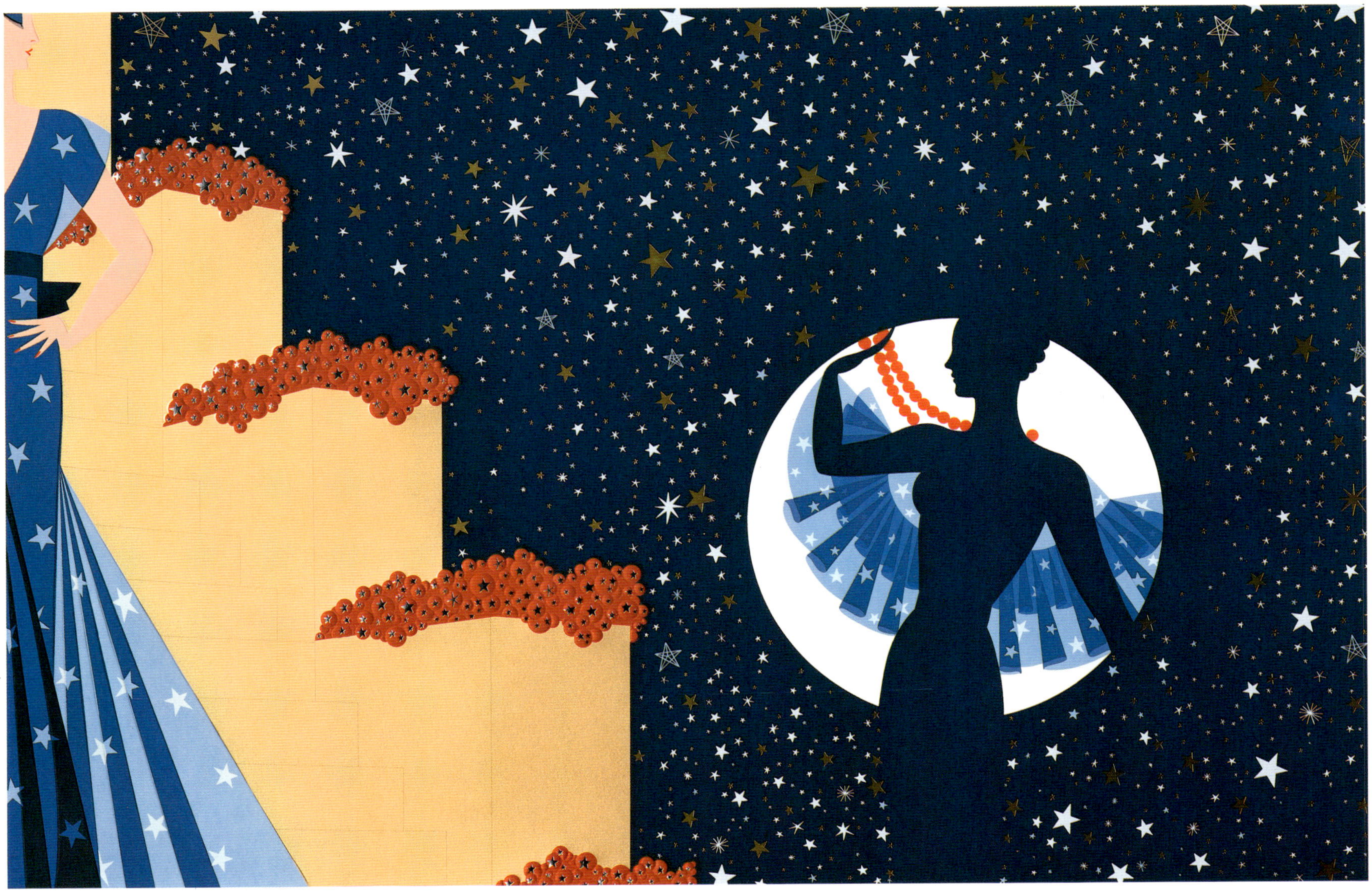

*

Star Spangled Night
Nuit pailletée d'étoiles
Notte stellata
Sternbesäte Nacht

SCULPTURE

INTRODUCTION

Erté at work on his last sculptures

DAVID ROGATH

Every great artist contributes something invariably characteristic of his persona to each of the works comprising his oeuvre, and when one writes about the creative genius of my late friend Erté, it remains difficult to separate his energy, enthusiasm, discipline, and determination from the bronzes illustrated in this book, the majority of which, I am proud to say, were published by our company during the past four years. Exquisite to behold, each sculpture of a strutting femme fatale, gliding geisha girl, prancing dancer, or romantic Renaissance beauty is as lively in spirit, stylish in manner, and innovative in approach as was the artist whom we at Chalk & Vermilion revered.

It is always exciting to view a newly cast, freshly patinated bronze on which one has collaborated, and this was especially true with these images, which comprise Erté's last sculpture series. From selecting the specific illustrations to preparing them for their three-dimensional application to analyzing each model for articulation to choosing the appropriate finishes, the process that I watched Erté follow to produce these sculptures was both arduous and aesthetically rewarding.

This sculpture series was inspired by the artist's pen-and-ink drawings and gouaches, particularly those executed between 1918 and 1933, when Erté was the celebrated illustrator for *Harper's Bazaar,* as well as the featured costume and set designer for French music hall revues, Broadway shows, and, briefly, Hollywood films. As he often noted, he chose illustrations whose images were dynamic and appealing, whose costumes conveyed his stylistic development from luxury and grace to wit and flamboyance, and whose figures could be precisely and accurately rendered in bronze.

Once each selection was made, Erté then readied it for its translation from a two-dimensional to a three-dimensional work of art. If his original image faced forward, Erté would describe the back for our notation or provide a small sketch and consider the kind of base to be used for his future statue. These were scrutinized for their overall balance and rhythm, adjusted for further detail, and reviewed for their ideal dimensions. A clay model was next created for the lost-wax process that was to be employed; it was studied and modified, and the final finishes were determined.

The renowned twentieth-century artist Henry Moore once said, "Every sculpture must have its own life", and such was the case as we prepared each of Erté's editions. In fact, rarely was a sculpture adapted exactly from its original illustration or more recent serigraph. Occasionally, as in the piece entitled *Michelle,* with its newly white dress panels and pumps, Erté would elect to use a different color to balance better with his image's once-pale, now-bronze skin tone. Or he might apply more electric, eye-catching colors to a freestanding work and replace a wine, gray, and white combination with a mauve, silver, and gold one, as he did in *Ermine Brocade.*

In most instances, Erté manifested his flair by making more substantial modifications to the plans for his bronzes. To achieve an all-around graceful line, he would taper the arms, legs, and neck of his *Arabian Fan* slave girl, more gently angulate the arms of his *Rose Dancer,* or perhaps extend the billowing headdress of his *Bal Tabarin* performer. Once adjusted or repositioned, the artist might then add further style to such figures as his *Printemps,* by substituting for their connecting floral bough a glittering, gold-plated sash, incorporate faux pearls into the sumptuous gown in *Radiance,* or finish his Deco dress with delicate crystal pendants.

Satisfied with these and other adaptations for his images, this master of *mise-en-scène* next applied his enormous talents to designing bases on which they would stand. This was a particularly pleasing exercise for

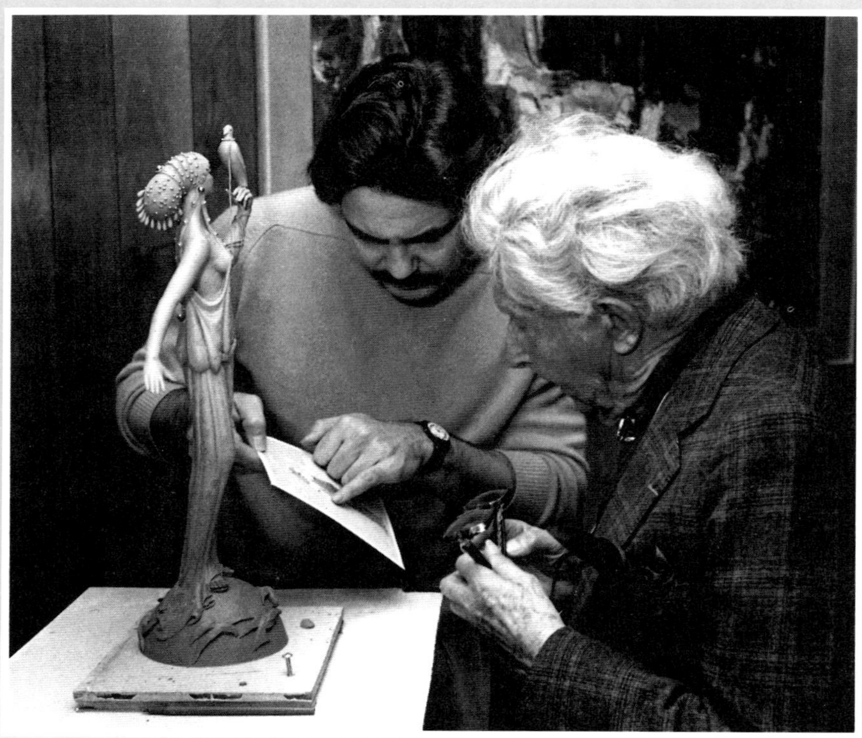

David Rogath and Erté discussing corrections on the clay model of Love Goddess

Erté, as he had always considered the total environment for every one of his creations, and now he could again express his original concept for each figure's individual stage production or fashion layout to an audience that had, most likely, never seen either. Consequently, he set his mythological *Golden Fleece* figure atop an inverted classical cornice, placed his sprightly *Bacchante* upon a plump cluster of ripe red grapes, and put his dazzling *Rose Gown* debutante on an upended, barely open bud.

As he worked on the plans for his bronzes, the artist occasionally recalled how the costumes for his theatrical projects looked in the limelight of their postwar stages and how the audiences received the spectacles. The model for his bronze *Starfish,* created for a 1919 Folies-Bergère tableau entitled "Fonds de la mer", prompted many such memories. Erté lucidly described how he outfitted the other members of the troupe as entrancing lobsters, rays, octopuses, and goldfish and how these dancers were almost magical in maneuvering on that house's notoriously narrow stage with its eighteen steps. He also beamed at the fact that he was now producing bronze figures bedecked in the original costumes that once inspired the sculptures by his Art Deco contemporaries, Démetre Chiparus and Joé Descomps among them.

Once Erté completed his plans for each sculpture, the laborious task of producing its edition began. The individual, master clay model for the edition was created. After Erté's review and adjustments, a segmented negative rubber mold was then made from this model in order to produce a plaster mold, which would then be examined and refined according to Erté's specifications. A new, negative polysulfide rubber mold would then be made from this plaster mold; from it the mother epoxy form was created to make the production molds for the wax replicas. Each wax casting then made would be refined, fitted with gates and vents for the subsequent passage of molten bronze, and covered with protective layers of fine sand, which would be left to cure into a shell. The foundry would then heat the shell, whereby the enclosed wax replica would melt to create the cavity into which the molten bronze would then be poured. Once cooled, the ceramic shell would be broken and removed, and the new cast-bronze figure would be cleaned, cleared of faults, chased, patinated, and, if required, polished and gold-leafed.

A complicated process by technical necessity, the production of bronze castings and the application of their patinas was made even more so by Erté's aesthetic demands for results that were not within the foundry's normal range of possibilities. In the area of patination alone, brilliant new colors such as verdi green and mauve were developed, transparent patinas were devised, and unique contrasting gold-leaf finishes were incorporated onto the surfaces of single sculptures.

The procedure of examining, correcting, and approving the models, casts, and patinated bronzes—of which there are 105 illustrated in this book—was an enormous undertaking. It was difficult not only to execute but to coordinate with the artist's tight schedule, as he moved frequently between such widely divergent locations as Paris, London, Barbados, New York, and Majorca, where he was building a home and spent two months every year. We also had to contend with previously slated month-long tours to art galleries across the United States and Europe.

This problem was overcome by a great deal of travel by those involved in the endeavor. Besides myself, my wife and partner, Leslee, Sal Estorick, and Ray Perman would deliver models or photographs to Erté, discuss their progress with him, and note any changes he wished to

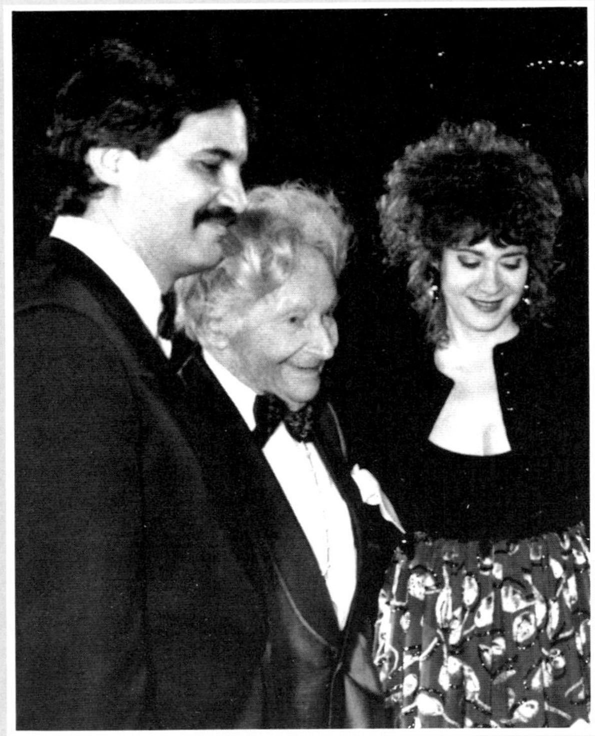

Erté with David and Leslee Rogath

make on his work. The four of us were saved from exhaustion by Erté's long stay each winter with the Estoricks in Barbados, where the majority of the review and approval work was accomplished, by the directives the artist gave us while in Majorca, and by his twice-yearly trips to New York, where he would not only work on the various stages of his sculptures, but would also visit the foundry, where he put to use fresh ways to achieve enriching sculptural details. To effect the sleek satin lining that he once suggested in *Harper's Bazaar* for his *Faubourg St. Honoré* cloak, the artist designated that this section of this sculpture be finished with polished bronze, and to impart a brocade pattern to his now-bronze *Cabaret* gown Erté inventively applied antique metal filigree stampings to its master cast.

The Romanian sculptor Constantin Brancusi is credited with saying "Create like a god, command like a king, work like a slave". But it may well have been the precept that best expressed Erté's spirit, for he never stopped considering and improving the visual imagery on which we worked.

At the time of his death the artist had approved all the masters for the sculptures illustrated in this book. Many had been cast in bronze and were patinated. In each case, Erté had given instructions to guide the foundry in completing the patinas. In most cases, besides written instructions, his thoughts about each piece were conveyed to us in extensive discussions, so that we could proceed with completing the patination confident that the result would have met Erté's approval.

Leslee and I cherish dearly the ten years that we were fortunate enough to work with Erté, first to publish his graphics and later his sculptures. Every moment of our association with this creative dynamo produced a new and unique idea. It had the exciting magnitude of a constantly changing world that unfortunately ended suddenly and sadly.

ERTÉ
21, RUE GUTENBERG
92100 BOULOGNE s/SEINE
TÉL. 46 05 26 89

16-5-89

Dear Leslee and David
thank you very much for your kind letter and the photos

1) „Motherhood"
I think this sculpture can be good when finished.
The pedestal is very good.

2) „Faubourg St Honoré"
Please note all the corrections indicated on the photographs.

3) „Chinchilla Sleeve"
Not clear enough to make a jugement.

4) „Firebird"
Impossible to have an opinion with the feathers and the trousers missing.

ERTÉ
21, Rue Gutenberg
92100 Boulogne s/Seine
Tél. 46 05 26 89

26-2-88

Dear Leslee and David
many, many thanks for the two sculptures and all the graphics.
The sculpture „Glory" is beautiful, but I don't like the patina of the front panel in silver.
I should like a copper patina with the sun in shiny light gold.
The black marble base is wonderful.
We should change the title of this sculpture, as Dyansen has already a sculpture called „Glory" — I should like to call her „Triumph".
As to the clay models:—

1) The „Arctic Sea" seems beautiful but the icecles on the top should be pointed exactly like on the image and to have no round base behind.

2) „The Mother of Pearl" seems nice, but I should prefer her sitting in the shell and even with the bearers, like on the graphic — without the schell it is very dull and has no meaning.

3) I have made a change in „The Wave" by adding two small waves in the front to make it more stable and exagerate the movement.

Love and Kisses

Romain

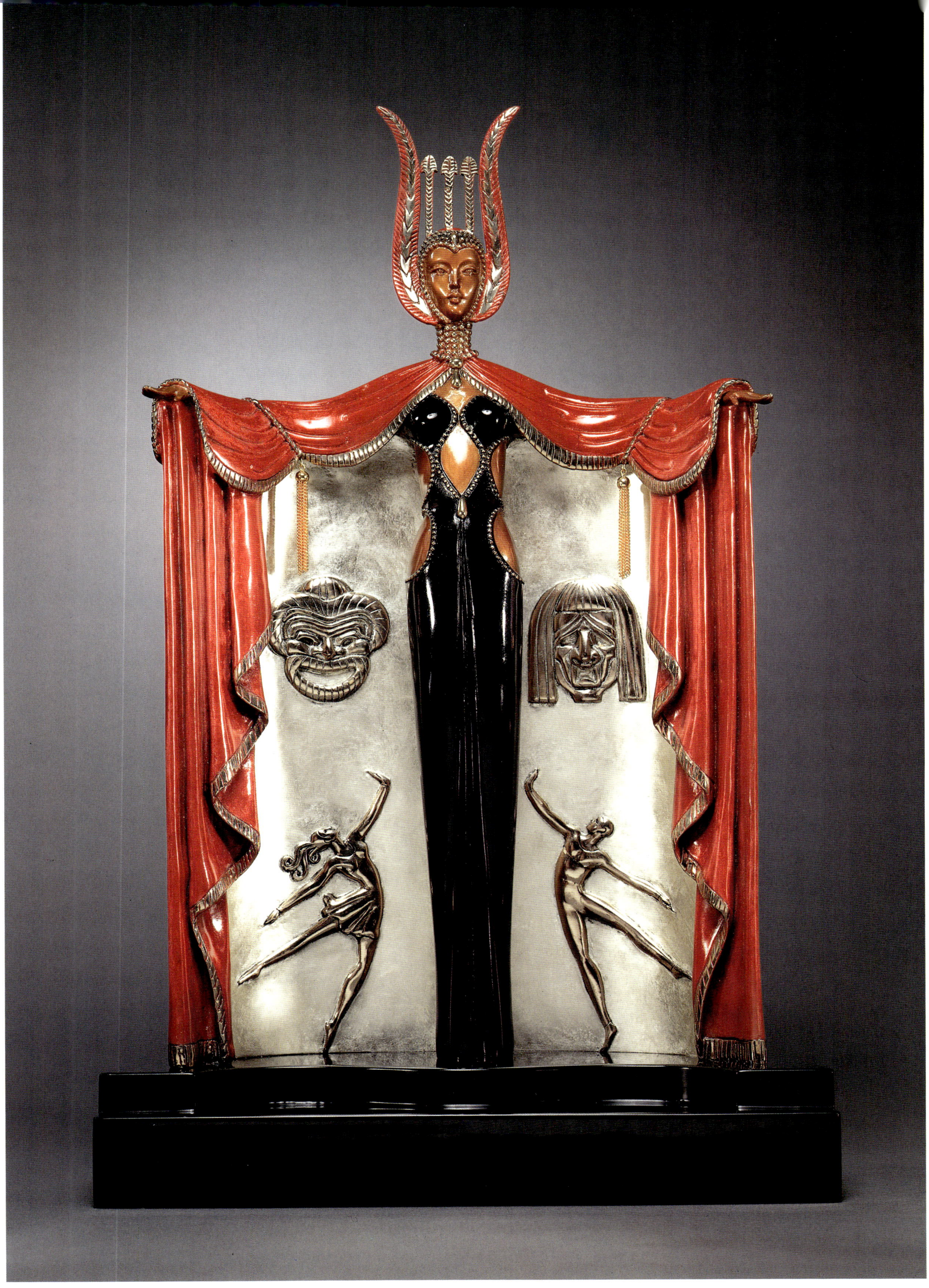

Broadway's in Fashion
Broadway's in Fashion
Broadway's in Fashion
Broadway's in Fashion

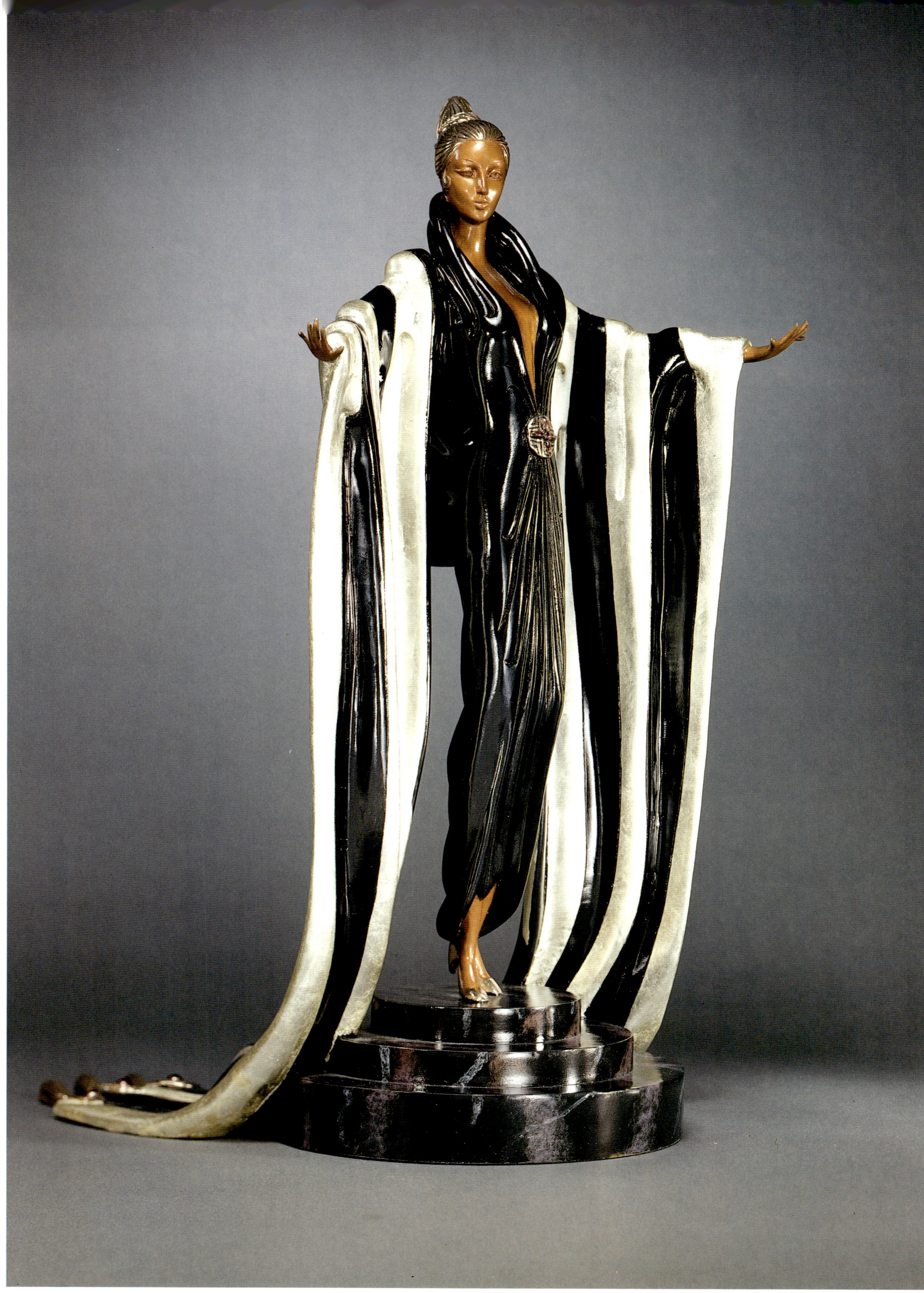

Monaco
Monaco
Monaco
Monaco

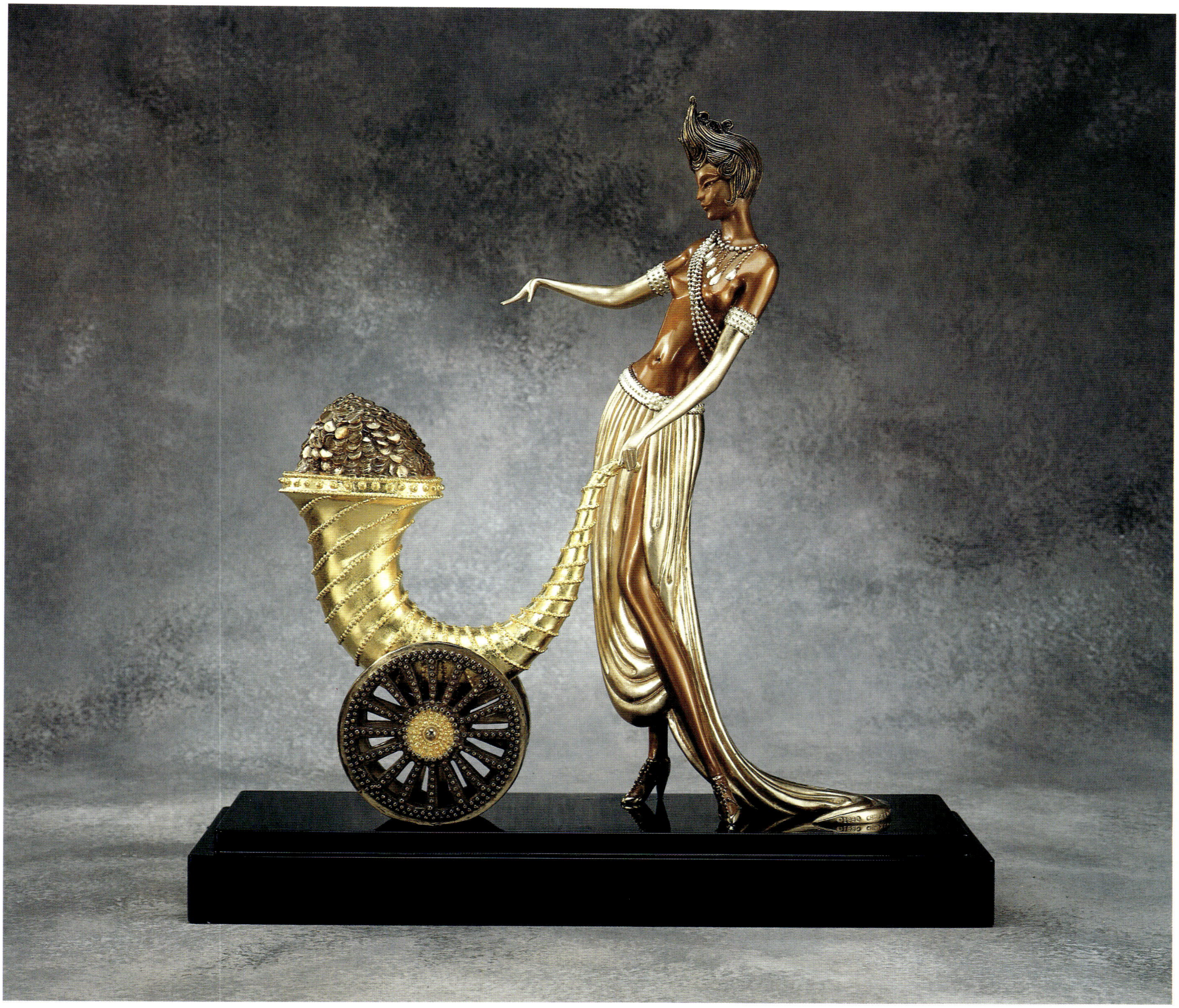

Cornucopia
Corne d'abondance
Cornucopia
Füllhorn

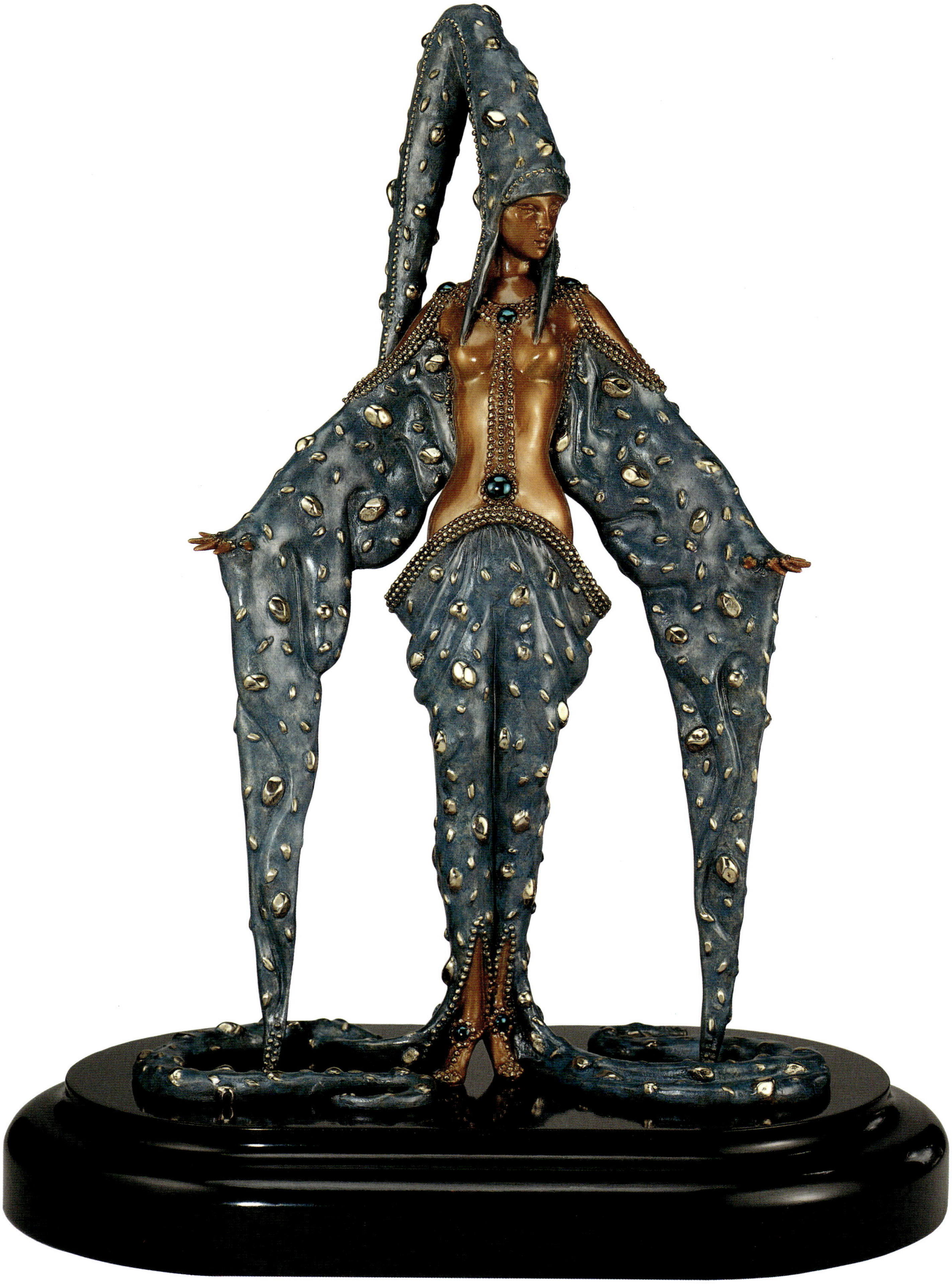

Starfish
Étoile de mer
Stella di mare
Seestern

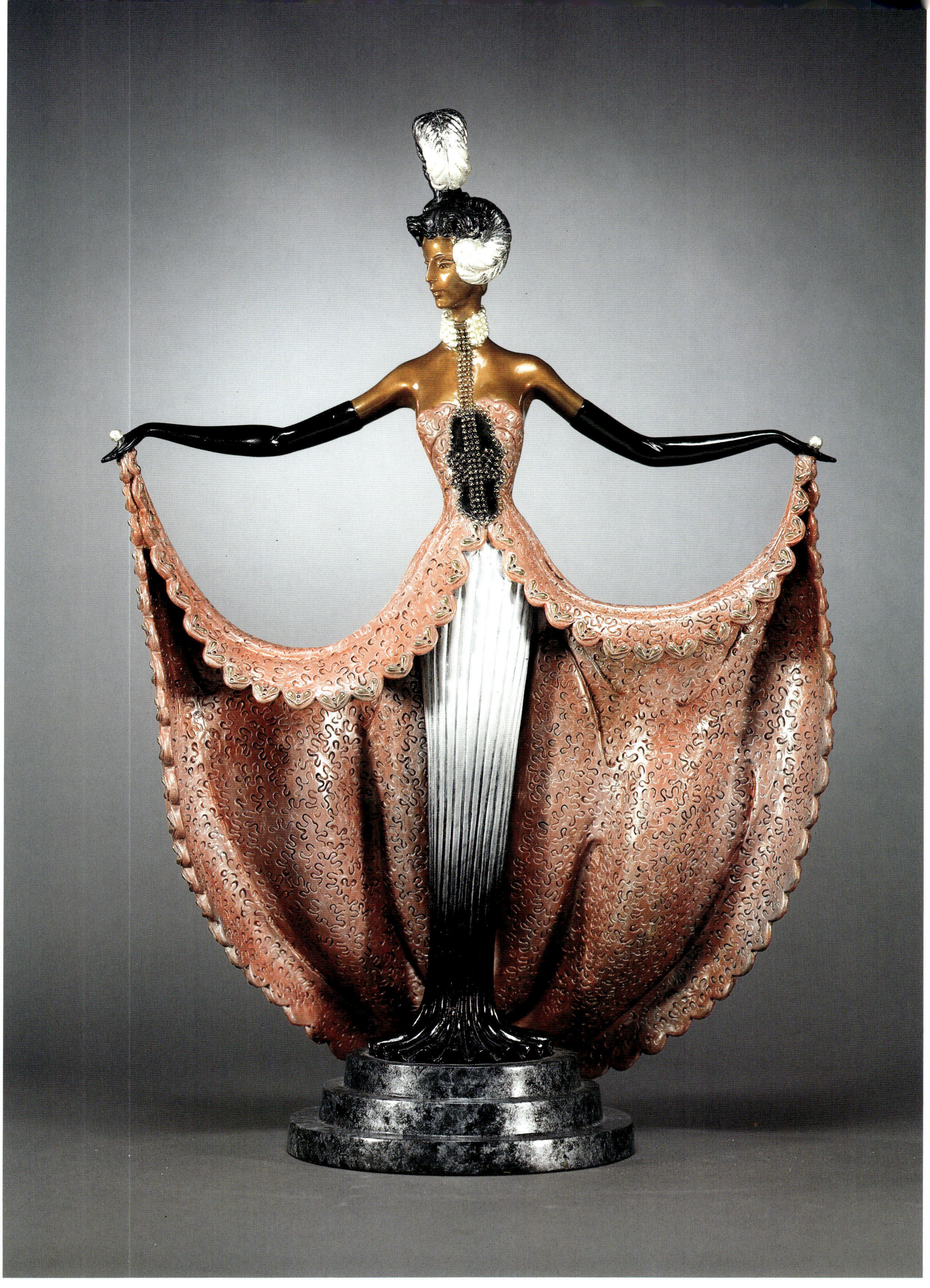

Cabaret
Cabaret
Cabaret
Kabarett

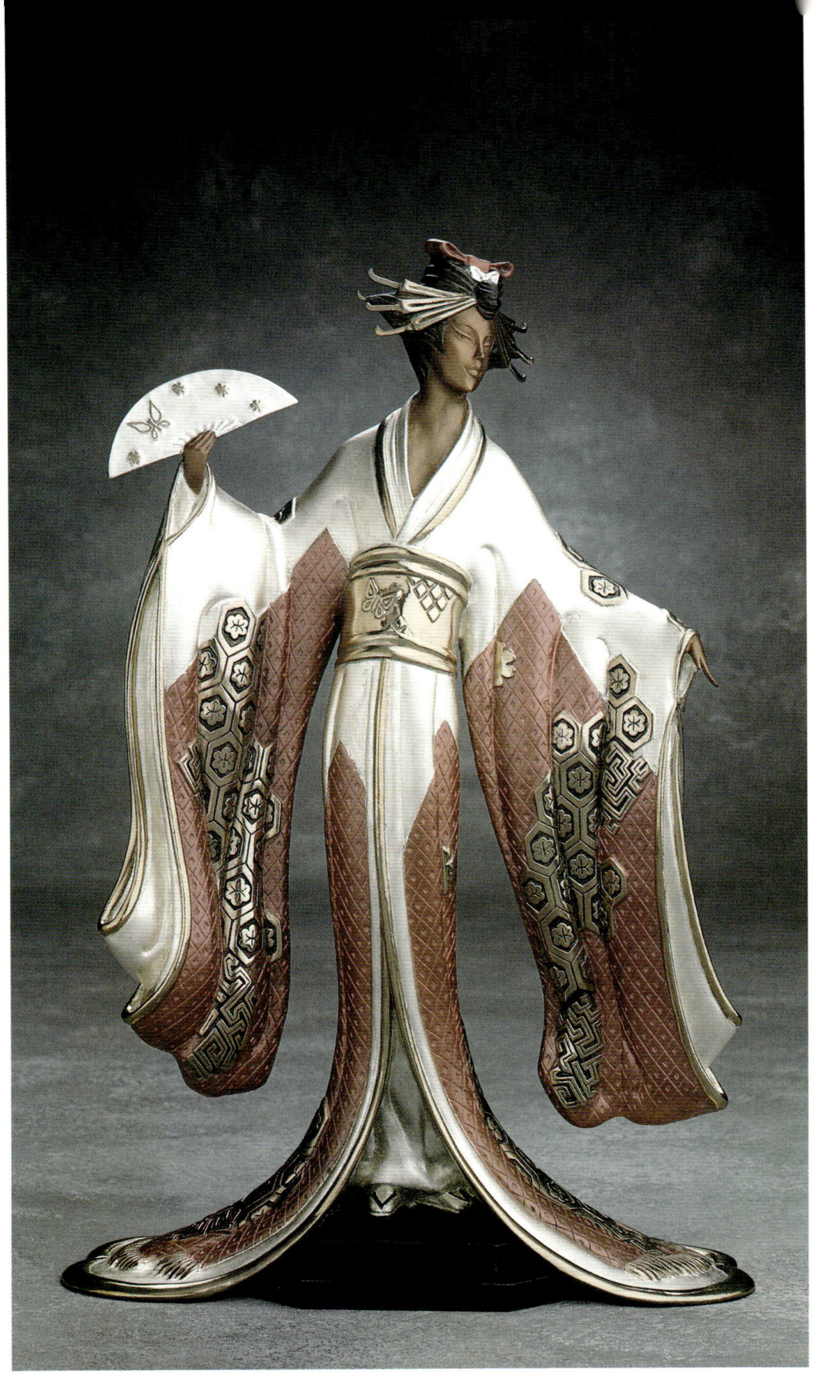

Madame Butterfly
Madame Butterfly
Madame Butterfly
Madame Butterfly

Iras
Iras
Iras
Iras

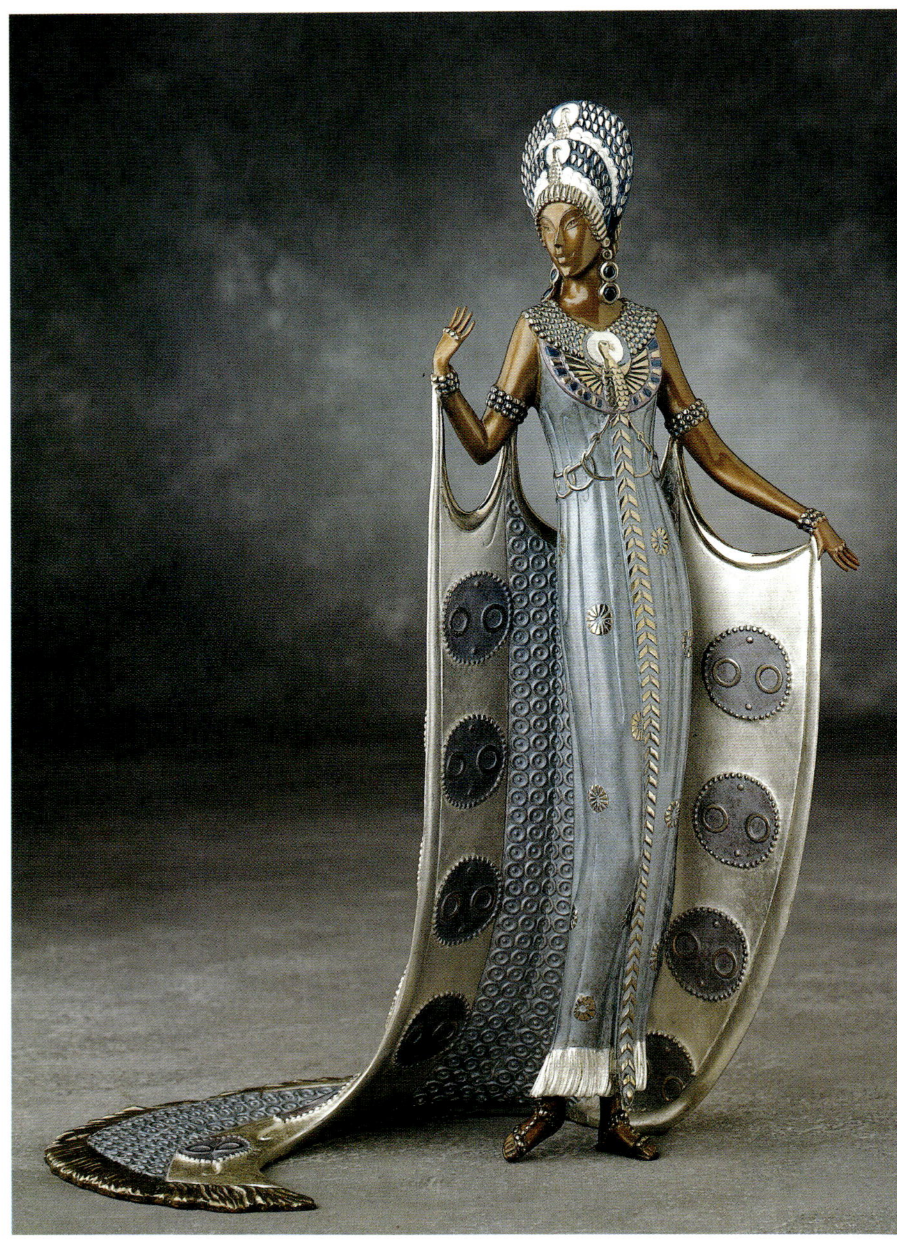

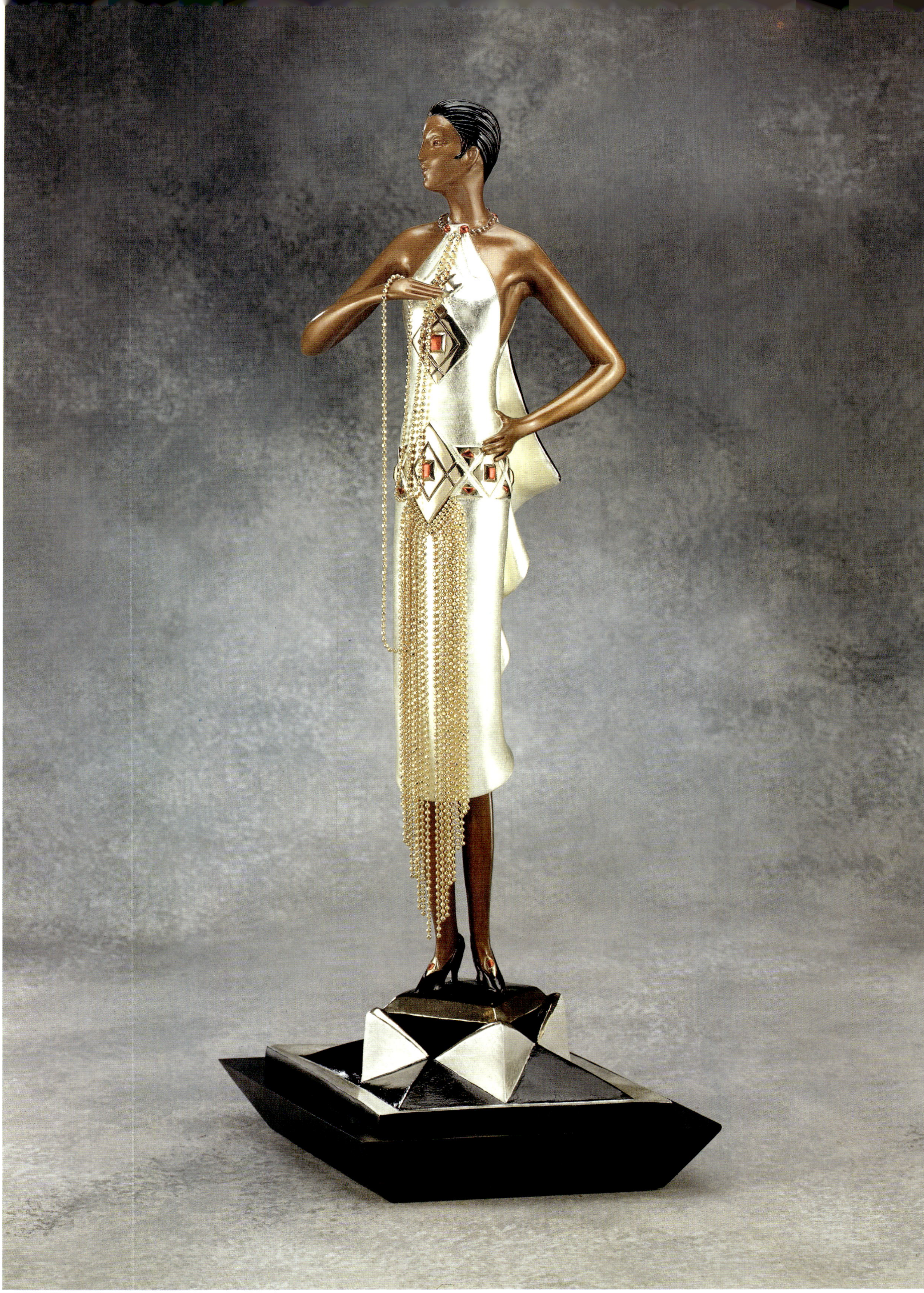

Cafe Society
Café Society
Cafe Society
Kaffeegesellschaft

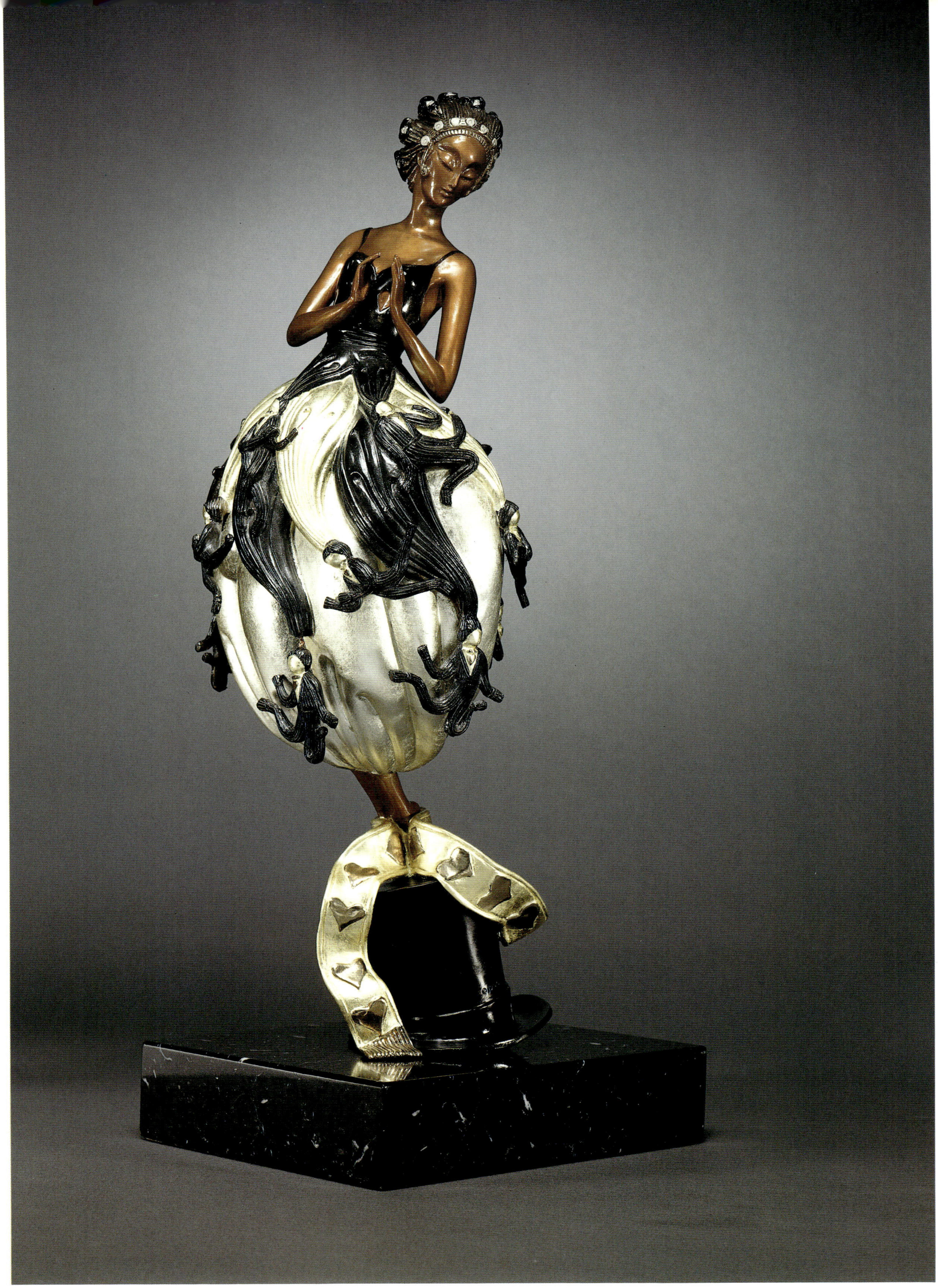

Tuxedo
Smoking
Smoking
Tuxedo

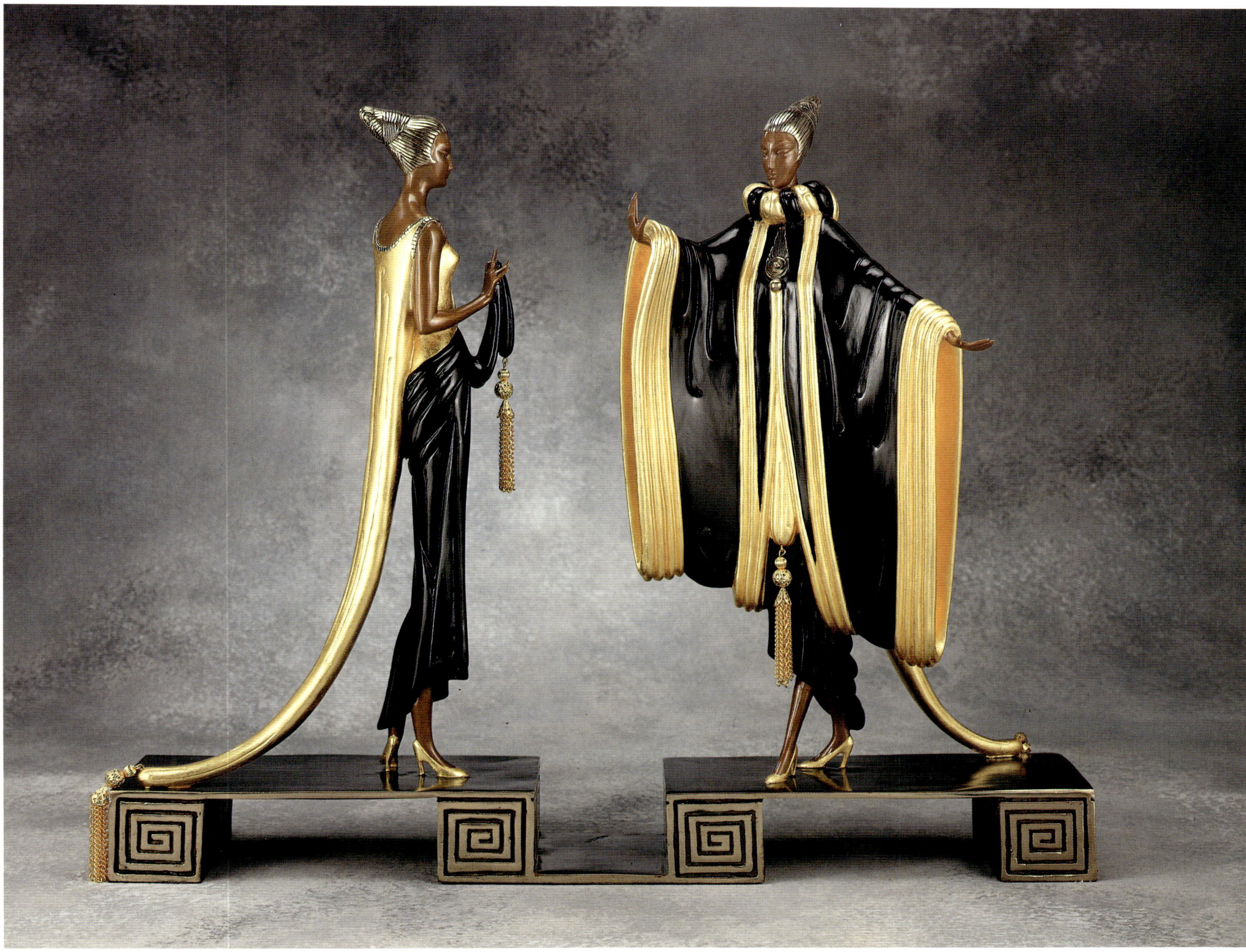

Ready for the Ball
Prête pour le bal
Pronta per il ballo
Bereit für den Ball

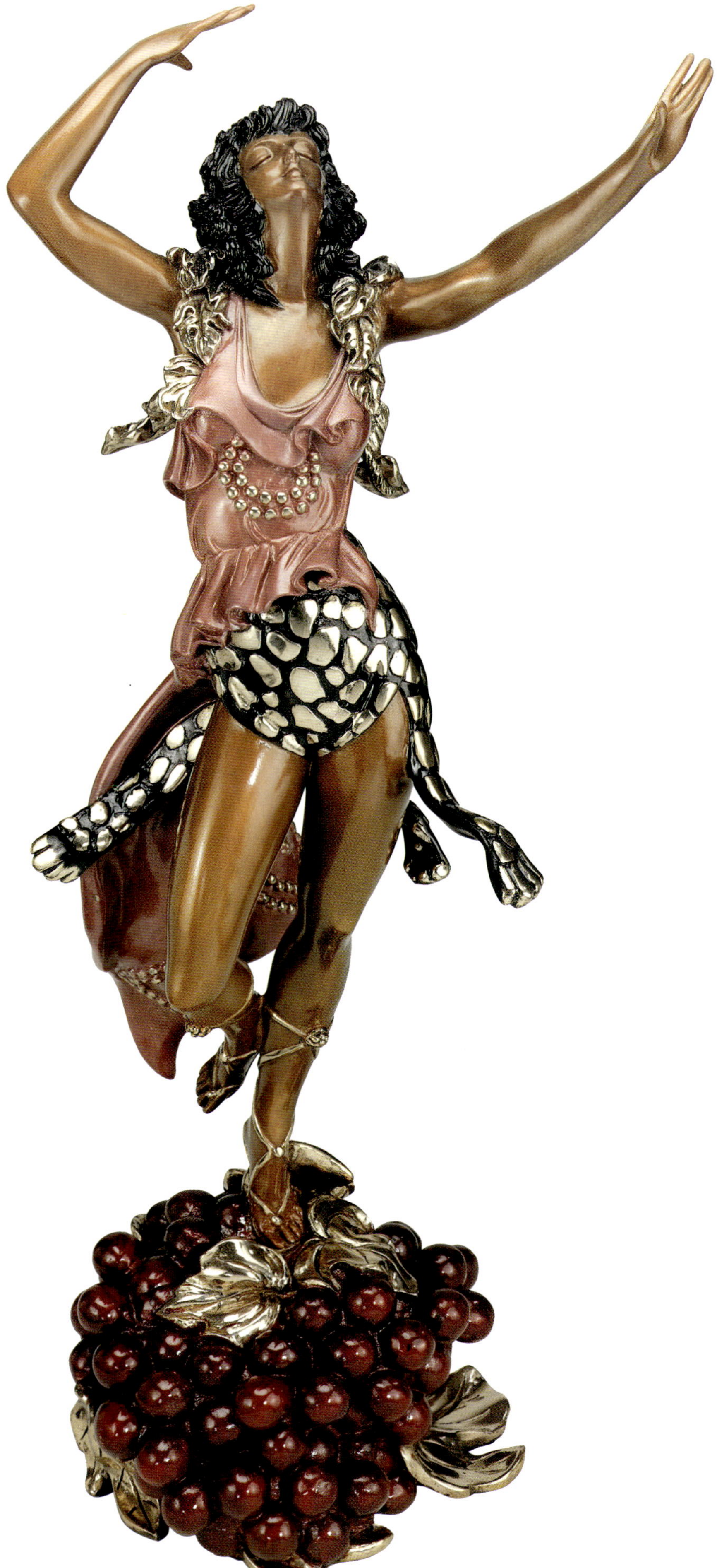

Bacchante
Bacchante
Bacchante
Bacchantin

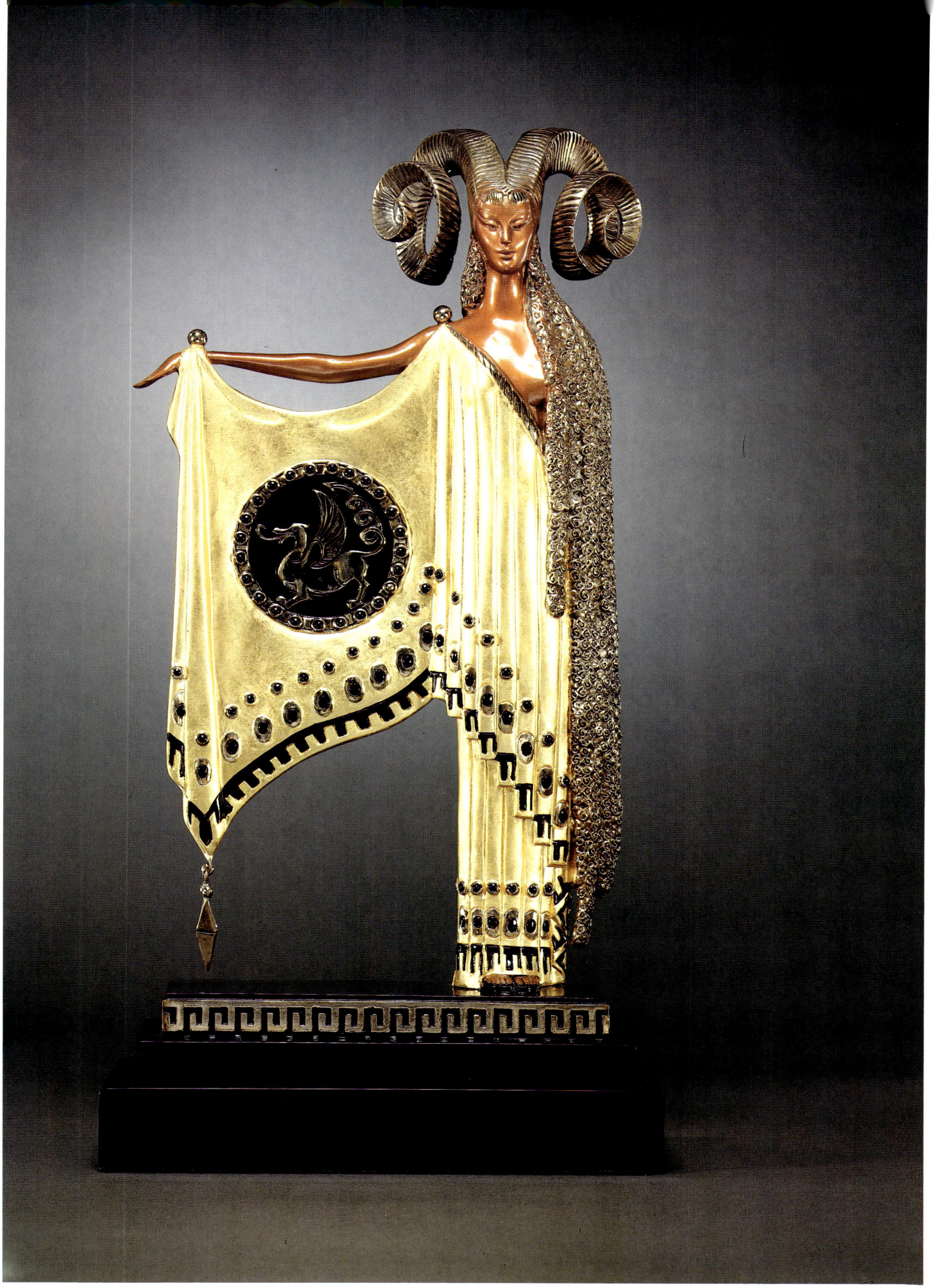

Golden Fleece
Toison d'or
Il vello d'oro
Das Goldene Vlies

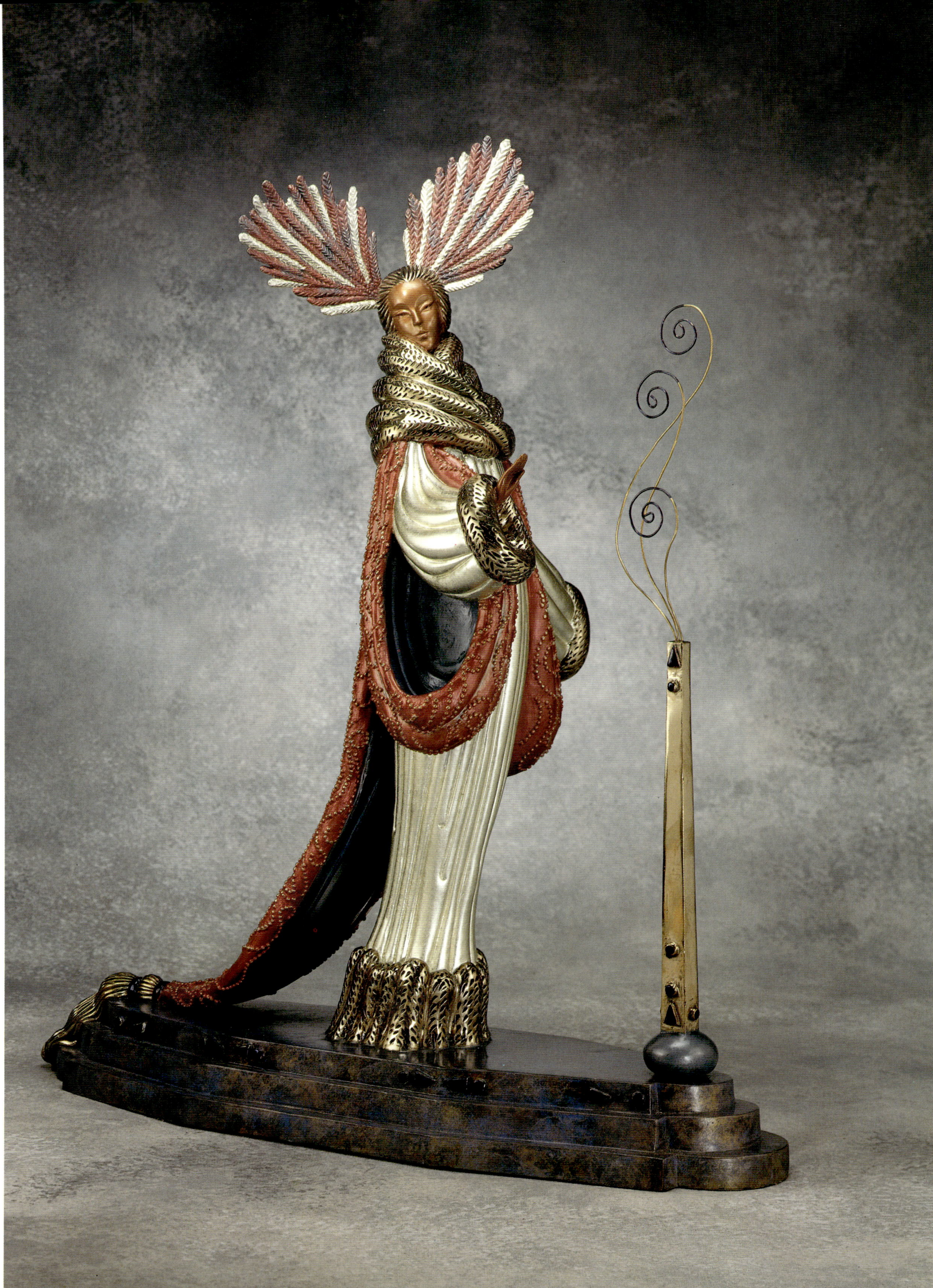

Ermine Brocade
Brocart d'hermine
Broccato d'ermellino
Hermelin-Brokat

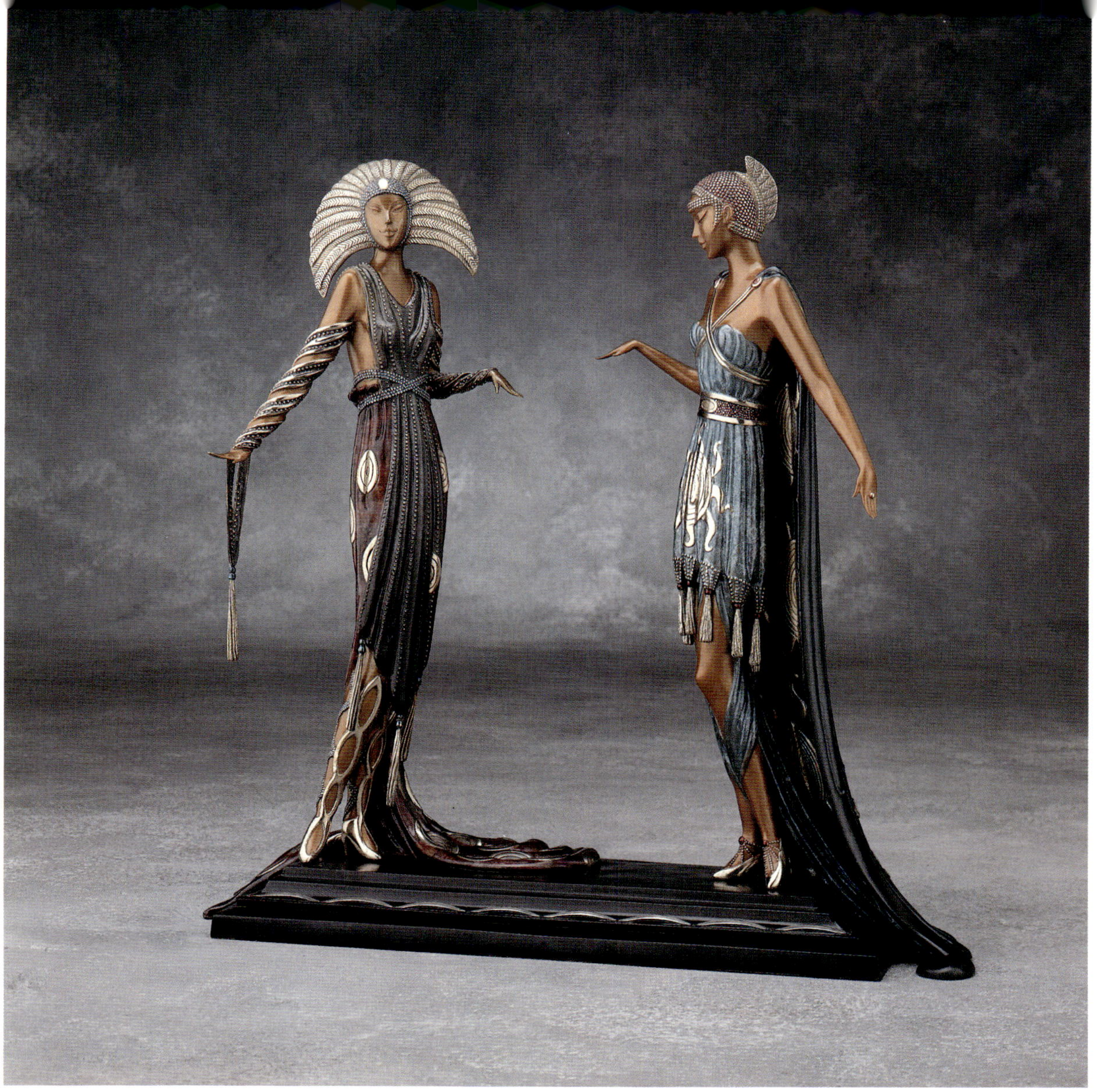

Two Vamps
Les deux allumeuses
Due donne fatali
Zwei Vamps

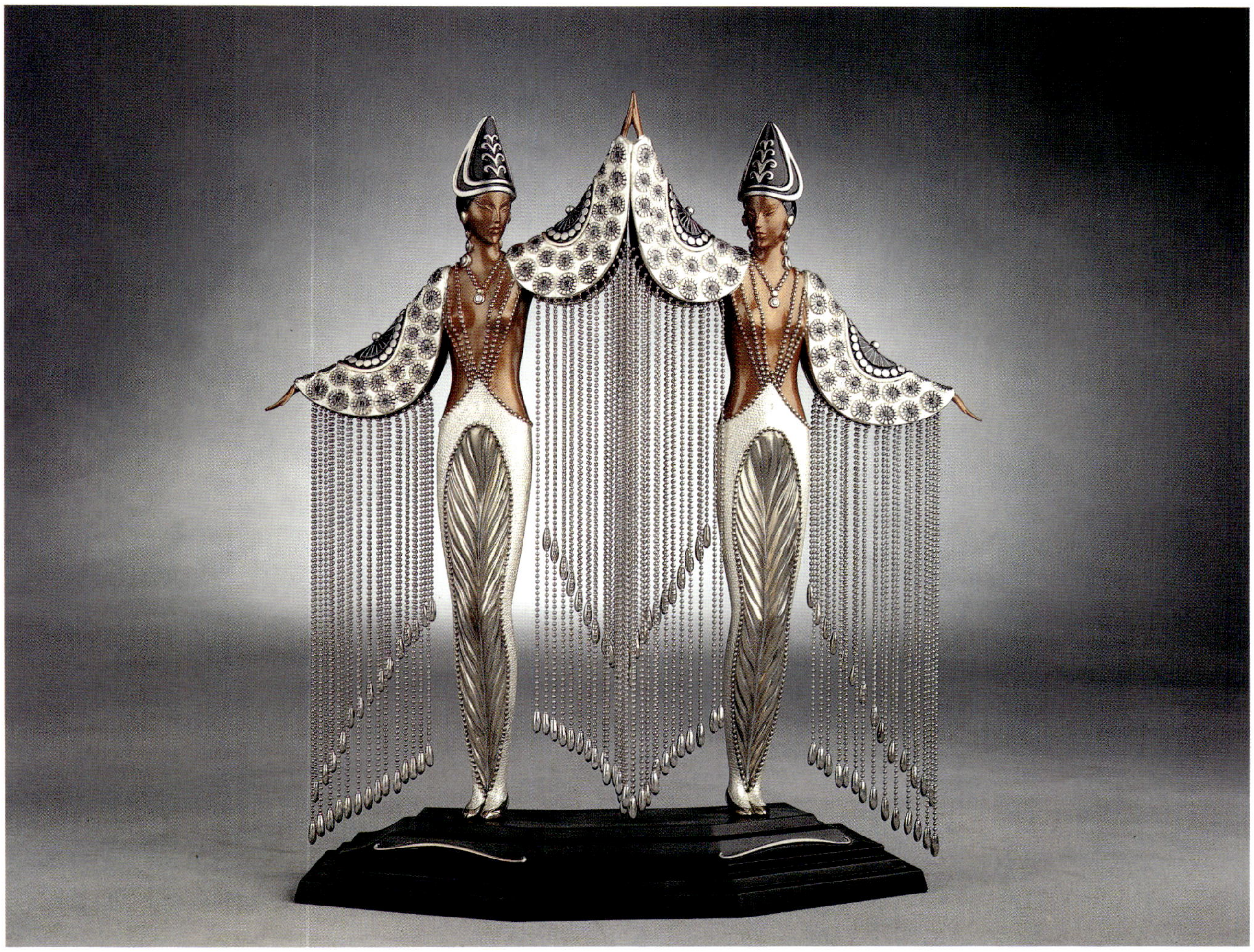

Les Bijoux de perles
Les Bijoux de perles
Gioielli di perla
Perlenschmuck

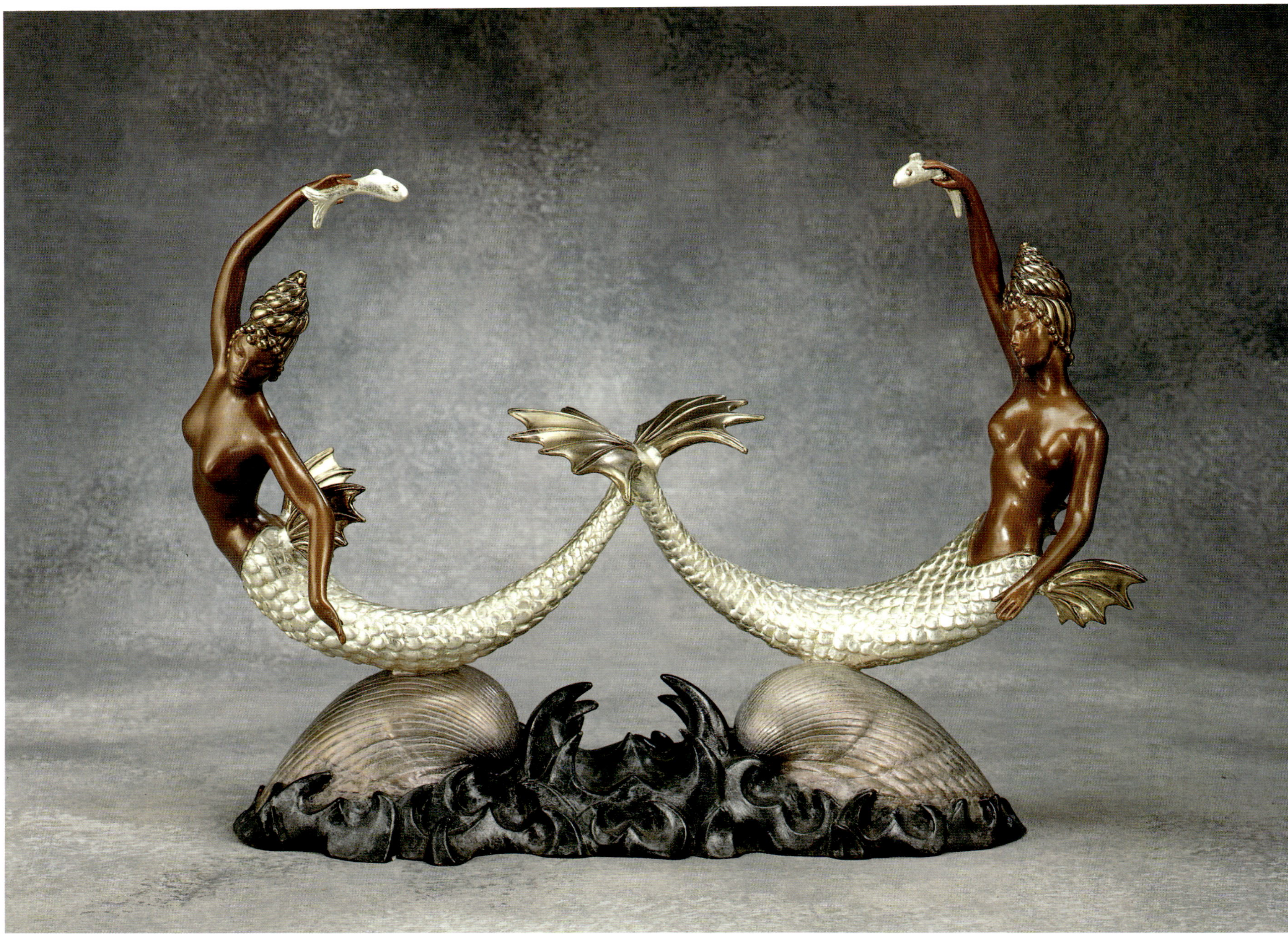

Sirens
Sirènes
Sirene
Sirenen

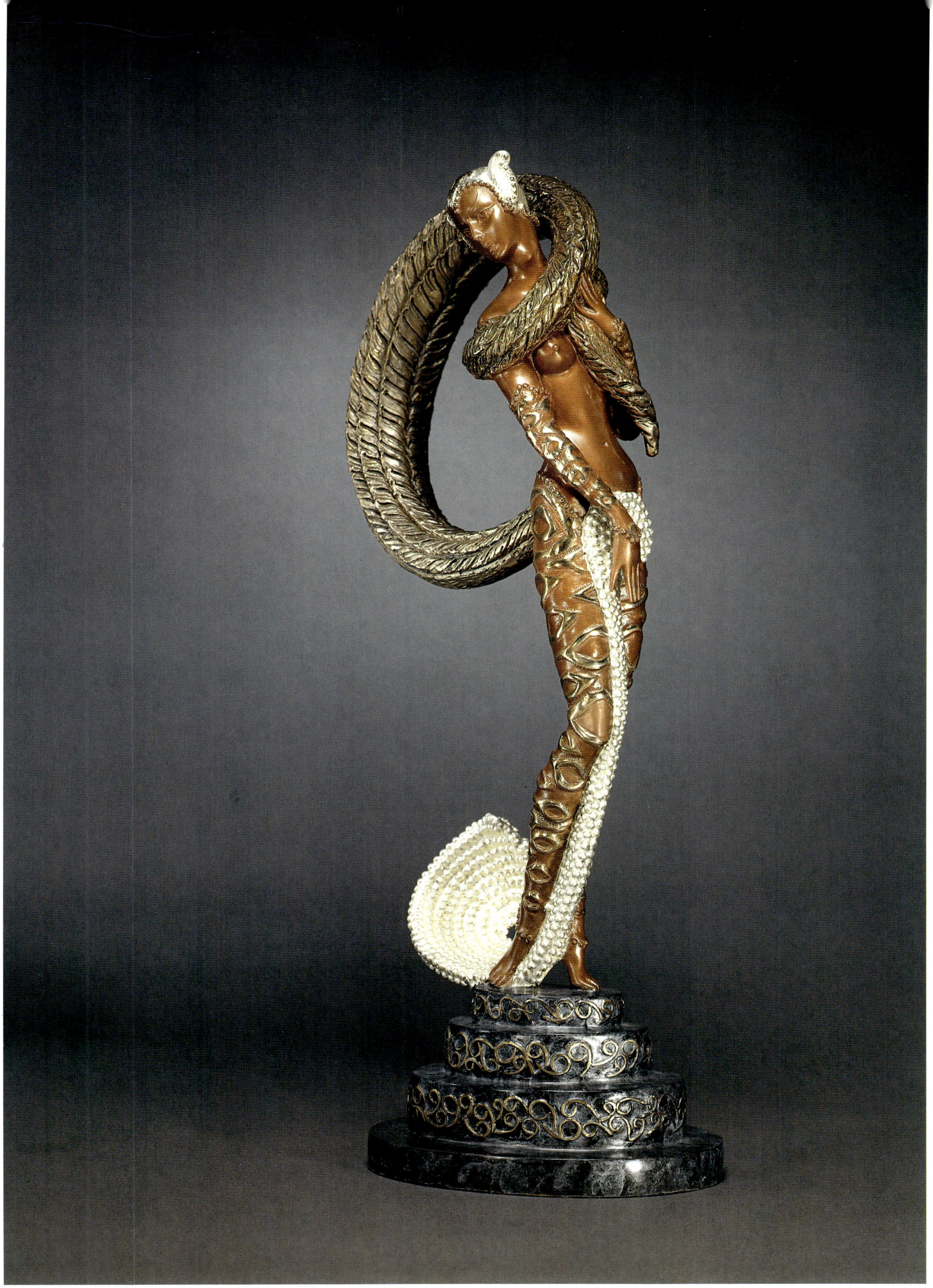

Masquerade
Mascarade
Mascherata
Die Maskerade

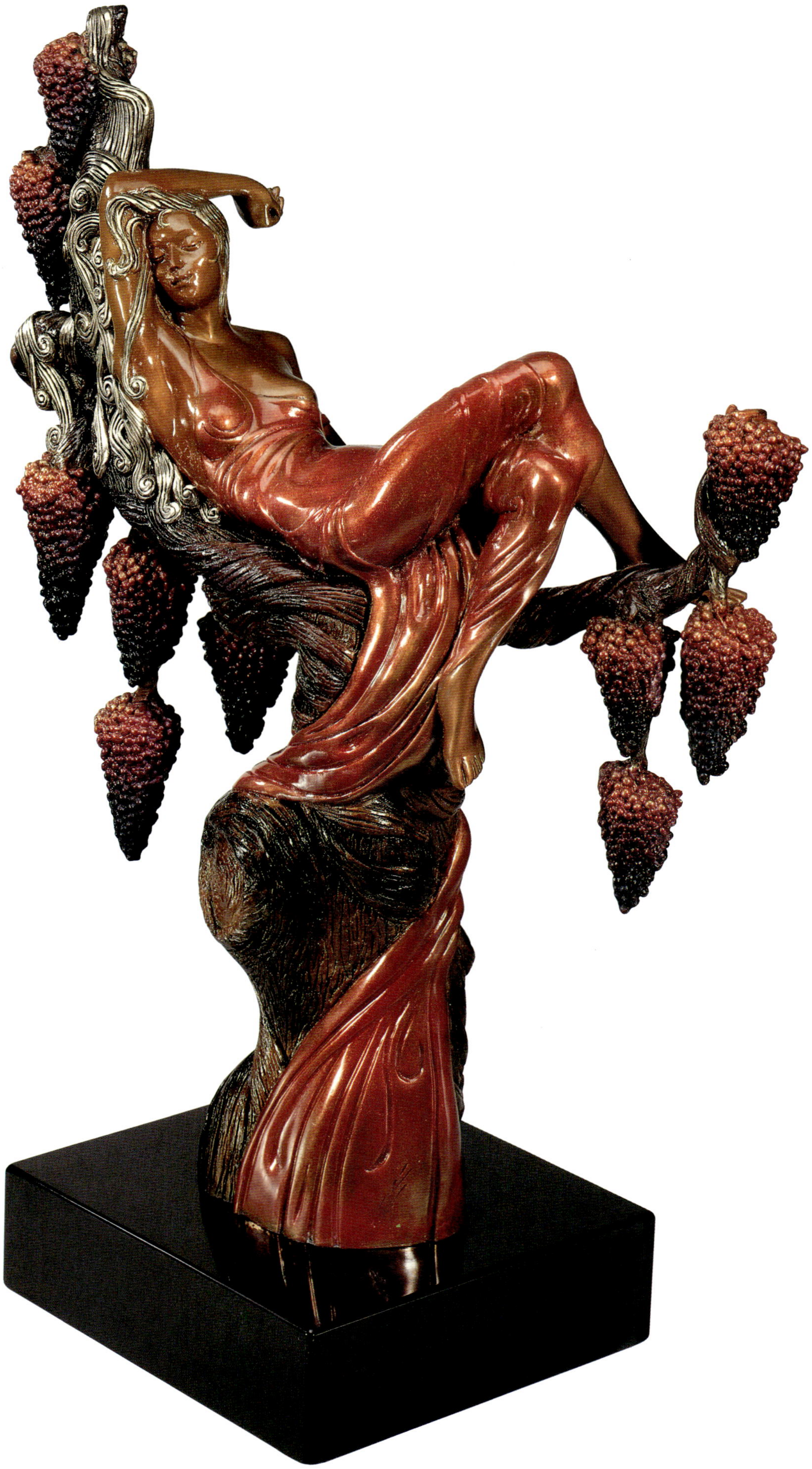

Heat
Chaleur
Calore
Hitze

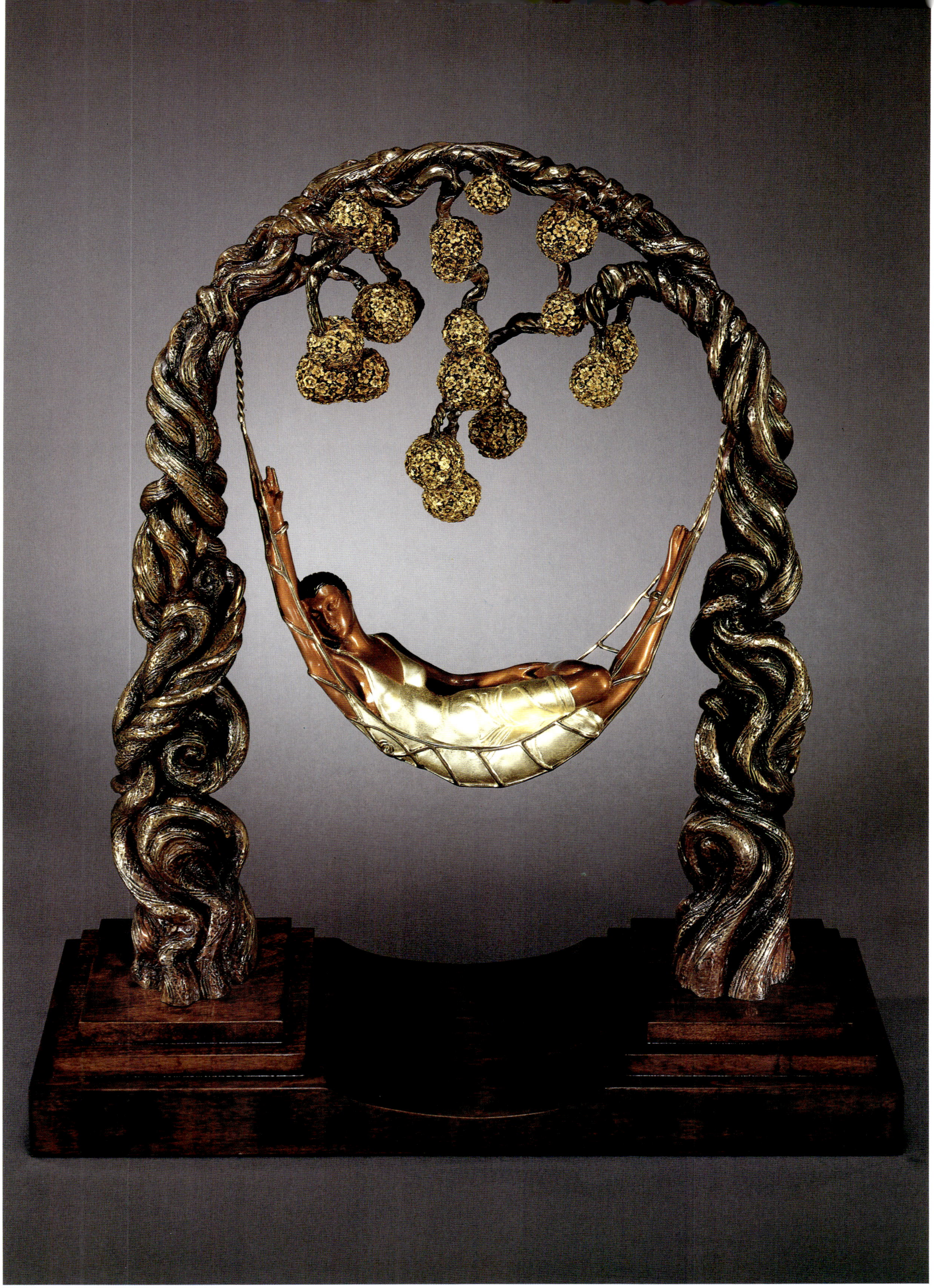

Spider Web
Étoile d'araignée
La Ragnatela
Spinnengewebe

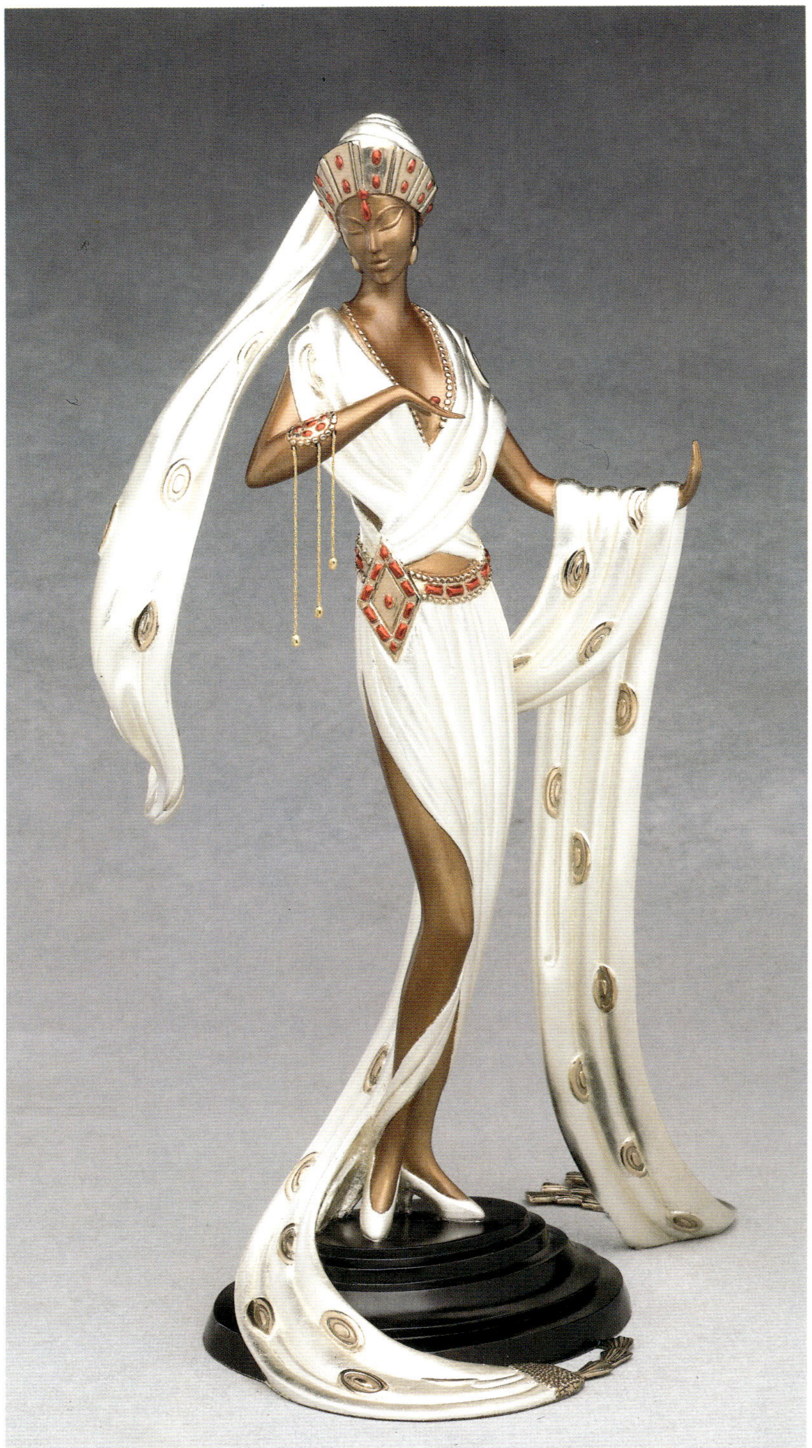

Scheherezade
Schéhérezade
Schéhérazade
Scheherezade

Belle du bal
Belle du bal
La bella del ballo
Ballschönheit

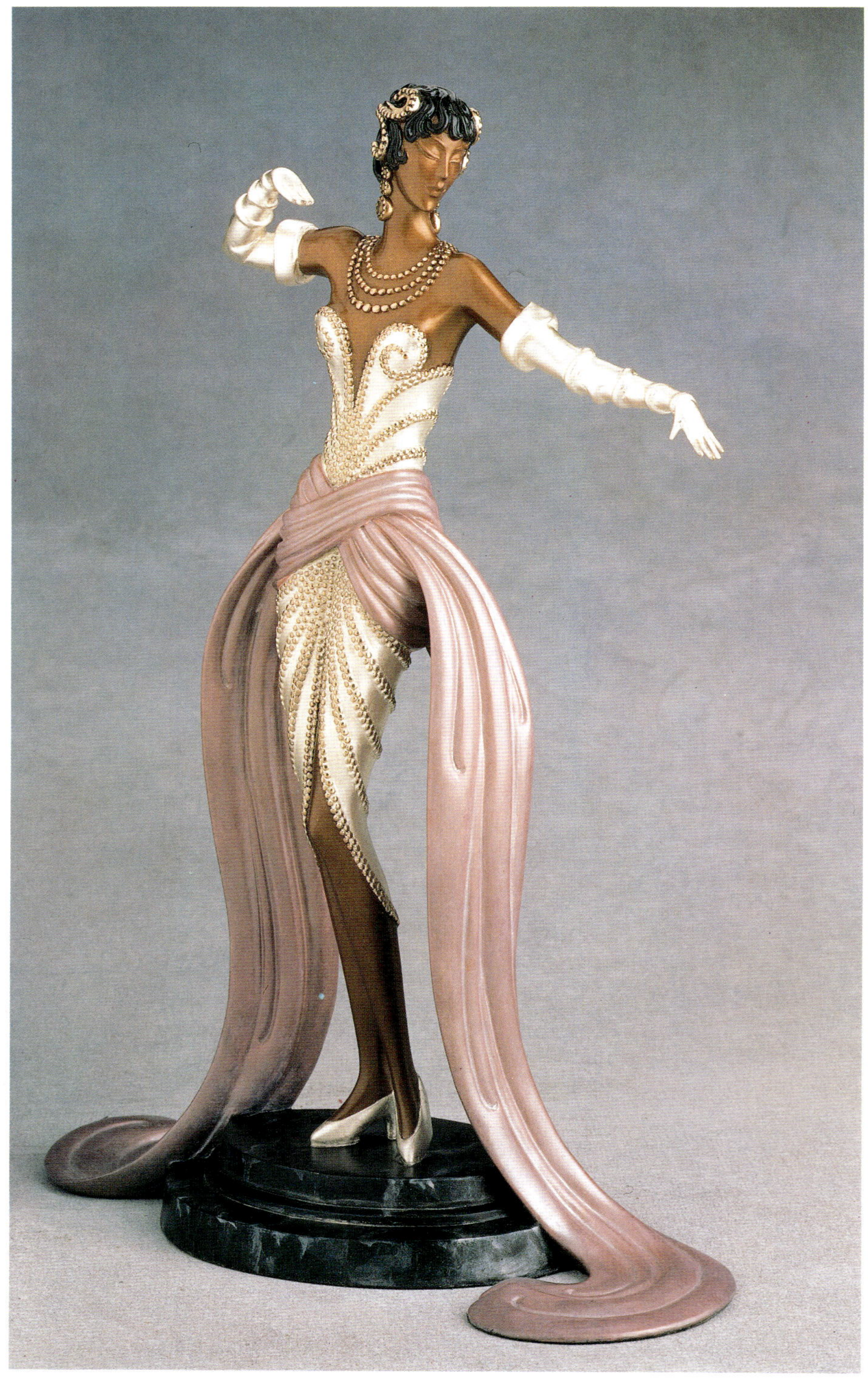

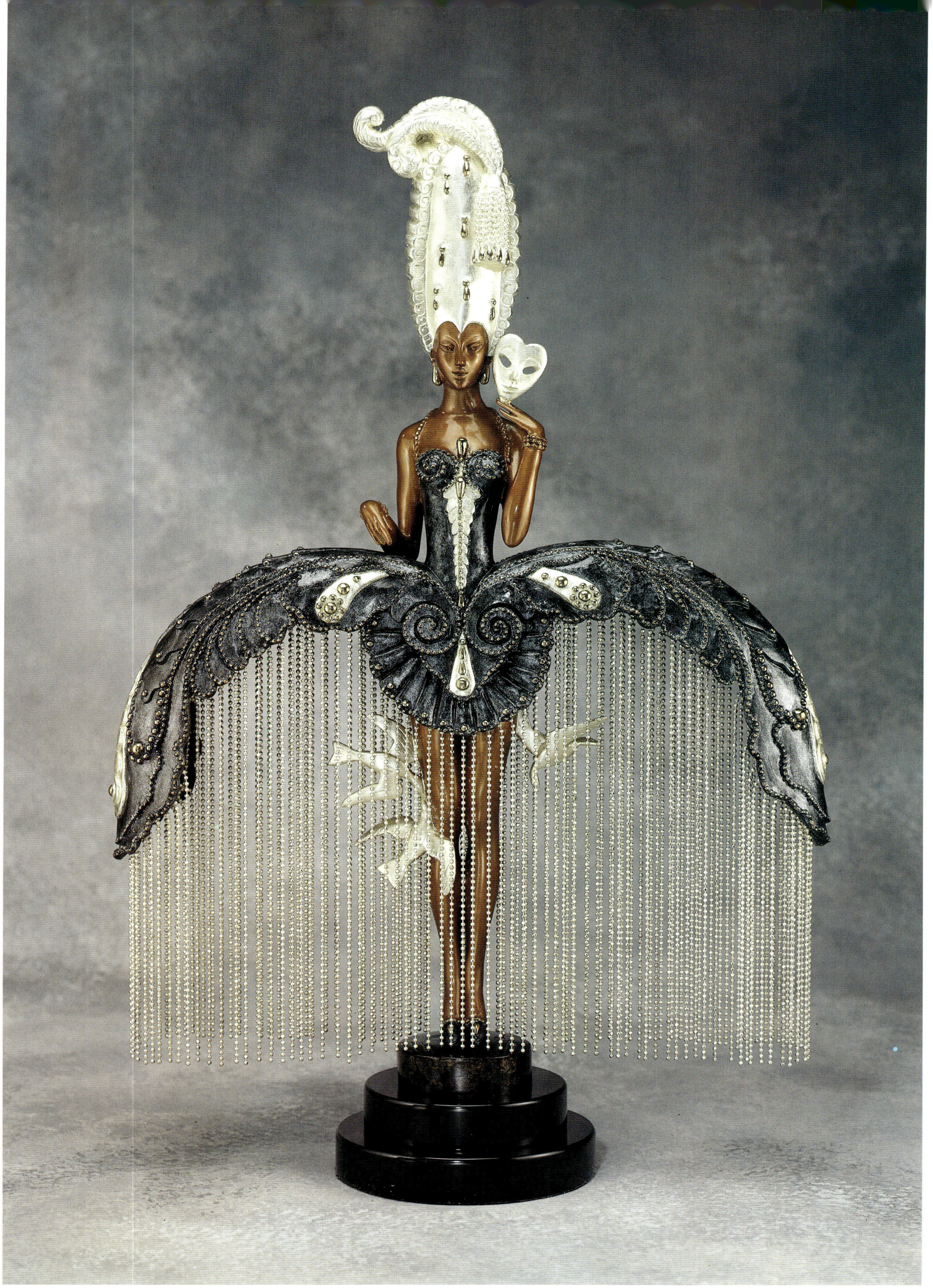

Her Secret Admirers
Admirateurs clandestins
I suoi ammiratori segreti
Ihre heimlichen Bewunderer

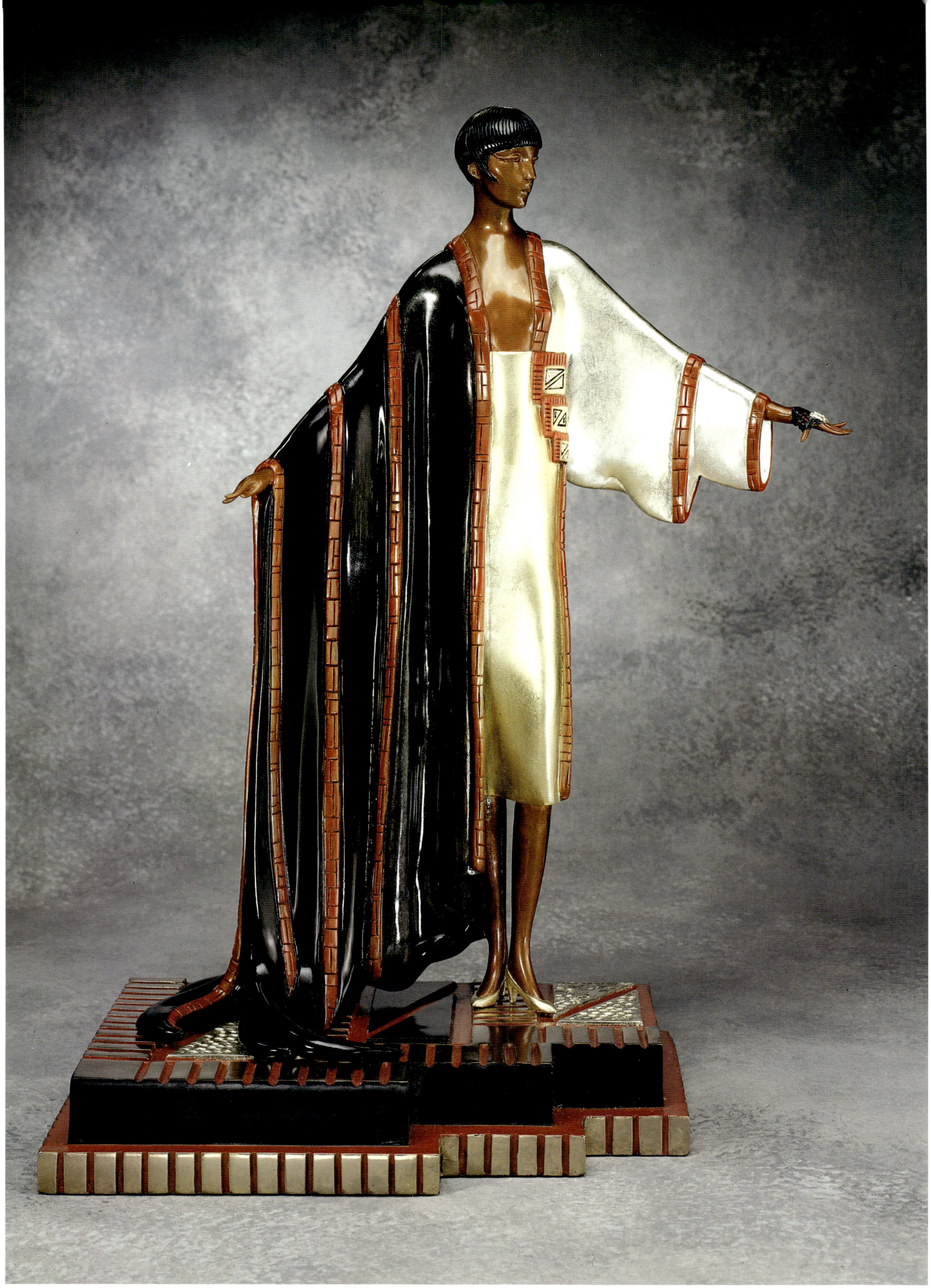

Michelle
Michelle
Michelle
Michelle

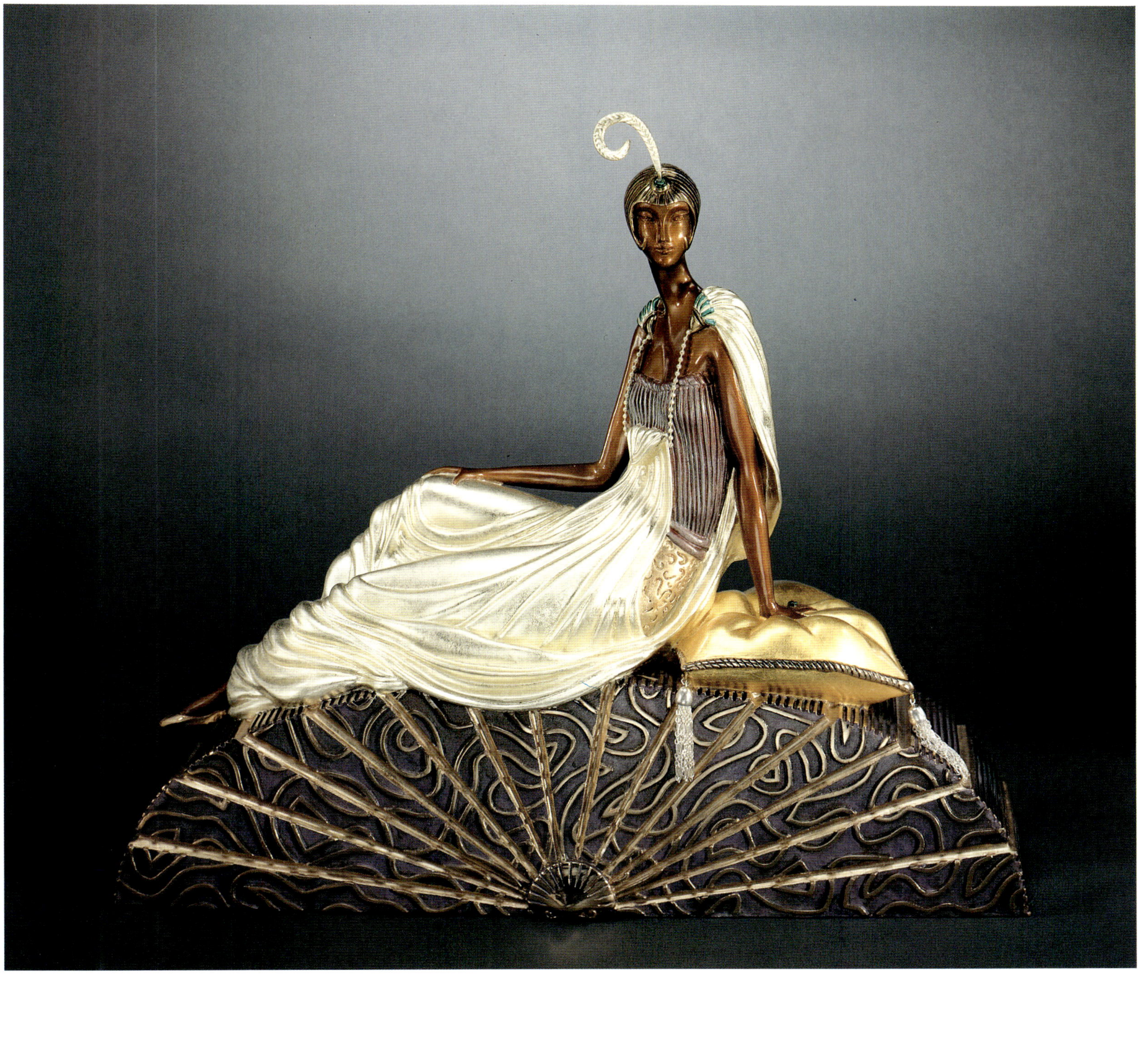

King's Favorite
La Favorite du Roi
La favorita del re
Die Favoritin des Königs

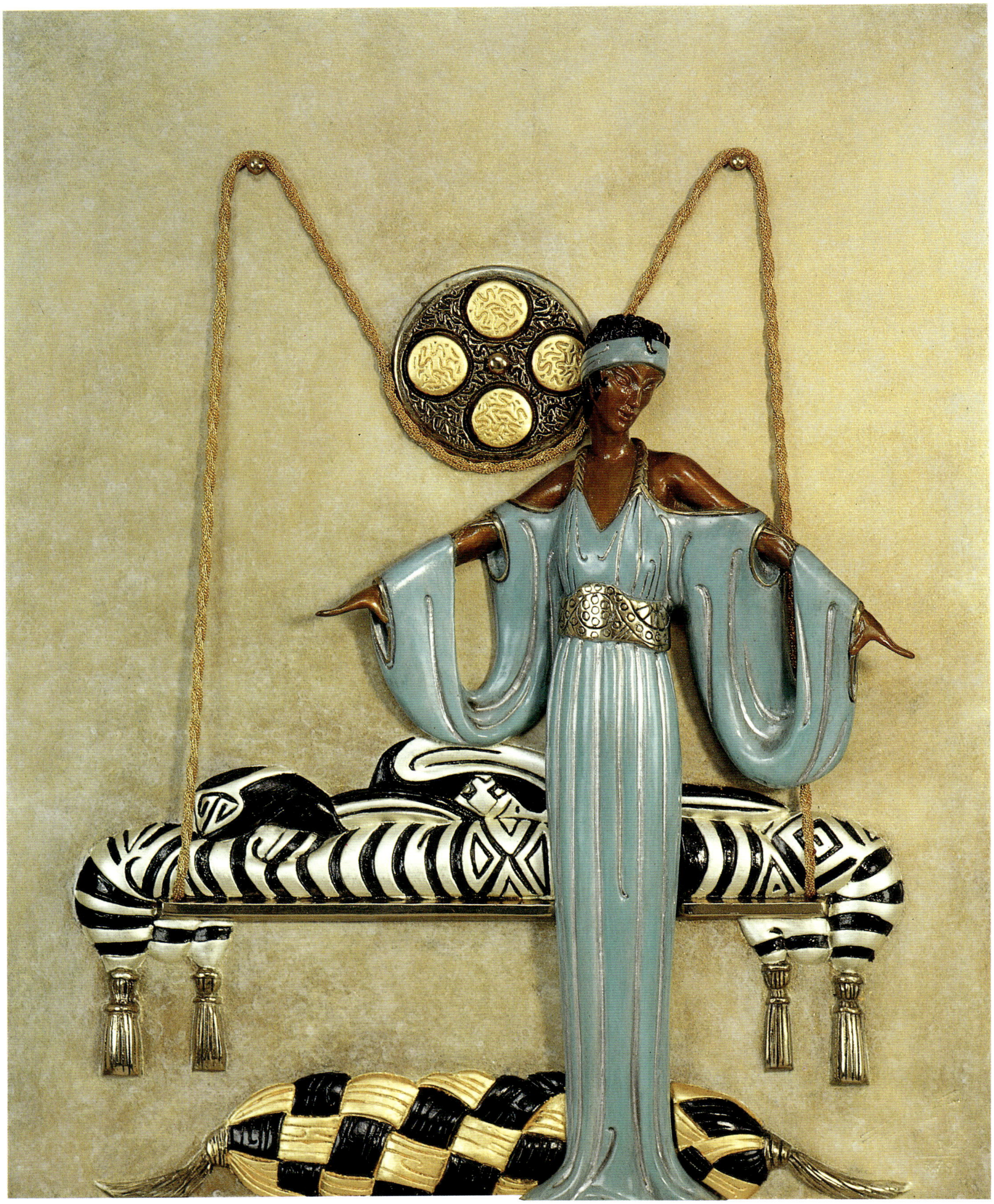

Pillow Swing
Escarpolette à coussin
Dondolo di cuscini
Liegeschaukel

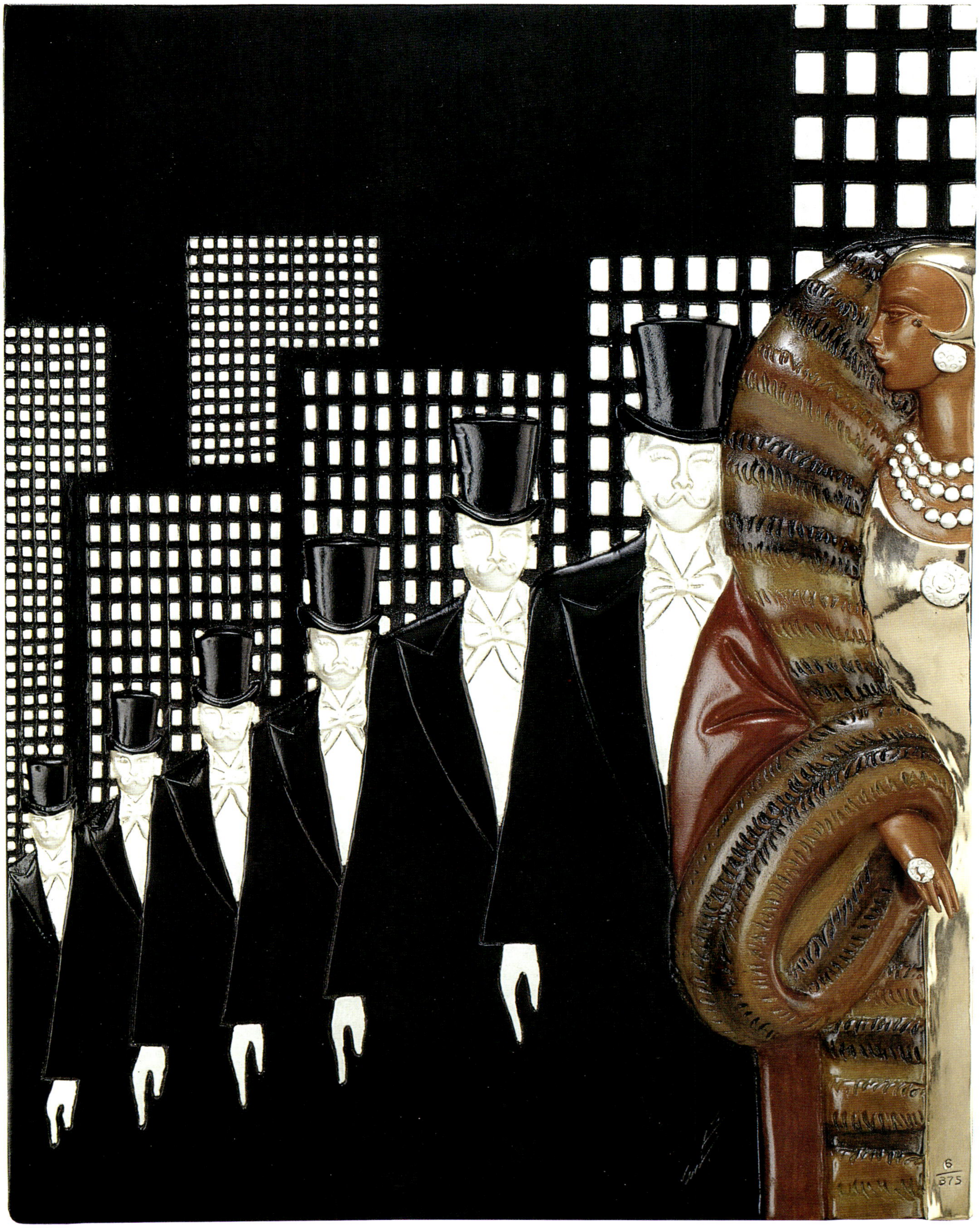

Top Hats
Hauts-de-forme
Cappelli a cilindri
Zylinderhute

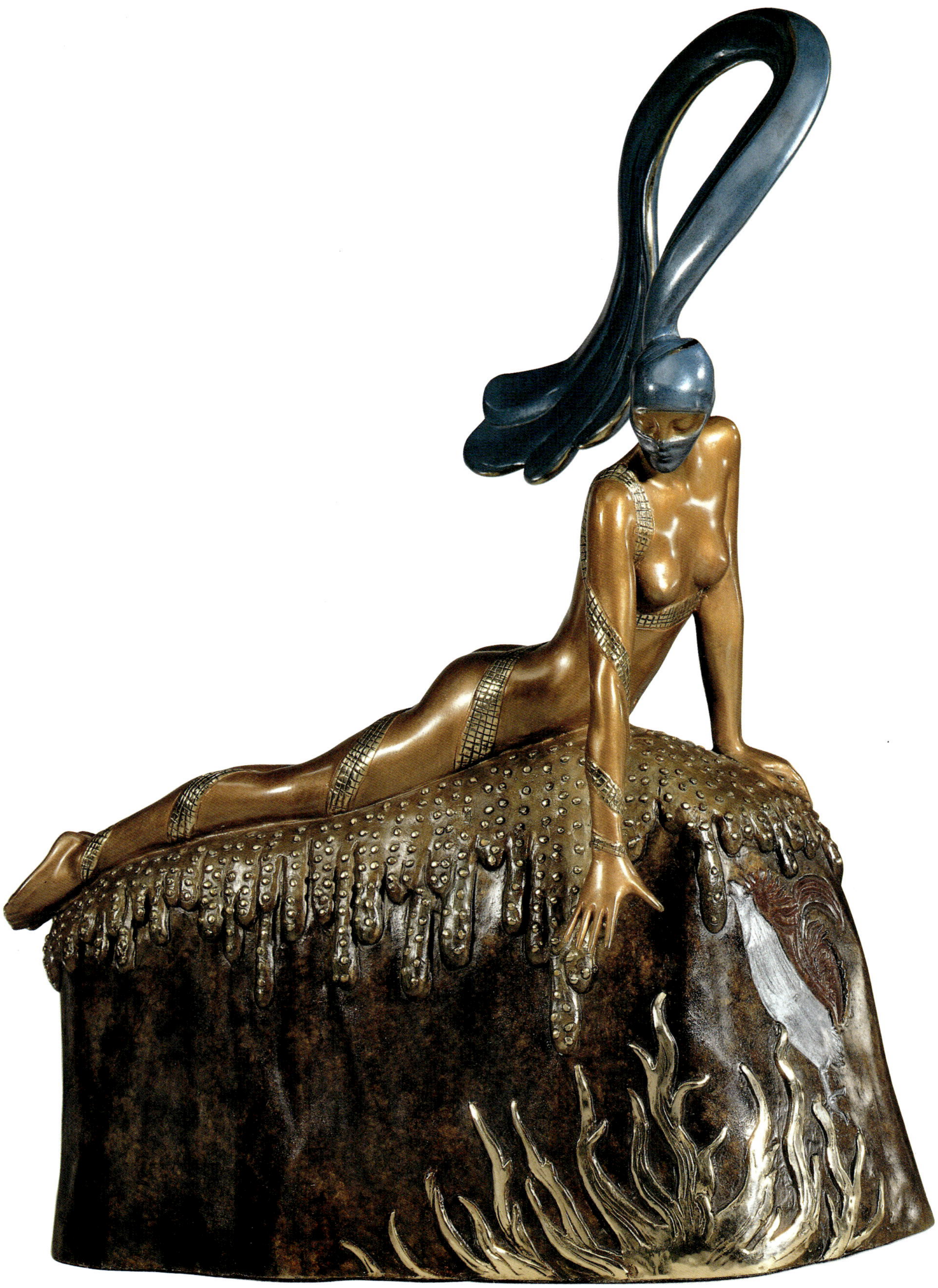

French Rooster
Le Coq français
Il gallo Francese
Der Französische Hahn

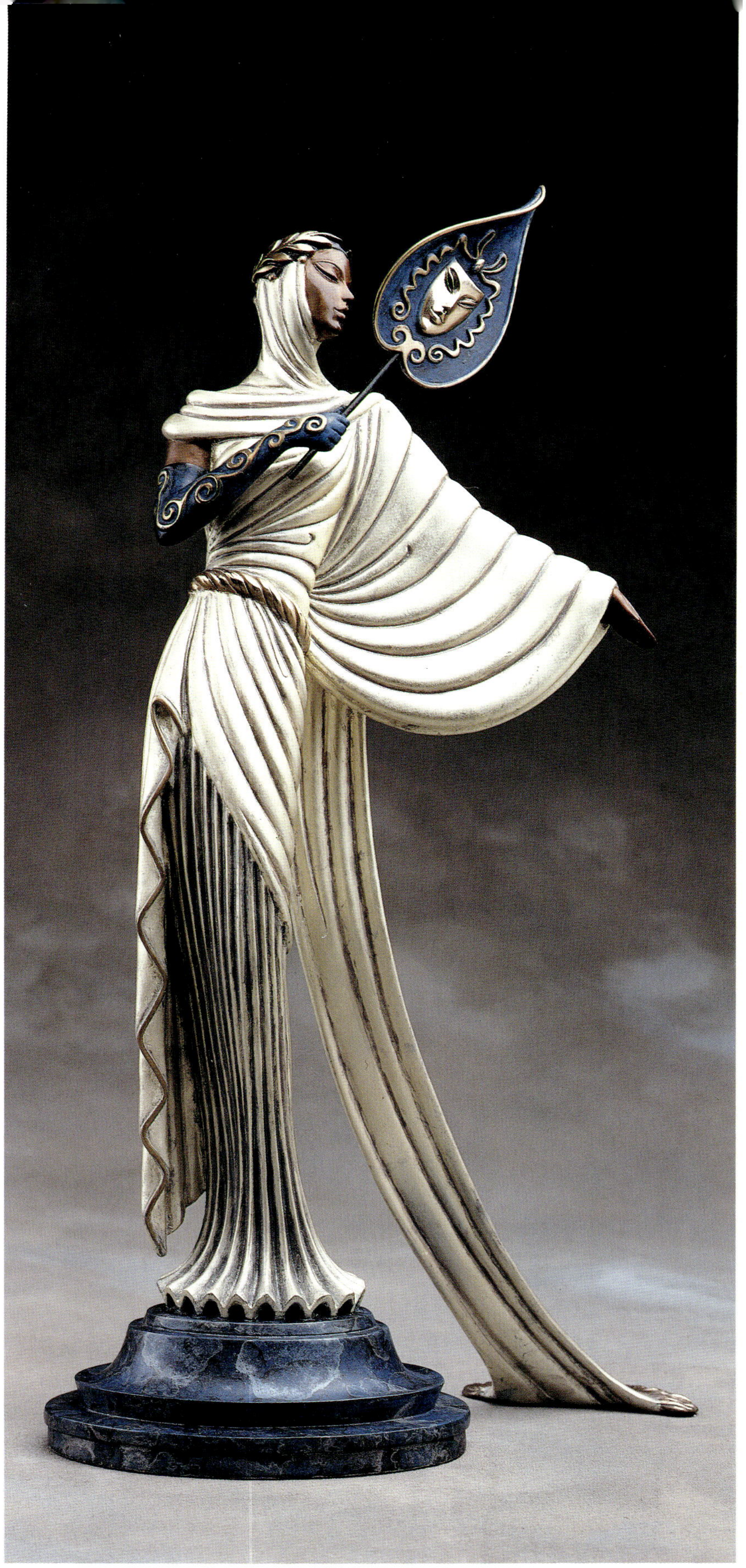

Tanagra
Tanagra
Tanagra
Tanagra

Ecstasy
L'Extase
L'estasi
Ekstase

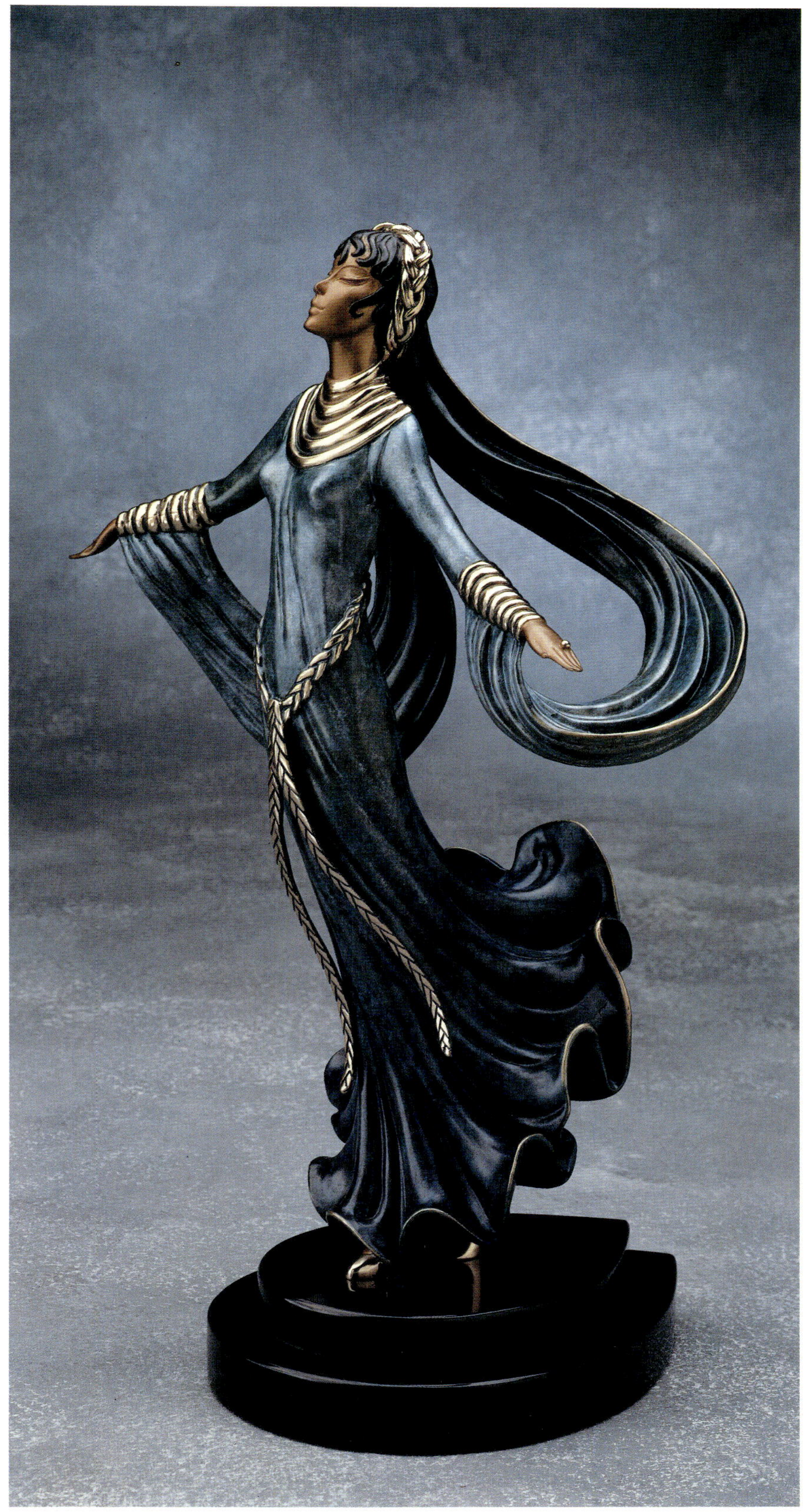

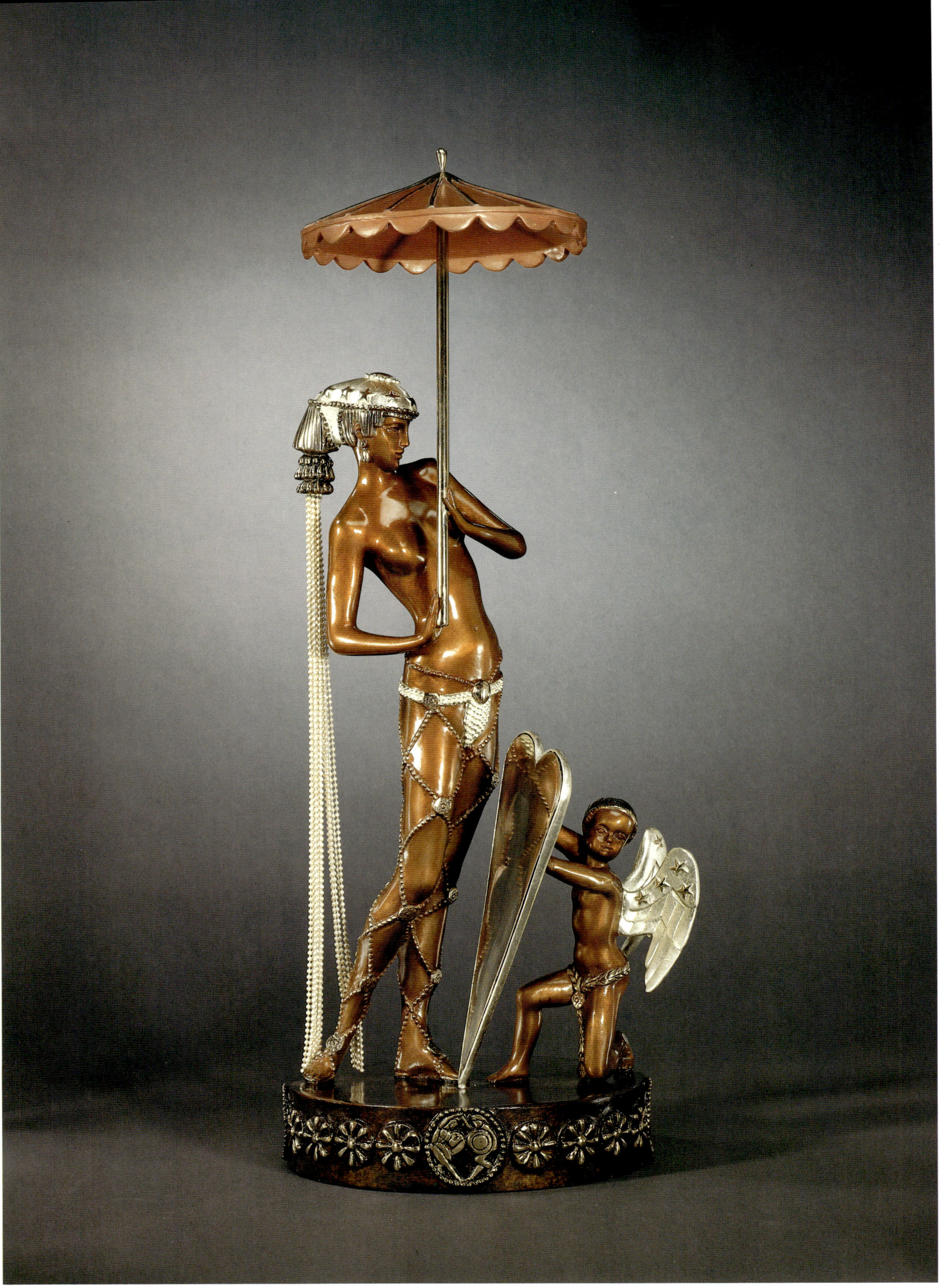

Helen of Troy
Hélène de Troie
Elena di Troia
Helene von Troja

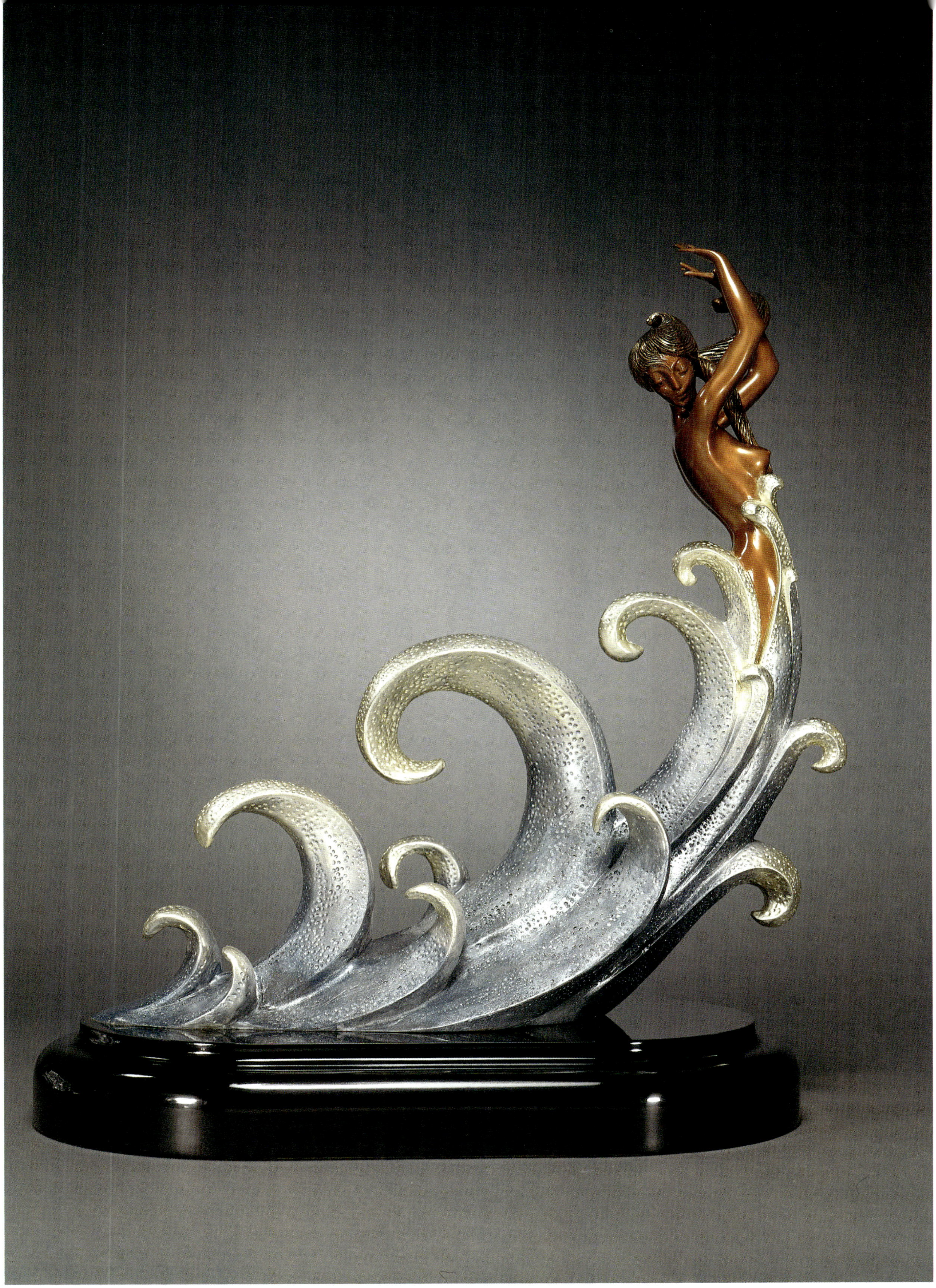

The Wave
La Vague
L'Onda
Die Welle

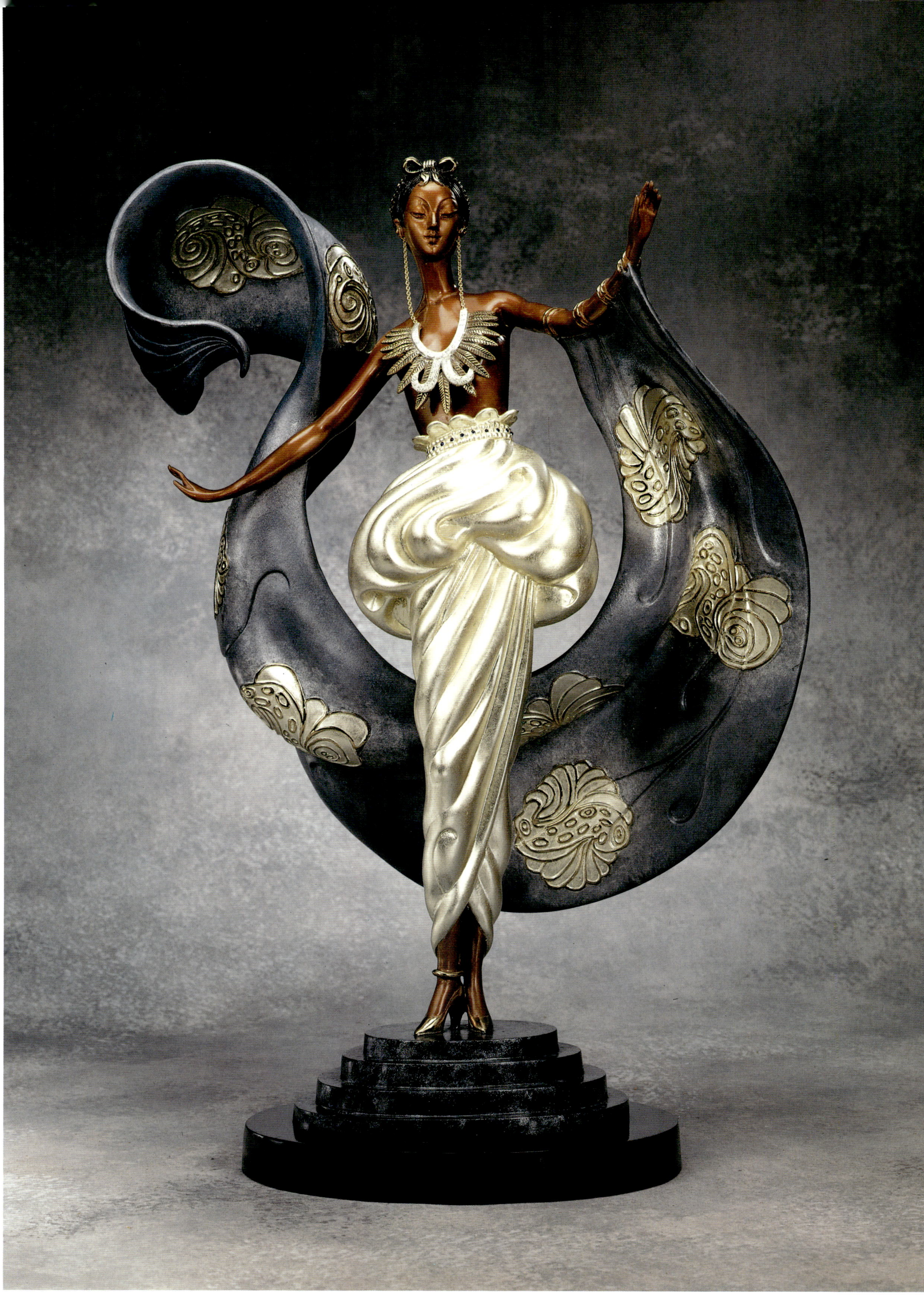

Dream Girl
Femme fantasme
La ragazza dei sogni
Traummädchen

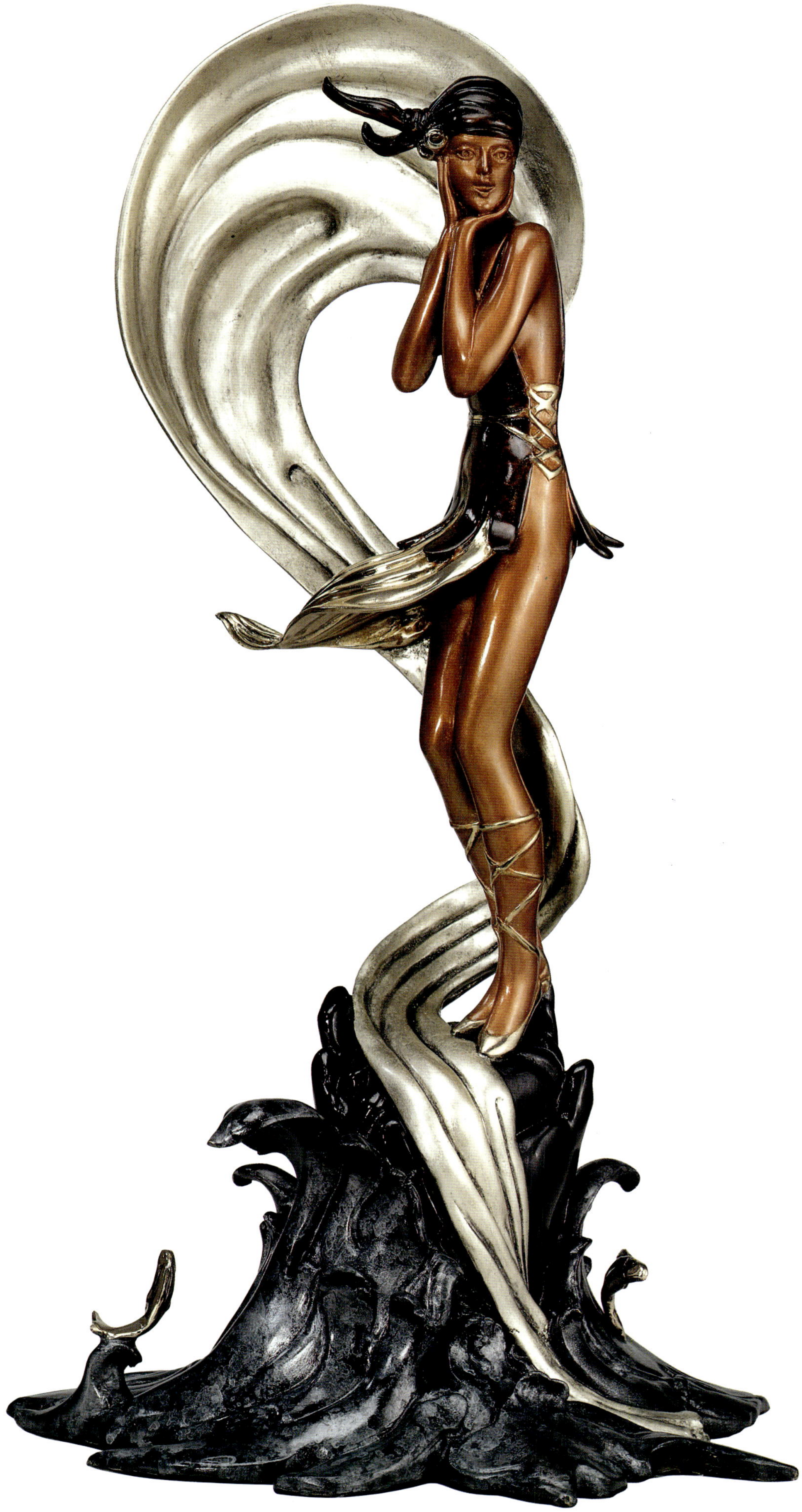

Stranded
Echouée
Incagliata
Gestrandet

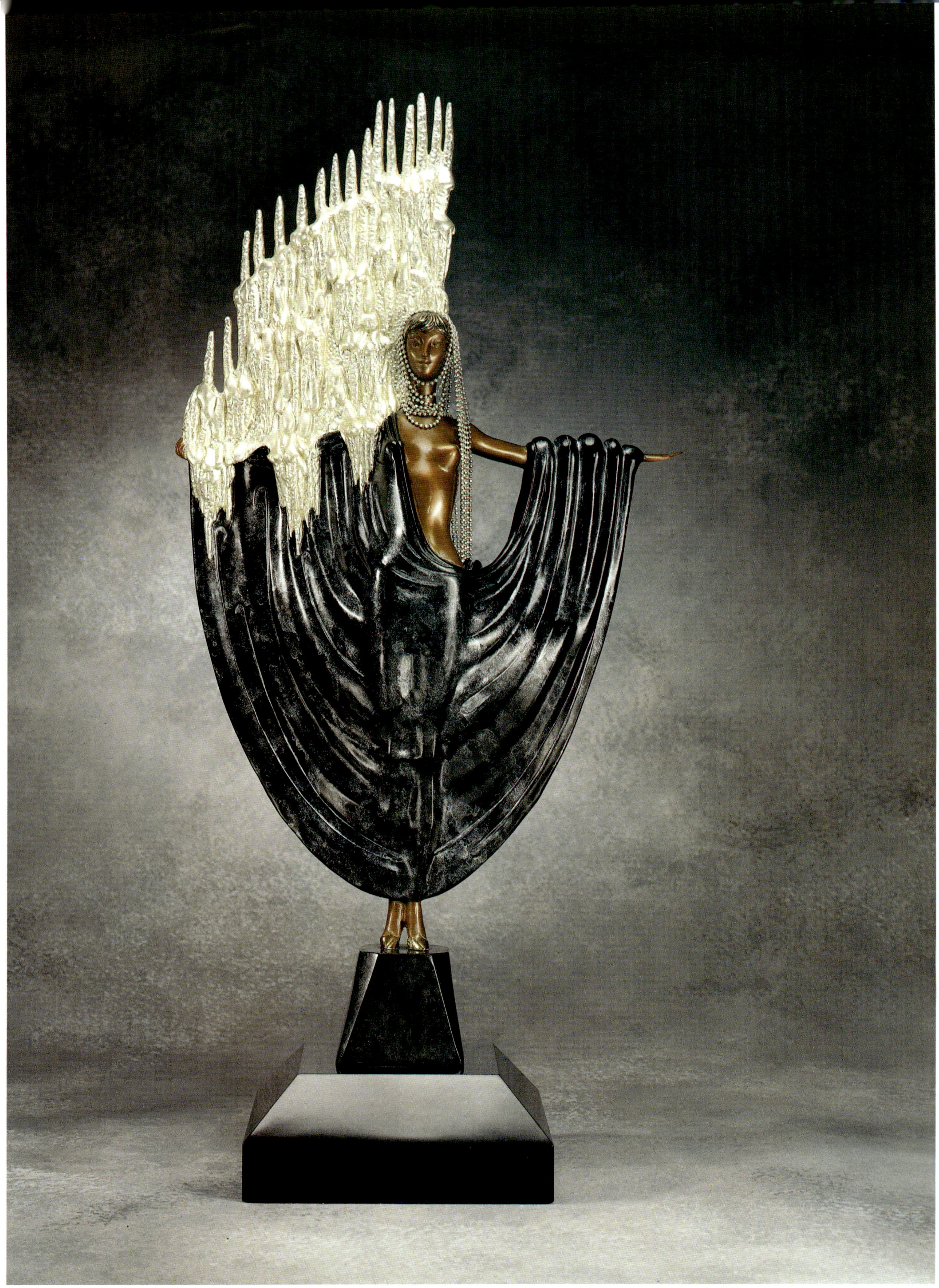

Arctic Sea
L'Océan Arctique
Il Mare Artico
Das Polarmeer

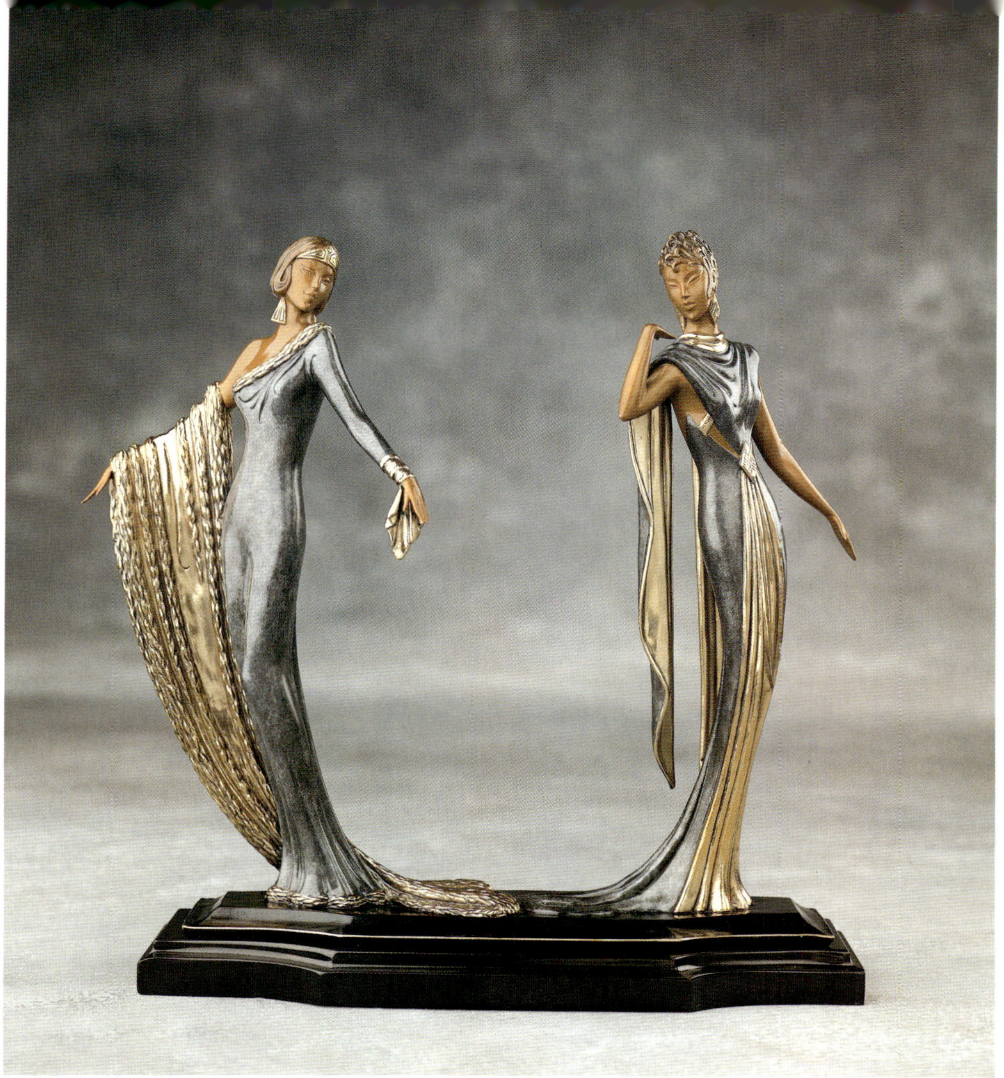

Duetto
Duet
Duetto
Duett

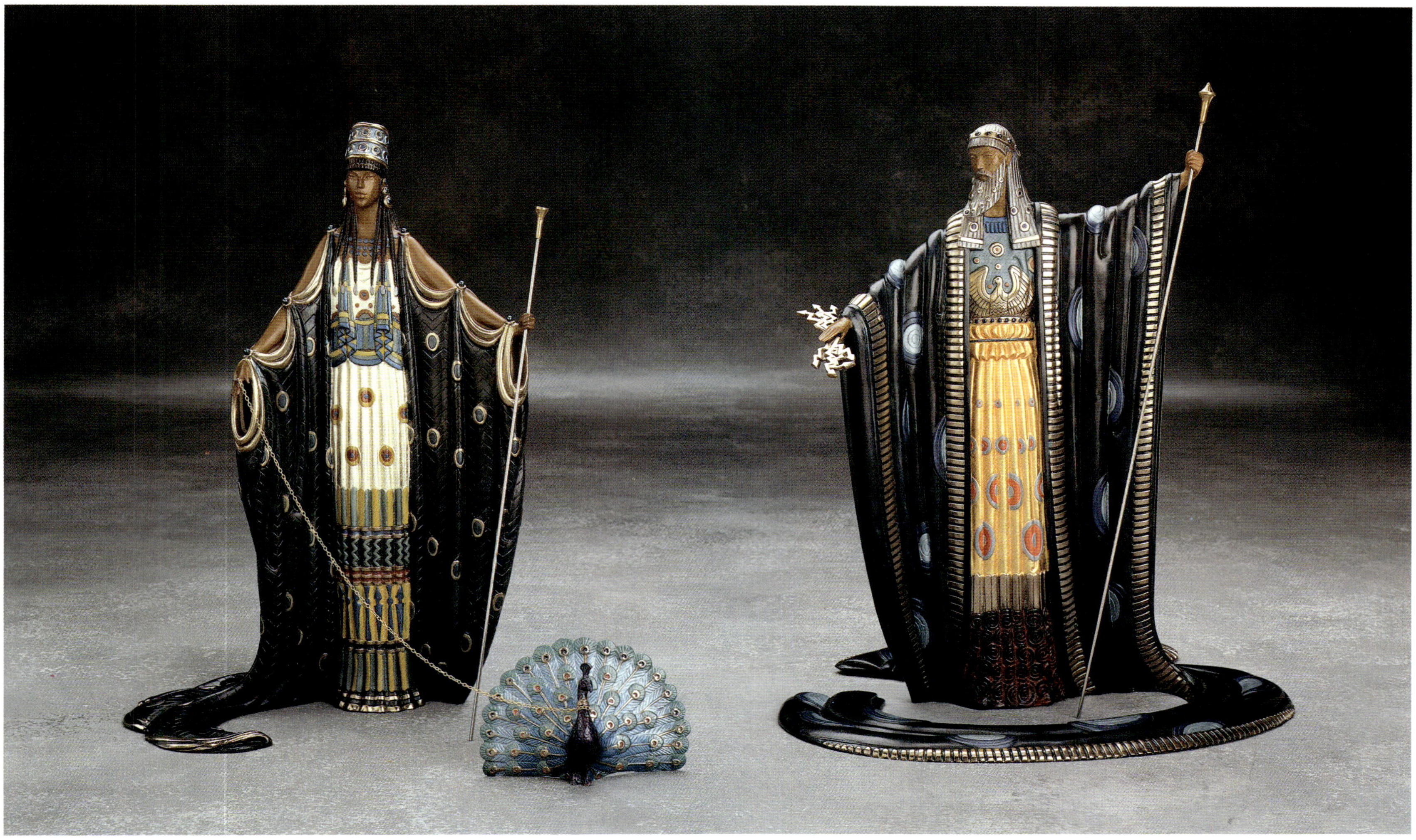

Hera and Zeus
Hera et Zeus
Era e Zeus
Hera und Zeus

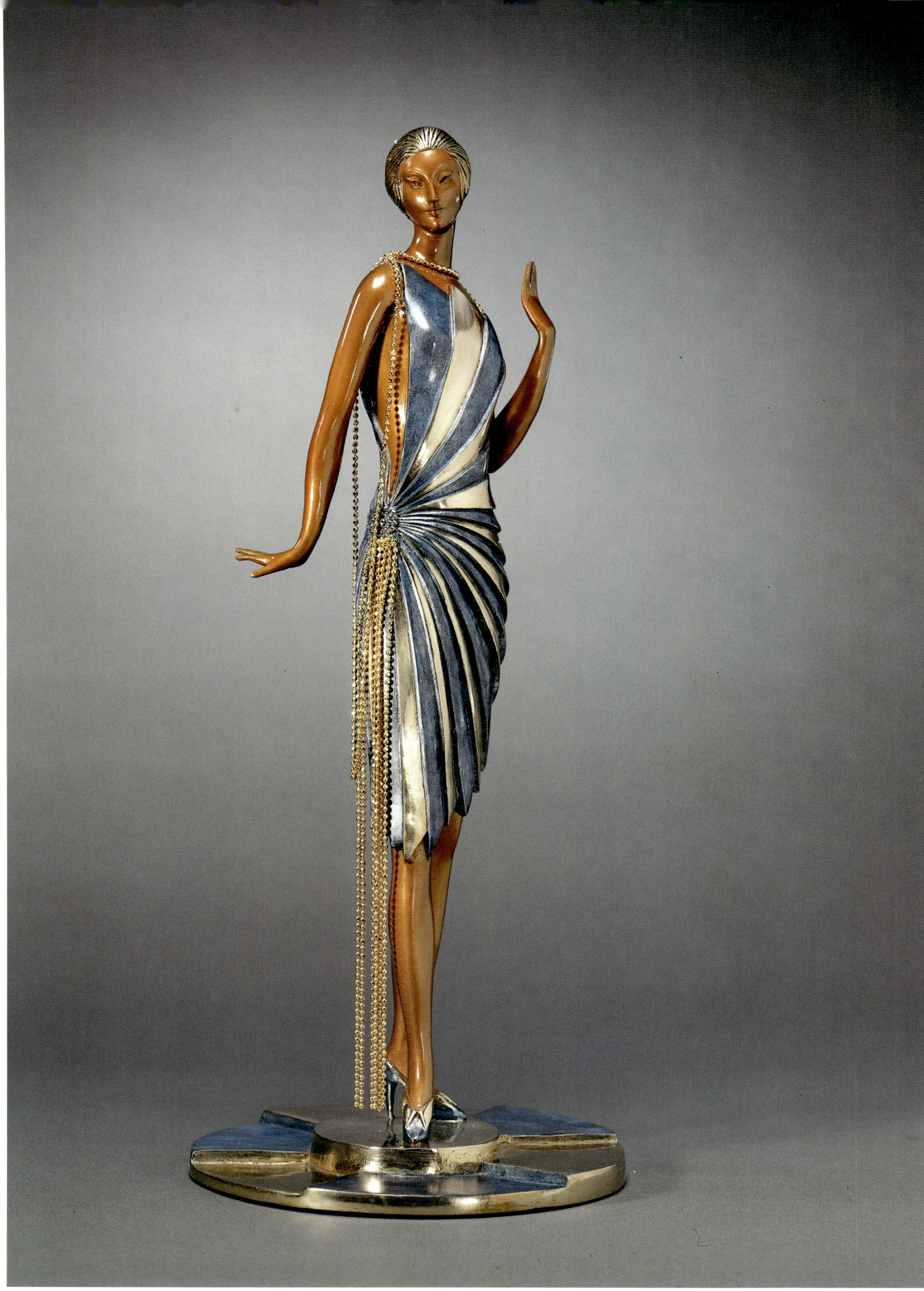

Roaring Twenties
Les Vingtièmes rugissants
I ruggenti anni venti
Die wilden zwanziger Jahre

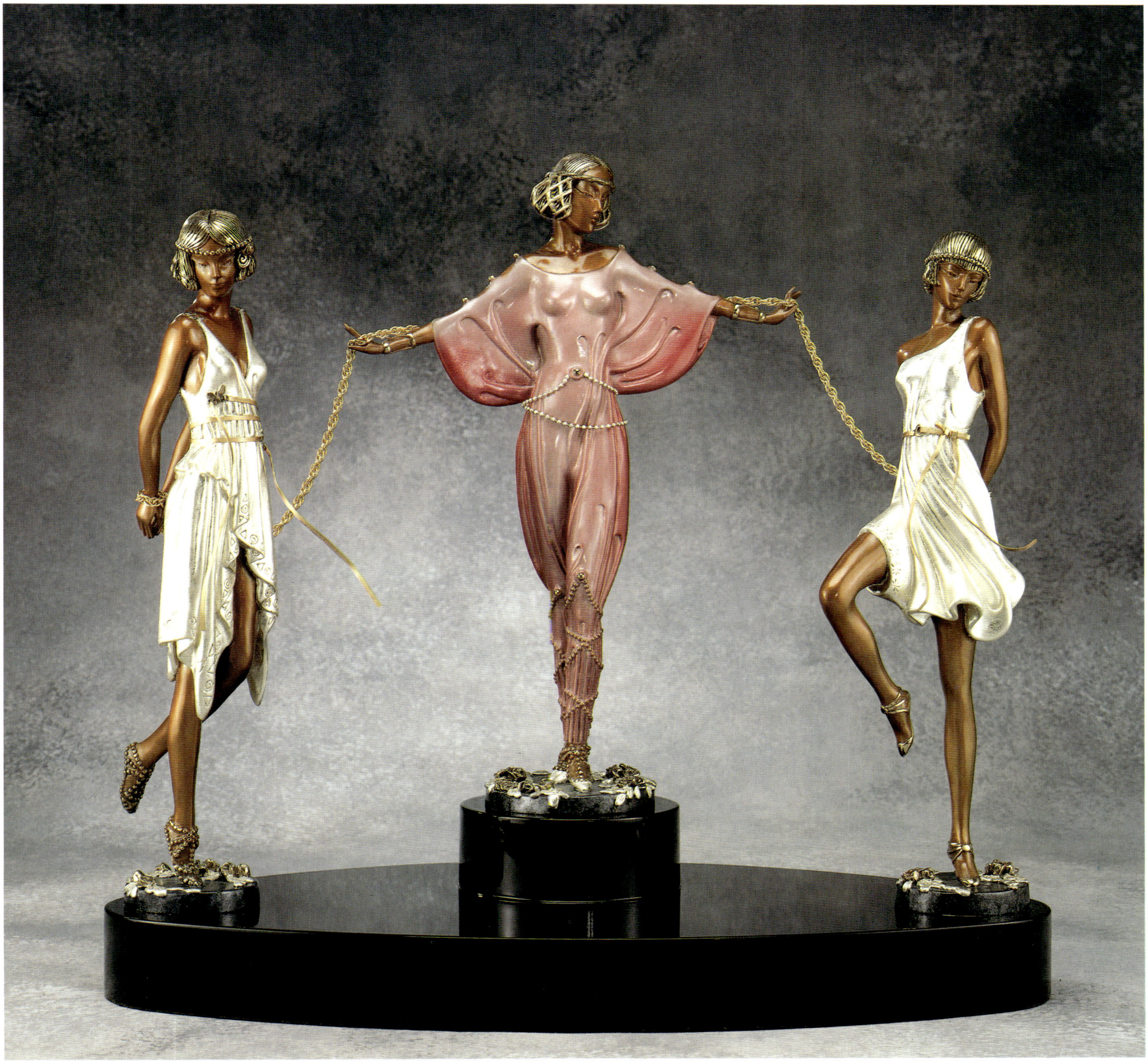

Printemps
Printemps
Primavera
Frühling

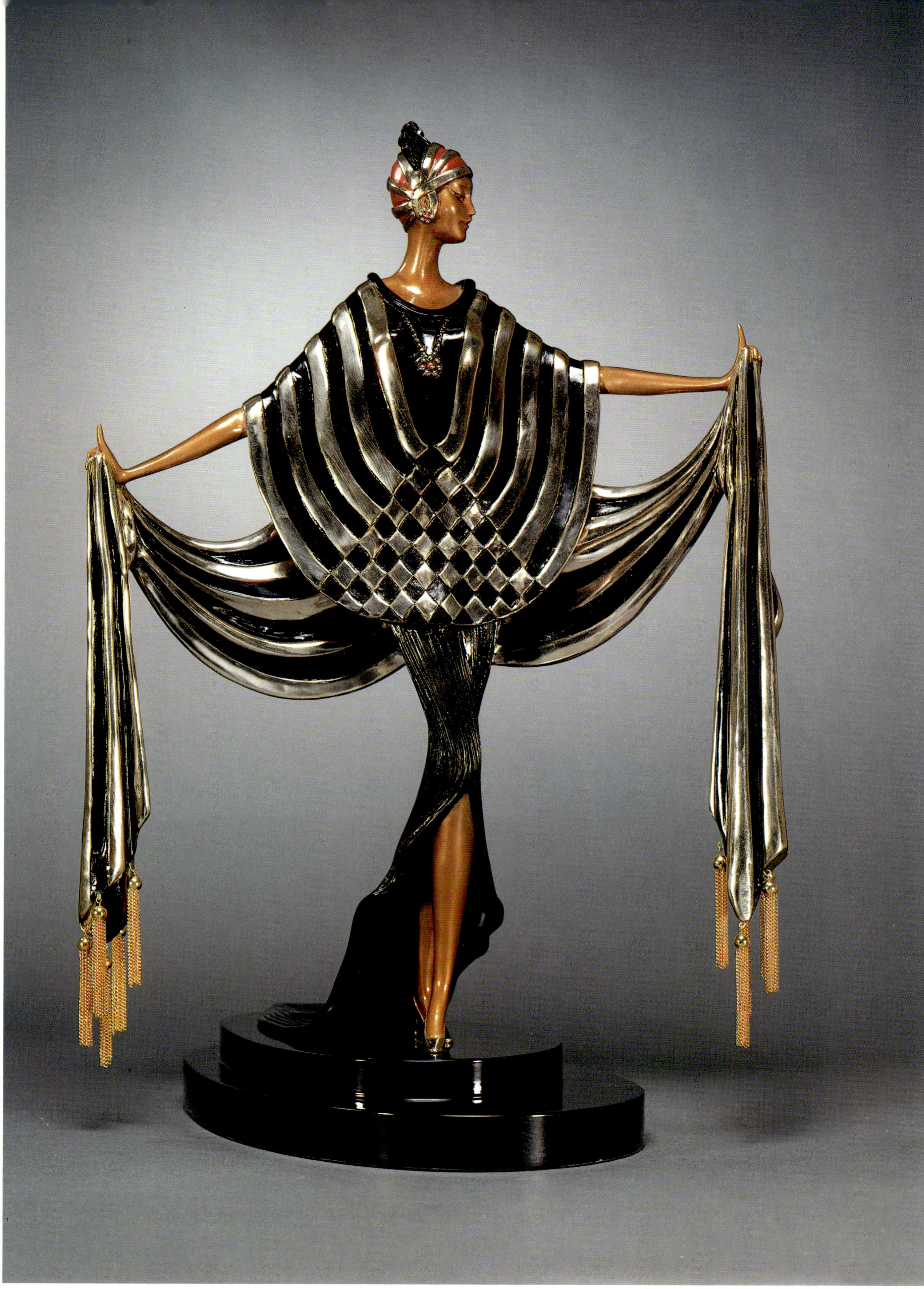

Opening Night
Première de gala
La sera della prima
Premiere

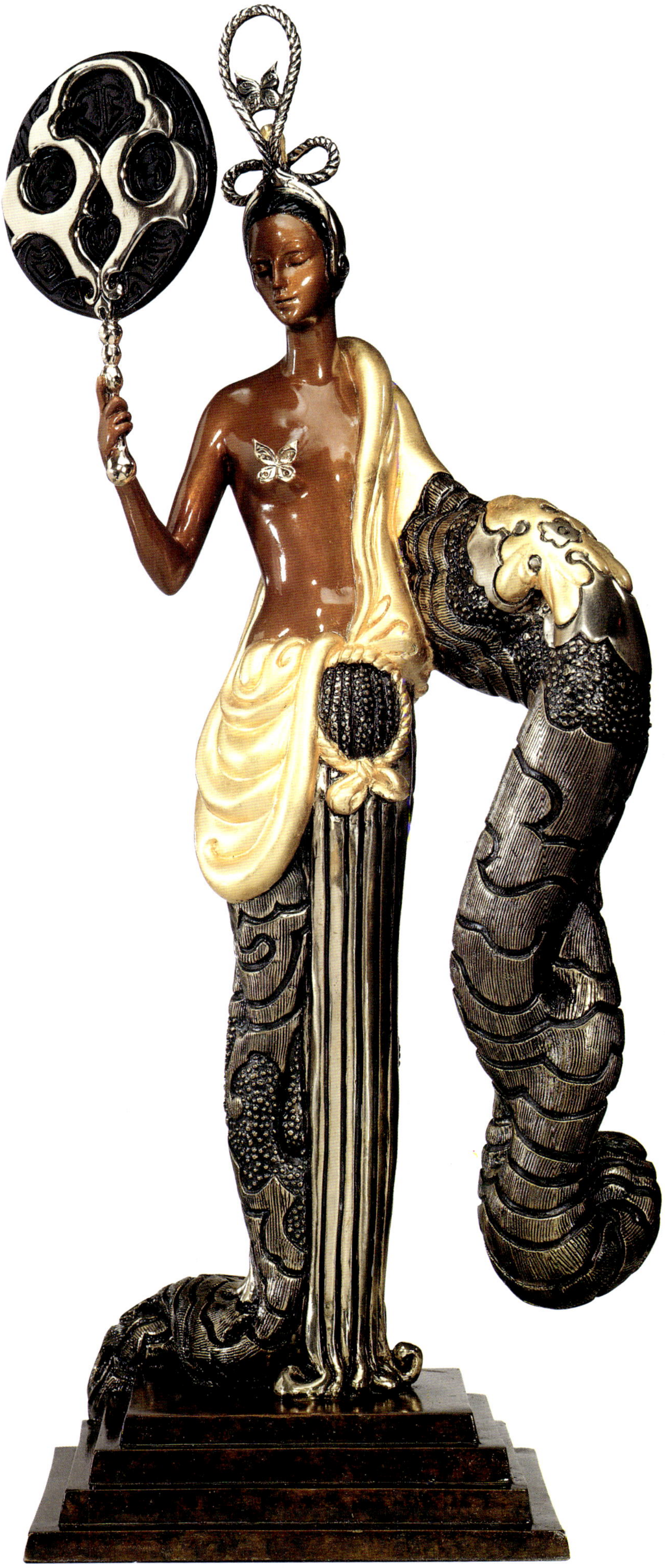

Bamboo
Bambou
Bambú
Bambus

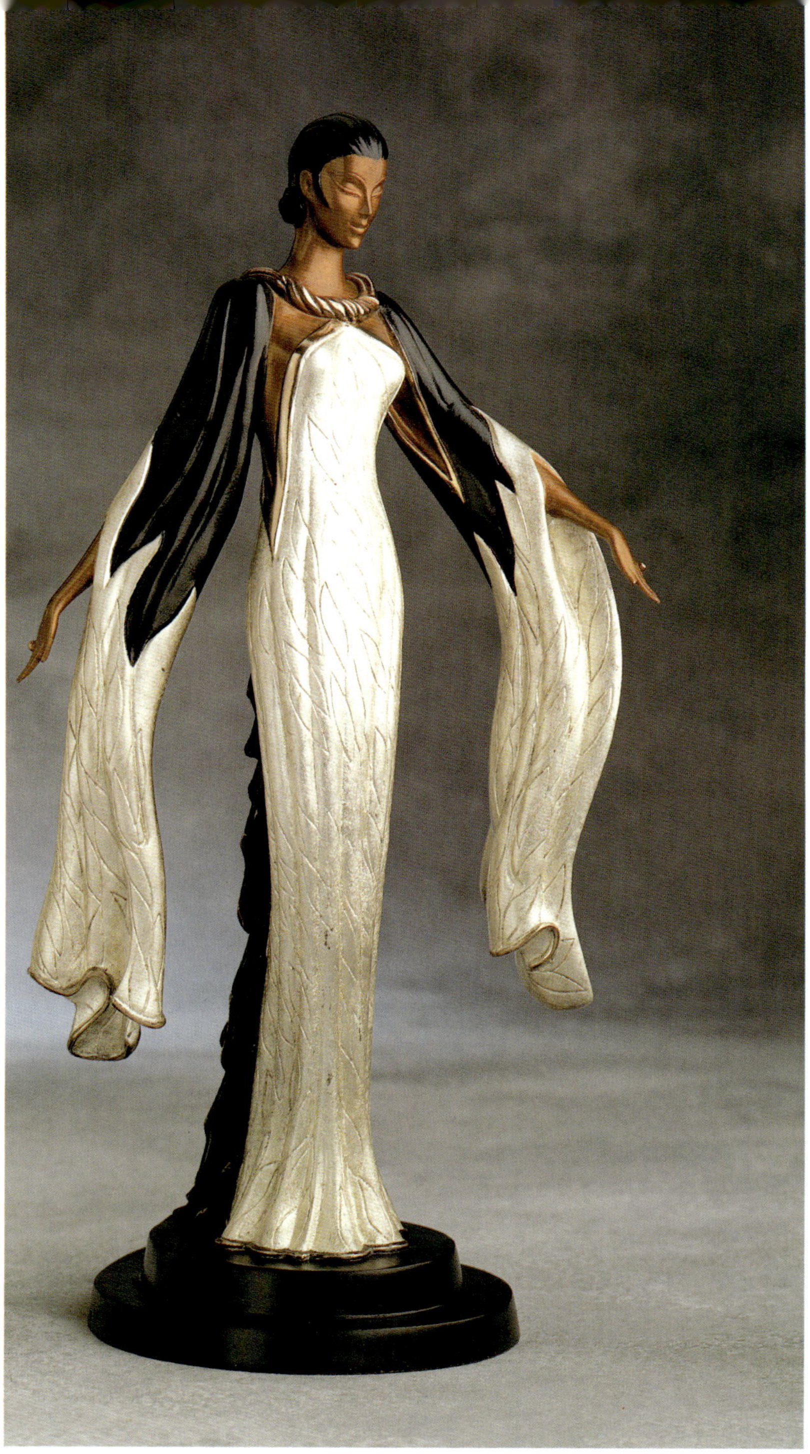

Fireleaves
Feu de feuilles
Foglie di fuoco
Feuerblätter

Je l'aime
Je l'aime
Io l'amo
Ich mag ihn

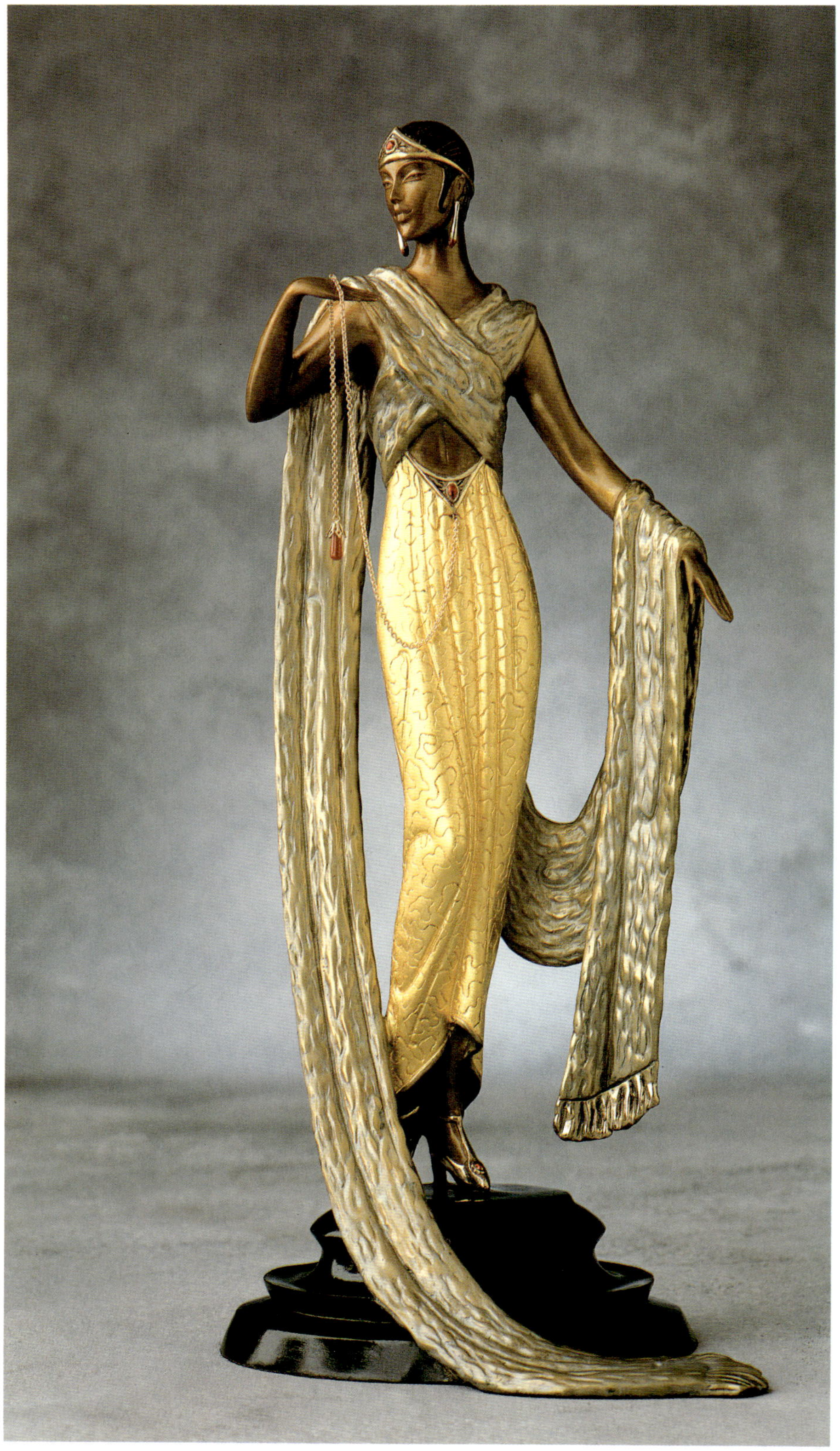

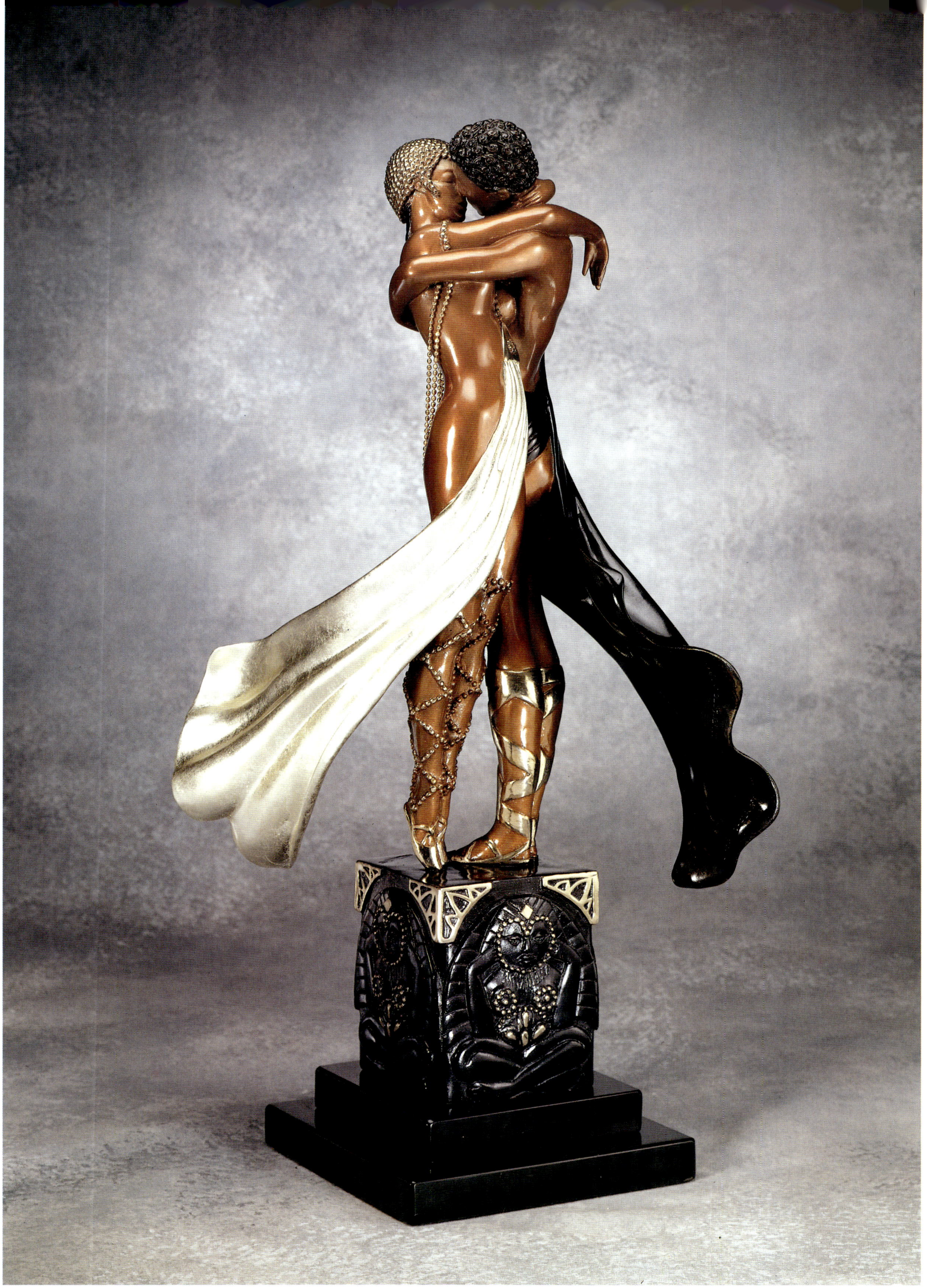

Lovers and Idol
Amants et idole
Amanti e idolo
Liebhaber und Idol

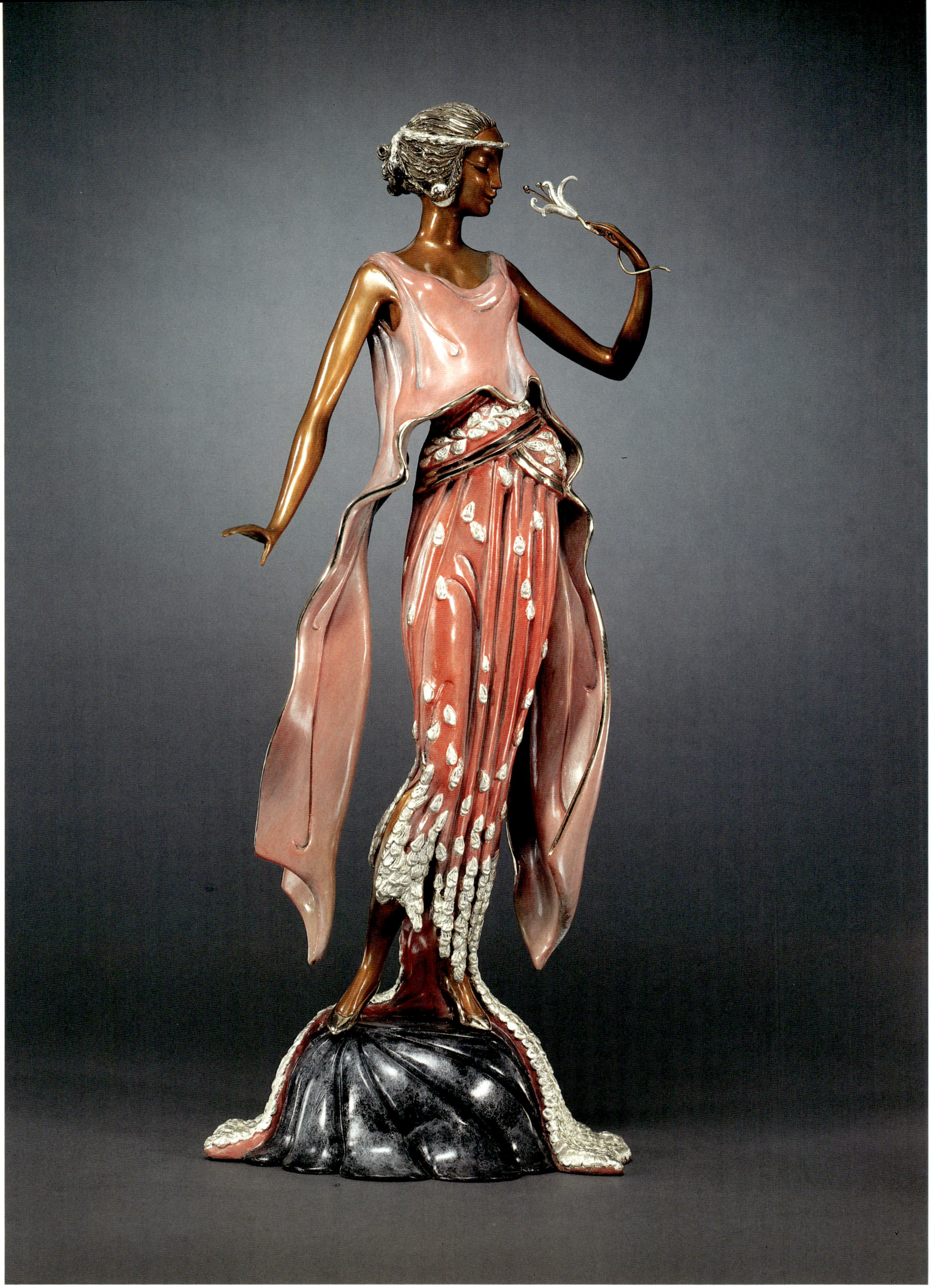

Flower Petal Gown
Robe à pétale de fleurs
Abito con petali di fiori
Blüttengewand

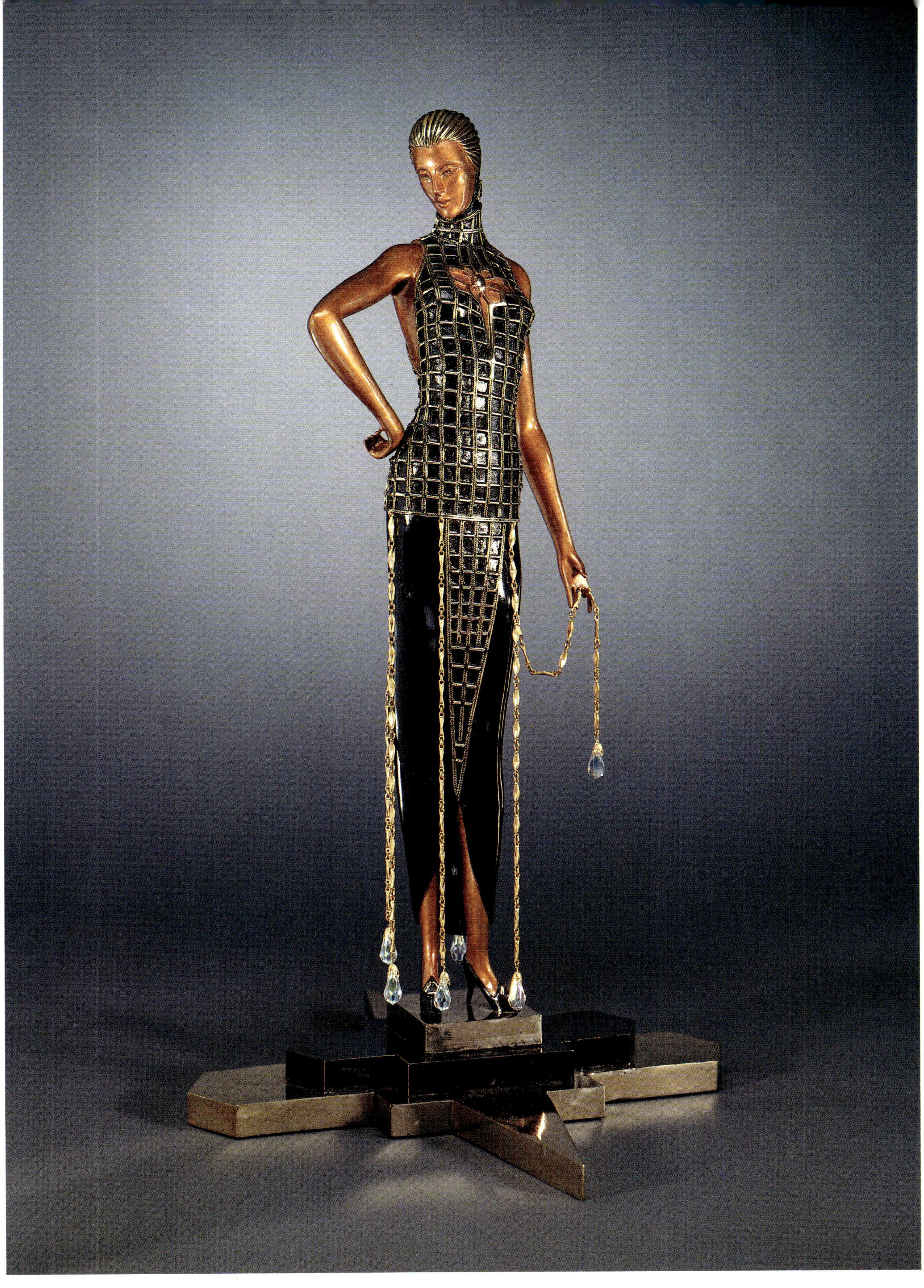

Deco
Deco
Deco
Deco

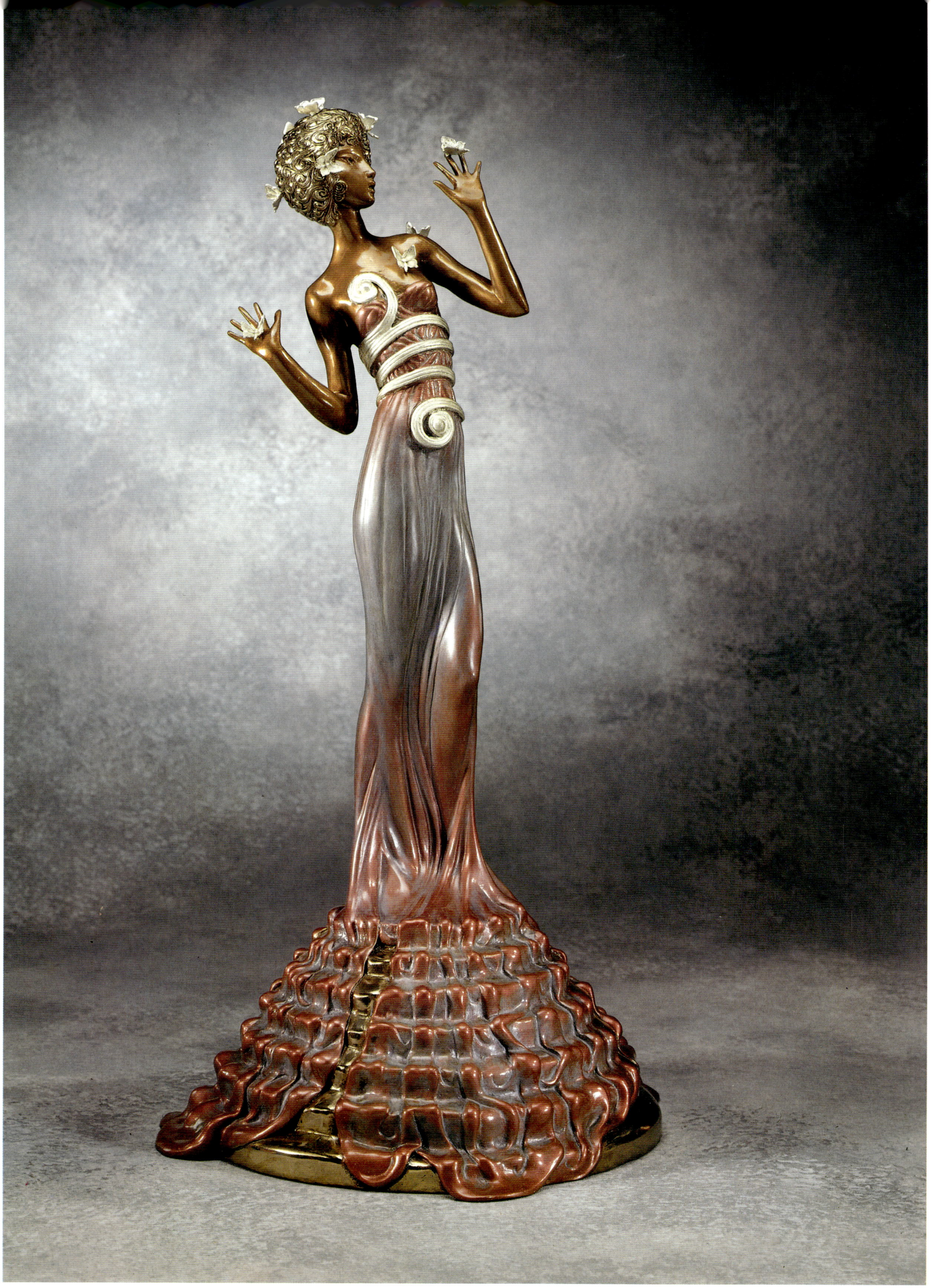

Fantasia
Fantaisie
Fantasia
Phantasie

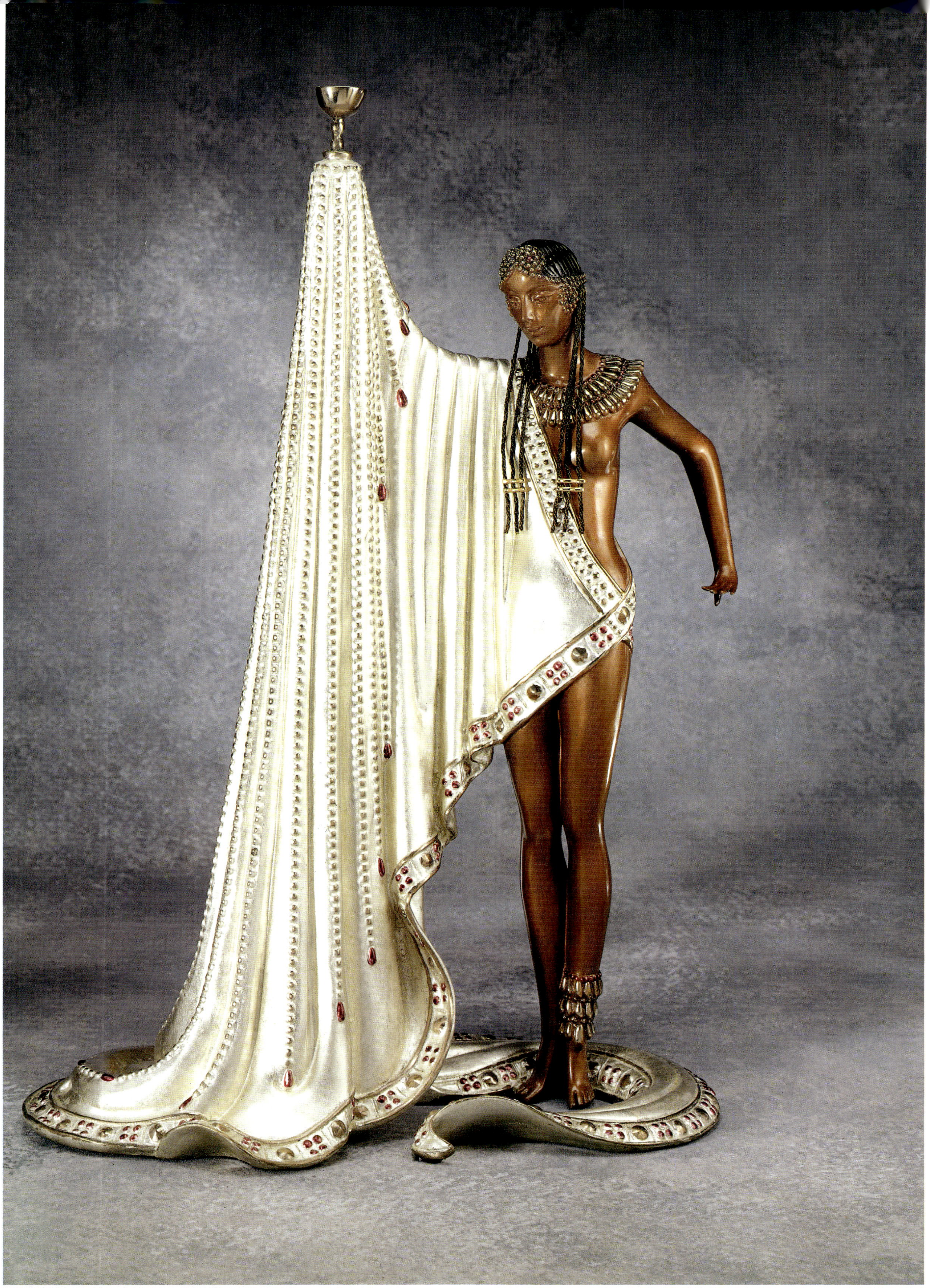

The Slave
L'Esclave
Lo schiavo
Der Sklave

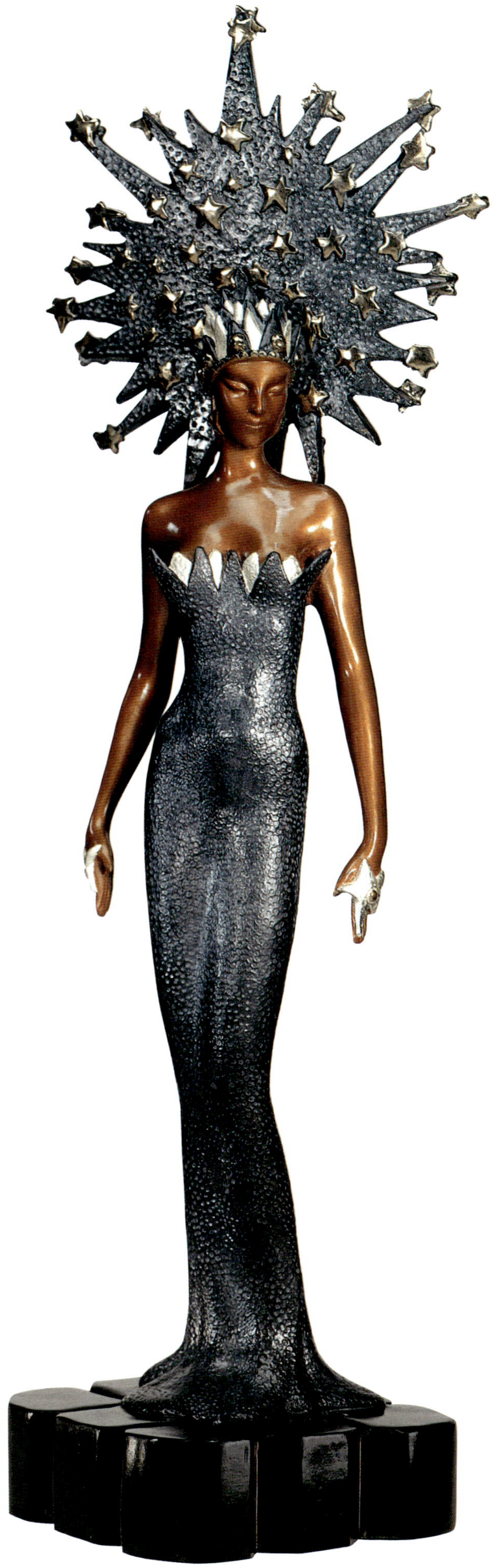

Starstruck
Bouquet d'étoiles
In un turbine di stelle
Von Sternen getroffen

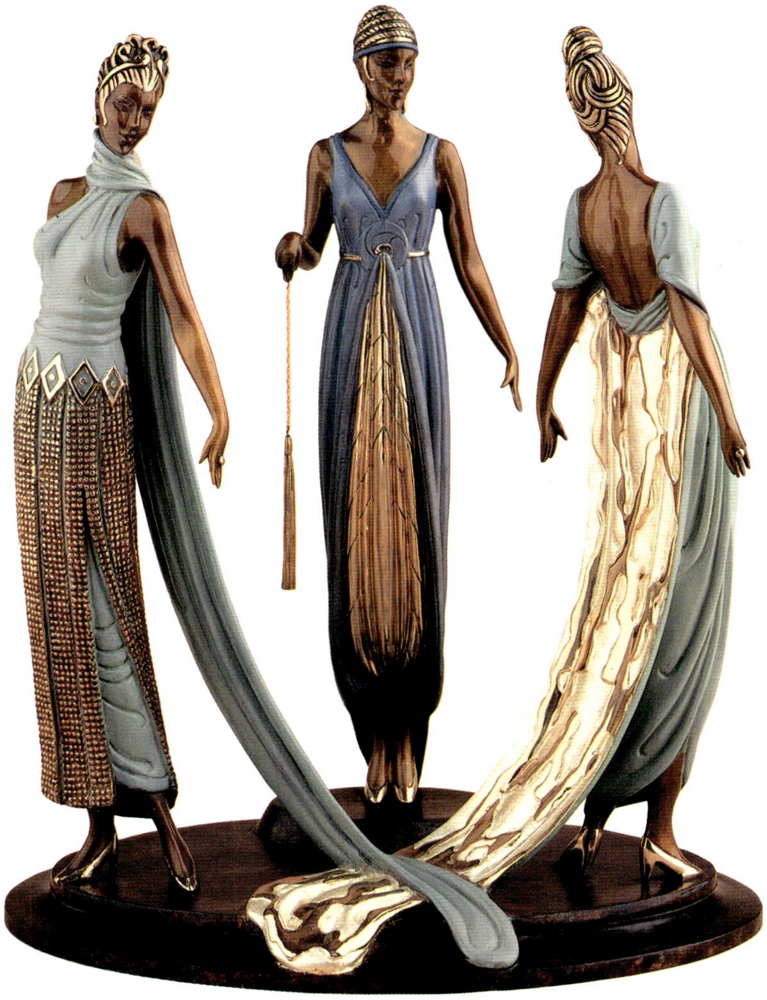

The Three Graces
Les Trois Grâces
Le tre grazie
Die drei Grazien

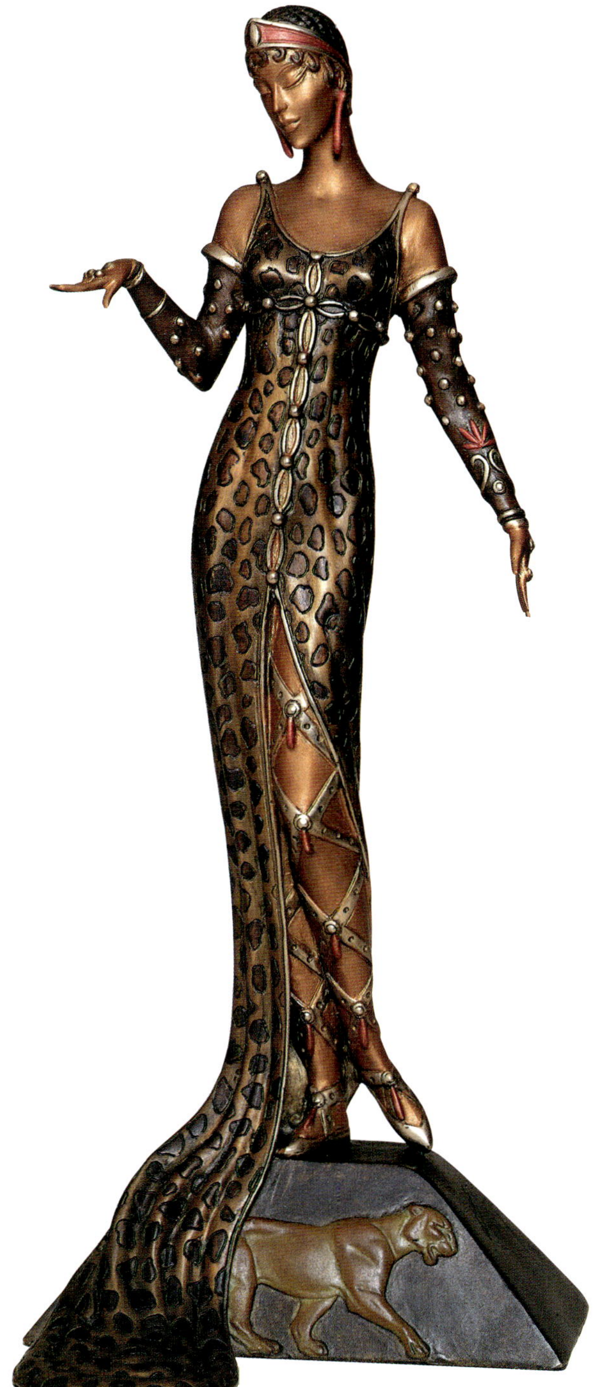

Julietta
Julietta
Guilietta
Julietta

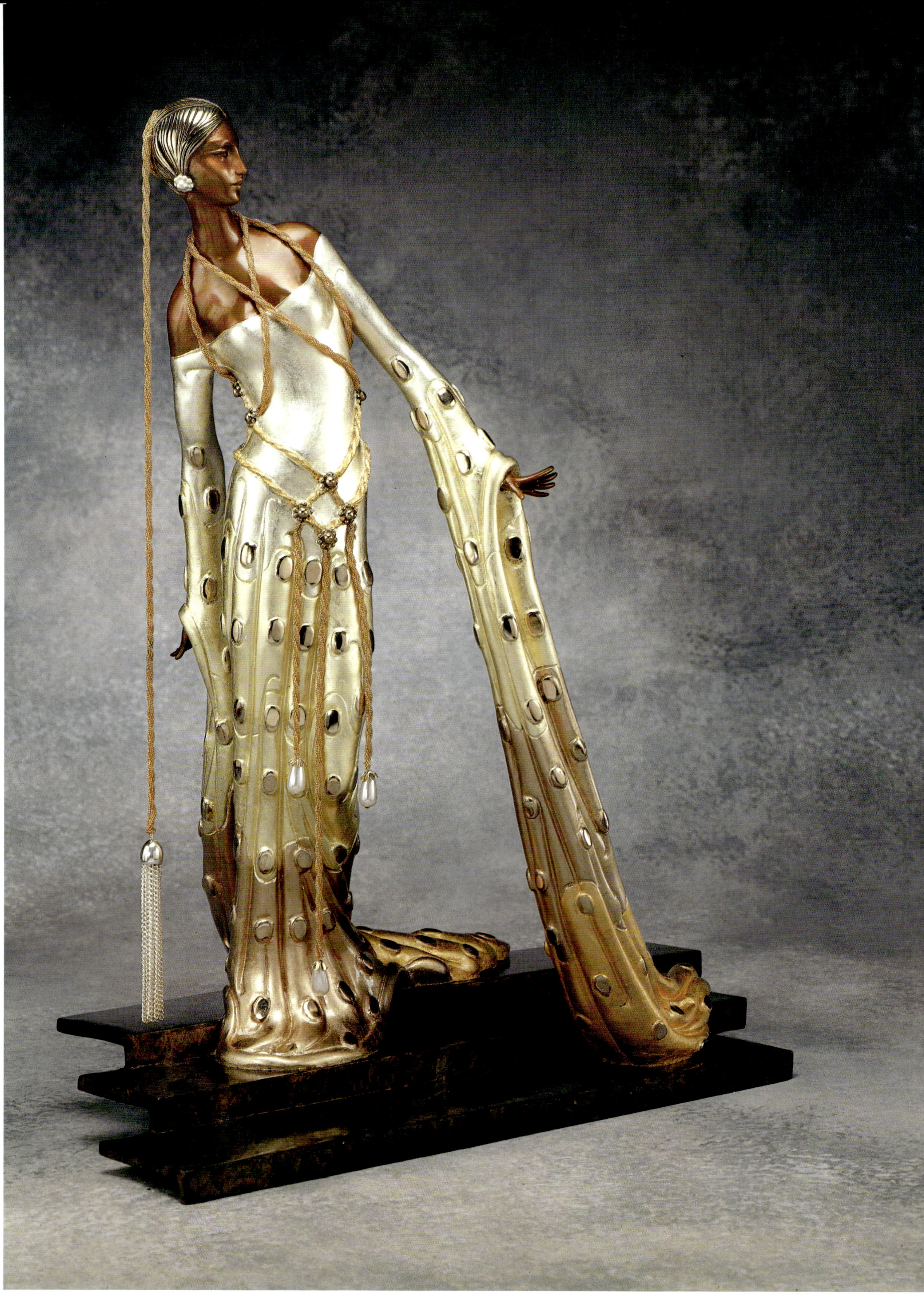

Melisande
Melisande
Melisande
Melisande

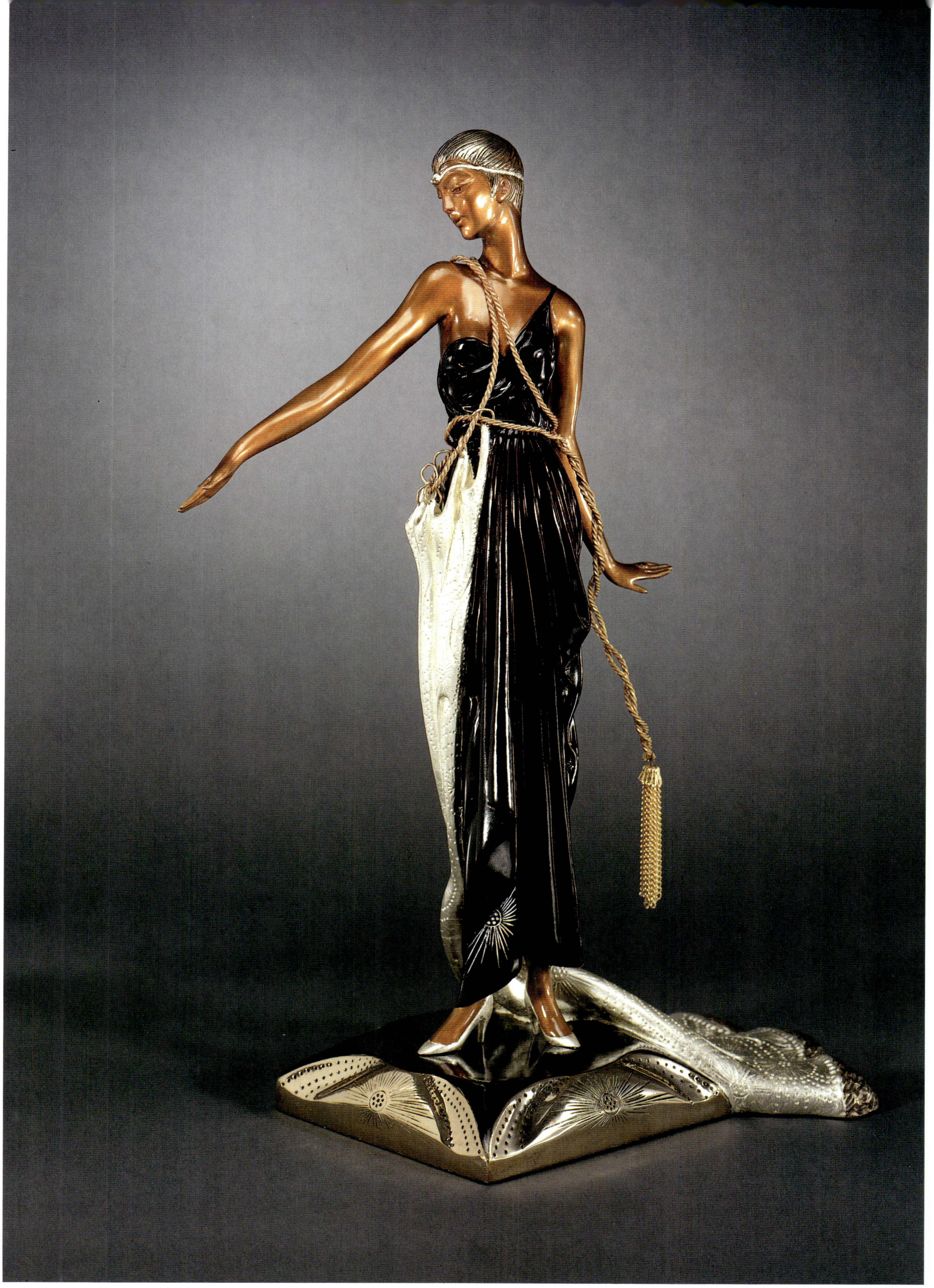

Soleil de nuit
Soleil de nuit
Sole di notte
Nachtsonne

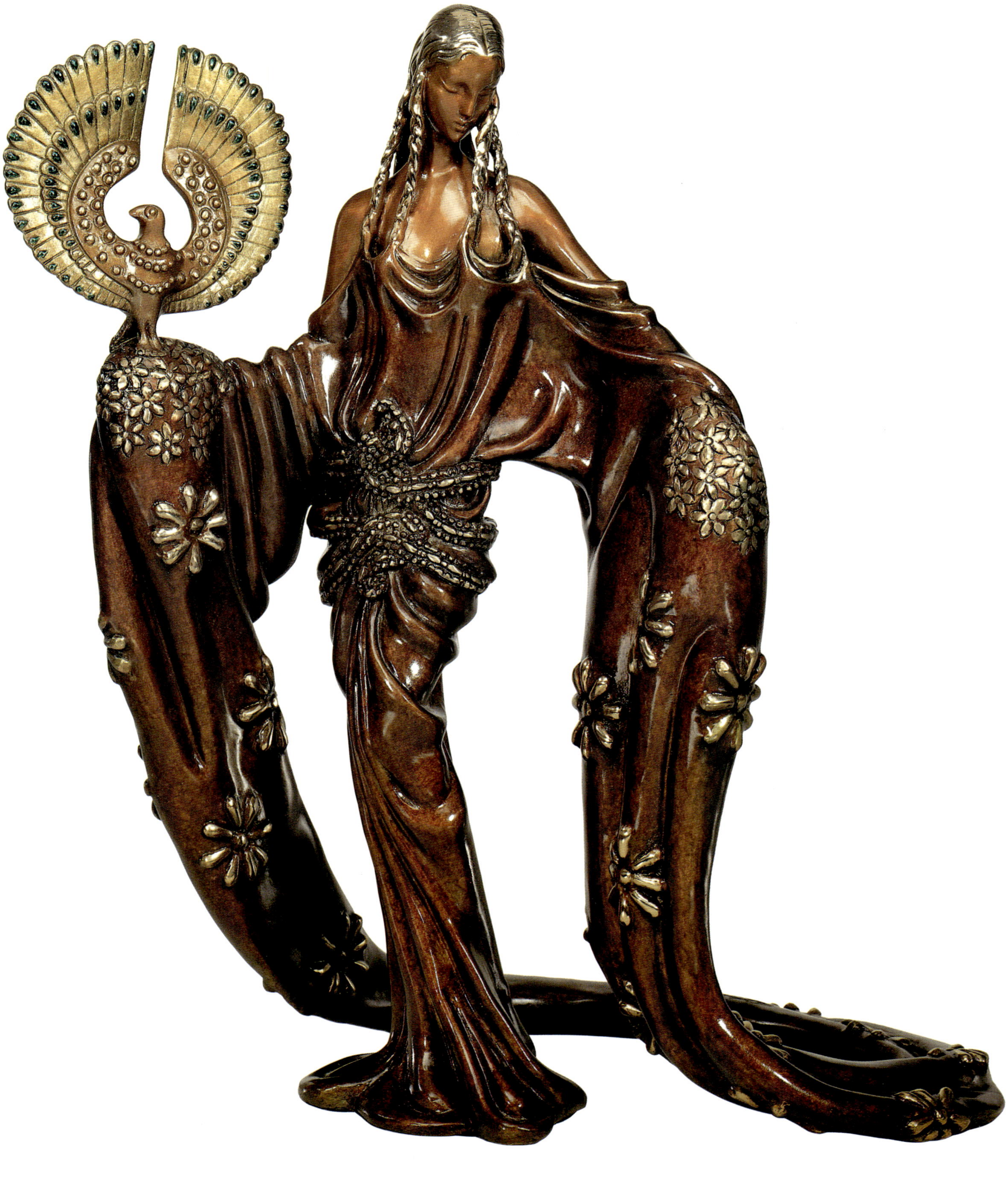

Wisdom
Sagesse
Saggezza
Weisheit

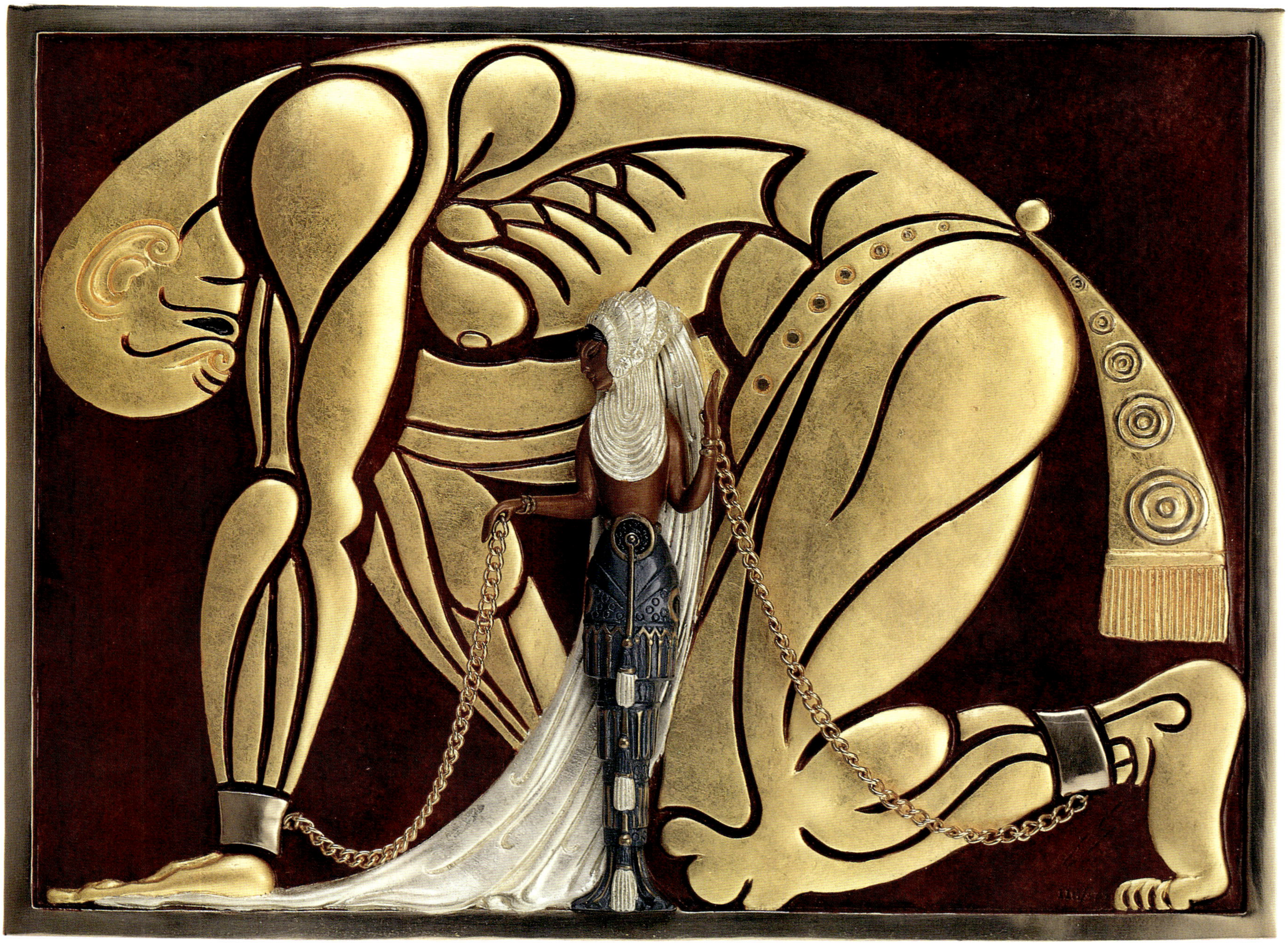

Samson and Delilah
Samson et Dalila
Sansone e Dalila
Samson und Delilah

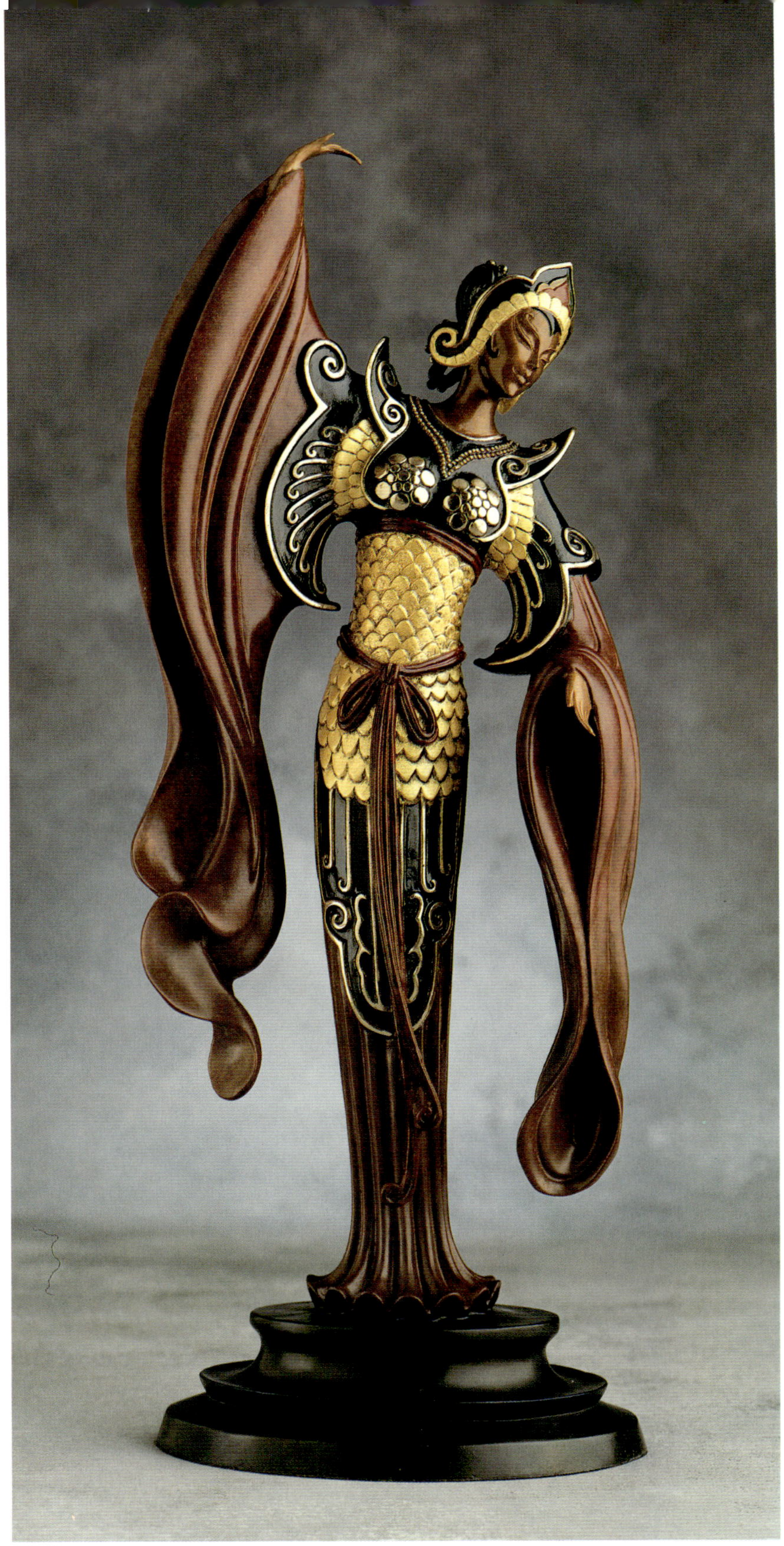

Chinese Legend
Légende Chinoise
Leggenda cinese
Chinesische Sage

Fedora
Fedora
Fedora
Fedora

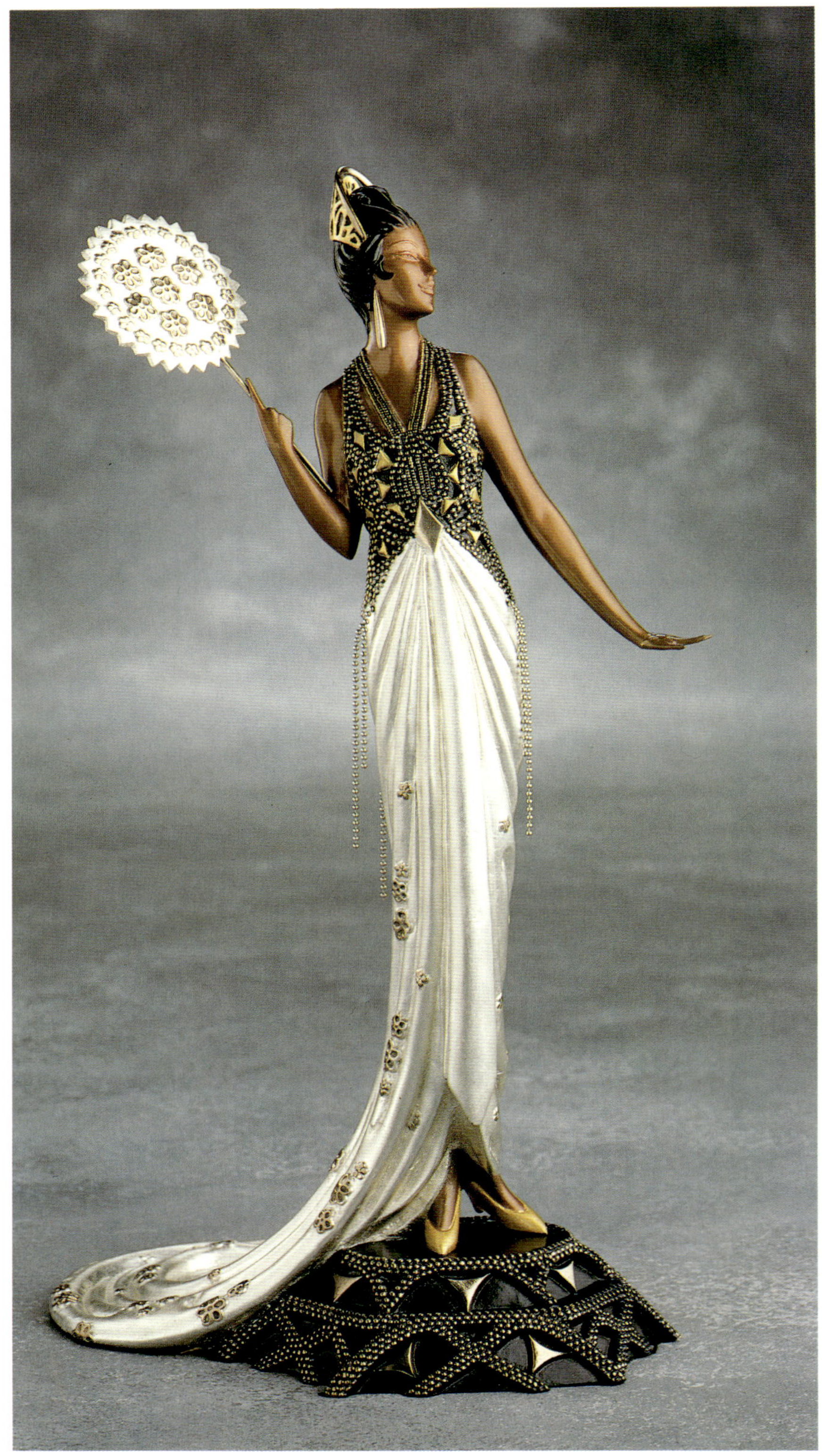

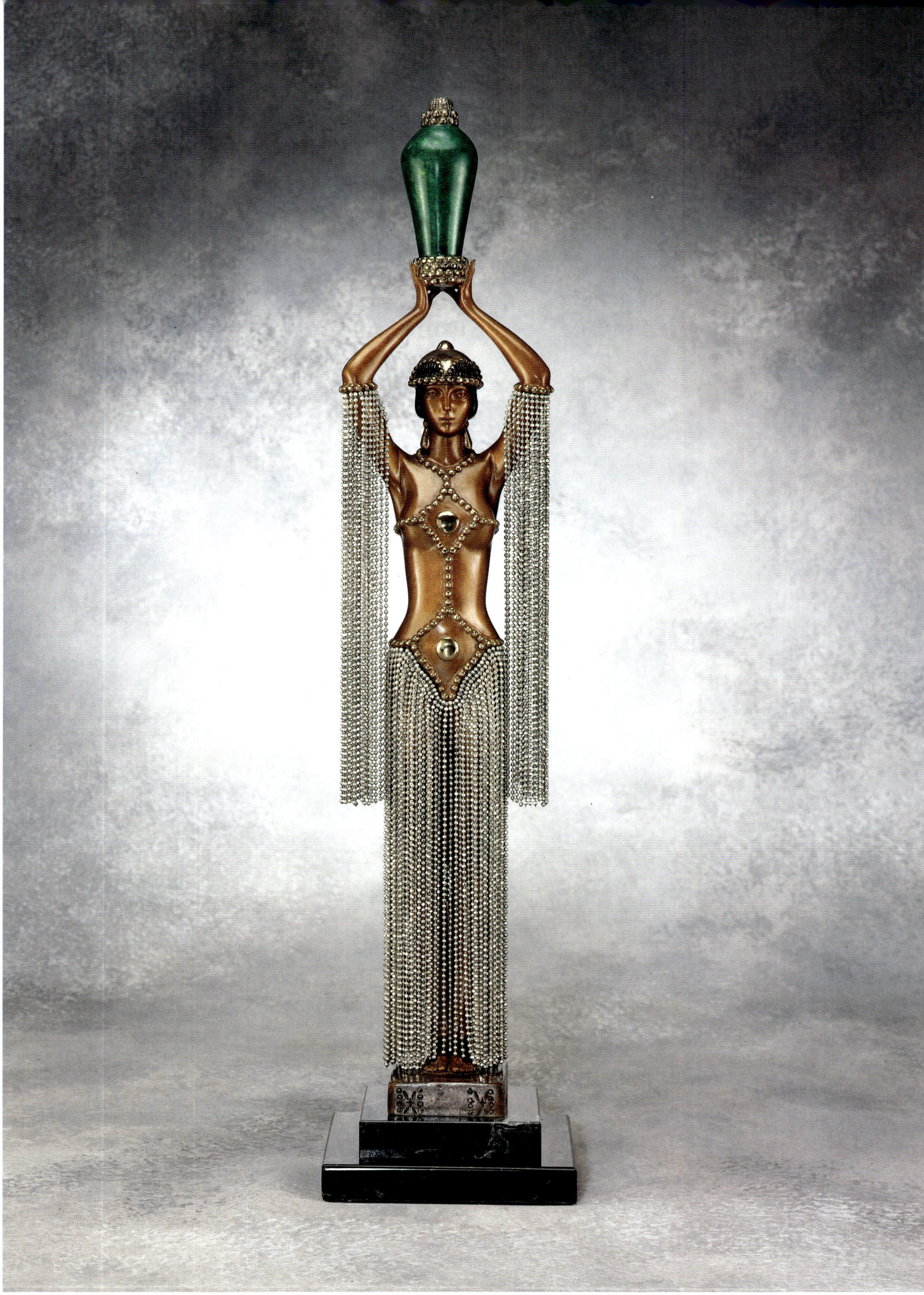

Emerald Vase
Vase d'émeraude
Vaso di smeraldo
Smaragdvase

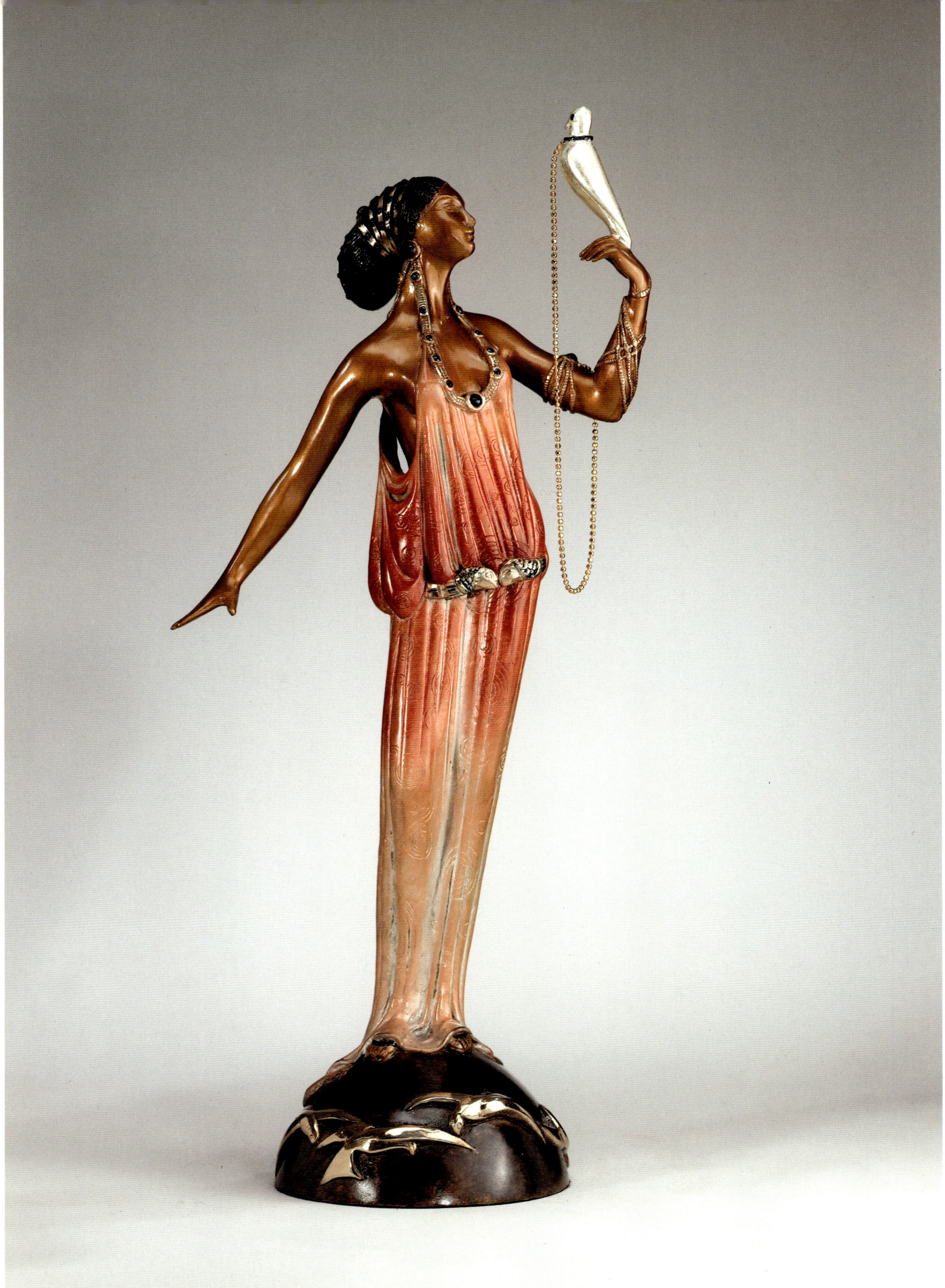

Love Goddess
Déesse de l'Amour
Dea dell'amore
Liebesgöttin

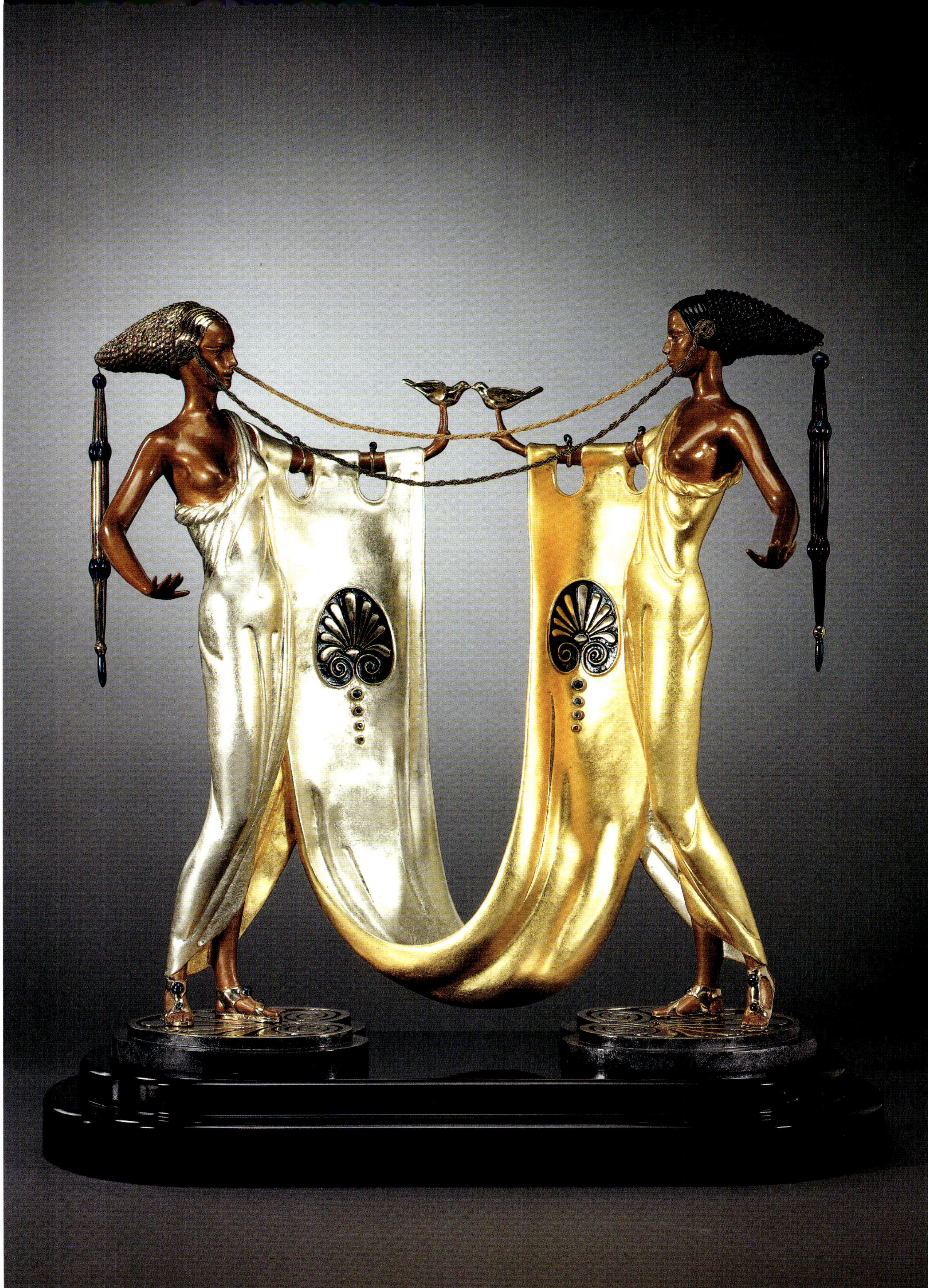

Sisters
Soeurs
Sorelle
Schwestern

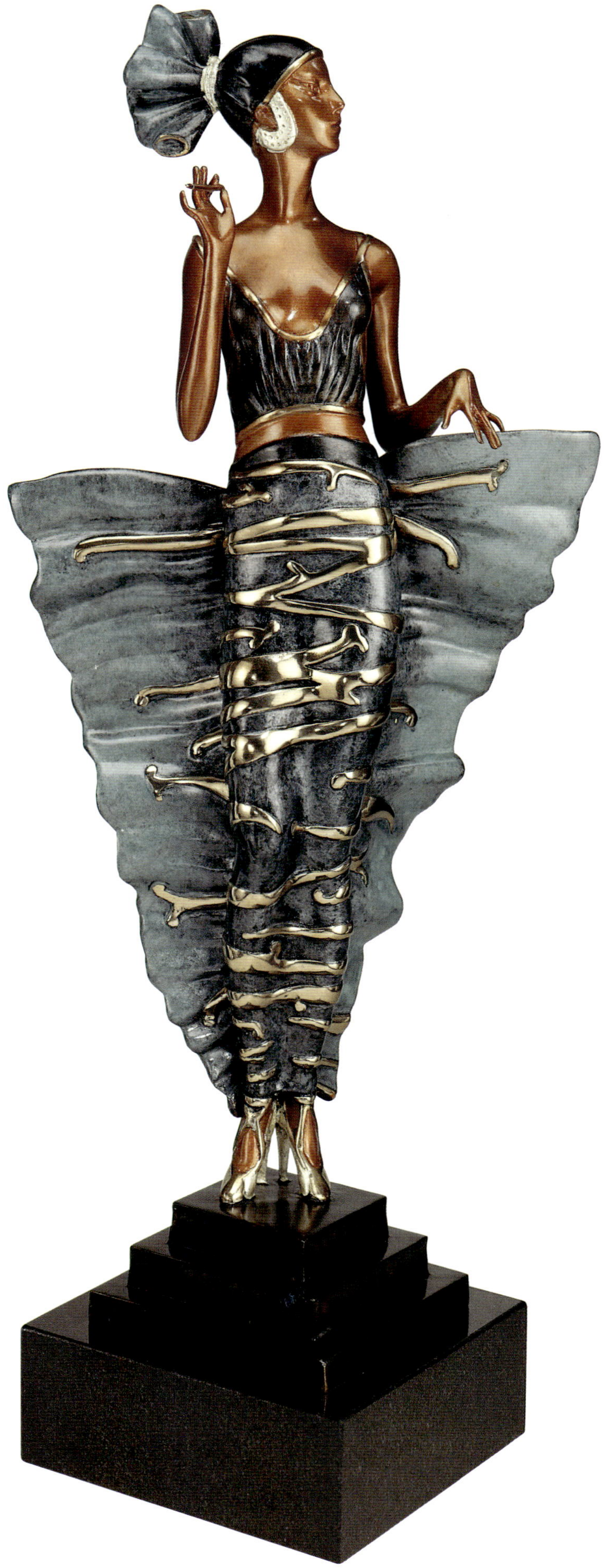

Femme fatale
Femme fatale
Donna fatale
Femme Fatale

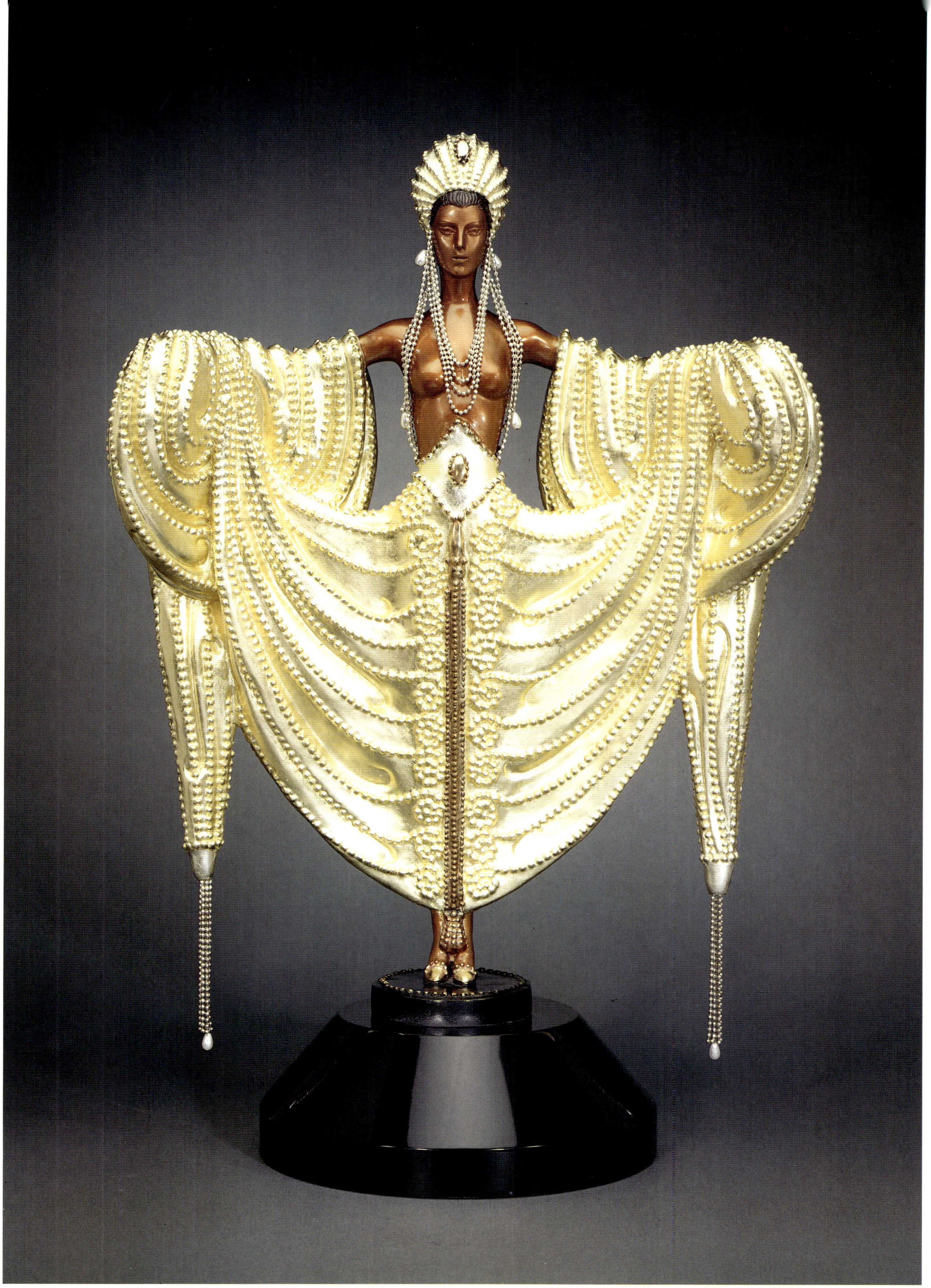

Radiance
Rayonnement
Fulgore
Erleuchtung

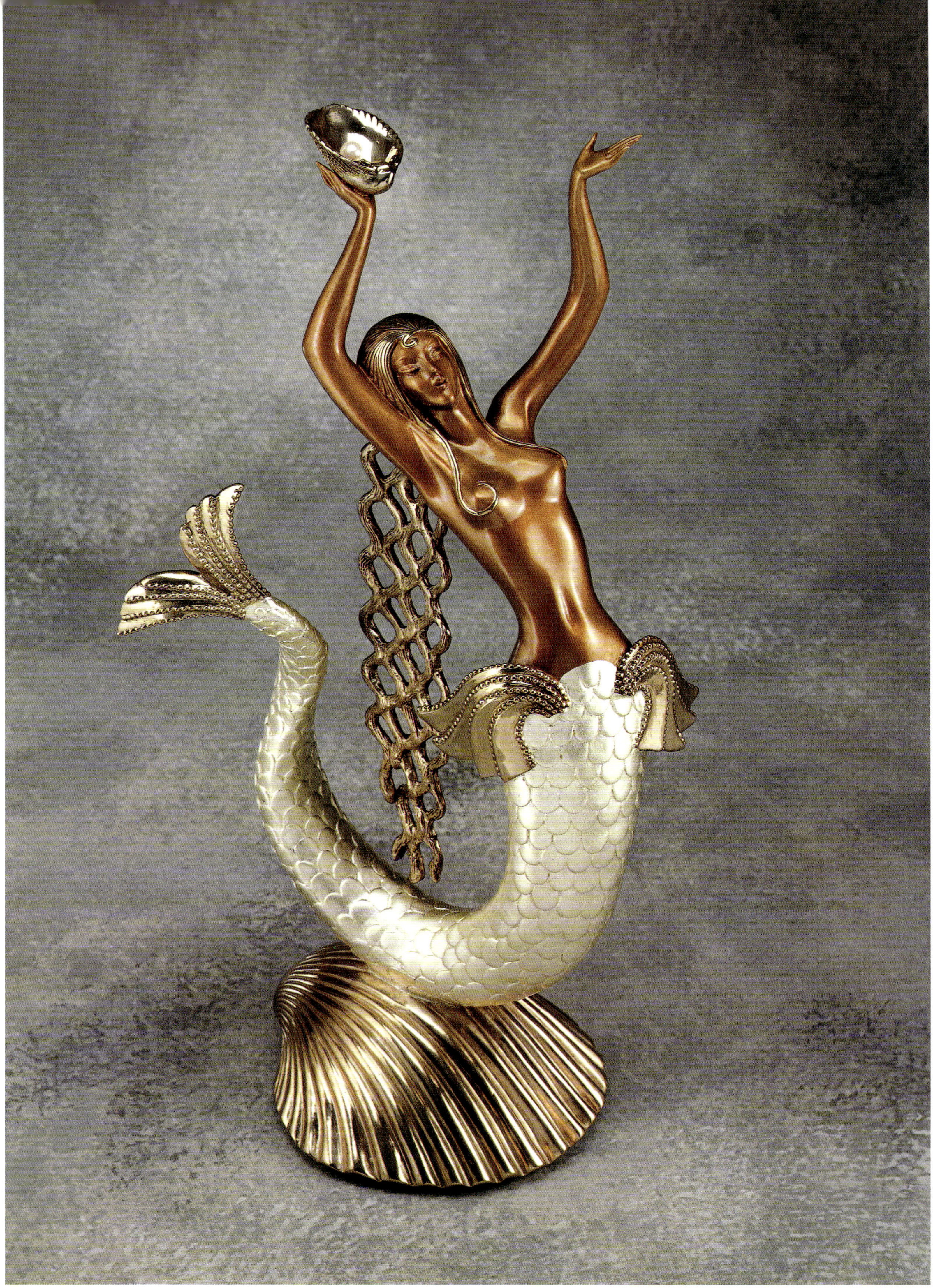

Mermaid
Sirène
Sirena
Wassernixe

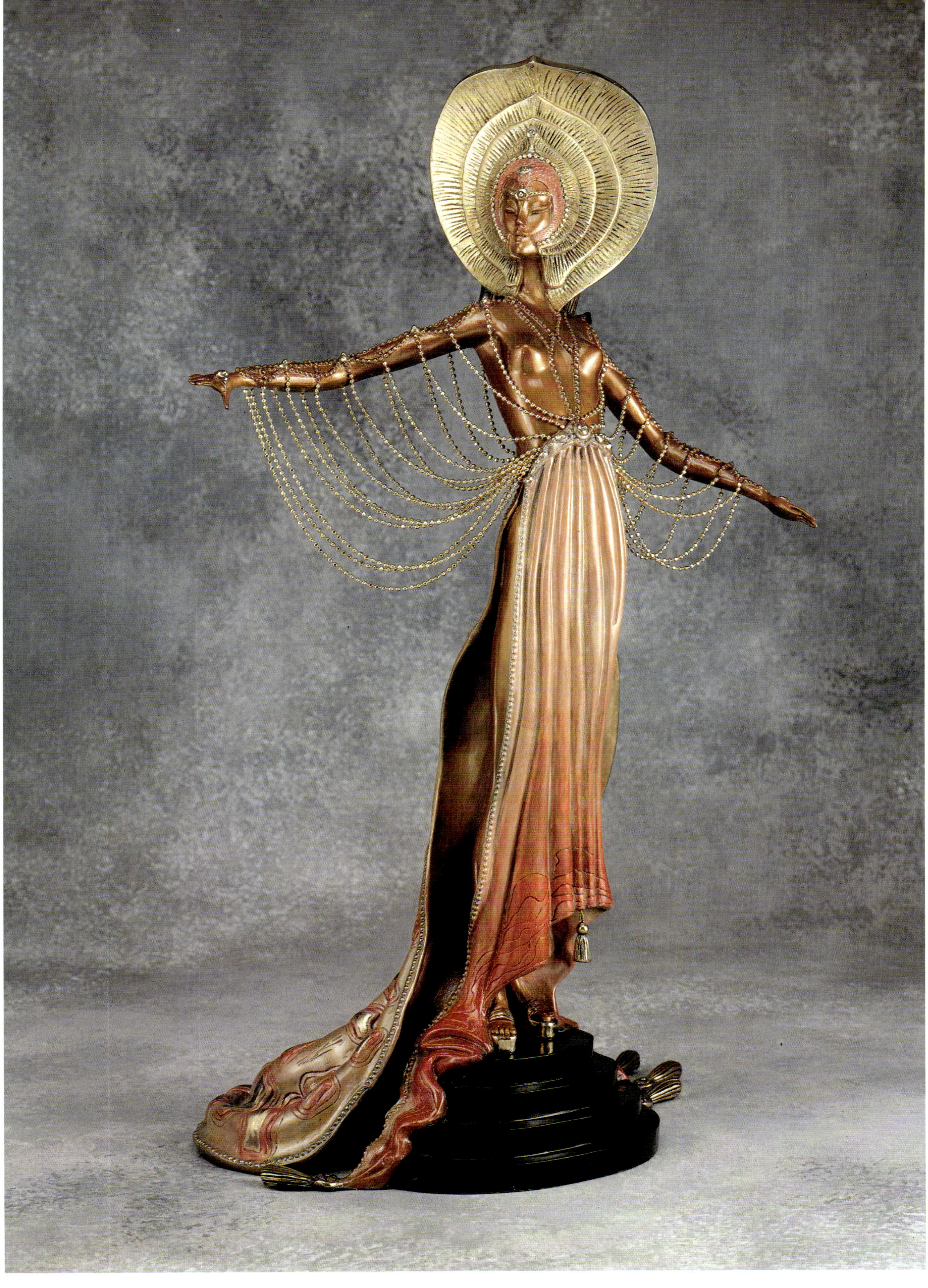

L'Orientale
L'Orientale
L'orientale
Die Orientalin

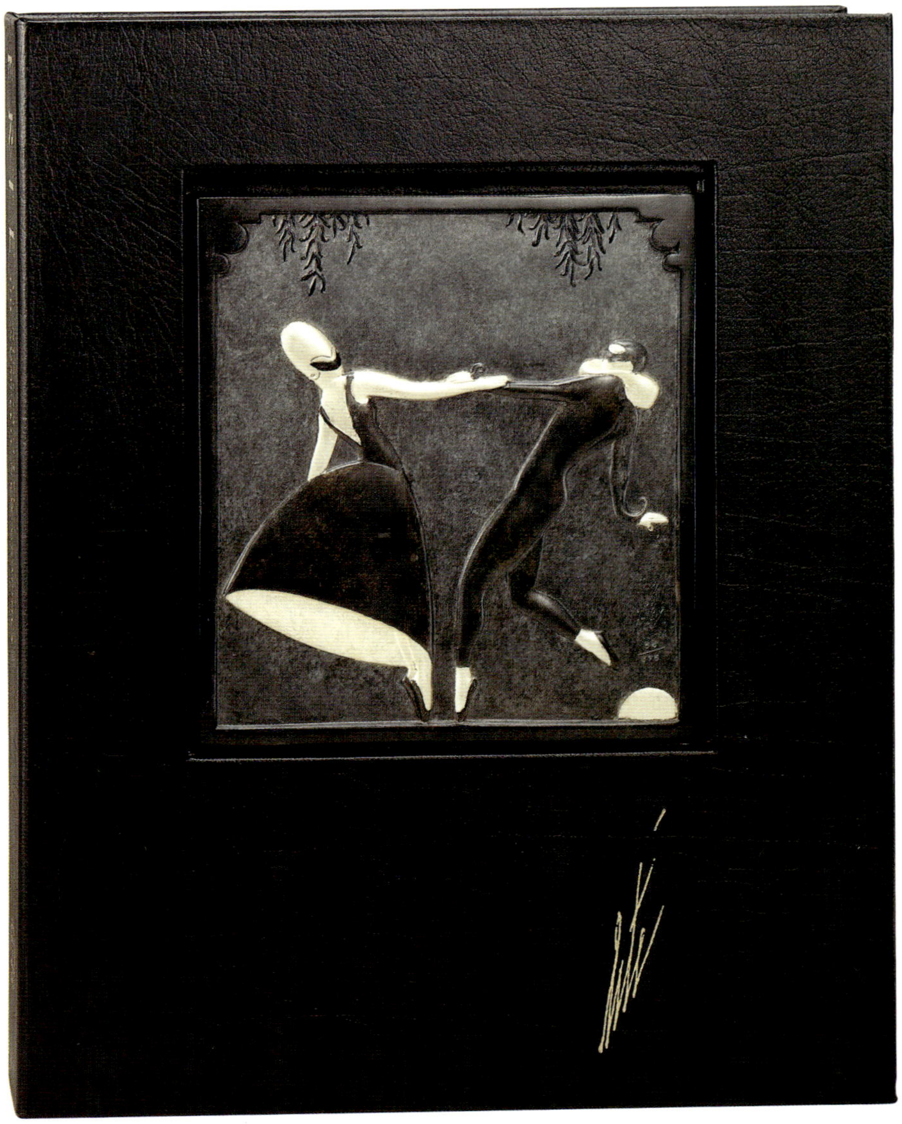

Pas de deux
Pas de deux
Pas de deux
Pas de deux

Rigoletto
Rigoletto
Rigoletto
Rigoletto

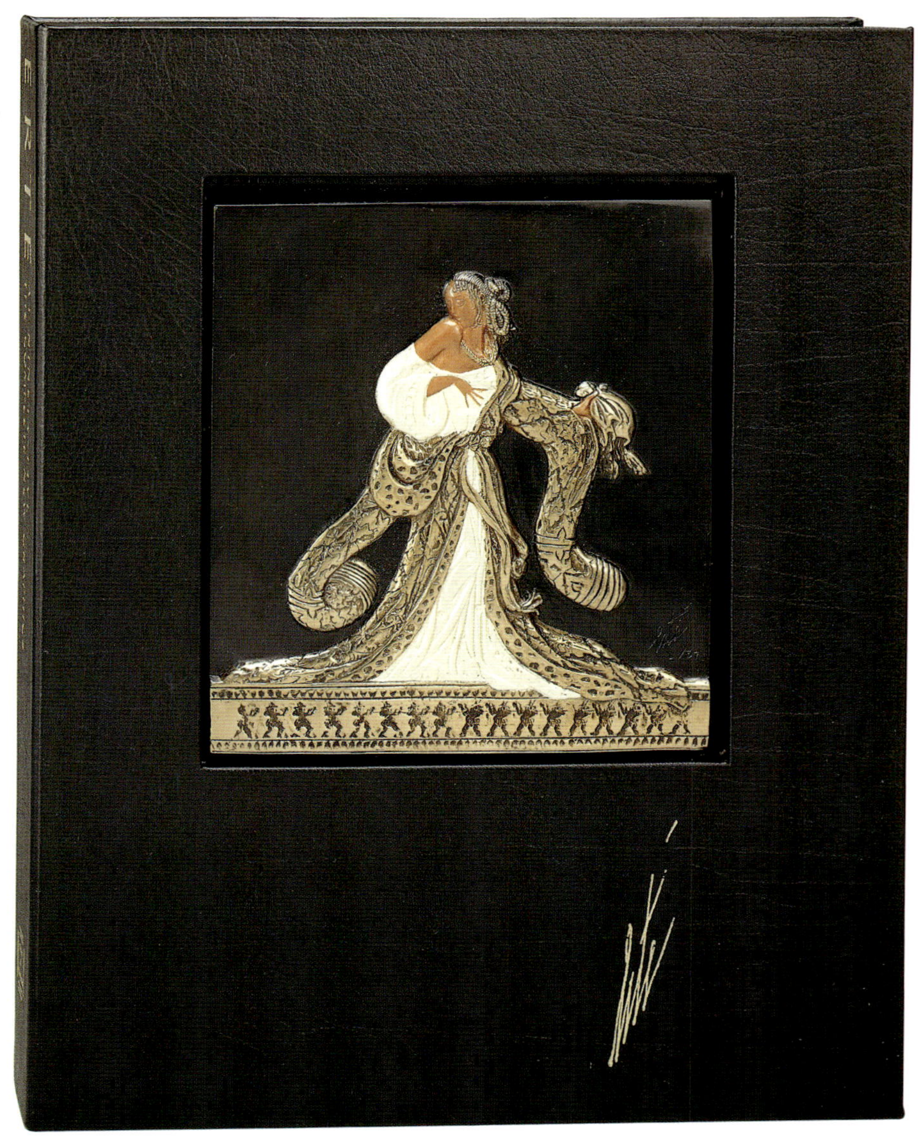

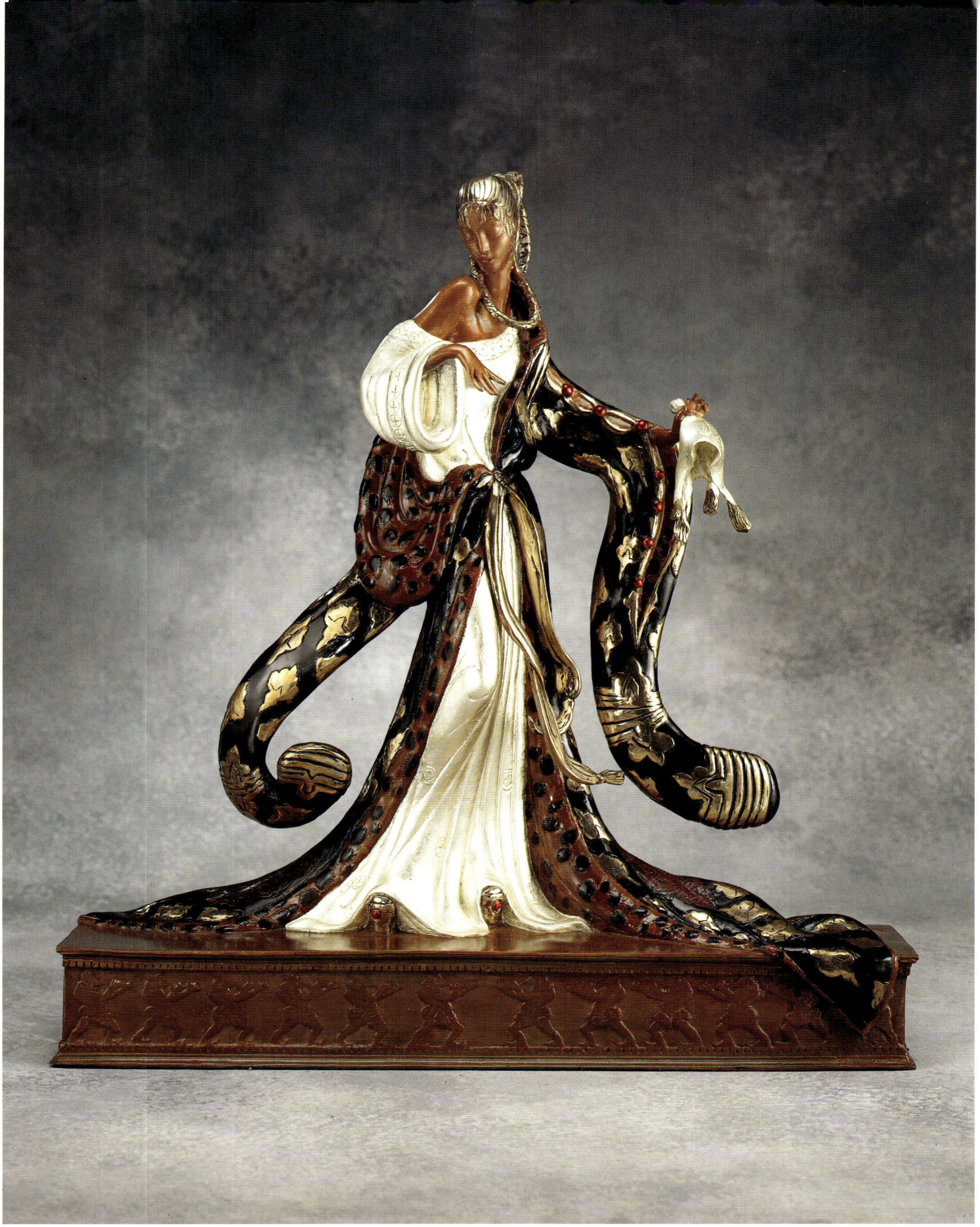

Rigoletto
Rigoletto
Rigoletto
Rigoletto

Astra
Astra
Astra
Astra

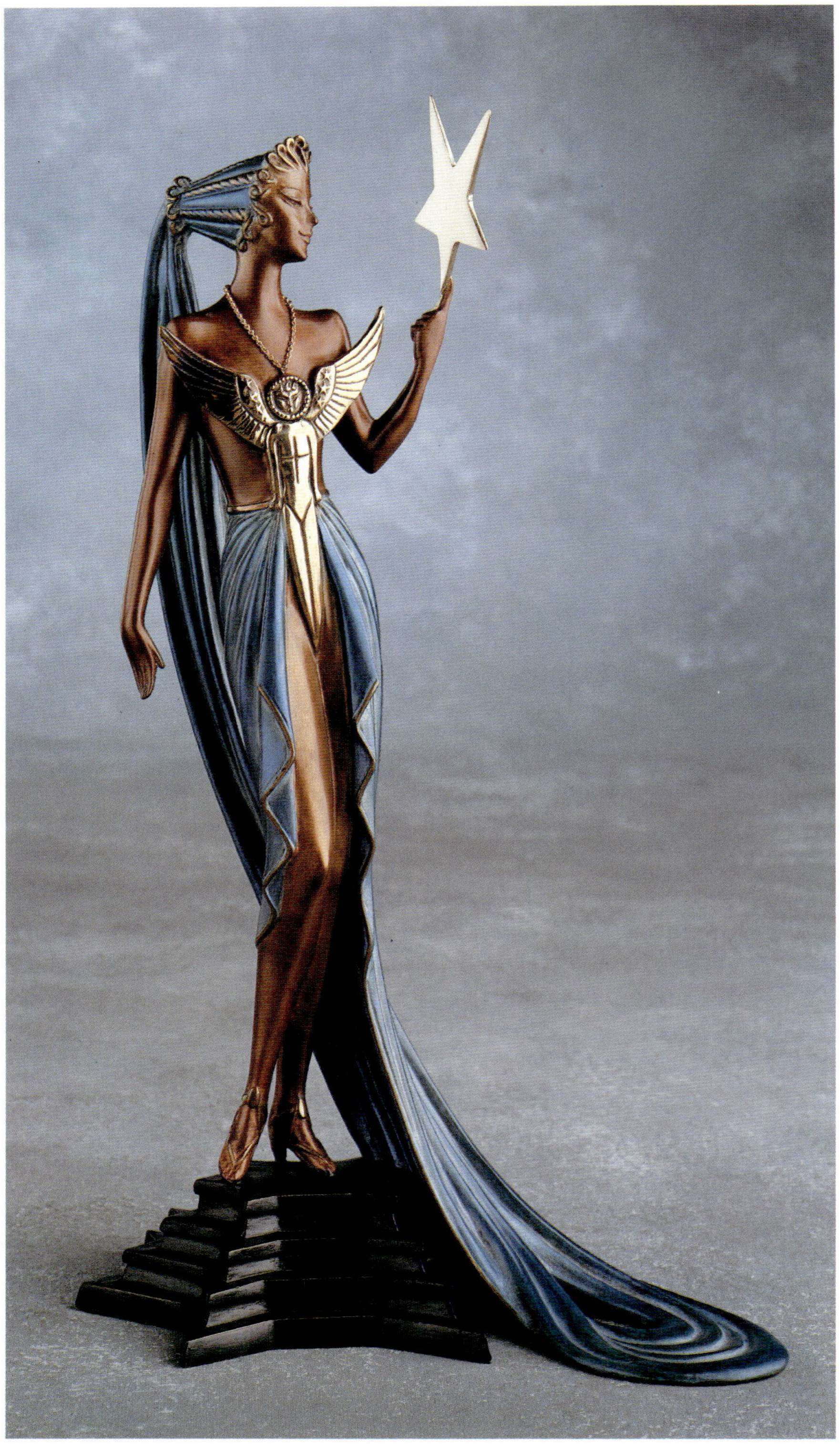

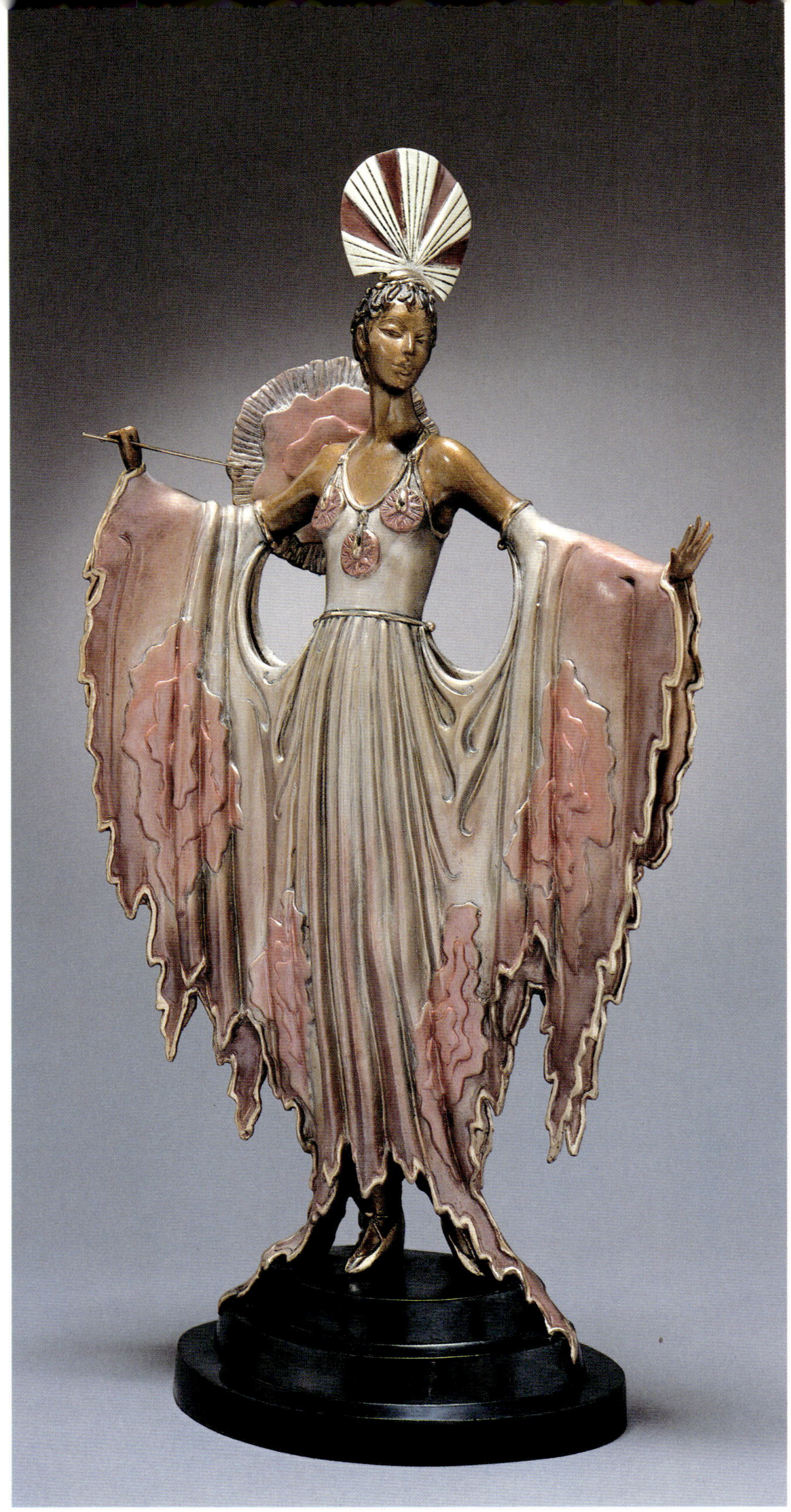

Twilight
Crépuscule
Crepuscolo
Zwielicht

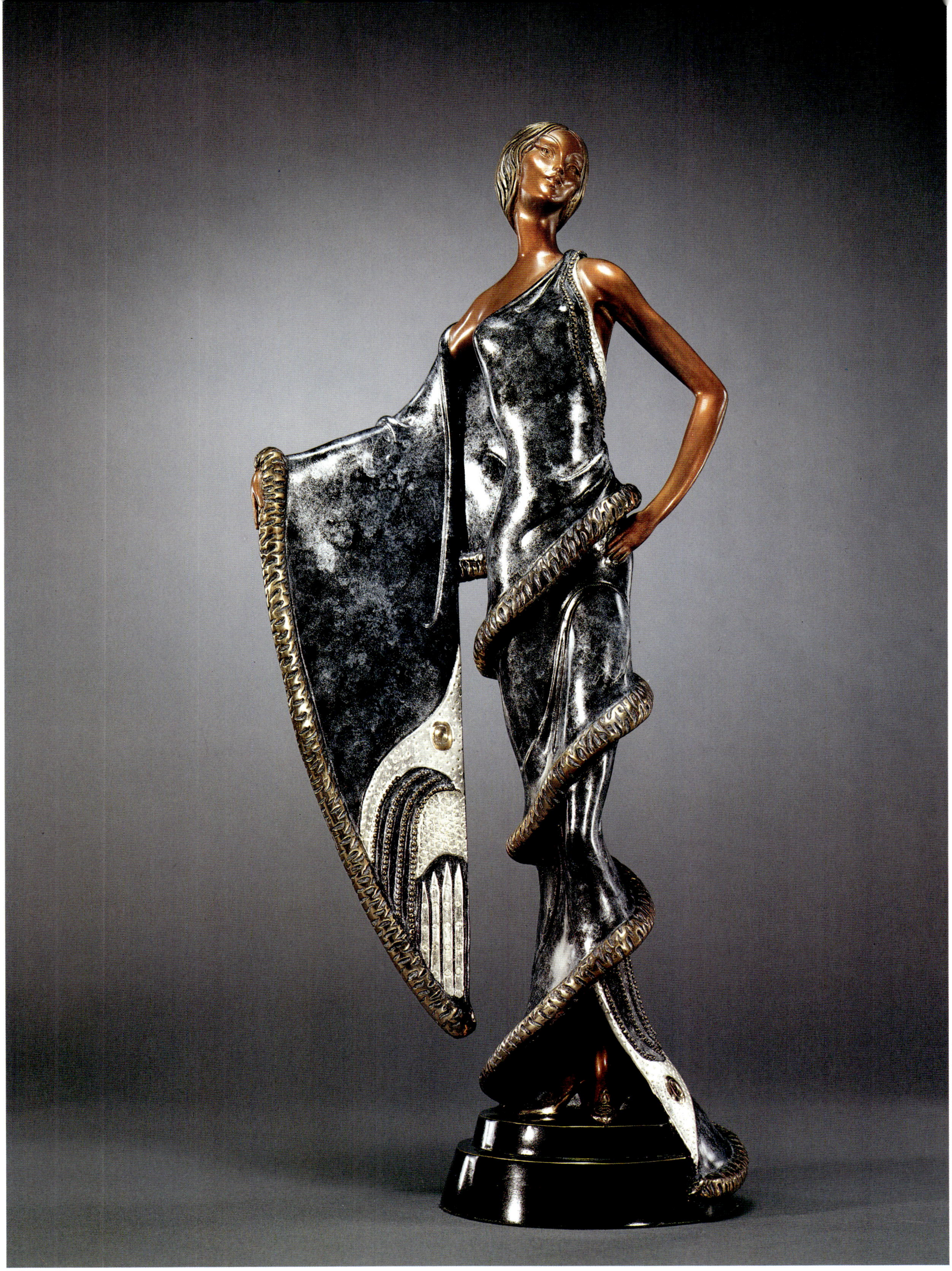

Chinchilla
Chinchilla
Cincilla
Chinchilla

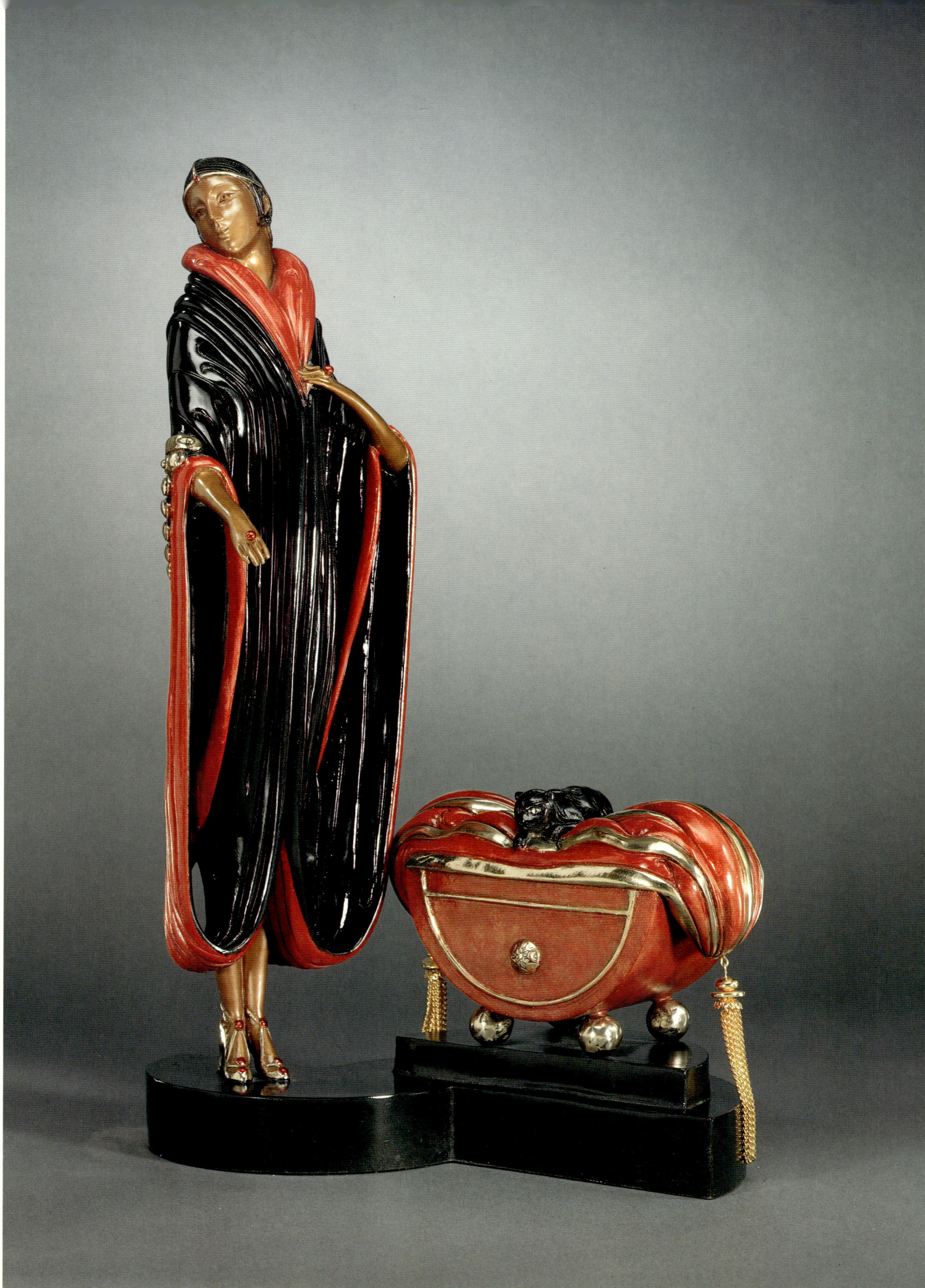

Caramelle
Caramelle
Caramelle
Caramelle

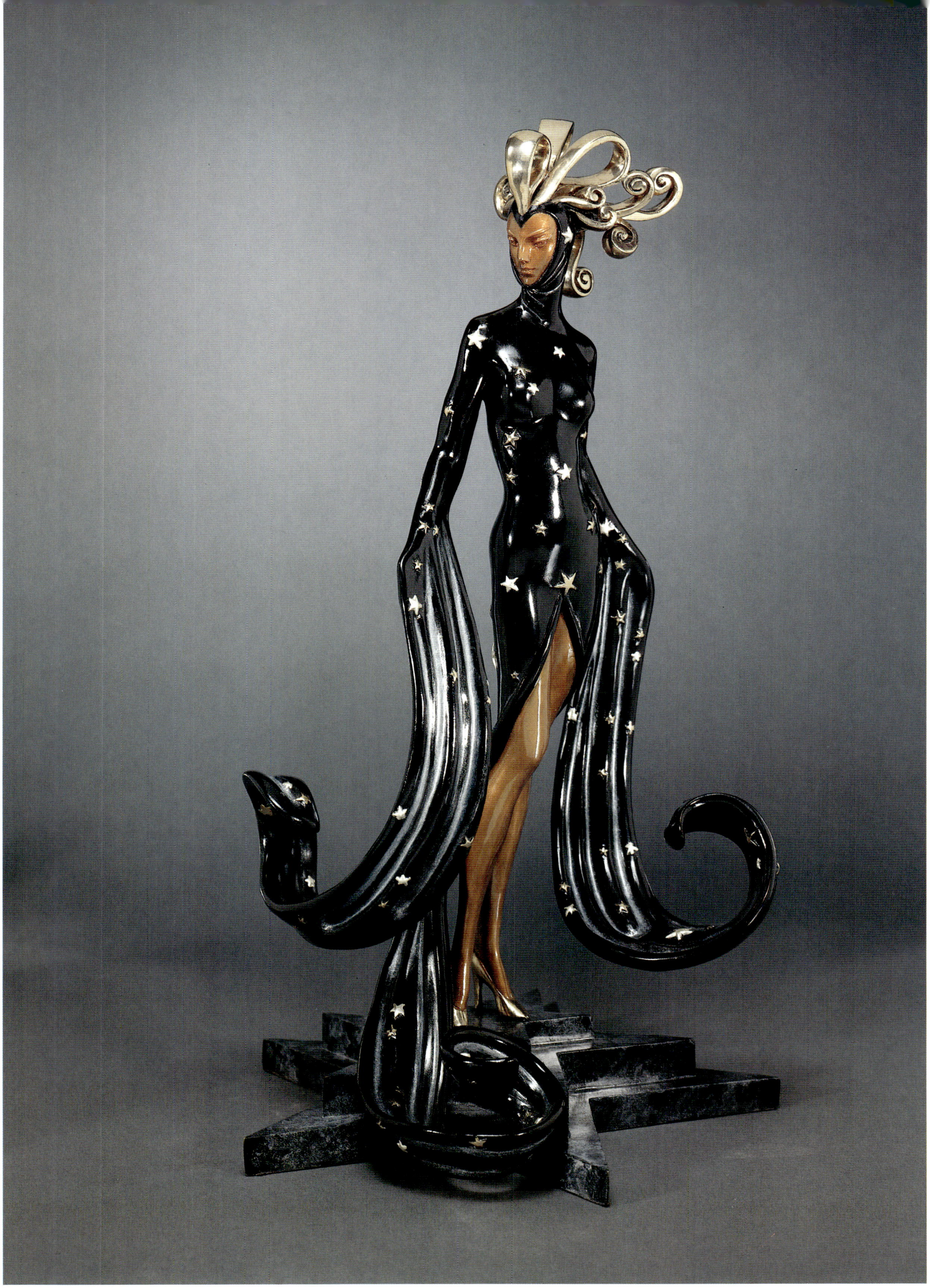

Bal Tabarin
Bal Tabarin
Bal Tabarin
Bal Tabarin

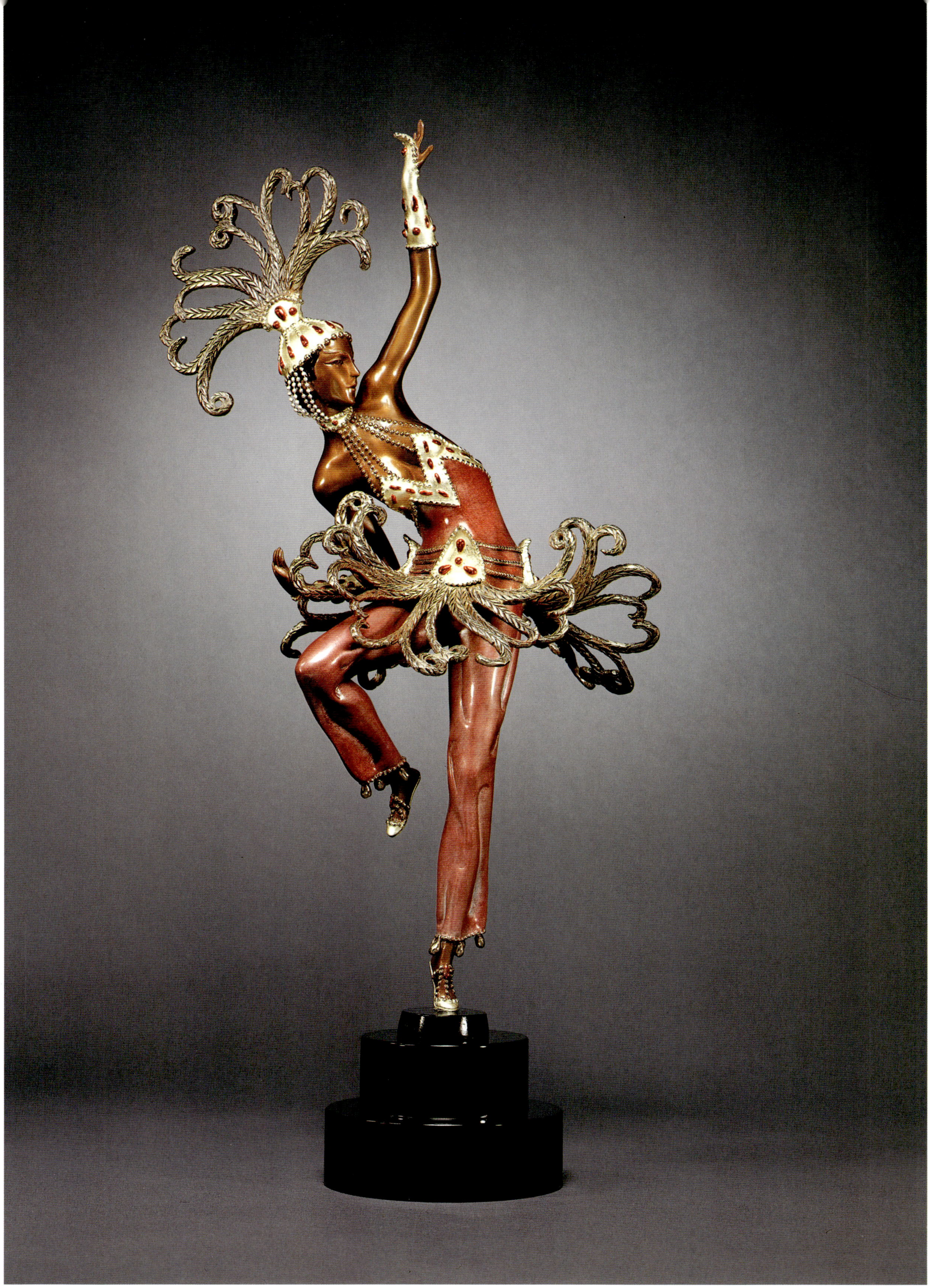

Fire Dancer
Danseur de feu
Danza del fuoco
Feuertänzer

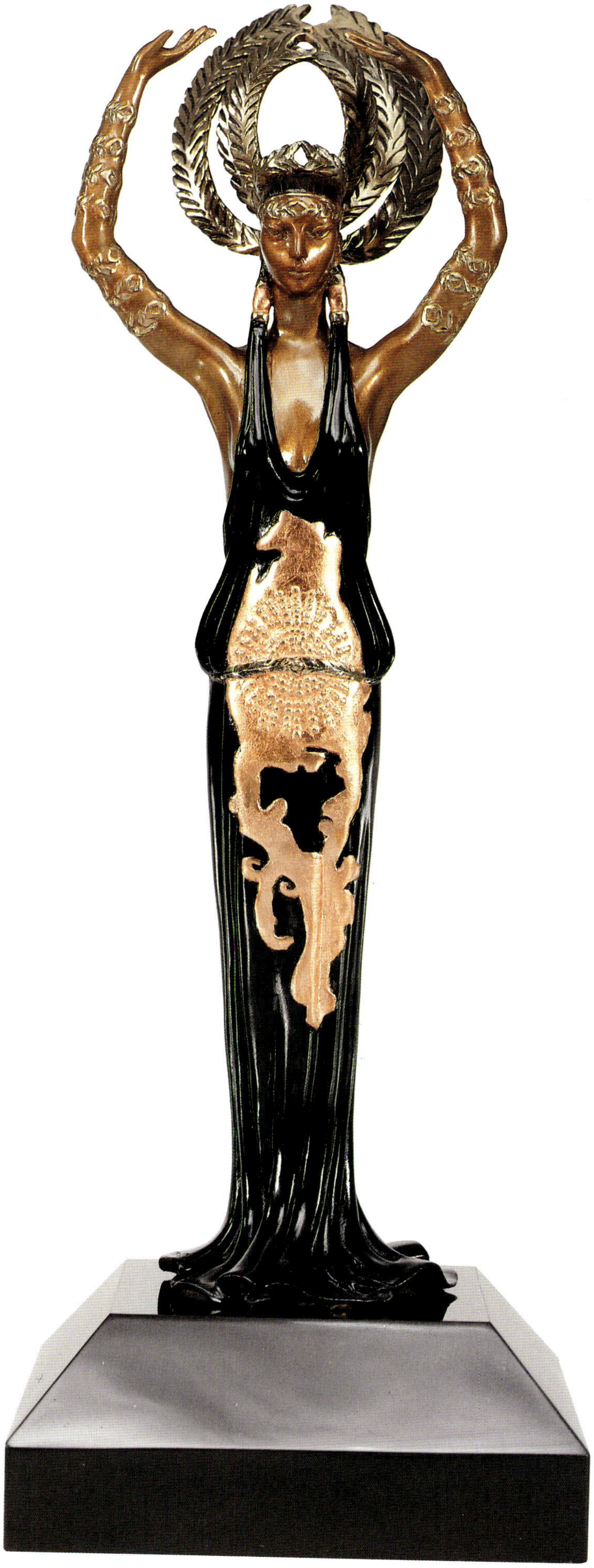

Triumph
Triomphe
Trionfo
Triumph

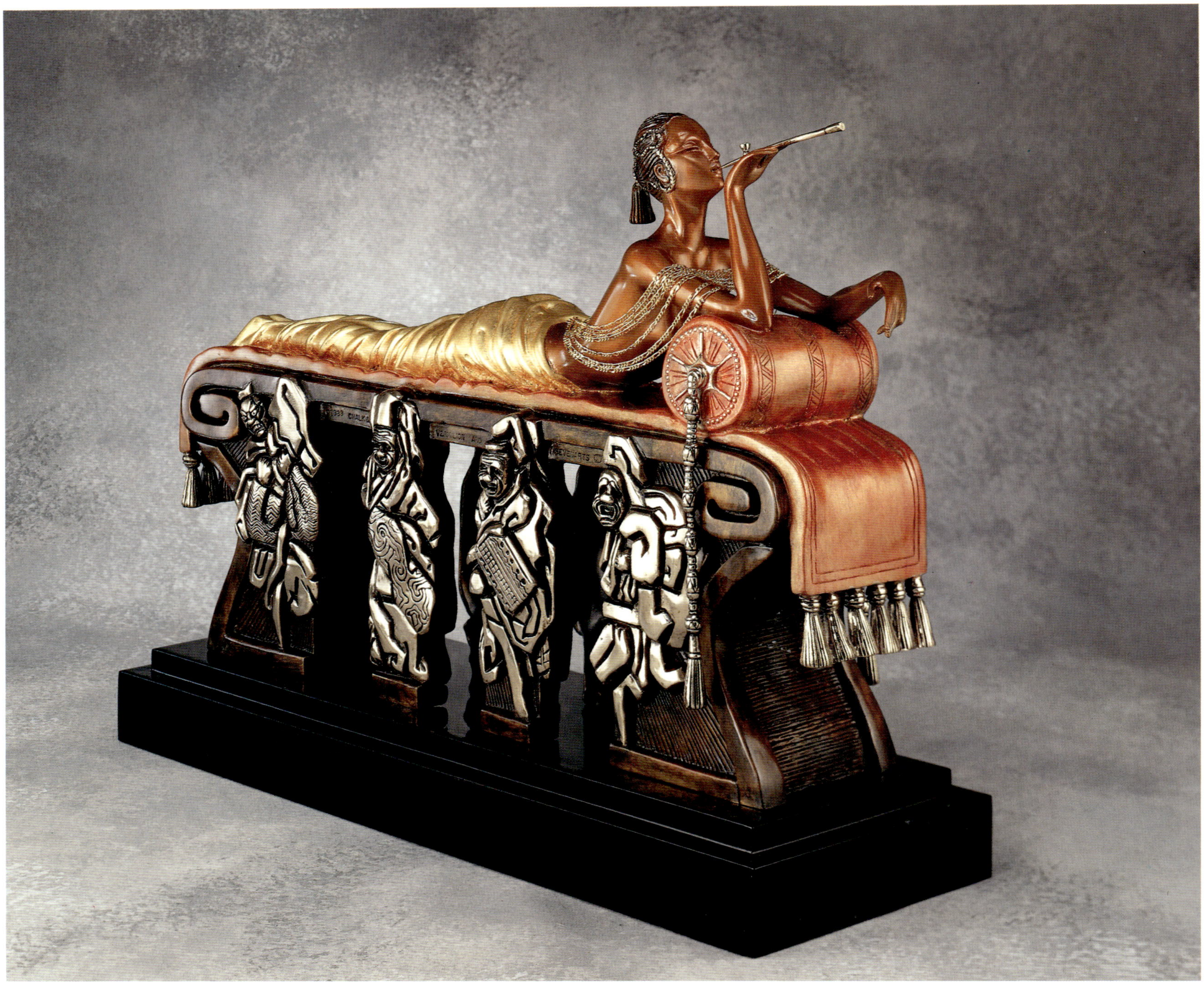

Daydreams
Rêveries
Sogni ad occhi aperti
Tagträume

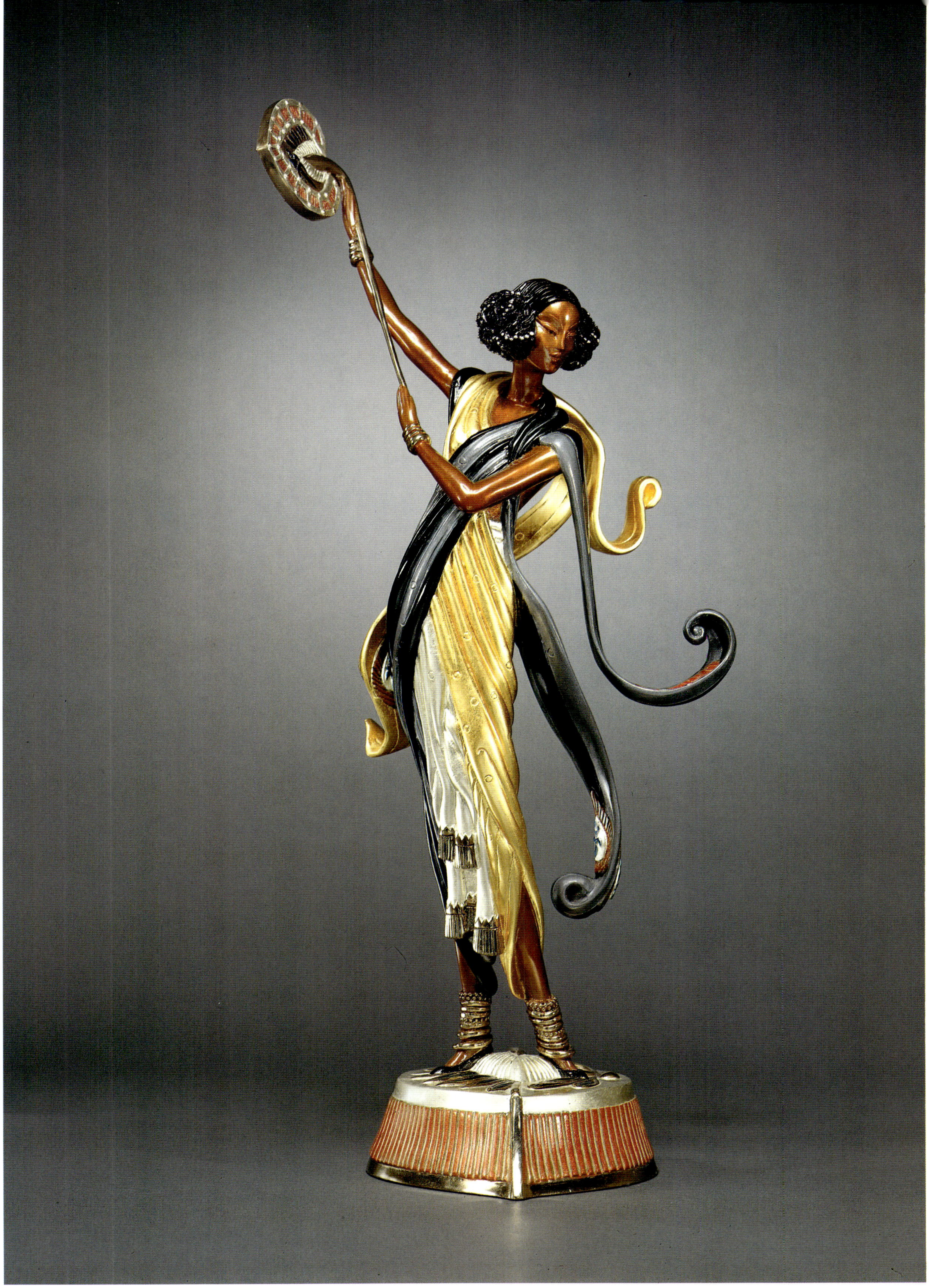

Arabian Nights
Les Mille et Une Nuits
Notti Arabe
Arabische Nächte

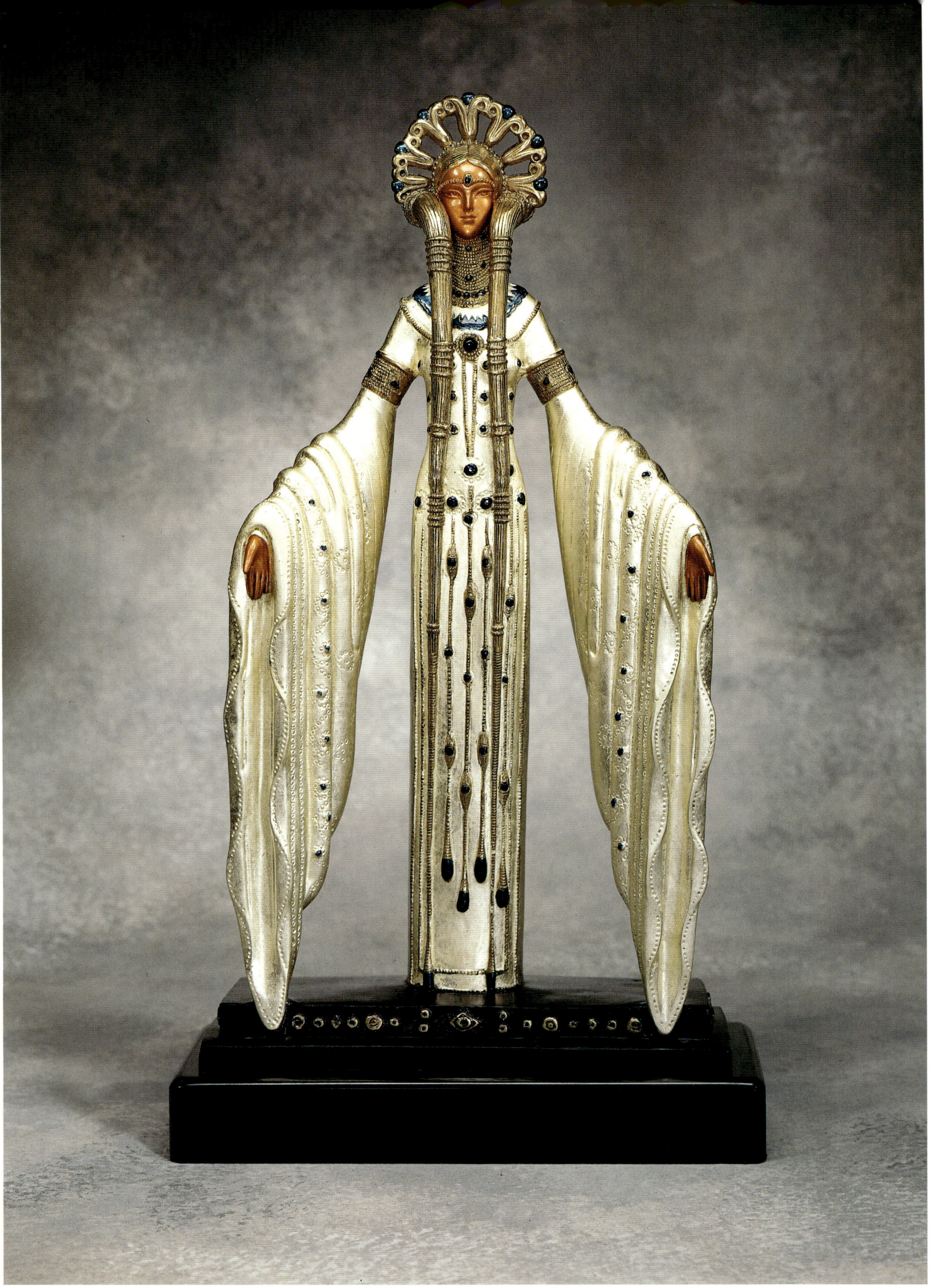

Byzantine
Byzantin
Bizantina
Byzantinerin

Femme de luxe
Femme de luxe
Femme de luxe
Luxusfrau

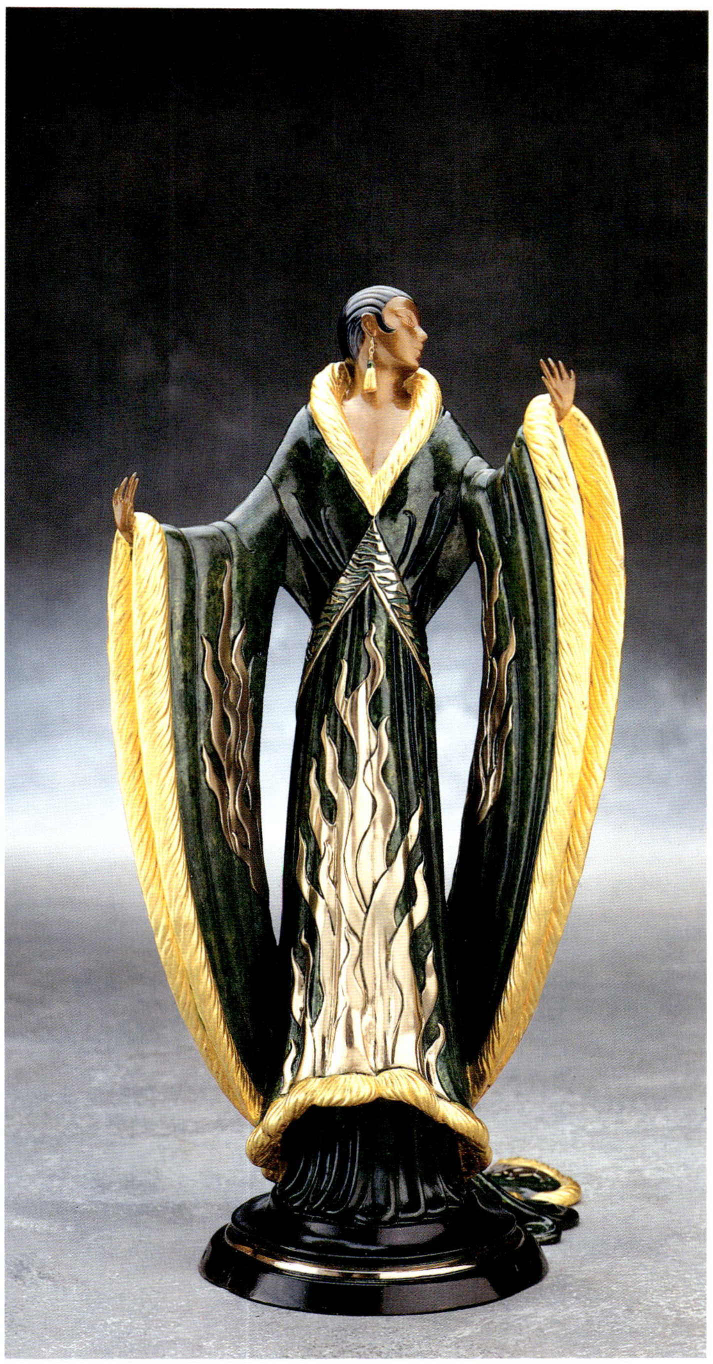

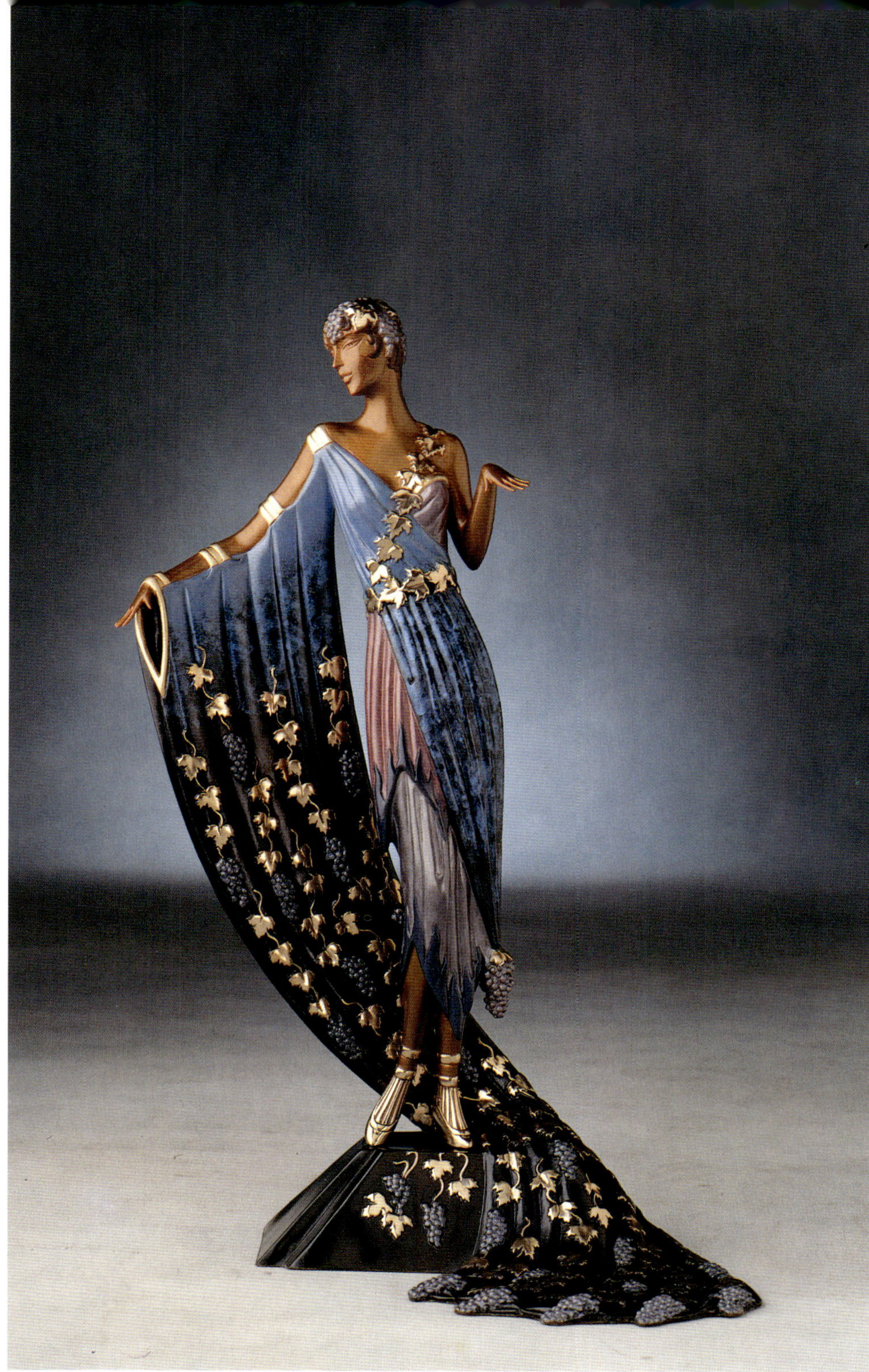

L'Amour du vin
L'Amour du vin
L'Amore del vino
Weinliebhaber

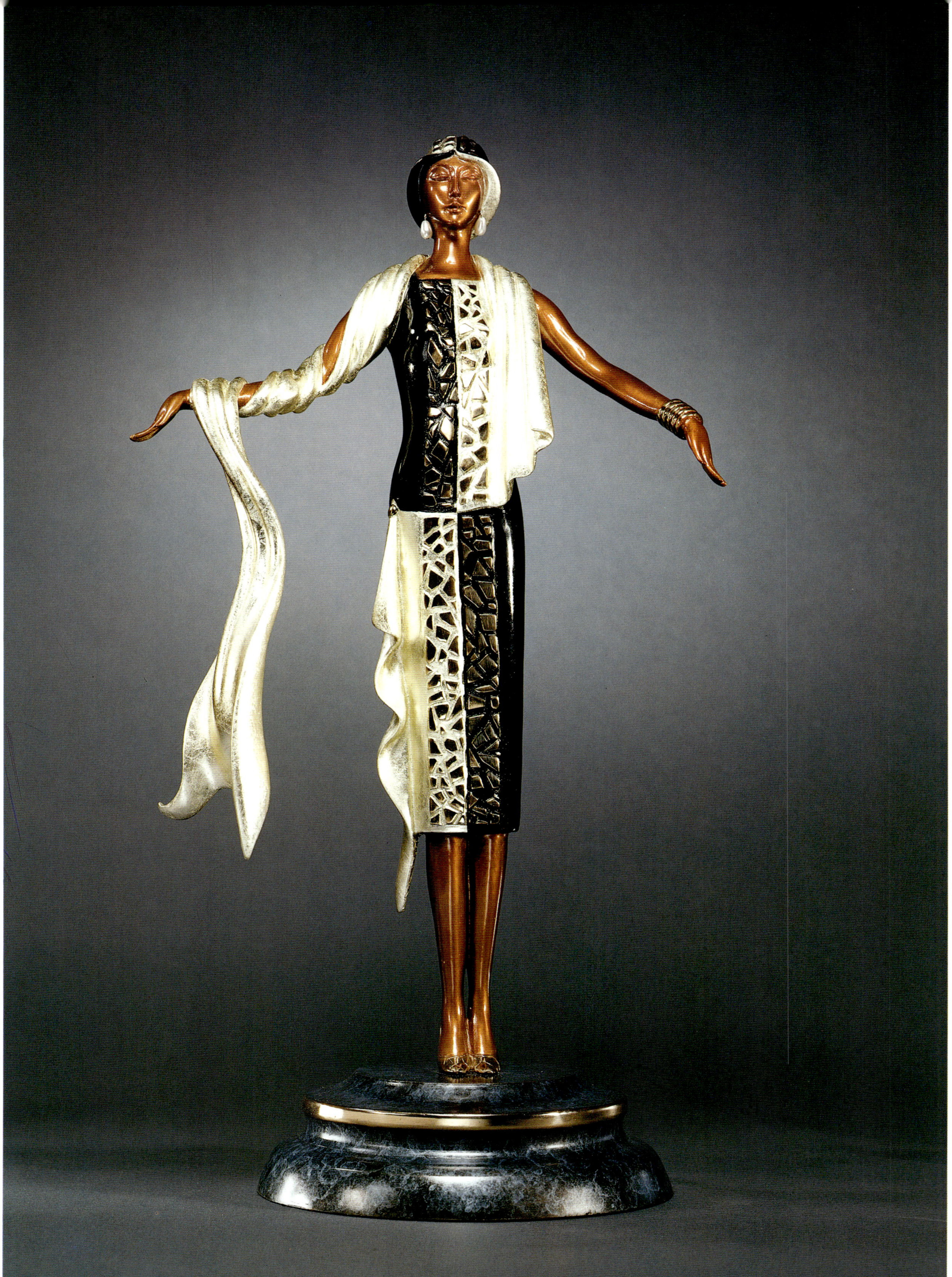

On the Avenue
Sur l'Avenue
Lungo il viale
Auf der Avenue

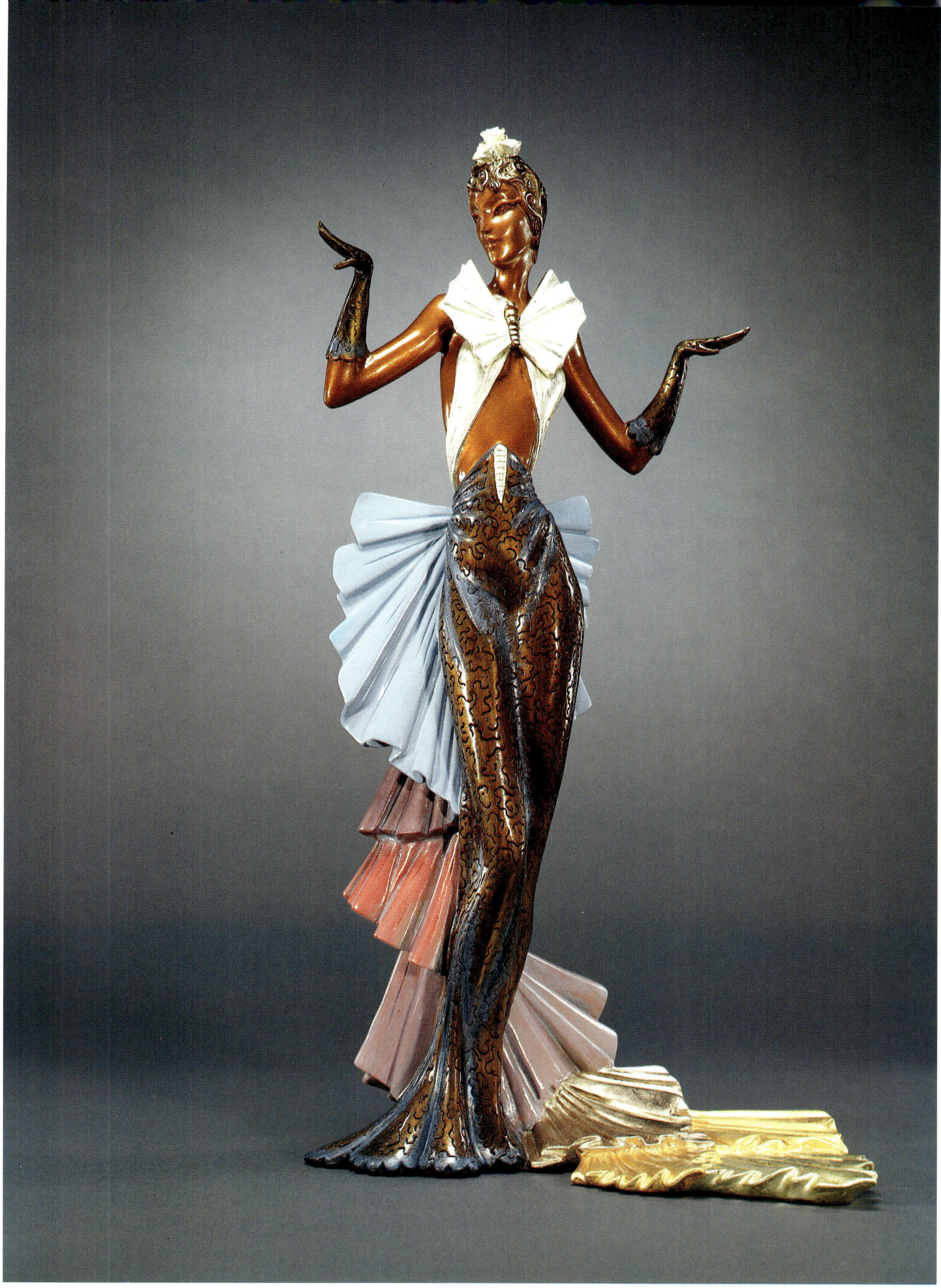

Copacabana
Copacabana
Copacabana
Copacabana

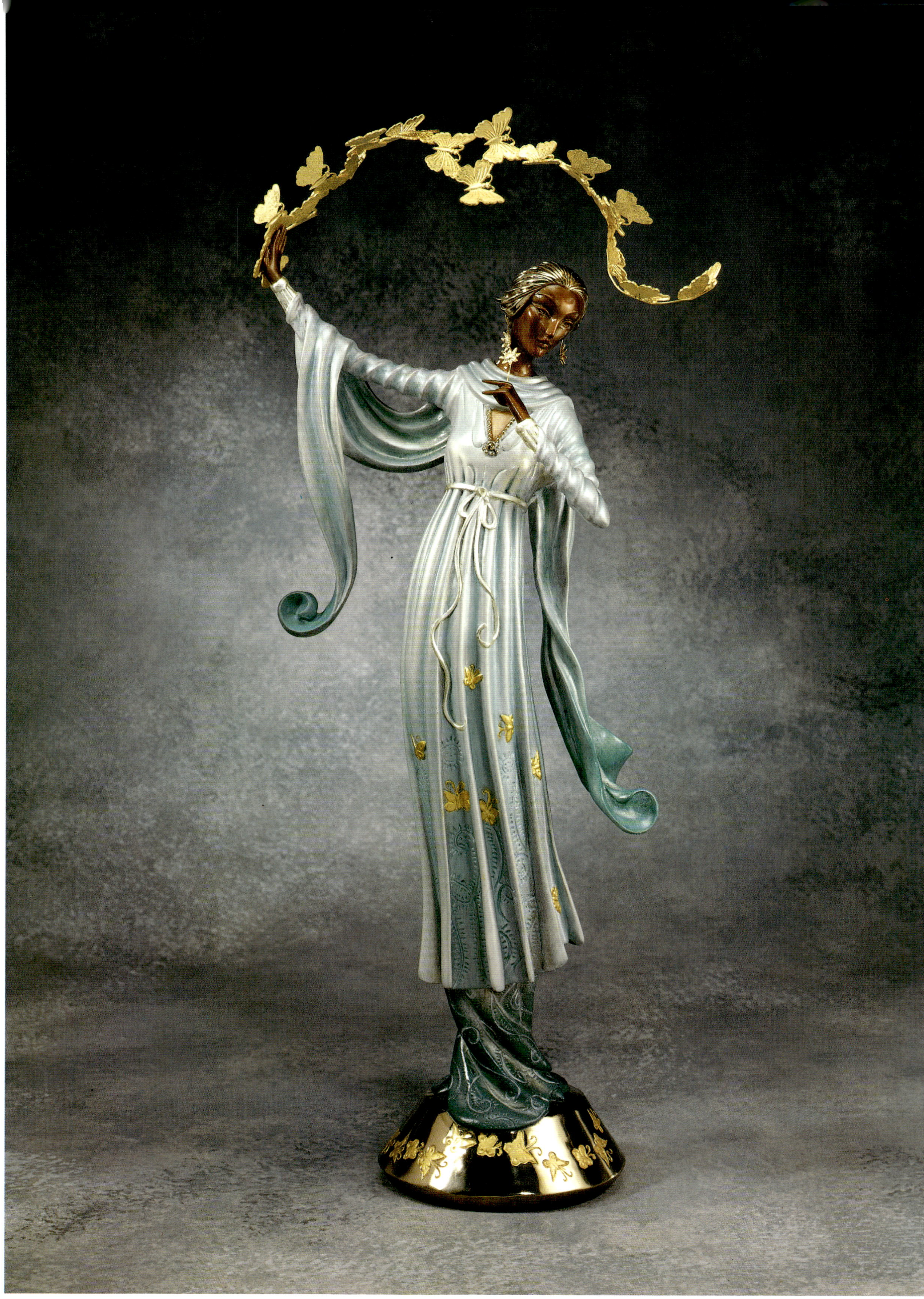

Joie de vivre
Joie de vivre
Gioia di vivere
Lebensfreude

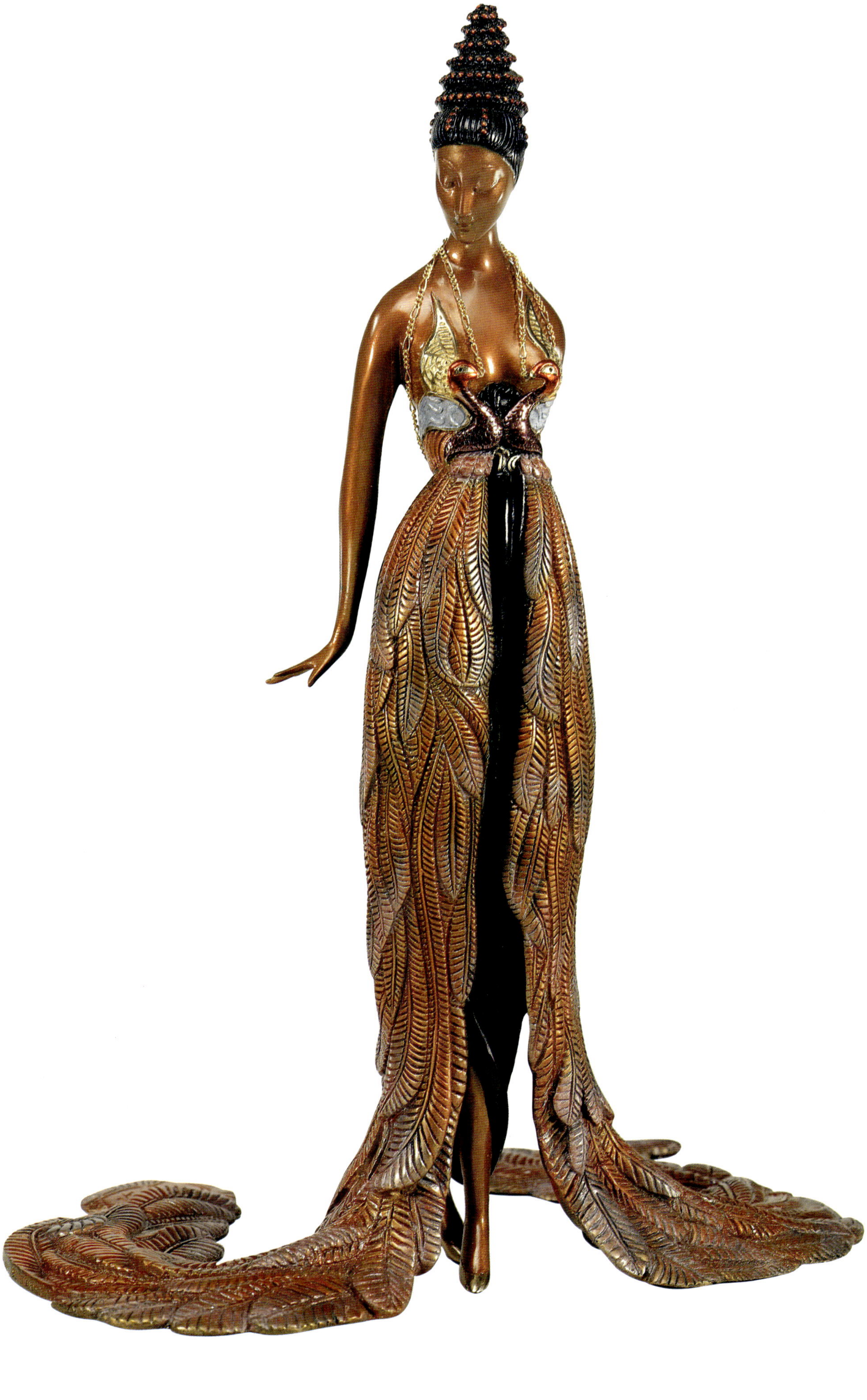

Feather Gown
Robe de plume
Abito di piume
Federkleid

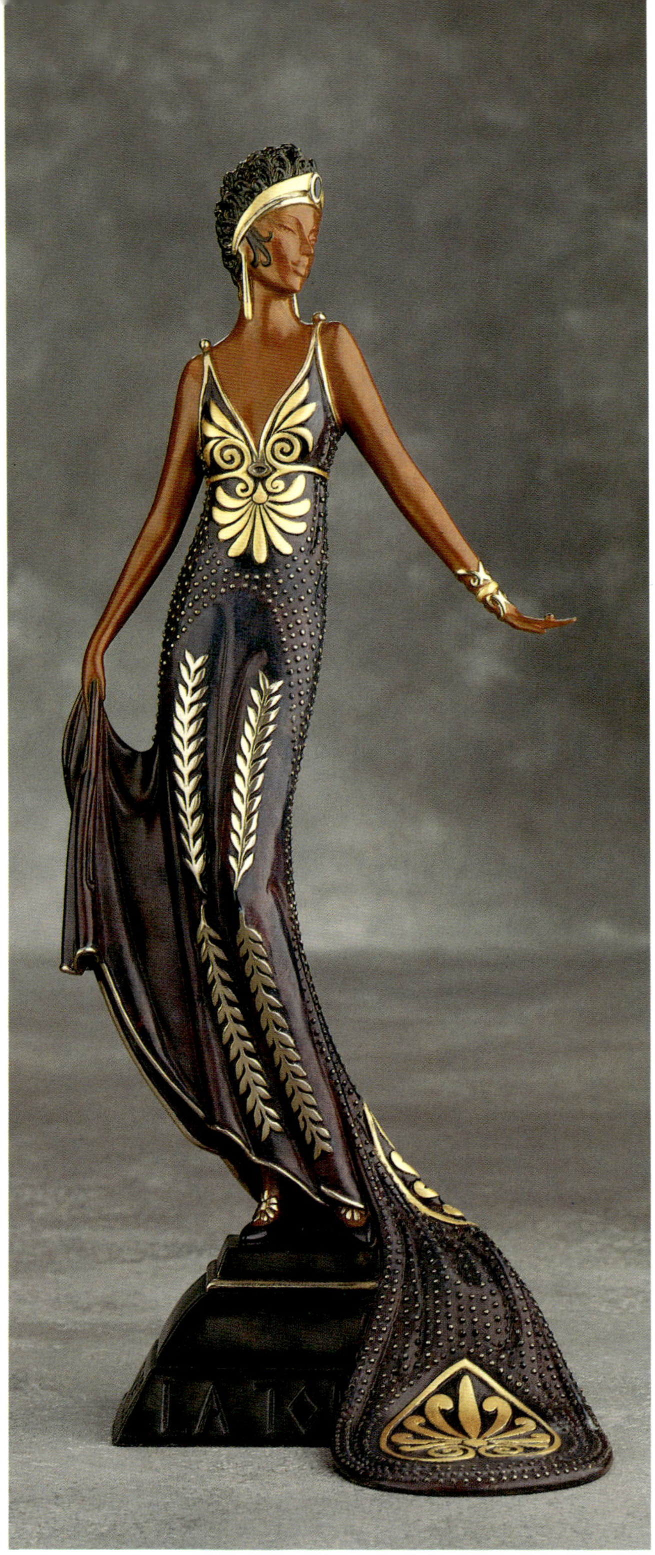

La Tosca
La Tosca
La Tosca
Tosca

Dreambirds
Oiseaux de rêves
Uccello dei sogni
Traumvögel

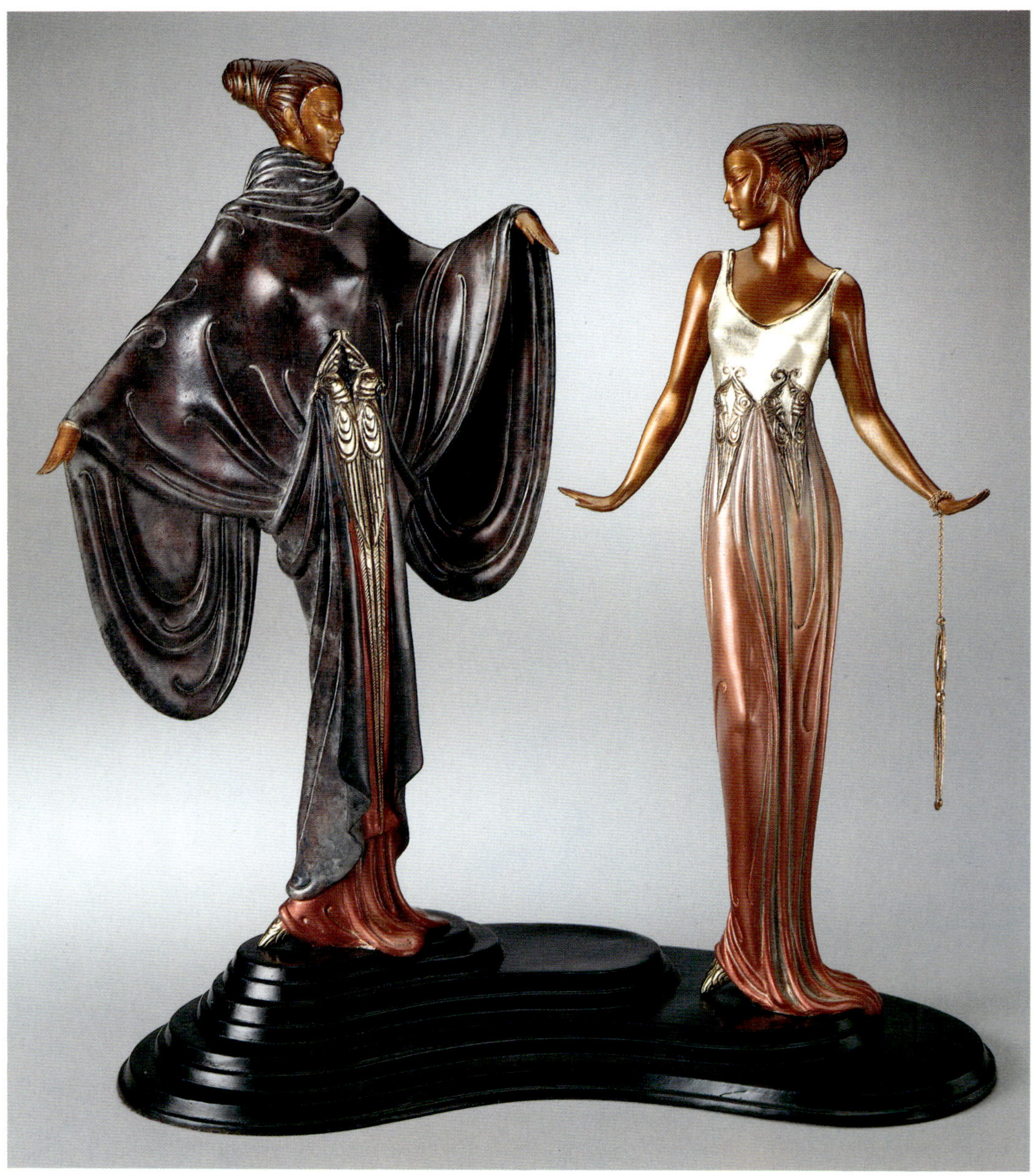

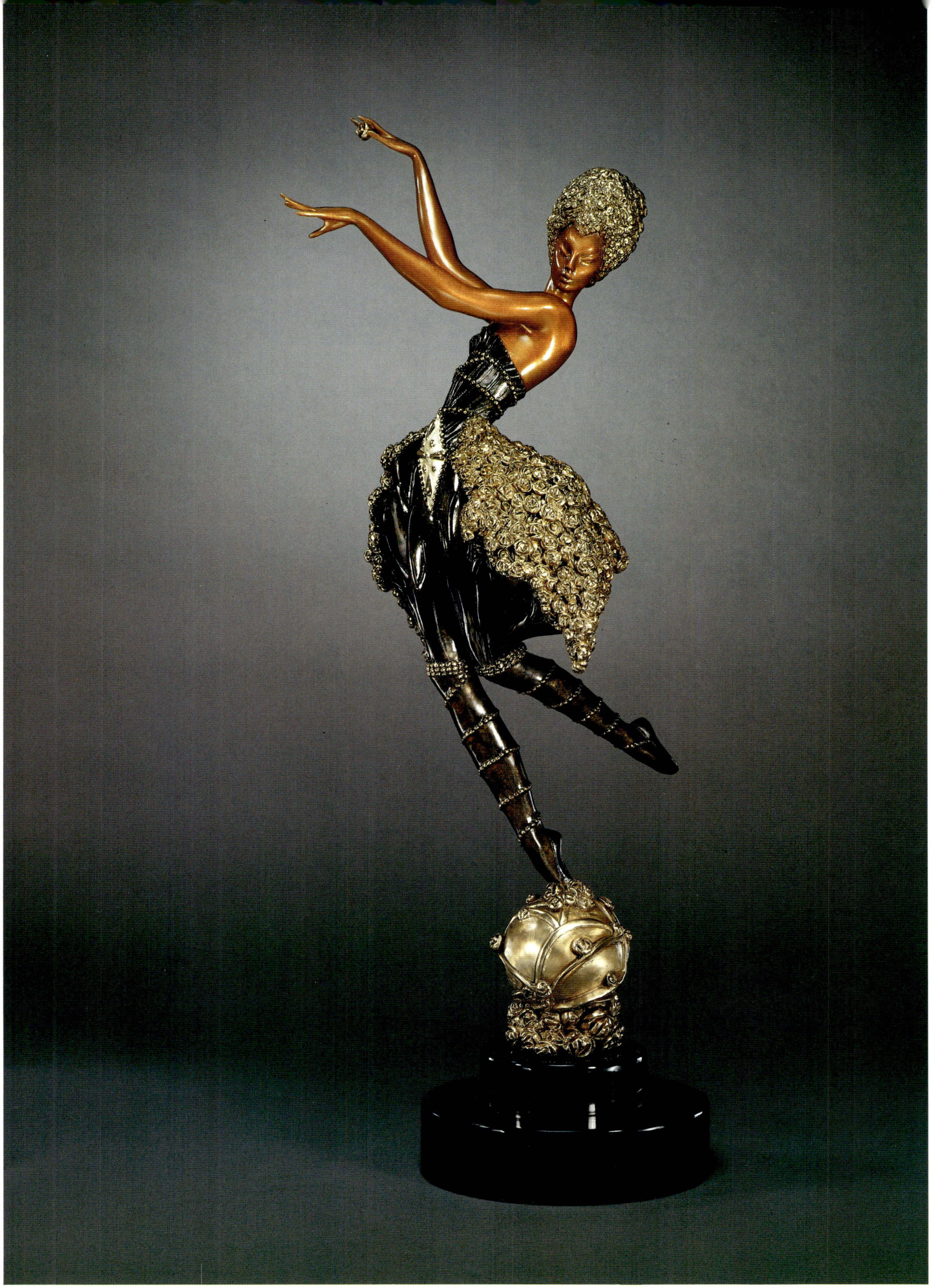

Rose Dancer
Rose dansante
Danzatrice rosa
Rosentänzerin

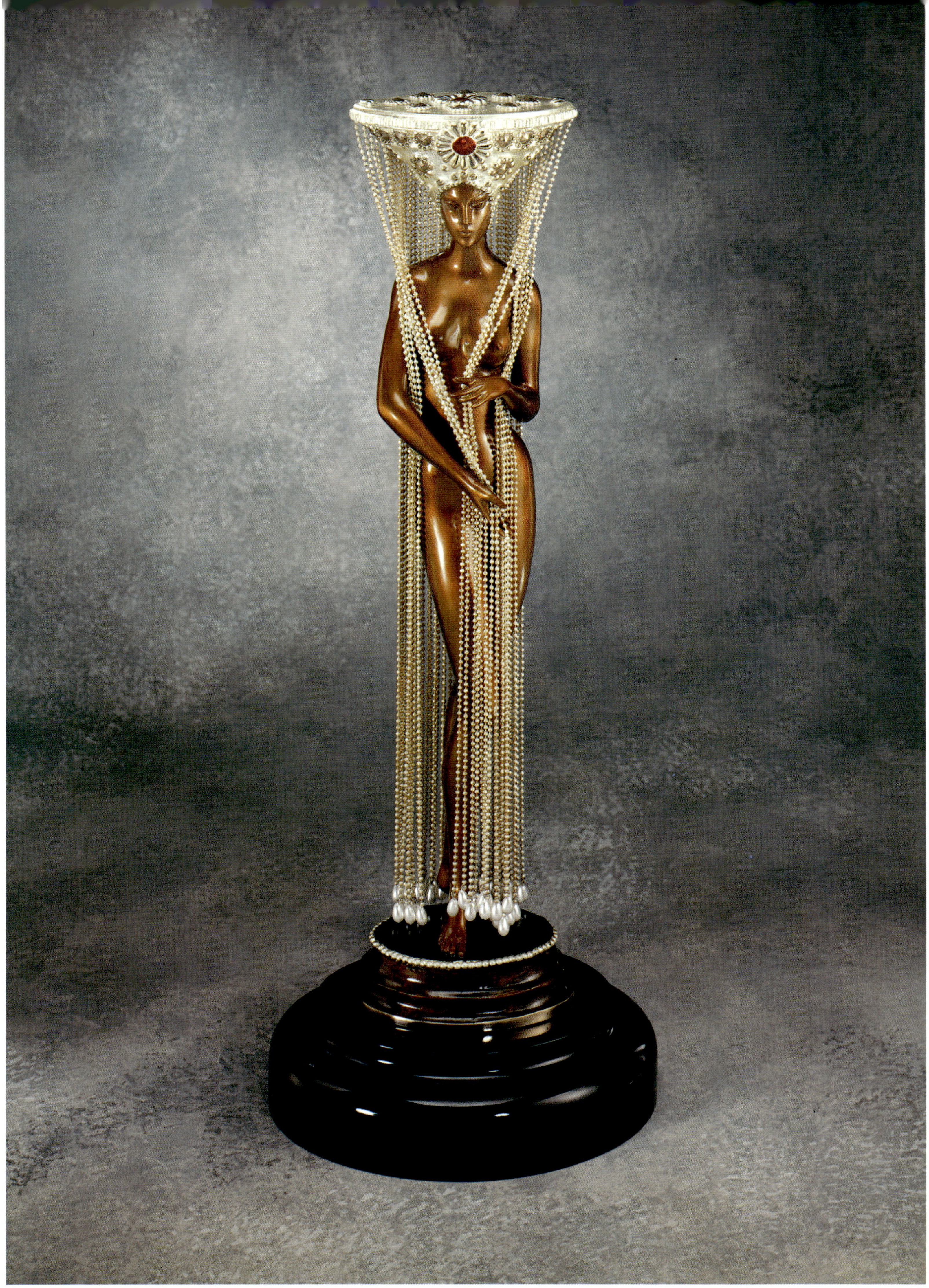

No. 1
Nr. 1
N. 1
Nr. 1

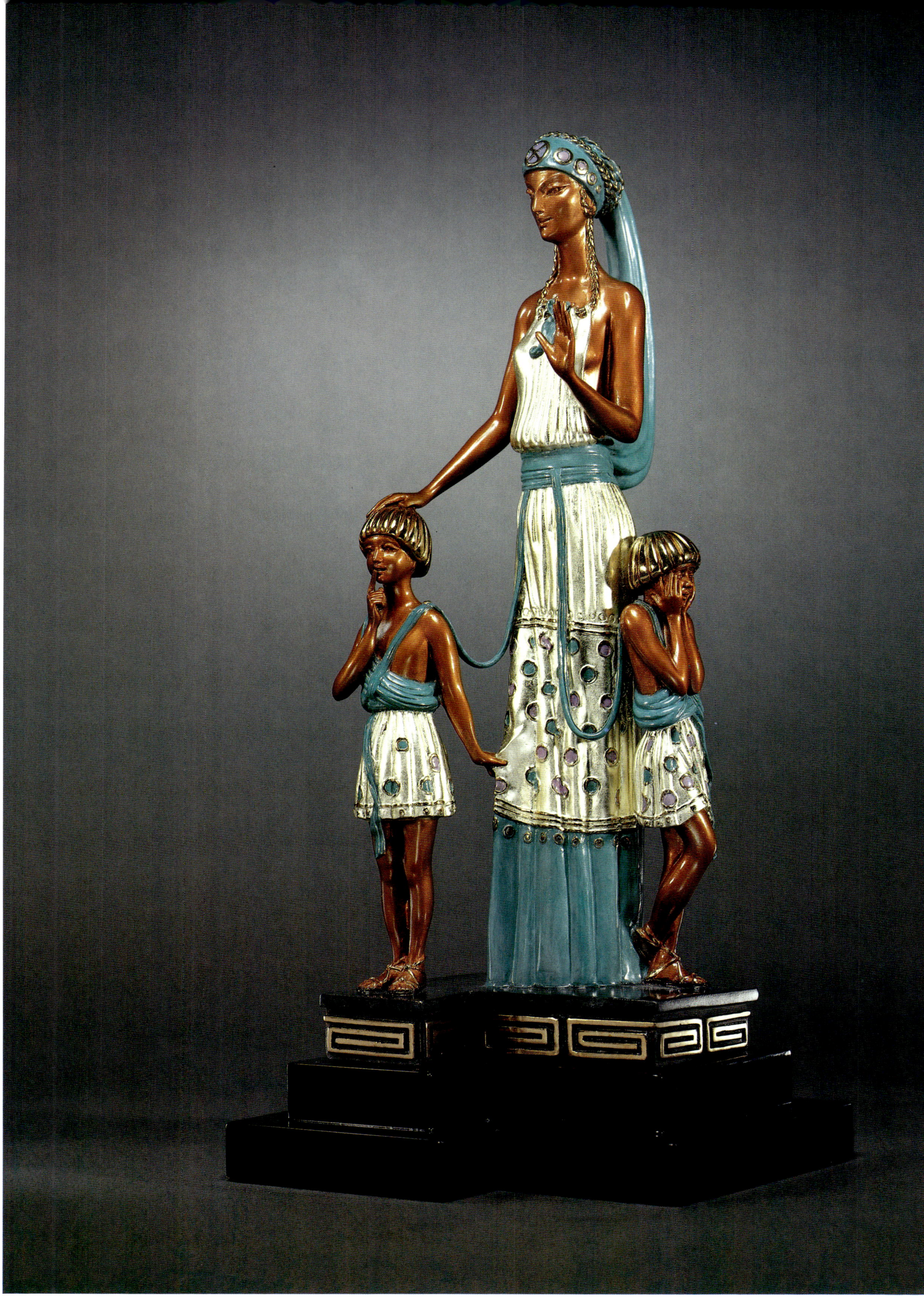

Motherhood
Maternité
Maternitá
Mutterschaft

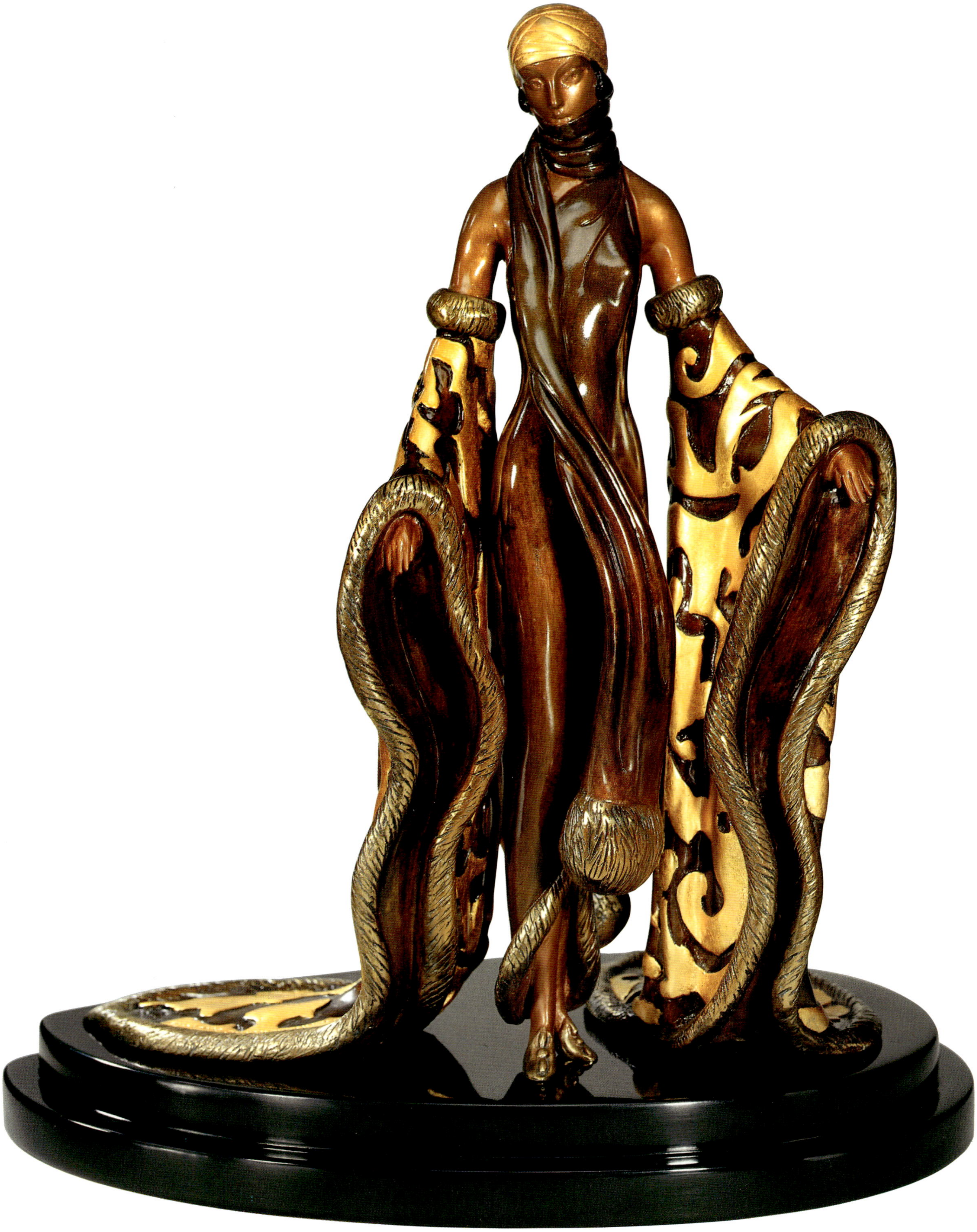

The Mystic
Le Mystique
Il mistico
Der Mystiker

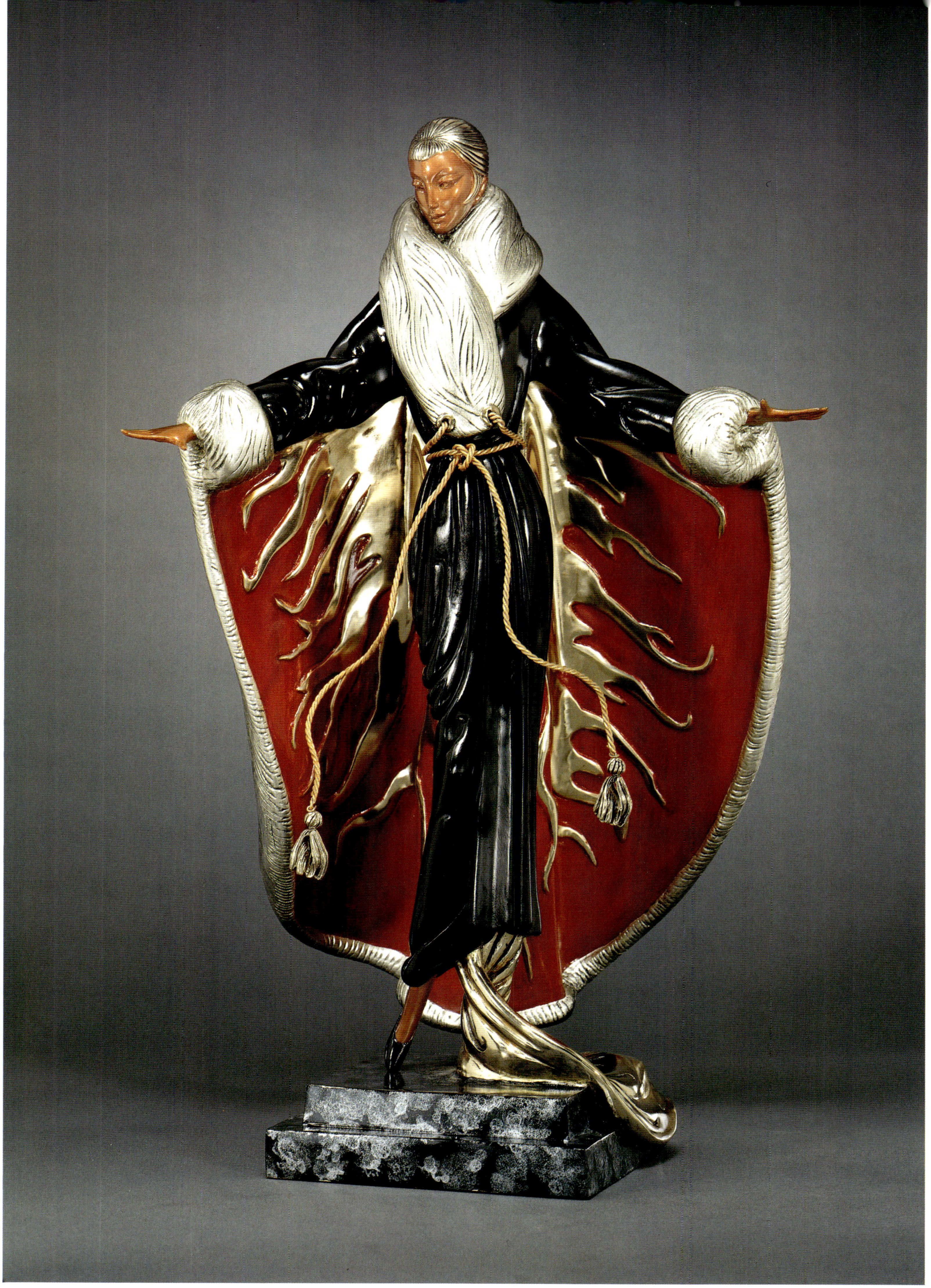

Faubourg St. Honoré
Faubourg St. Honoré
Faubourg St. Honoré
Faubourg St. Honoré

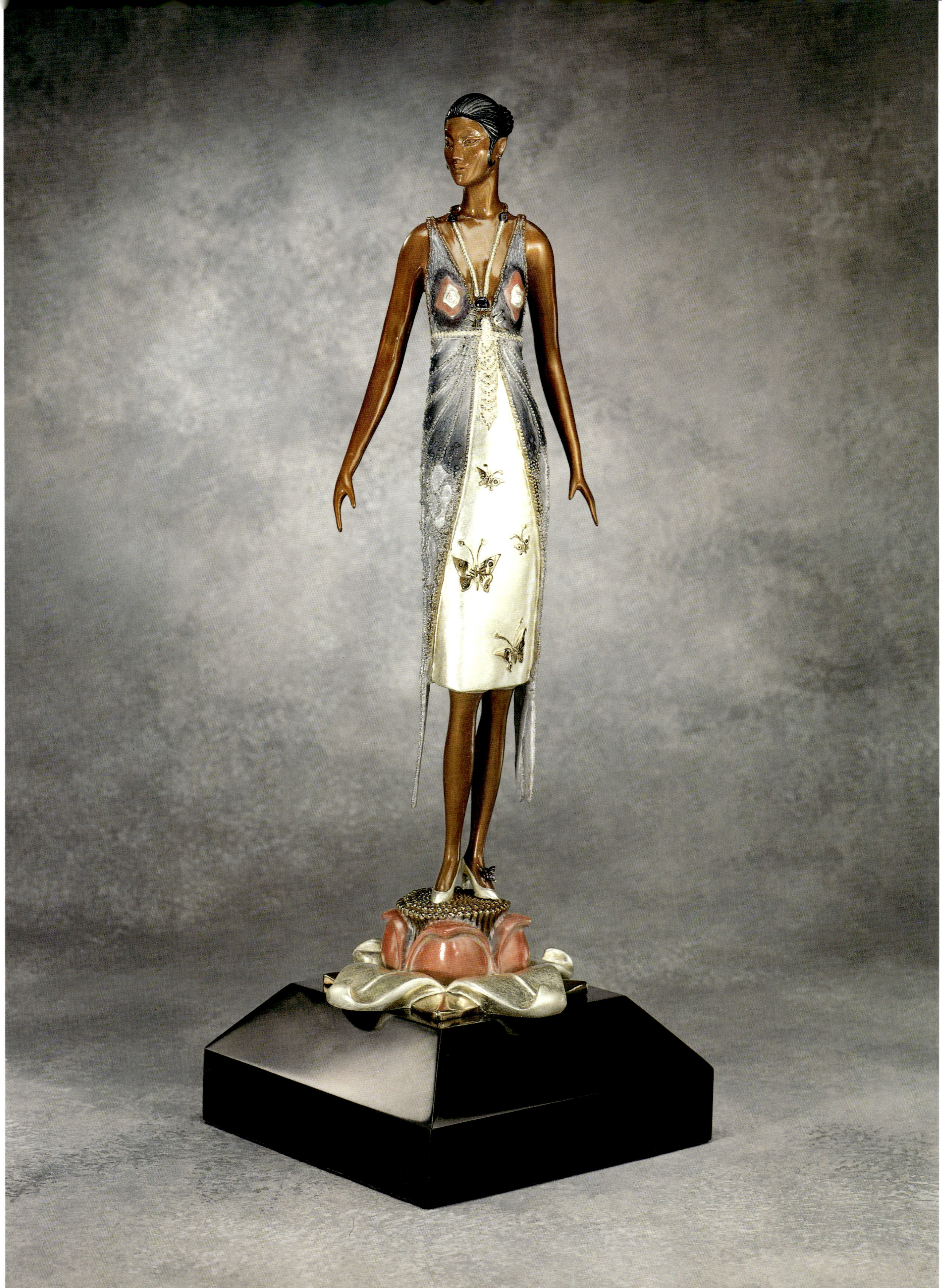

Butterfly Lady
La Femme papillon
La donna farfalla
Schmetterlingsfrau

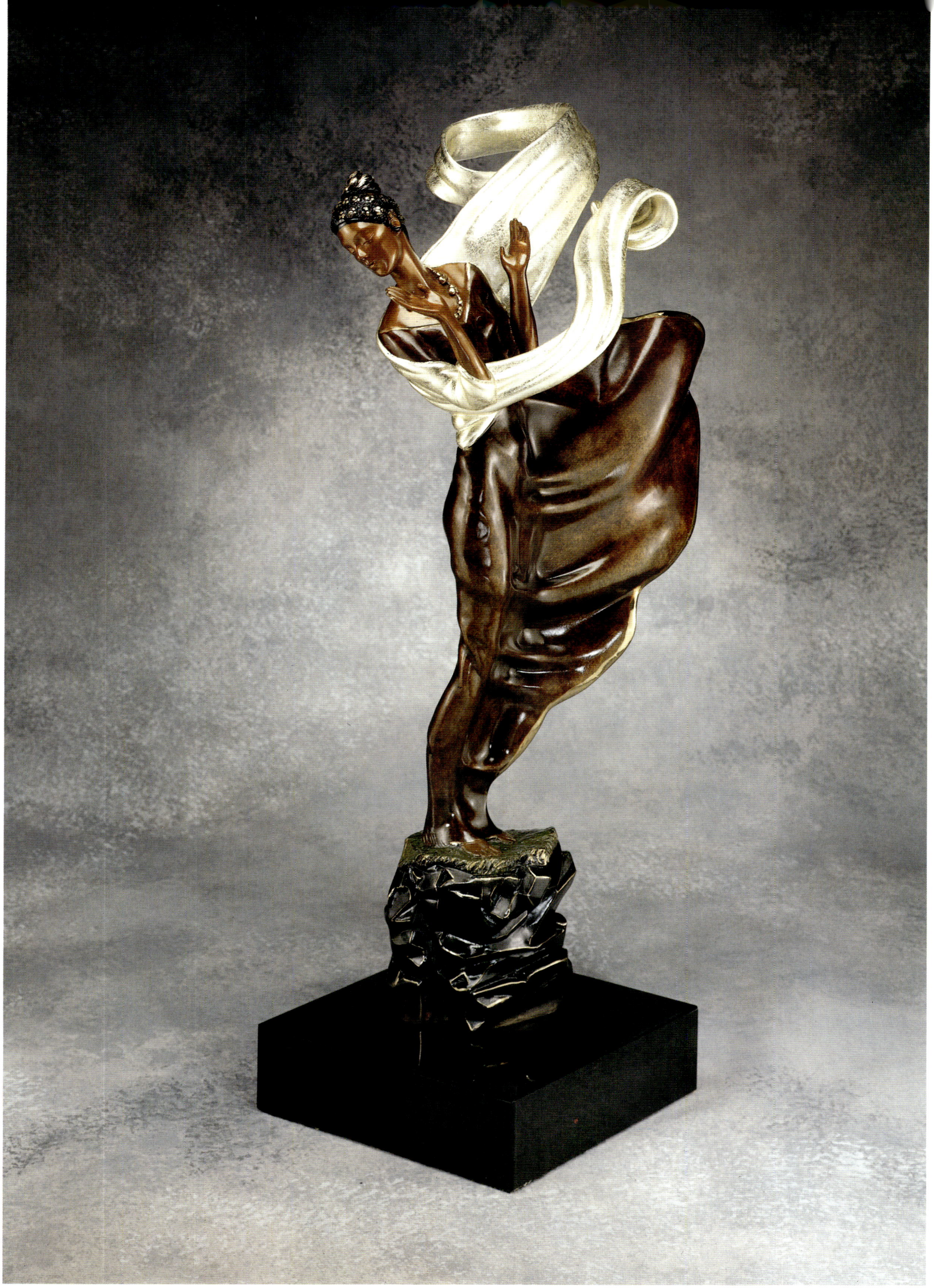

Summer Breeze
Brise d'été
Brezza estiva
Sommerbrise

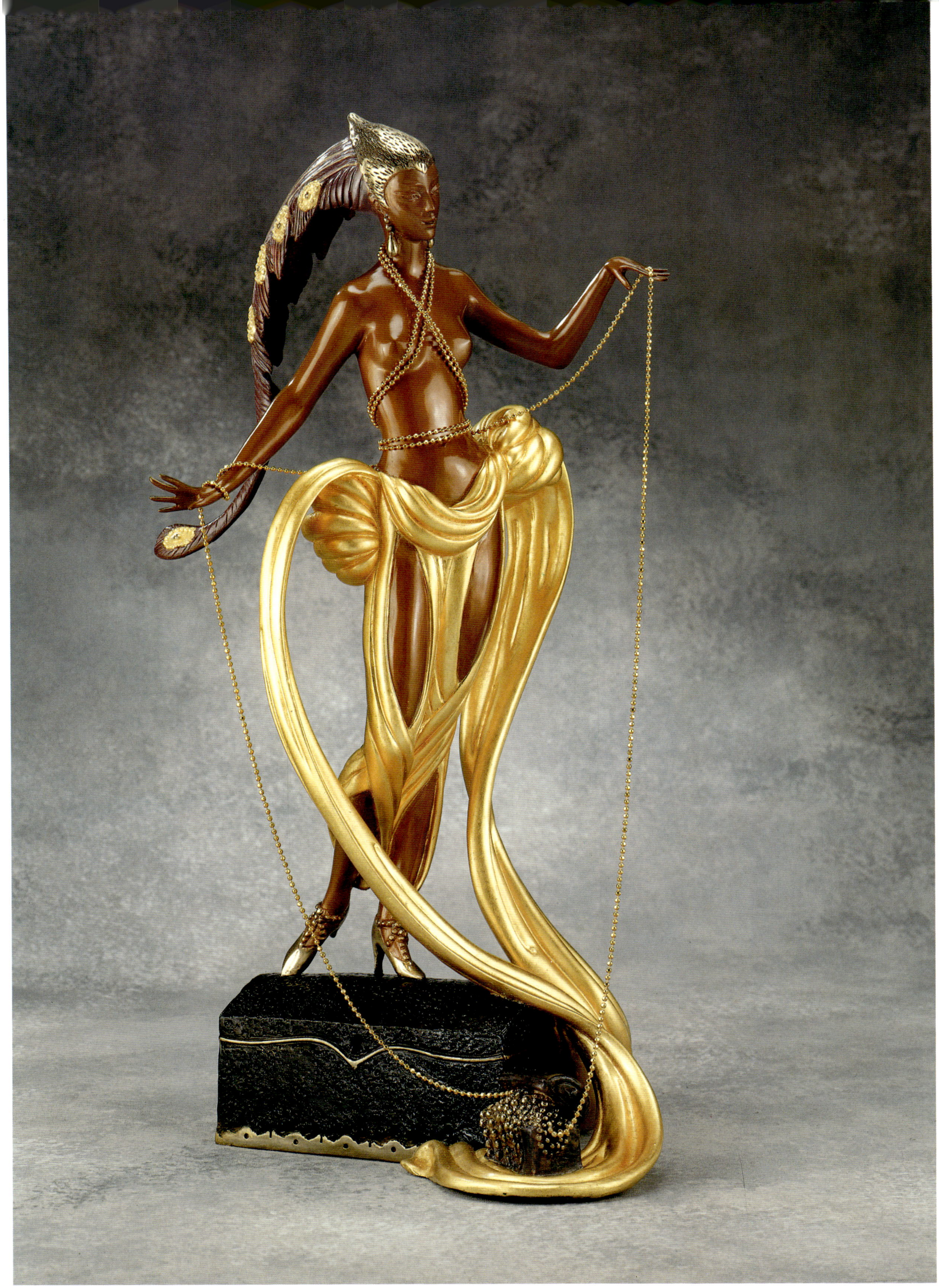

Pleasure of the Courtesan
Plaisir de courtisane
Il piacere della cortigiana
Das Vergnügen der Kurtisanin

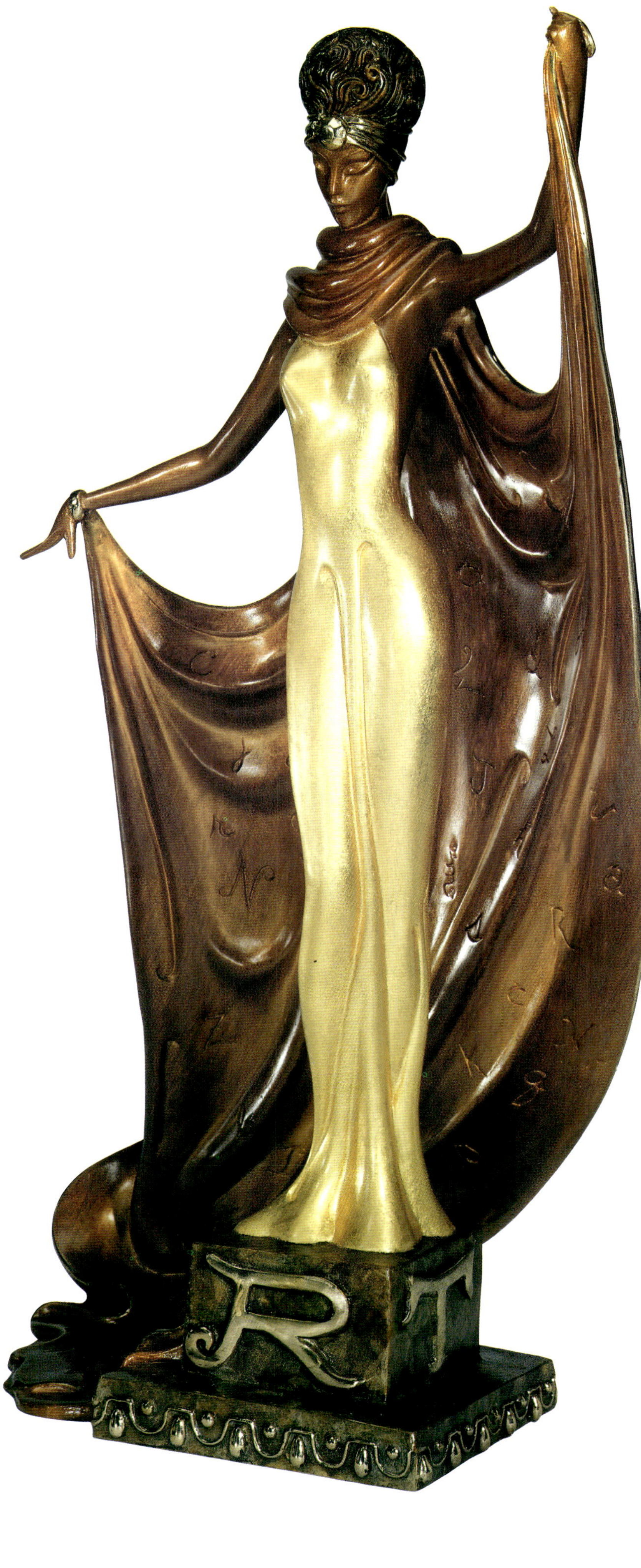

Alphabet Lady
La Femme alphabétique
La donna alfabeto
Alphabet-Dame

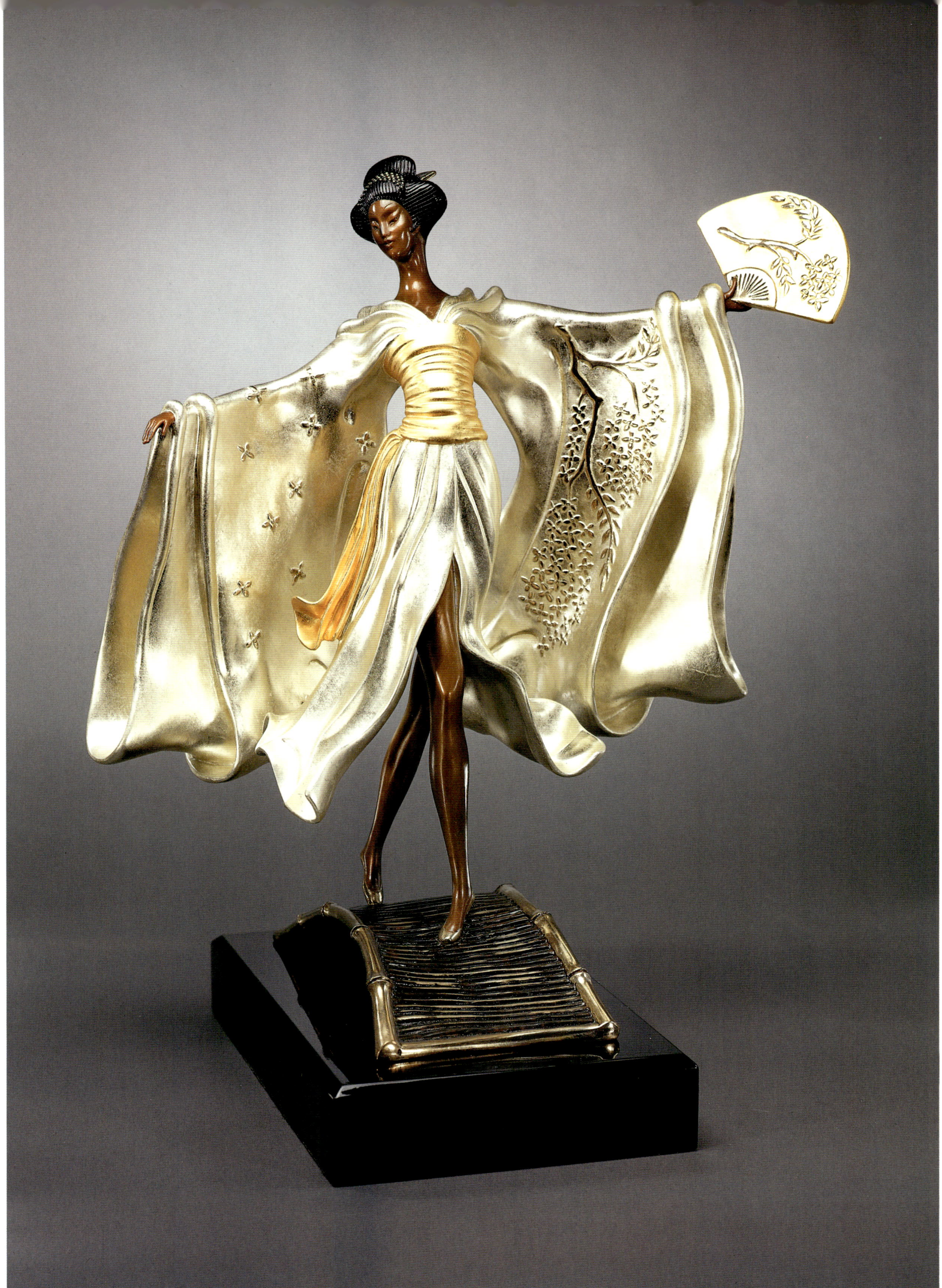

Asian Princess
Princesse Asiatique
Principessa Asiatica
Asiatische Prinzessin

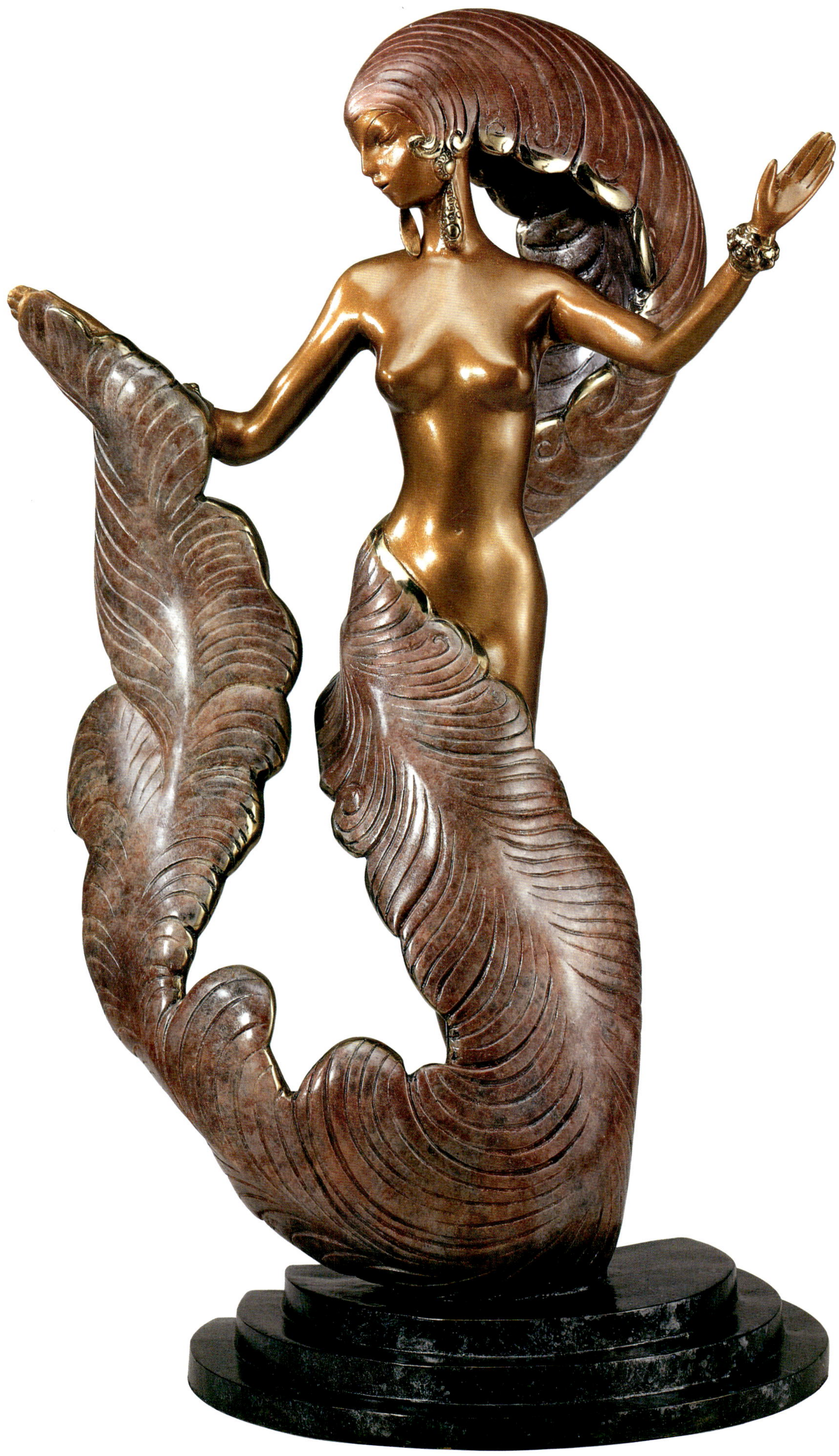

Folies-Bergère
Folies-Bergère
Folies-Bergère
Folies-Bergère

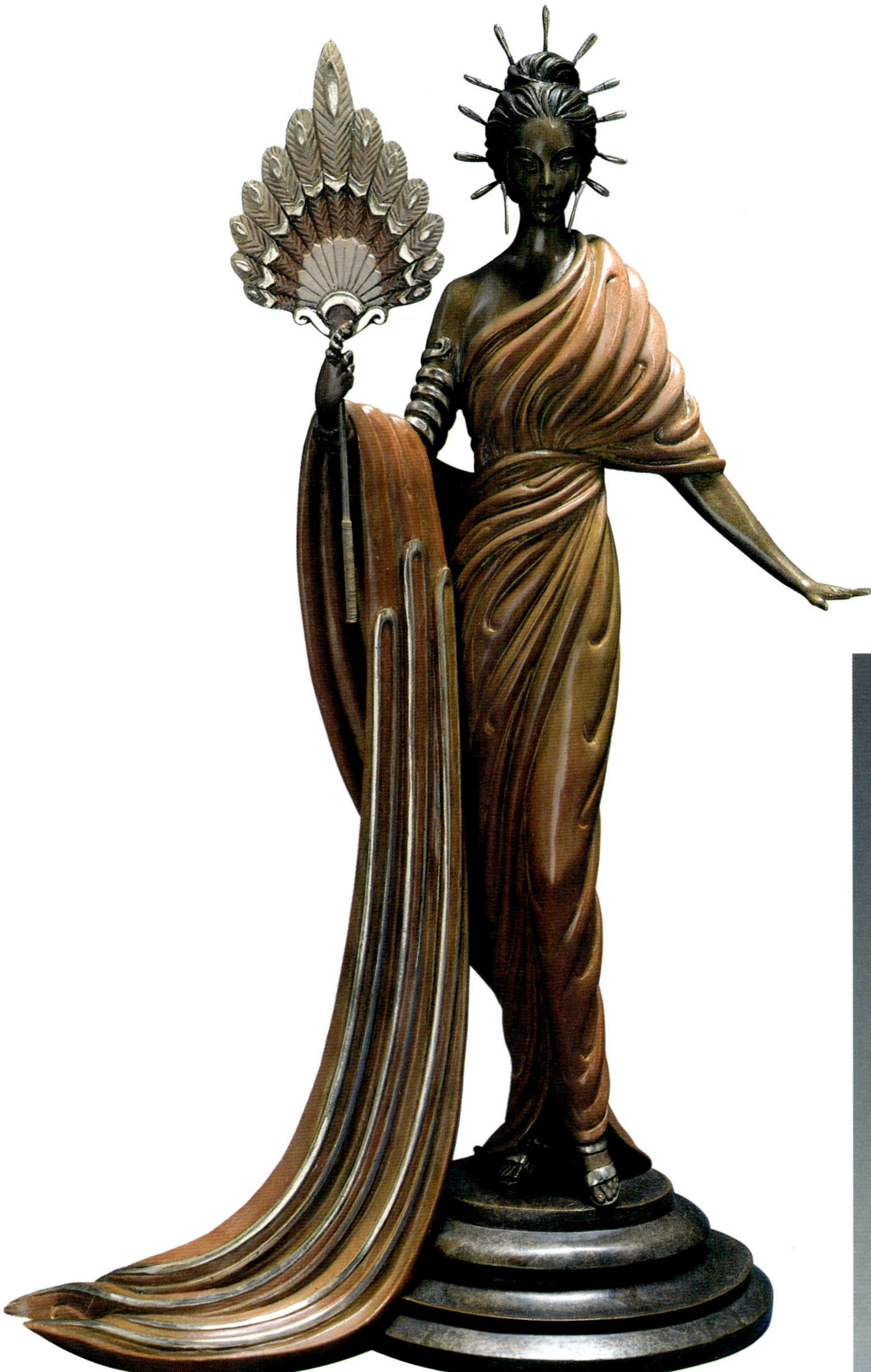

Aphrodite
Aphrodite
Aphrodite
Aphrodite

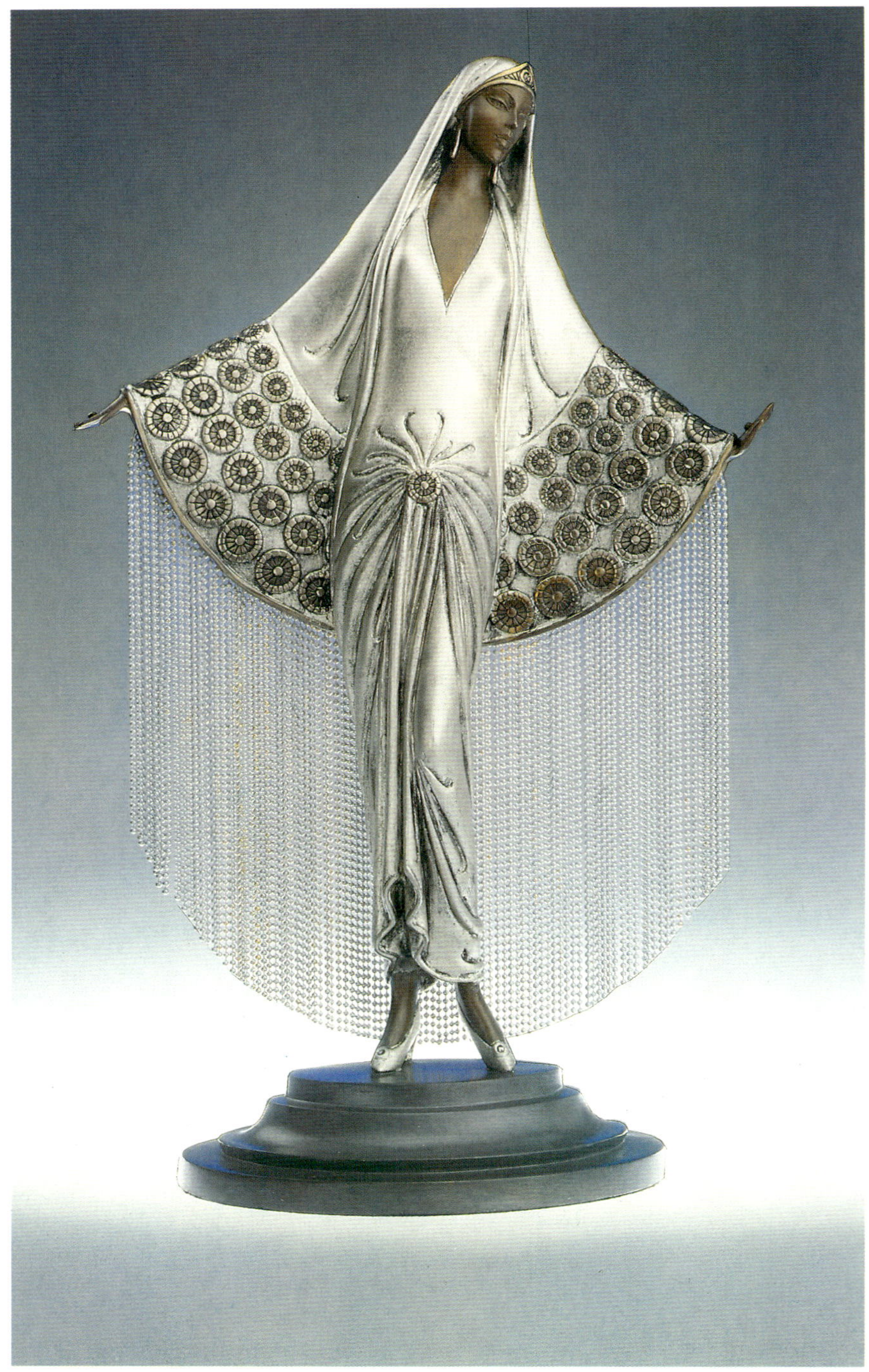

Beloved
La Bien-aimée
L'amata
Geliebte

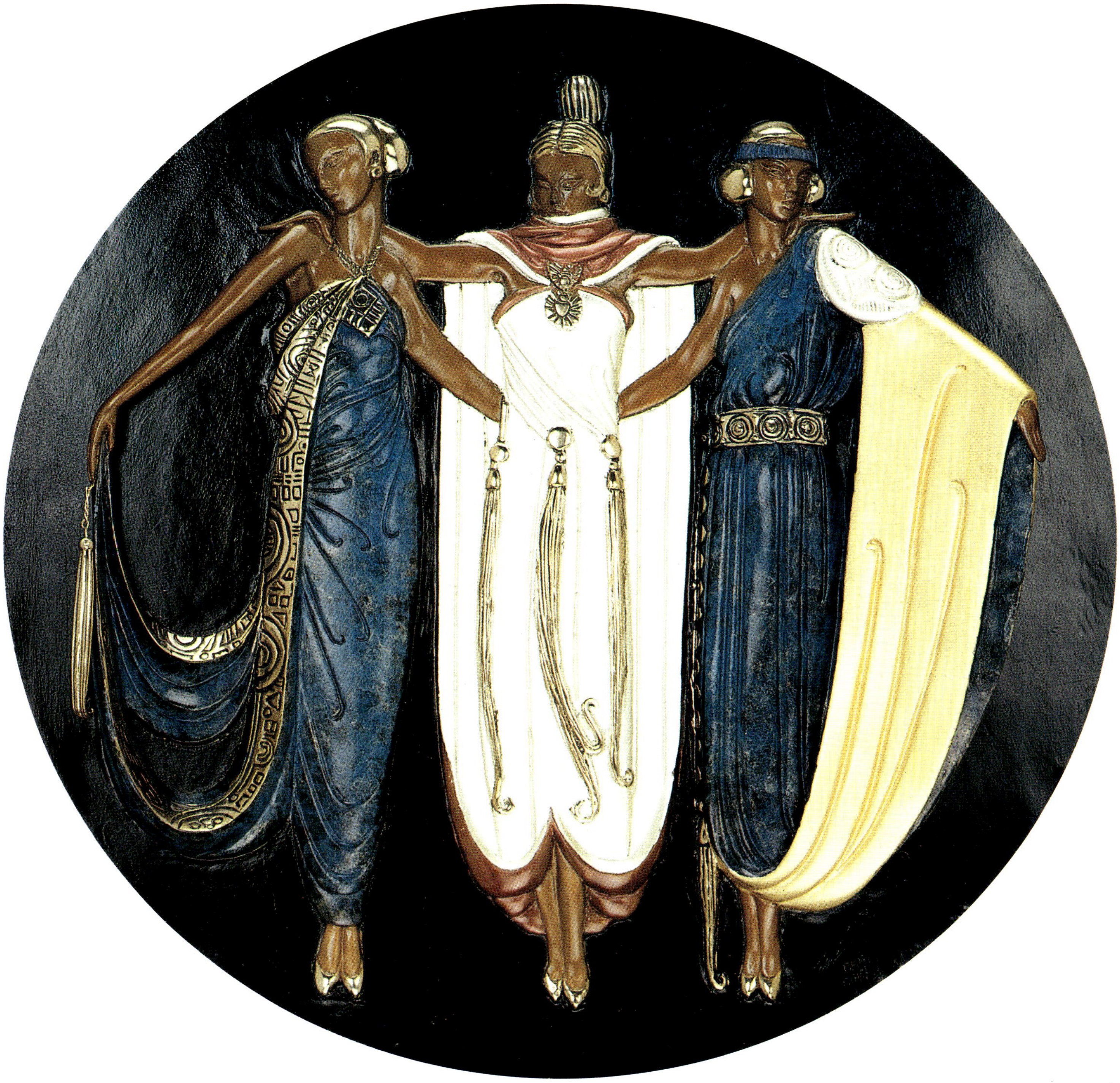

Ladies in Waiting
Les Dammes d'honneur
Damigelle
Hofdamen

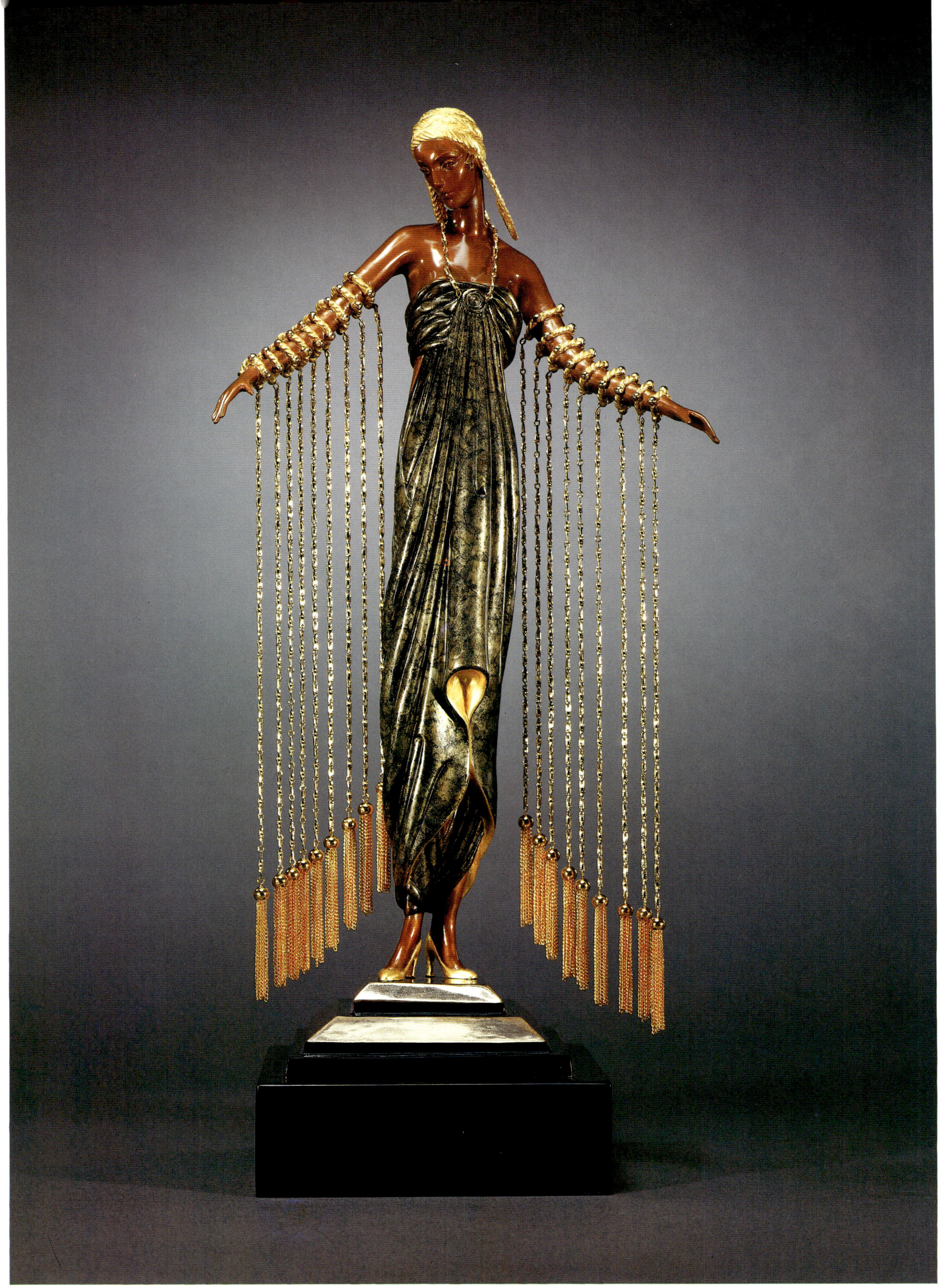

Zobeide
Zobeide
Zobeide
Zobeide

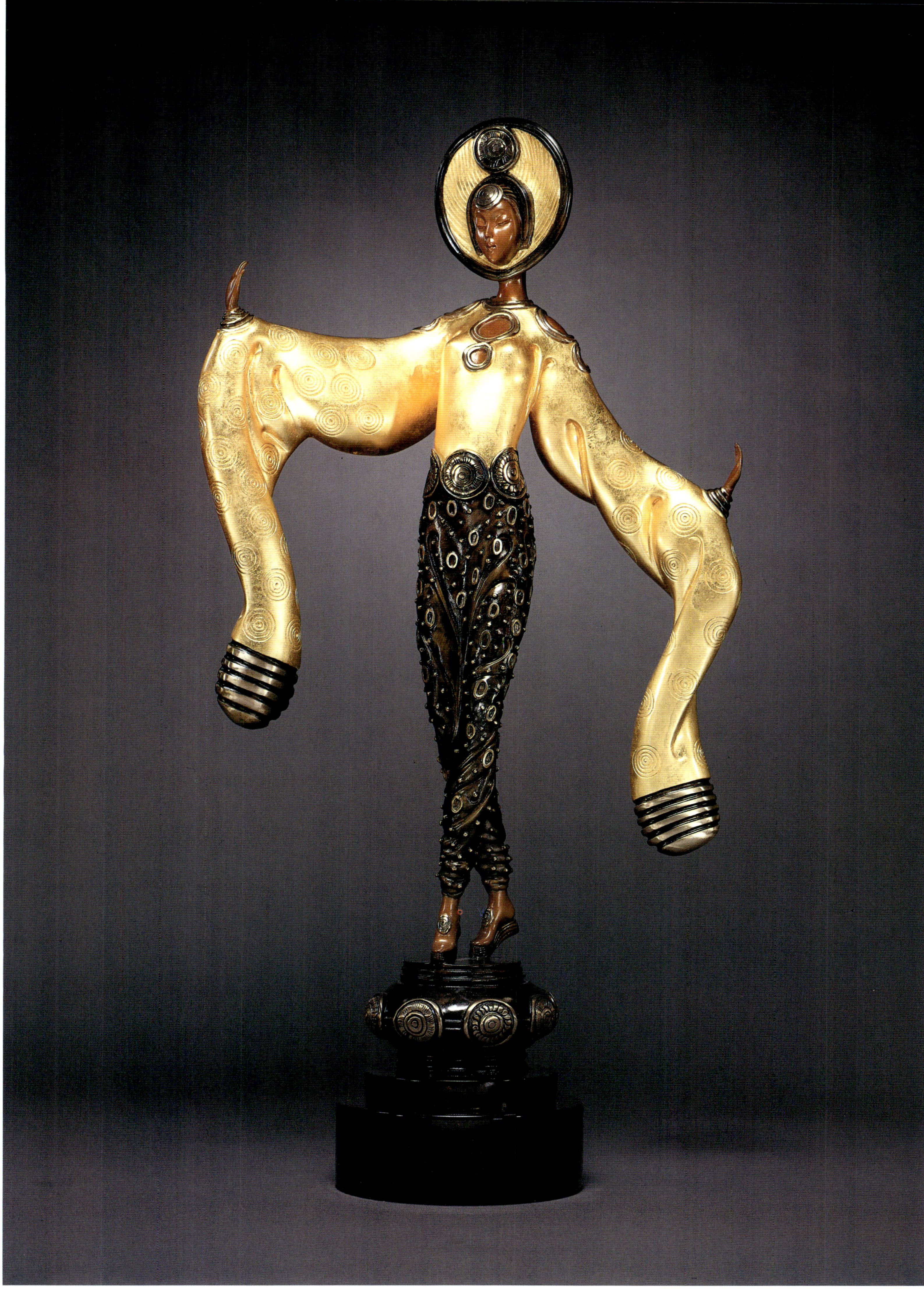

Willow Tree
Le Saule
Salice
Weide

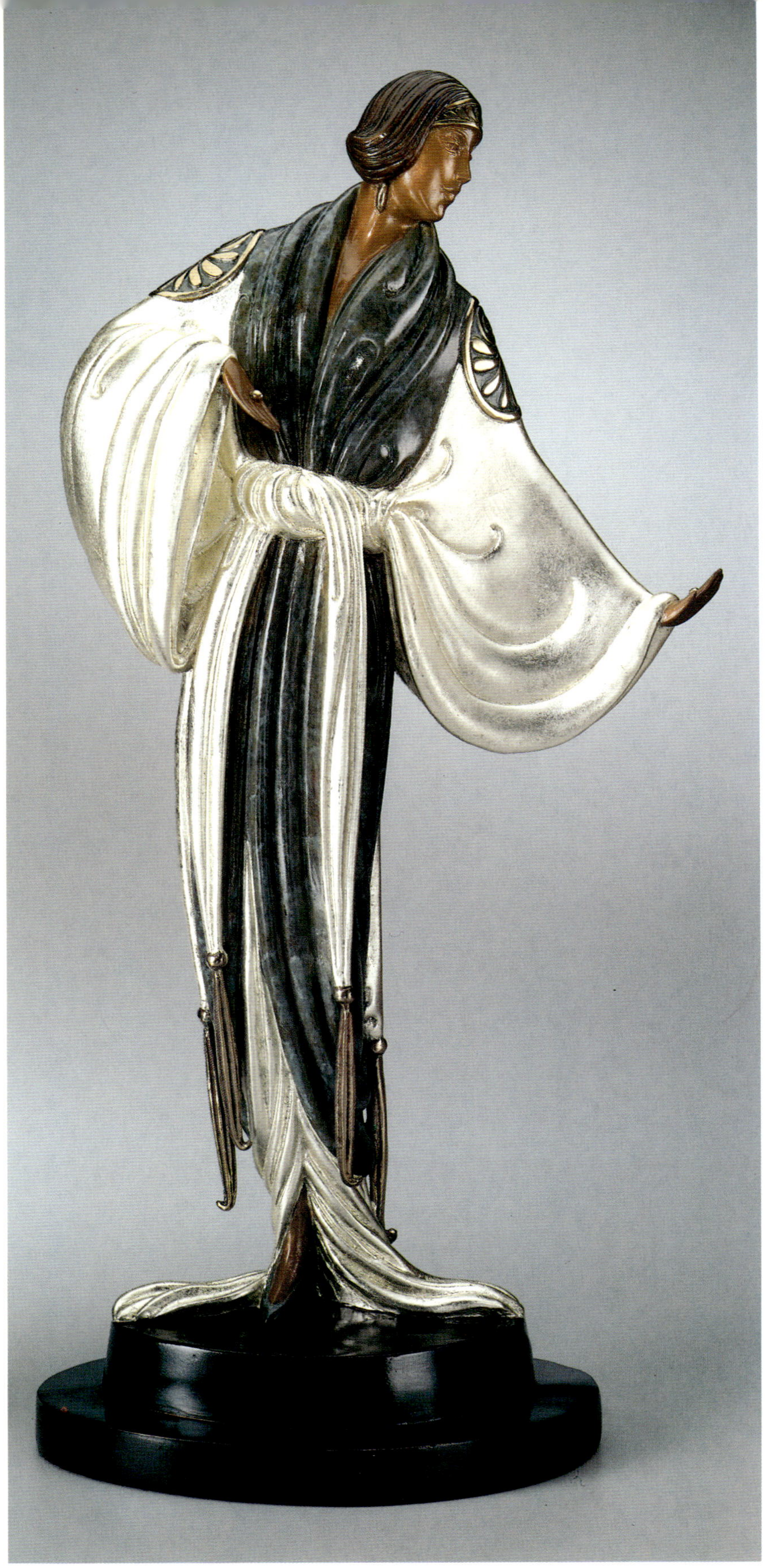

Belle de nuit
Belle de nuit
La bella di notte
Schönheit der Nacht

Rue de la Paix
Rue de la Paix
Rue de la Paix
Rue de la Paix

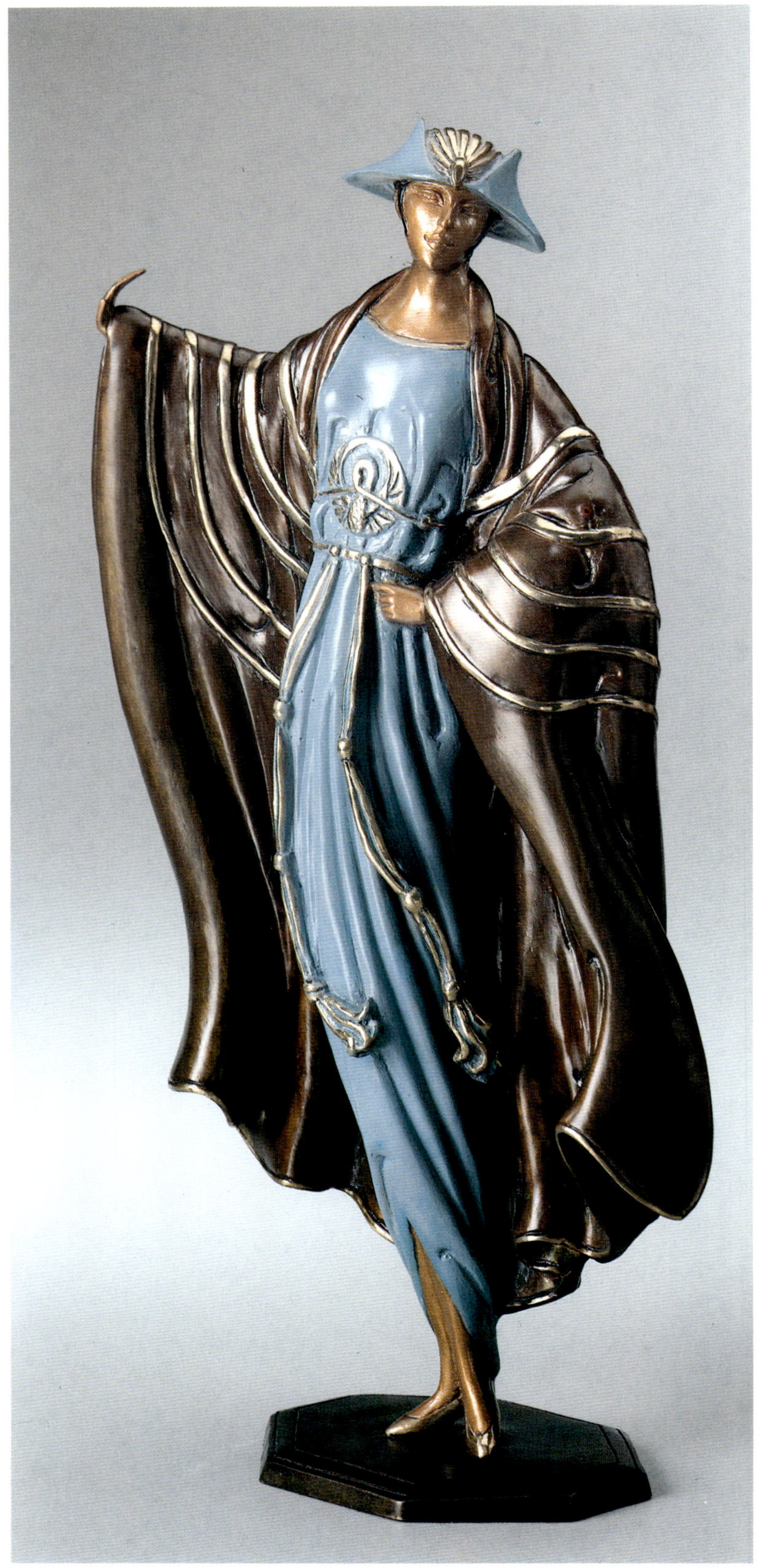

APPENDIX

NOTES

on the sources of selected graphics

(Listed in order of appearance in the Plates)

THE BALCONY: Based on a fashion design for *Harper's Bazaar,* February 1920.

PEARLS AND EMERALDS: Based on a costume for the scene "Les Décolletes", George White's *Scandals,* 1925.

PARIS BOUTIQUE: Based on a drawing for *Harper's Bazaar,* 1919.

PRINTEMPS: Based on costume designs for *Les Rois des légendes* at the Folies-Bergère.

BIRD IN A GILDED CAGE: Based on an illustration for Richard Le Galliene's novel *There Was a Ship,* serialized in *Harper's Bazaar,* 1929.

TANAGRA (Red, Blue, Turquoise): Based on 1940 costume designs for *Madame Phidias.*

ROSES DE NUIT: Based on a 1915 evening dress design for Henri Bendel.

ROSE GOWN: Based on an evening dress design created for Henri Bendel in 1915.

CALIFORNIA (Turquoise Dress): Originally a costume design for the *American Millionairess Revue* at the Théâtre Femina, Paris, 1917.

FLORIDA (Pearl Dress): Originally a costume design for the *American Millionairess Revue* at the Théâtre Femina, Paris, 1917.

MADAME BUTTERFLY: Based on a set design for the scene "Madame Butterfly" in George White's *Scandals,* 1928.

MOTHERHOOD: Based on a 1924 costume design for *Les Idoles* at the Théâtre Sarah Bernhardt, Paris.

LES PRÊTRESSES: Based on a design for the production *Porteurs de pierreries* at the Folies-Bergère, 1927.

GOWN ORIENTALE: Based on a costume design for the *American Millionairess Revue,* Théâtre Femina, Paris, 1917.

CAPE À LA RUSSE: This image was created originally as the back view of the costume on which *Gown Orientale* was based.

CASBAH: Based on a 1929 stage set for the Folies-Bergère production *Aladdin.*

BALINESE: Based on a design for a slave costume for *Les Rois des légendes.*

CRYSTAL MASK: Based on a costume design for *Phi-Phi,* an operetta at the Théâtre des Bouffes Parisiens, Paris, 1940.

FEDORA FAN: FEDORA FUR:

FEDORA BUTTERFLY: Based on costume designs for the singer Ganna Walska in the 1919-1920 Chicago Opera Company production of Giordano's *Fedora.*

ANGEL MELODY: Based on a 1926 design for a costume called "Blue Angel Musician" for the George White's *Scandals* production of George Gershwin's *Rhapsody in Blue.*

SUMMER/WINTER: Based on a fashion drawing for *Harper's Bazaar,* February 1923.

A GLANCE: Based on a fashion drawing for *Harper's Bazaar,* August 1922.

ONYX COIFFURE: Based on a design for a hair ornament for *Harper's Bazaar,* 1922.

RED HAT: Based on a fashion drawing for *Harper's Bazaar,* August 1923.

BRACELETS: Based on a jewelry drawing for *Harper's Bazaar,* January 1924.

HAT AND CHAIN: Based on a fashion drawing for *Harper's Bazaar,* 1922.

BIRD PIN: Based on a drawing of an enameled hatpin for *Harper's Bazaar,* 1922.

TASSEL HAT: Based on several drawings of hat designs in *Harper's Bazaar,* 1922 and 1923.

NEW YEAR'S EVE: Based on a drawing for *Harper's Bazaar,* May 1920.

SEDUCTION: Based on a design for a sun hat for *Harper's Bazaar,* 1922.

ONYX SLEEVE: Based on a design for a bracelet of pearls and polished jade for *Harper's Bazaar,* 1922.

CHIGNON: Based on a fashion drawing for *Harper's Bazaar,* January 1924.

ROSE FAN: Based on a drawing of a wedding bouquet for *Harper's Bazaar,* 1920.

CAMEOS: Based on a design for coiffures and earrings for *Harper's Bazaar,* 1920.

REPOSE: Based on a design for *Harper's Bazaar,* 1919.

WINTER IN PARIS: Based on a drawing for *Harper's Bazaar,* 1919.

FLAPPER: Based on a costume design for *Manhattan Mary,* Majestic Theater, New York, 1927.

THE LOOKING GLASS: Based on a design for *Harper's Bazaar,* 1921.

LYRE: Based on a curtain design for "La Lyre", George White's *Scandals,* 1926.

APRIL: Based on the center figure in *Printemps.*

MAY: Based on the left figure in *Printemps.*

JUNE: Based on the right figure in *Printemps.*

WINTER PROMENADE: Originally a fashion drawing for *Harper's Bazaar,* December 1915.

FLOWER PETAL GOWN: Based on a fashion design for *Harper's Bazaar,* April 1920.

SCANDINAVIAN PRINCESS: Based on a costume design for the film *Restless Sex,* Cosmopolitan Productions, 1920.

RIBBON DRESS: Based on a dress design for *Harper's Bazaar,* 1921.

INGENUE: Based on a dress design for *Ladies' Home Journal,* 1924.

MILLINERY SHOP: Based on a drawing for *Harper's Bazaar,* April 1919.

ARCADIA: Based on a triple costume design called "Marriage" for the scene "Les Mariages", George White's *Scandals,* 1924.

MAXIM'S: LE CIRQUE:

LAURENT: Based on costume designs for *Manhattan Mary* at the Majestic Theater, New York, 1927.

ISIS: Based on costume designed for Carmel Myers in the film *Ben Hur,* 1925.

BOUDOIR: Based on a design for *Harper's Bazaar,* November 1920.

STAR SPANGLED NIGHT: Based on a cover for *Harper's Bazaar,* August 1934.

NOTES

on the sources of selected sculptures

(Listed in order of appearance in the Plates)

EMERALD NIGHT: Originally a fashion illustration for *Harper's Bazaar,* March 1918.

AMERICAN MILLIONAIRESS: Originally a costume design entitled "Texas" for the 1917 New York stage production of *The American Millionairesses.*

VENUS: Based on a costume design for the Folies-Bergère production of *Les Idoles* in 1924.

STARFISH: Originally a costume design for the Folies-Bergère production of "Fonds de la mer", 1919.

MADAME BUTTERFLY: Based on a costume for "Madame Butterfly" in George White's *Scandals,* 1928.

IRAS: Based on a costume design for Carmel Myers in the 1925 MGM film *Ben Hur.*

GOLDEN FLEECE: Originally a costume design for a Folies-Bergère scene entitled "The Golden Fleece" and a 1926 George White's *Scandals* scene entitled "La Toisen d'or".

ERMINE BROCADE: Originally an evening coat design for Poiret in 1913 and redrawn for *Harper's Bazaar* in 1913.

TWO VAMPS: Based on costumes for the Folies-Bergère, 1929.

SIRENS: Based on the lithograph *No.* from Erté's *Numerals* series.

MASQUERADE: Originally a fashion drawing for *Harper's Bazaar.*

SCHEHEREZADE: Based on a design for a 1975 Robert Hoseein production of the same name.

BELLE DU BAL: Based on a costume for *Cendrillon,* London Palladium, 1945.

HER SECRET ADMIRERS: Originally a gouache painted in 1930 as a design to show the latest fashion in hosiery.

TOP HATS: Based on a cover for *Harper's Bazaar,* November 1933.

FRENCH ROOSTER: Based on a cover for *Harper's Bazaar,* January 1918.

ECSTASY: Based on a design for the 1940 ballet *Unfinished Symphony.*

DREAM GIRL: Originally created as a design for *Le Reveil des elégances parisiennes,* 1919.

STRANDED: Based on a cover for *Harper's Bazaar.*

ARCTIC SEA: Based on a costume design from a 1925 George White's *Scandals* scene of the same name. The image was first used for a serigraph of this title.

DUETTO: Based on a costume created for *The Mystic,* an MGM film, 1925.

HERA AND ZEUS: Based on costumes commissioned by William Randolph Hearst for the film *Restless Sex,* starring Marion Davies, 1920.

PRINTEMPS: Originally a costume design for the scene "Les Rois des légendes" at the Folies-Bergère.

OPENING NIGHT: Originally a fashion design for *Harper's Bazaar,* February 1920.

BAMBOO: Based on a costume design for a 1924 George White's *Scandals* scene entitled Mah Jongg.

LOVERS AND IDOL: Based on a 1917 cover for *Harper's Bazaar.*

FANTASIA: Based on a cover for *Harper's Bazaar,* July 1920.

THE SLAVE: Based on a costume design for a slave of Salomé in the scene "Femme Fatales" in the 1926 production of George White's *Scandals.*

THE THREE GRACES: Inspired by "Beauty", "Charm", and "Elegance" in mythology.

SAMSON AND DELILAH: Originally a set design for the 1926 George White's *Scandals* scene entitled "Famous Heroines" and used later at the Folies-Bergère in a scene entitled "Les Princesses de légende".

CHINESE LEGEND: Based on a design for the George White's *Scandals* production of "Aladdin", Paris, 1927.

FEDORA: Based on a costume design for prima donna Ganna Walska in the Chicago Opera production of the opera *Fedora,* 1919.

EMERALD VASE: Based on a 1928 costume design for the George White's *Scandals* scene "Precious Stones".

SISTERS: Inspired by a gouache painting entitled *Les Baisers pervers ou la brune et la blonde,* 1921.

FEMME FATALE: Based on a drawing that originally appeared as a *Harper's Bazaar* fashion design in the 1920s.

PAS DE DEUX: Inspired by a gouache representing Harlequin and Columbine.

RIGOLETTO: Based on a 1920 costume design for the singer Ganna Walska as Gilda in Verdi's opera *Rigoletto.* Erté wrote, "Here is Gilda coming out of the Duke's bedroom in tears, dressed in his dressing gown over his shirt."

ASTRA: Inspired by an Erté gouache painting representing Venus admiring herself in a star-shaped mirror.

CARAMELLE: Originally a fashion drawing for *Harper's Bazaar,* September 1920.

TRIUMPH: Inspired by a gouache painting by Erté.

FEMME DE LUXE: Based on an illustration for *Harper's Bazaar,* January 1916.

L'AMOUR DU VIN: Based on a costume design for the "Bal des Arts" sequence in the silent film *Restless Sex,* 1919.

JOIE DE VIVRE: Originally a costume design for Ganna Walska in the opera *Fedora,* 1919.

FEATHER GOWN: Originally a costume design.

DREAMBIRDS: Based on a fashion design in *Harper's Bazaar,* 1922.

MOTHERHOOD: Originally a costume design for *Les Idoles* at the Théâtre Sarah Bernhardt in Paris.

THE MYSTIC: Based on a costume design for Aileen Pringle in the 1925 film entitled *The Mystic.* The image was first used for the serigraph *Fox Fur.*

FAUBOURG ST. HONORÉ: Originally a fashion drawing for *Harper's Bazaar,* January 1918.

SUMMER BREEZE: Based on a cover for *Harper's Bazaar,* May 1919.

PLEASURE OF THE COURTESAN: Based on Erté's design for a scene in the spectacle entitled *Les Baisers* at the Théâtre Femina, Paris, 1921.

FOLIES-BERGÈRE: Inspired by a poster Erté designed for the Folies-Bergère in the late 1960s.

LADIES IN WAITING: Originally a fashion drawing for *Harper's Bazaar,* April 1922.

BELLE DE NUIT: Based on a fashion design for *Harper's Bazaar,* March 1921.

RUE DE LA PAIX: Based on a fashion design for *Harper's Bazaar.*

BIOGRAPHICAL OUTLINE

1892: Romain de Tirtoff, son of an admiral, born in St. Petersburg, Russia

1898: Designs a dress for his mother that she has made into a ballgown.

1900: Visits World's Fair in Paris with his mother and sister. Decides he wants to live there someday.

1906: Studies painting with portraitist Ilya Repin.

1912: His parents consent to let him study art in Paris. Studies at Académie Julian with historical painter Jean-Paul Laurens, but dislikes the regimented structure of classes and leaves after several months to become a fashion designer. Contributes sketches to Russian fashion magazine *Damsky Mir.*

1913: Works for one month with the dressmaker Caroline. She tells him he has no talent for designing. He then submits fashion sketches to Paul Poiret. Poiret recognizes his talent and hires him as one of two full-time designers. Creates costumes for his first theatrical production, *Le Minaret,* featuring Mata Hari. Contributes drawings to *La Gazette du Bon Ton,* leading fashion magazine of Paris. First use of signature "Erté".

1914: Poiret closes because of war. Erté designs for Henri Bendel and Altman's in New York. Submits designs to *Harper's Bazaar.*

1915: *Harper's Bazaar* publishes first cover design (January) and designs on interior pages, beginning a twenty-two-year collaboration.

1916: Erté contributes work to *Vogue* magazine. After six months, William Randolph Hearst, owner of *Harper's Bazaar,* signs ten-year exclusive contract with Erté to prevent him from creating more designs for *Vogue.* First costume and set designs for a music hall: Madame Rasmini's Théâtre Bataclan in Paris.

1917: Creates costumes for revue, *Marvels of the Orient,* starring Maurice Chevalier and Mistinguett at Théâtre Femina, Paris.

1919: Designs costumes for Gaby Deslys, Théâtre Femina. First designs for Folies-Bergère. Works with Max Weldy, head of Folies-Bergère costume workshop, and thoroughly learns architecture of theater and mechanics of stage. Will continue costume and set designs for Folies-Bergère for eleven years.

1920: Costumes for Ganna Walska of Chicago Opera Company for *La Bohème, I Pagliacci,* and *Faust,* among others. Costumes for Mary Garden of Chicago Opera Company for *L'Amore dei Tre Re.* His costume designs used in film *Restless Sex,* starring Marion Davies (Cosmopolitan Films). Exhibition at Knoedler Gallery, New York.

1921: Costume designs for Anna Pavlova.

1922: Costume and set designs for George White's *Scandals,* Irving Berlin's *Music Box Revue,* and Winter Garden in New York. Costume designs for Ganna Walska in *Rigoletto* at Paris Opera.

1923: Costume and set designs for *Ziegfeld Follies,* New York. Illustrations for *La Gazette du Bon Ton.* Fashion drawings for *Ladies' Home Journal.*

1924: Costume designs for *Le Secret du Sphinx* by Maurice Rostand at Théâtre Sarah Bernhardt, Paris. Illustrations for *The Sketch,* London, and *Ladies' Home Journal.*

1925: Goes to Hollywood, under contract to Metro-Goldwyn-Mayer, to design sets and costumes for film *Paris.* Costume and set designs for *George White's Scandals.* Exhibition at Madison Gallery, New York. *Paris* production delayed, and Erté designs costumes for other films, *The Mystic, Dance Madness, A Little Bit of Broadway,* and King Vidor's *La Bohème,* starring Lillian Gish.

1926: Returns to France, dissatisfied with caricature the producers of *Paris* have created. Makes cover designs and illustrations for Paris magazine *Art et Industrie.* Signs second ten-year contract with *Harper's Bazaar.* Costume and set designs for *George White's Scandals* and Folies-Bergère.

1927: Costume designs for Lucrezia Bori in *Pelléas et Mélisande, L'Amore dei Tre Re,* and *Les Contes d'Hoffmann* at Metropolitan Opera. Costume and set designs for George White's musical comedy *Manhattan Mary* at Majestic Theater, New York. Exhibition at Studio Gallery, Brussels.

1929: Article and illustrations for *The Encyclopaedia Britannica* (14th ed.). Costume and set designs for *La Princesse Lointaine* by Edmond Rostand at Théâtre Sarah Bernhardt. Exhibition at Galerie Charpentier, Paris, and William Fox Gallery, New York. Illustrations for *International Cosmopolitan* and *The Sketch.* Collection of fabric designs for Amalgamated Silk Corporation, New York.

1930: Second collection of fabric designs for Amalgamated Silk. Illustrations for *Art et Industrie, International Cosmopolitan,* and *The Sketch.*

1931: Costume and set designs for Folies-Bergère. Costume designs for Ganna Walska in *Pelléas et Mélisande* (Chicago Opera Company).

1932: Set designs for *Faust* and *Don Pasquale* at Riga Opera.

1933: Designs for Bal Tabarin, Paris.

1934: Costume and set designs for *Au Temps des Merveilleuses* at Théâtre du Châtelet, Paris. Costume designs for *Les Travaux d'Hercule,* operetta by Claude Terrasse at Théâtre des Capucines, Paris. Exhibition at Waldorf-Astoria Hotel, New York.

1935: Costume and set designs for Théâtre Alhambra and Bal Tabarin, Paris, and French Casino, New York.

1937: Costume and set designs for *Plaisir de France,* Bal Tabarin; *It's in the Bag,* by Cecil Landeau, Saville Theatre, London; and Scala Theatre, Berlin. Resigns from *Harper's Bazaar* in dispute with editor Carmel Snow.

1938: Costume and set designs for *London Symphony,* Palladium, and *Fleet's Lit Up,* Hippodrome, London.

1939: Costume and set designs for George White's show at San Francisco Exposition. Costume and set designs for *Un Vrai Paradis,* Bal Tabarin, and *Black Velvet,* Palladium, London.

1942: Costume and set designs for Lecocq's operetta, *Les Cent Vierges,* Théâtre de l'Apollo, Paris; Lido, Paris; and André Messager's operetta, *Coupe de Roulis,* Théâtre Marigny, Paris.

1943: Costume and set designs for Van Parys's operetta, *Une Femme par Jour,* Théâtre des Capucines; *Belamour,* Théâtres des Nouveautés; Lido; and Bal Tabarin; all Paris. Decoration of windows of Au Printemps department store, Paris.

1945: Costume and set designs for Rossini's *The Barber of Seville* for French television. Costume and set designs for Lido and Bal Tabarin.

1947: Costume and set designs for Francis Poulene's opera *Les Mamelles de Tirésius,* at Opéra-Comique, Paris. Costume and set designs for Bal Tabarin, and a revue at Opera House, Blackpool.

1948: Costume and set designs for Maurice Ravel's ballet *Ma Mère l'Oye,* at Opéra-Comique, Paris, and *Sueños de Viena* at Teatro Comico, Barcelona.

1949: Costume and set designs for *Puss in Boots* at Palladium, London.

1951: Costume and set designs for *La Traviata,* Paris Opéra; *Fancy Free,* Prince of Wales Theatre, London; *Histoires d'Eve,* La Nouvelle Eve, Paris; *Happy Go Lucky,* Opera House, Blackpool; and *La Leçon d'Amour dans un Parc,* a musical comedy by Guy Lafarge at Théâtre des Bouffes Parisiens.

1952: Costume and set designs for *Pelléas et Mélisande* and Albert Roussel's *Padmavâti,* at Teatro San Carlo, Naples; Mozart's *Cosi fan Tutti,* Opéra-Comique, Paris; *Ring Out the Bells,* Victoria Palace, London; *Bet Your Life,* Hippodrome, London; and *Les Filles d'Eve,* at La Nouvelle Eve. Costume and set designs for *Maske in Blau* for Bavaria-Films, Munich.

1953: Costume designs for *Die Geschiedene Frau,* for Bavaria-Films. Costume and set designs for *Caccia al Tesoro,* Teatro delle Quattro Fontano, Rome.

1955: Costume and set designs for Jacques Ibert's opera, *Gonzague,* at Cannes and Rouen opera houses; *Campañas de Vena,* Teatro Comico, Barcelona; and *La Plume de Ma Tante,* Garrick Theatre, London.

1957: Costume and set designs for Richard Strauss's *Capriccio,* Opéra-Comique, and *Pommes à l'Anglaise,* Théâtre de Paris.

1958: Costume and set designs for Massenet's opera, *Don Cezar de Bazan,* Rouen Opera; *La Plume de Ma Tante,* Royal Theatre, New York; and revues at Drap d'Or and Folies-Pigalle, Paris.

1959: Costume and set designs for Donizetti's *Don Pasquale,* Opéra-Comique, Paris, and *Crown Jewels,* Victoria Palace, London.

1960: Costume and set designs for Racine's *Phèdre,* Théâtre du Vieux Colombier, Paris; set designs for Robert Thomas's *Piège pour un Homme Seul,* Théâtre des Bouffes Parisiens. Costume and set designs for ballet films of Louis Cuny: *Le Coiffeur-Miracle* and *Édition Speciale.*

1961: Costume and set designs for Rameau's *Castor et Pollux,* Théâtre Antique de Fourvières, Lyons Festival and Moulin Rouge, Paris. Set designs for *Olé,* Deutschlandshalle, West Berlin.

1963: Costume and set designs for Latin Quarter, New York.

1964: Costume and set designs for *Wonderworld,* New York's World's Fair; Terence's *The Eunuch,* Comédie de Paris; and Latin Quarter, New York. Exhibition of Formes Picturales (metal sheet sculpture decorated with oil pigment) at Galerie Ror Volmar, Paris.

1965: Exhibitions at Galerie Motte, Paris, and Galleria Milano, Milan.

1966: Exhibition, "Les Années 25", at Musée des Arts Décoratifs, Paris, commemorating 1925 exhibition that marked emergence of Art Deco movement. Exhibition at Galerie Jacques Perrin, Paris, and "100 Years of Harper's Bazaar", New York.

1967: Costume and set designs for "Flying Colors", Expo '67, Montreal. Exhibition at Grosvenor Gallery, New York; this entire exhibition of 170 works was purchased by Metropolitan Museum of Art, New York. Exhibition at Grosvenor Gallery, London, with numerous works purchased by Victoria and Albert Museum. Exhibition at Galerie Jacques Perrin, Paris; Galleria Viotti, Turin; and Galleria d'Arte Cavalletto, Brescia.

1968: Costume designs for *The Silent Night,* a ballet for television, New York. First lithographs, *The Numerals,* published by Grosvenor Gallery. Exhibitions at Metropolitan Museum of Art; Neues Kunst-Zentrum, Hamburg; Galleria Paolo Barozzi, Venice.

1969: Illustrations for two books, *Ermyntrude and Esmeralda,* by Lytton Strachey, and *The Beatles Illustrated.* Exhibition at Galerie René Drouet.

1970: Awarded title "Chevalier du Mérite, Artistique et Culture!" by French government. Costume and set designs for *Zizi Jeanmaire Show,* produced by Roland Petit, Casino de Paris. Exhibition at Galeria Arvil, Mexico City.

1971: Exhibitions at Galleria della Rocchetta, Parma; Galleria Marino, Rome; Galerie Proscenium, Paris; and Club dei Bibliofili of Milan, Bologna, and Palermo.

1972: Costume and set designs for *Zizi, je t'aime,* produced by Roland Petit, Casino de Paris. Exhibition at Rizzoli Gallery, New York.

1974: Creates *Splendeur,* his first serigraph. This begins collaboration with Circle Fine Art as his publisher of prints. Exhibition at Galerie Proscenium, Paris. Costume and set designs for *Ragtime Ballet,* Ballet Théâtre, Angers. Poster designs for Alcazar nightclub and Folies-Bergère.

1975: Costume designs for *Schéhérazade,* produced by Robert Hossein. Publication of autobiography, *Things I Remember.*

1976: Awarded title "Officer of Arts and Letters", by French government. Exhibition at Shiseido Gallery, Tokyo.

1977: Honored with Ziegfeld Award of Excellence at the Ziegfeld Ball, New York. Publication of *The Alphabet* portfolio, combining lithography and serigraphy. Graphics retrospective exhibitions at Circle Galleries, New York, Los Angeles, San Francisco, San Diego, Chicago; Gallery in the Square, Boston; and Cherry Creek Gallery of Fine Art, Denver.

1978: Honored by Eugene O'Neill Foundation at gala "Broadway's in Fashion" celebration, New York. CBS-TV film on Erté, narrated by Diana Vreeland. Exhibition of Erté costumes for New York's Latin Quarter, Boston Center for the Arts.

1979: French documentary, *Erté—Or a Magician in the Twentieth Century,* released. Smithsonian Institution organizes traveling retrospective exhibition that tours the United States, Canada, and Mexico for three years.

1980: Costume and set designs for Glyndebourne Opera Company's performance of *Der Rosenkavalier* by Richard Strauss. Honored at the French Cultural Mission, New York City. Erté Sculpture Collection introduced by RKP International and Dyansen Corporation. Jewelry series based on Erté designs begun by Circle Fine Arts.

1981: Erté 90th Birthday Retrospective at the Dyansen Gallery, New York.

1982: Major Erté exhibition in Copenhagen, Denmark. Awarded Medaille de Vermeil de la Ville de Paris. Chalk & Vermilion begins publishing Erté graphics. Honored with retrospective exhibitions and galas in New York City by Chalk & Vermilion and the Dyansen Galleries at 90th Birthday. Publication of *Erté at Ninety,* showing all Erté graphics since 1968.

1983: Collaborated on a musical autobiography, *Erté.* Participated in designing a collection of women's haute couture clothing and millinery. Exhibition at Fashion Institute of Technology, New York.

1984: Designed Christmas packaging for a Swiss hosiery company. Created new posters for Folies-Bergère and Campari. Chalk & Vermilion hosts 92nd birthday gala at Plaza Hotel, New York. Honored at the 92nd Birthday Retrospective Gala by the Dyansen Galleries at Trump Tower in New York.

1985: Costume and set designs for Arthur Schnitzler's *Anatol,* opening in Los Angeles. Awarded the Legion of Honor by France.

Honored at 93rd birthday Gala in New York by Chalk & Vermilion.

1986: Commission to design cover of January 1987 *Playboy* magazine. Commission to design official poster for new Theatre Museum, London. Commission to design a bottle for Courvoisier cognac. Retrospective exhibition Boulogne-Billancourt (Paris), "75 Ans de Création, 1911–1986." Ninety-fourth birthday exhibition, Grosvenor Gallery, London. Chalk & Vermilion retrospectives across United States. Dyansen Galleries host 94th Birthday Retrospectives in New York, Los Angeles, San Francisco. Erté is subject of lecture series by Alastair Duncan of *Christie's*. *Erté Sculpture* book published. "Homage to Erté" evening, Valledemosa Chopin Festival, Majorca.

1987: Major 95th birthday retrospective exhibitions sponsored by Chalk & Vermilion and at Dyansen Galleries throughout U.S. 95th birthday celebration and exhibition, Circle Gallery Soho, New York. Introduction of the "Treasures in Bronze" and "Visions in Bronze" sculpture collection. Exhibition of Erté's American productions at Grosvenor Gallery, London. "Erté Ball", Loewe Museum, Miami. Publication of *Erté at Ninety-five*, showing graphics published since 1982.

1988: 96th Birthday Gala hosted by Dyansen Galleries at the Pierpont Morgan Library, New York. Respective exhibitions sponsored by Chalk & Vermilion and Dyansen Galleries throughout U.S. Commissioned to design bottles for Courvoisier cognac. Begins design of medallion collection. Begins design of bas-relief collection. Publication of *Erté at Ninety-five: Extended Edition* with new graphics.

1989: Erté honored at Gala in The Rainbow Room by Chalk & Vermilion and at ribbon-cutting ceremony at Dyansen Gallery Trump Tower in New York City. Reception for Erté by Donald Trump at Trump Castle, Atlantic City. Sevenarts Tokyo, "The Erté Gallery", opens in Tokyo. Chalk & Vermilion sponsors retrospective exhibitions throughout U.S. and Japan. Release of "Theater in Bronze" sculpture collection. Costumes and set designs for new production of musical *Stardust* produced by Louise Westergaard. Costumes and sets for 1990 Easter Show, Radio City Music Hall, New York.

1990: Erté died on April 21, 1990.

BIBLIOGRAPHY

Barthes, Roland. *Erté.* Franco M. Ricci, Milan, 1972 (lim. ed.).

Blum, Stella. *Designs by Erté.* Dover, New York, 1976.

Cox, John. (Introduction) *Erté's Costumes and Sets for "Der Rosenkavalier".* Dover, New York, 1980.

Erté. *Erté Fashions.* St. Martin's, New York, 1972.

______. *Erté—Things I Remember.* Quadrangle, New York, 1975.

______. *Erté: My Life/My Art: An Autobiography.* E. P. Dutton, New York, 1989.

Erté's Fashion Designs. Dover, New York, 1981.

Estorick, Salomé. (Preface) *Erté Graphics.* Dover, New York, 1978.

______. (Preface) *Erté's Theatrical Costumes.* Dover, New York, 1979.

______. (Preface) *New Erté Graphics.* Dover, New York, 1984.

Johnston, Susan (Rendered by). *Erté Fashion Paper Dolls of the 20s.* Dover, New York, 1980.

Lee, Marshall (Editor). *Erté at Ninety: The Complete Graphics.* E. P. Dutton, New York, 1982.

______. *Erté Sculpture.* E. P. Dutton, New York, 1986.

______. *Erté at Ninety-Five: The Complete New Graphics.* E. P. Dutton, New York, 1987.

______. *Erté at Ninety-Five: The Complete New Graphics.* Extended Edition. E.P. Dutton, New York, 1988.

______. *Stardust.* Harry N. Abrams, Inc., New York, 1990.

______. *Erté: Art to Wear/The Complete Jewelry.* Dutton Studio Books, New York, 1991.

Spencer, Charles. *Erté.* Clarkson N. Potter, New York, 1970, rev. 1981.

Walters, Thomas. *Erté.* Rizzoli, New York, 1978.

INDEX

Alphabetical list of the works with technical data

GRAPHICS

The data are given in the following order:

title (series)
medium (size of edition) date printed
sheet size
printer
page

All the graphics are published by Chalk & Vermilion Fine Arts except those whose title is followed by a slash / which are published by Sevenarts, Ltd.

The asterisks following some titles indicate whether the work is a "facsimile signature print" (**) or a "Studio Edition" (*).

SCULPTURES

The data are given in the following order:

title
size of edition
date of publication
dimensions (heightxwidthxdepth)
foundry(s)
page

An asterisk (*) following the date indicates that the work was not released at the time of this book's publication. In these cases, the date given refers to when the artist approved the master.

SCULPTURE PUBLISHERS

All 105 of the sculptures shown are published by Chalk & Vermilion Fine Arts except those published by Dyansen Corporation, which are illustrated on the following pages: 110, 117, 122, 129, 135, 140, 147, 152, 162, 171, 176, 188, 192.